# AN INQUIRY INTO THE EXISTENCE OF GUARDIAN ANGELS

# AN INQUIRY

## INTO THE

# EXISTENCE

## OF GUARDIAN

# ANGELS

Pierre Jovanovic

M. Evans and Company, Inc.
New York

M. Evans and Company, Inc.
216 East 49th Street
New York, New York 10017


**Library of Congress Cataloging-in-Publication Data**

Jovanovic, Pierre, 1960–
    [Enquête sur l'existence des anges guardiens. English]
    An inquiry into the existence of guardian angels / Pierre Jovanovic ; translated by Stephen Becker. — 1st ed.
        p.    cm.
    Includes bibliographic references and index.
    ISBN 0-87131-781-8 : $21.95
    1. Guardian angels. 2. Angels. I. Title.
BT966.2.J68    1995                                                94-49563
291.2'15—dc20                                                      CIP


Typeset by Not Just Another Pretty Face, New York City

Manufactured in the United States of America

First Edition

9  8  7  6  5  4  3  2  1

This book is particularly dedicated
to four marvelous women:
Marie, Gemma, Gabrielle, and Georgette;
and to the Creator of the Subject.

In homage to two angelologists emeriti,
Gustav Davidson and Vincent Klee.

# PERMISSIONS

# Acknowledgments

From the bottom of my heart I thank the following for the help and, above all, the encouragement they offered me:

Gerard Adamis
Serge de Beketch
Michael Auriel
Lieutenant Claude Boucherville
Joachim Boufflet
Father François Brune
Martin Caidin
Gérard Coste
Father Jean Derobert
Muriel Dzu
George Gallup, Jr.
Father Guy Girard
Jacinta Gonzales
Michael Grosso
Jean-Yves Guizouarn
Carole Hennebault
Francis Jeffrey

Dr. Elisabeth Kübler-Ross
John Lilly
Robert Monroe
Dr. Melvin Morse
Father Alessio Parente
Dr. Maurice Rawlings
Kenneth Ring
Dr. George Ritchie
Evelyne-Sarah Mercier
Father Stephen Schneir
Kimberley Sharp
Monsignor Sheridan
Father Paul-Francis Spencer
Terry Taylor
Philippe Tesson
Dave Wallis

The Dominican Libraries in Paris
The Los Angeles County Library
The J. Paul Getty Museum in Malibu
The French, Swiss, Italian, American, and Canadian publishers who sent me, always with great good nature, thc books I needed.

Jack and Nikki Singleton who were truly my American Guardian Angels when I arrived in the United States.

Oriel Malet and her swimming Angel.

# CONTENTS

# AN INQUIRY
## INTO THE
# EXISTENCE
## OF GUARDIAN
# ANGELS

# FOREWORD

FOR THE LAST TEN YEARS, SINCE SERIOUS RESEARCH ON THE MATTER OF Near Death Experience began, remarkable—and for many—unexpected facts and theories have come to light. We know now that when we die we enter a tunnel, that we are often accompanied on this journey by a "being," and that it is a journey from which we don't want to return, and never would if not urged to do so by the "being."

The researchers in the field have been, up to this point, people like myself who have been through the experience of NDE, and doctors like Melvin Morse and Raymond Moody, who have based their findings and beliefs on their own experiences, the experiences of their patients and their colleagues' patients. Now Pierre Jovanovic, a reporter, a man whose professional training teaches him to be always skeptical, has given us a look at this field from a new perspective—a journalist's investigative report into the existence of guardian angels.

Pierre told me that his interest began when he encountered a seemingly unexplainable phenomenon; and as a reporter—a digger for *facts*—he felt he had to arrive at a true answer. He had been saved by death or at least by serious injury by literally being pushed by an unseen force out of the way of a bullet speeding at him. Was it real? he asked himself. Was it his imagination? Was it coincidence? So almost reluctantly Pierre found himself drawn deeper into the investigation of this phenomenon.

Driven by an urgent need to understand, he began a spiritual inquiry by beginning to explore angel experiences and the nature of angels. He interviewed people who made it their life work to explore the phenomenon of near death experience, investigated the lives of saints, and arranged to interrogate stigmatics from their sick beds.

Out of the jumble of raw data came his account of an investigative reporter's search for the who, what, why, when, and where of angels and their appearances to mostly unassuming individuals throughout the centuries.

Pierre told me that he concluded after all his research that angels are real, very powerful and often very funny. It is my firm belief that no one will be able to read this book without being moved—and changed—in some fundamental way.

—Betty J. Eadie
Author of *Embraced by the Light*

CHAPTER 1

# Of the Angels' Influence
# on Daily Life

ONE AFTERNOON IN AUGUST 1988, AT FREMONT IN THE HEART OF Silicon Valley, I had just ended a visit to the assembly plant of Grid portable computers. My lady friend and I hopped into our rental car, and after hunting for ten minutes or so we finally found Highway 880, to take us back to San Francisco. On the highway everything seemed normal and calm. It was a sunny day, and not being the driver I looked at the big rigs we were passing, so American with all their shiny chrome, and suddenly, without thinking, I flung myself to the left. One second later a bullet pierced the windshield, smack in the middle of the passenger side. My side. An hour later, with a statement (obligatory for the insurance) from the Highway Police, who assured us that it was a relatively common (sic) incident of sniper fire, I was wondering why I had flung myself to the left *before* the bullet hit the windshield. Later, while talking with other journalists, I discovered that I wasn't the only one to experience this sort of phenomenon. Other colleagues—reporters or press photographers—told me how at the very moment of inevitable death something inexplicable had saved their lives, some million-to-one shot. And most of them explained to me that time had suddenly stood still, and they had begun to see their whole lives unfold, as if *"outside of time."* An inexplicable phenomenon, so they tuck it away in a corner of memory. But the memory pops up again when some other person talks about such matters: *"Listen, something just like that happened to me in Lebanon,"* or Iraq, or wherever.

I too forgot. But then after an investigation of life after death, I couldn't help connecting near death experience with these anecdotes from reporters, photographers, and pilots saved *in extremis* by an unexplained voice or event. What they all had in common was either *"time standing still"* or their *"lives unfolding in three dimensions,"* and sometimes both. So I dug deeper into near-death experiences, or near-life, if you prefer. An interview with the French Doctor Devawrin would convince me definitively: that physician had written his thesis in medicine on this subject from a particularly propitious observation post, the resuscitation unit at the hospital in Garches,[1] which receives serious accidents from the belt highways that ring Paris. To carry it further, I even proposed this topic during an editorial conference at the *Quotidien de Paris*, and it was accepted. This time, the inquiry into NDE became a prominent theme. I really wanted to know just what happened at the moment of death. After a few weeks of investigation, I was more than disturbed: accepting the principle of a life after death following this inquiry, I was confronted by a dilemma. If life did not cease with death, then the religious texts I had considered tall tales by bearded and boring old men were not so silly after all. I was plenty upset. Before that article, the Resurrection of Christ meant no more to me than a long weekend thanks to the Easter holiday. But in the end what do all these near death experiences represent, if not stories of modern resurrection? That bothered me so much that I did what everybody does. I preferred to forget about it. It required too much thought, and Catholic dolorism—deep and constant meditation on pain and death—had always horrified me.

But it all came crashing down on me again one night when I heard a song by Jean-Louis Murat about his guardian Angel. Stupidly I asked myself if I had a guardian Angel too, and the idea seemed as foolish as it was romantic. But less than an hour later, in a bookstore, I came across a book on Angels, entirely by chance. The topic piqued my interest, a purely intellectual interest, of course. But the deeper I plunged into the subject, the more the omens leapt out at me, in a chain of unlikely coincidences. That first question had lit the fuse of a bomb that would cost me a fortune in book money. Little by little I got the feeling that an invisible dialogue had begun between this supposed Angel and myself, a dialogue that Jung called synchronicity. It was not a matter of conversation in the strict meaning of the word, but more exactly of signs that make sense to you and no one else. Another example: one day I was walking home, trying to dismiss this angel business from my mind and I said to myself "I should stop believing in those stupidities." At that very second, a screeching of brakes broke into my thoughts. I had come within a hair of

1. A suburb of Paris.

being run down. The truck stopped within six inches of by body. It was a florist's van. Its name: *Michel-Ange Fleurs;* its make: Renault 4L, ie., four wings. Unbelievable, to be run down by a MichelAngelo Florist at the vey moment when I was, once again, trying to dismiss the idea that the Angels can exist…

The first time, you tell yourself it was only an accident. The second time, when someone gives you a book about the theme of Angels in art, you think it's a real coincidence. The third time, you receive a letter that begins "You were my guardian Angel" from someone you knew long before your sudden preoccupation, and you tell yourself that it's an incredible simultaneity. The fourth time leaves you speechless. After the tenth time, you surrender, and after the twentieth you start talking seriously to your Angel. From then on, the Angel's responses take you by surprise on a street corner, in a book, from a person or a letter or a phone call. I remember one day I answered the phone and at the other end a person I guessed was quite old asked me if she had reached the Church of Saint Mary of the Angels. I was dumbstruck.

Later on the Angel falls into the permanent habit of "talking" to you, always by interposed signs. Sometimes Cartesian rationality calls you to order, and once again you wonder sincerely if you haven't gone mad, if you're not seeing signs and omens where none exist. You even begin to doubt your own mental health. And just at that point an even more impressive omen literally stuns you. Exactly that happened to me in 1990 at Las Vegas, where Paris had sent me to cover the Comdex, a great convention all about computers. More than ever I "doubted," thinking I was out of my mind. One morning I was walking along the "Strip" when a cross on the "strip" caught my eye. This was my fifth trip to Las Vegas, but I had never noticed a church before. Just out of curiosity I approached, wondering what a church would be like in this capital of gambling and prostitution. When I read its name, "Guardian Angel Cathedral, Bishop of Nevada," I stood paralyzed for a full minute. Turns out it is the only church of that name in the United States.

Still, the more the signs came to me the less I believed, stubbornly insisting that it was all pure coincidence. And yet one day I thought I had really gone crazy. In a secondhand bookstore I found a magnificent Latin missal of the 19th century, called the "Missal of the Angels." Wanting to date it, and especially to learn more about the author or authors of this illuminated work, I asked the archbishopric of Paris for the name of a librarian who might be able to shed some light on it. They offered the name of a monk, whose order I will not reveal here. By telephone he gave me an appointment for the following Sunday, after services. On that day, after a Mass celebrated by a priest who kept talking about Angels, I asked a monk to introduce me to Brother X. When he pointed him out to me, I discovered to my pleased surprise that it was the officiating priest, a man in his thirties with a smiling face and a slightly feminine air. He led me to his office, took the missal, examined it with a jeweler's glass, and gave me some interesting information, warning me that this volume was new to him. I was not much further along. When I tried to turn him toward Angels, Brother X stopped me. He rose, indicating the end of the interview, and told me, *"Angels, apparitions of the Virgin and other such stupidities I do not believe in."* It was the coup de grâce that I had unconsciously been awaiting; I slipped behind the wheel of my car wondering why I should believe in Angels when even an ordained priest did not.

And yet somewhere (an odd term, that "somewhere": where?) this saddened me. I was attached, if not to my Angel at least to the idea of possessing one. And after that meeting it was as if he had vanished in a puff of smoke. It was the end of a beautiful, invisible friendship.

But we don't shake off a guardian Angel so easily. That incident was a sort of boomerang, a revelation. The Angel behaves like a girl we have broken up with, who watches for us at the doorway of our apartment building. Three days later, as I left a restaurant where I had lunched with my friend Gerard Adamis and told him about the incident with the monk, the Angel awaited me, like a thunderbolt.


I slipped into Gerard's Rolls-Royce and, as we started up, a cassette slipped out of the stereo (why hadn't it slipped out on the way over? A mystery). I glanced at it mechanically and, stunned, I read the title "Saint Michel, the Archangel." To my question about the cassette's origin, Gerard Adamis answered that Sunday (and therefore the same day as my interview) after the Mass in Paris he had seen this cassette, a collection of sermons on the Archangel, and had picked it up for me, knowing my interest in the subject. But after hearing side A, fairly boring, he had forgotten to mention it to me. Out of curiosity, I switched it to Side B and punched Play. After some sounds of breathing, an energetic male voice filled the vehicle, and the first words struck me like a dagger. It was a direct answer to what the priest told me, and in *his very words!*

*"I am not going to waste my time proving to you that there are angels,"* the voice declaimed. *"Open the Holy Scriptures to any page, and the evidence is abundant; it took all the stupidity of the progressives to reduce them to simplistic notions and I have no time to waste over such stupidities."*[2]

I never imagined that a priest would express himself so directly, calling his progressive colleagues "stupid." It was quite funny and yet rather surprising. Worse yet, the sermon came from the church of Saint-Nicolas du Chardonnet, Parisian fief of the traditionalists, a movement about which I felt more than doubtful. But this voice spoke of Angels with so much poetry, faith and certainty that I was left dazed. It was a truly strange situation. Gerard Adamis, as astonished and fascinated as I was, had parked the car in the shade of a locust tree so we could listen comfortably to this sermon, halfway between a course in philosophy and a course in theology. Doubtless, the brother's response had annoyed the "higher-ups;" doubtless it had made waves.

The synchronicity of this event plunged us into deep reflection. The priest who was an expert on missals, a progressive, had used the word "stupidity."[3] The priest on the tape used the same word in rebuking the progressives. . . . I couldn't get over it. On the spot my faith in my own guardian Angel, which had dropped to zero, shot up. I had just discovered that Angels very much dislike being mistaken for wild dreams.

But wild stories of this kind, whose synchronicity seems regulated to the precise second, can only be explained by the power of Angels, no doubt delighted that anyone really cares about them. And yet I was disappointed not to find a work that offered "proofs" of their existence. These books always consist of commentaries based on Biblical texts (when and where Angels appear in Scripture), or of reported testimonies (*"I was saved by an Angel"*), or of speculative writings (on the sex of Angels, of course), sufficient for those who have faith; but utterly insufficient for those who believe in nothing, and meaningless to those who would like to believe but require a sort of material, palpable "demonstration." In general,

2. Sermon of September 29, 1990, the Abbé Laguerie.

3. A few months later I discovered that the Italian writer Giovanni Sienna had come up against that same *"stupidity"*: *"One of our friends who is a monk,"* he tells us in *Padre Pio, voici l'heure des Anges, "had translated my book into his own language. And before sending it to press, he submitted it for ecclesiastical review. The book already had the Imprimatur in Milan and in Paris. It was now rejected with precisely this comment: 'Enough of these stupidities.'"*

Angels are discussed either by the most *nihil obstat* sort of priests, or by New Age authors on channeling (*"the Angel Saaparvada told me that . . ."*), or by cabalists (invocations of the Spirits of Goodness), or by unknowns who had an "angelic" experience, or by academics and theologians, for the most part abstruse. To understand their work one needs a dictionary of theology. They all adduce interesting details, but few give me the feeling that they could convince a harried businessman, or someone who was groping, searching, but had no desire to entrust himself to a priest. The position of the last-named is simple: *"The Church says that Angels exist, so we must believe in Angels,"* according to the progressives who have not relegated them to the realm of outdated dogmas. Well, if there is any intellectual approach that gets my goat, it's that one: the Church says that . . . The Church has proposed so many stupidities that we've reached the point of disbelief. Besides, didn't they put the *Grand Larousse Universel,* one of the world's great encyclopedia-dictionaries, on their Index?

So as a journalist I was looking for a book based on solid, strong foundations. But after much vain research, I had to yield to the evidence: that book did not exist. And yet my rational side insisted on finding material proofs of the existence of Angels and/or the testimony of people above all suspicion. Finally, after four years of reading in widely varied areas, I realized that I myself was capable of writing that book. But a problem rose immediately: how could I approach this topic from a journalistic angle, and conduct a multidisciplinary investigation, without making too much of a fool of myself as editor of a national daily? (I could imagine the comments of the press attachés: *"Oh, that's the idiot who believes in Angels,"* etc.)

Another problem arose immediately: to be credible, this book must include many interviews in the United States, which would mean traveling all over the country. At just that moment Paris was sending me to California, which took care of the logistical problem. So I was able to meet with the most eminent specialists in Near Death Experiences, like Dr. Elisabeth Kübler-Ross, Professor Kenneth Ring, and Dr. Melvin Morse; and those on the various levels of consciousness, like Dr. John Lilly; on out-of-body experiences like Robert Monroe; and on Angels, like Terry Taylor; and complete the research I had begun in France.

Cross-checking these various domains brought me original and enlightening insights on Angels, absolutely unexpected and unforeseen, and supplied rather extraordinary testimony, sometimes overwhelming proofs, as we shall see in the chapter "Mystics and

Angels." I have only one hope: that the fruit of several years' impassioned research may reconcile the reader with his guardian Angel, who is awaiting exactly that. Indeed, many are those (never mind the Confession) who consider God too remote, too inaccessible, and who hold Him responsible for horrors and injustices. On the other hand, the idea of possessing our own guardian Angel tempts us all the more because he *is* our own and we don't share him with anyone (egotists that we are . . .), contrary to God, who belongs to everyone, and whom everyone invokes and brandishes for any reason at all.

And that is why a relationship with our guardian Angel is the simplest to develop, the most intimate, and above all the most effective, for it immediately transforms, metamorphoses a life, spiritually as well as materially: a guardian Angel harbors an immense power, a power of which we have only a very vague notion.

It was Philip Faure, speaking of the writer Rainer Maria Rilke, who summed up in a few lines the power of an Angel and what occurs when the two meet: *"The Austrian poet's yearning for an Angel reveals itself when he comprehends the considerable distance that will separate man and Angel from now on, the full dimensions of which he intends to express: the celestial being is terrible, dazzling, and his encounter with man can only be violent.*[4]

It only remains to arrange an encounter with one's guardian Angel. At first that promises to wring tears from us. But later everything meshes as if by a miracle. One discovery of those who keep up a privileged relationship with their guardian Angels: their humor. Angels love to play jokes, a variety of celestial jokes composed of unique paradoxes and synchronicities. For example, one day in March 1992 in Paris I telephoned Rene Laurentin, author of many books and a journalist with *Le Figaro*, to ask for some advice and addresses. He greeted me between two appointments and explained that he had met a painter, a woman, who drew only Angels. He couldn't quite remember her name because it had been three or four years before, but he did remember her agent, a certain Malerbe-Navare, who lived in a street close to the Luxembourg Gardens in Paris. He wasn't even sure of the spelling of that name. With a map of Paris and a Minitel (a computer directory), I plunged into my search for Malherbe, Malsherbes, Navare, Navarre, etc. All my phone calls failed. They thought I was a lunatic: *"Good evening, sir, excuse me, I'm a reporter from the* Quoti-

4. In *Les Anges*, Cerf, pp. 68–69.

dien de Paris *and I'm looking for a Monsieur Malerbe-Navare who knows a painter who draws only Angels. Is it by any chance you?"* After half a day of trying, I gave up the notion of finding this mysterious artist.

That night in Paris I had a phone call from Los Angeles, from my colleague and most of all my neighbor Emmanuel Joffet, who had undertaken the difficult task of caring for my 90-pound Old English Sheepdog, and who wanted me to visit his grandparents in Paris.

Arriving at an apartment in the sixteenth arrondissement two days later, I was welcomed by a charming lady, Marguerite Bordet, who was herself a painter. Browsing in one of her catalogues, I discovered, rather wild-eyed, that it was she I had searched for so desperately via the name of her agent, Malherbe-Navarre Roger, two days earlier!

The grandmother of my neighbor who lived 7,000 miles from Paris! It was unbelievable. We both had the feeling that the Angels had played an immense intercontinental joke on us.

In short, after a few months' discussion with the Angel, we notice that all he desires really is one thing, a perfect communion with his protégé, since he knows his desires and problems better than anyone. The Angel does his best to fulfill desires, and in this "invisible" relationship I never felt anything but an immense complicity. And yet we read everywhere that Angels are only God's messengers, perfect and inhuman instruments, as it were, without feelings and without free will. Nothing could be more inaccurate, as the relationship between a guardian Angel and his protégé may be independent of God, which sets no problem because the role of the Angel consists precisely of bringing his protégé progressively toward God while respecting his free will. To believe in the Angel is already a tremendous step toward God. The French writer and poet Charles Peguy explained one day, in strict confidence, to his friend Joseph Lotte that he possessed an incredible guardian Angel: *"He's even shrewder than I am, mon vieux!"* Peguy said. *"I am closely guarded. I cannot escape his guard. Three times I've felt him grab hold of me, tear me away from desires, from premeditated, prepared, willed actions. He plays incredible tricks."*

And indeed, who has not heard a friend say, *"You know, sometimes I have the feeling that I'm being watched over,"* or *"You'd think Heaven was watching over me,"* or *"By a miracle I never boarded that plane."* People become aware of it but don't try to dig deeper, to explain this mysterious feeling, out of fear that they will make fools of themselves or, more rarely, lose that "protection" by trying to pierce his mystery.

That's another curious phenomenon: the incredulity of one's peers. If you say to someone, *"I believe in God,"* he won't think it abnormal even if he's an atheist. On the other hand, if you explain that you believe in your guardian Angel, he will stare at you goggle-eyed, as if you'd said, *"I believe in Santa Claus."* That has happened to me several times, mainly in Catholic bookstores where, when I asked a saleswoman or the owner,[5] *"What have you on the Angels?"* All I got by way of answer was a smile of the *"poor simpleton"* variety, while in New Age or esoteric book shops they answered, *"Yes indeed, right there behind you in the right-hand aisle."*

Still more curious is the reaction of practicing Catholics, above all the traditionalists, who, when you mention Angels to them, respond by throwing the Devil in your face: *"Are you sure you haven't been led astray by the Evil One?,"* as if being interested in Angels rather than God demonstrated the formal proof of my diabolical possession. Aren't Angels the common denominator of the greatest religions? You find them in the Old Testament as well as the New; in the Koran; the Torah; and among the Hindus, who call them "the shining ones," the devas. Are they not also *"the tools with which God amuses Himself and acts, by and with which He reveals eternal forces and wonders, and leads them in a game of love?"*[6]

Abruptly my interest in Angels, those *"immaterial beings, pure spirits, intermediaries between man and God,"* as the dictionary tells us, *"who are to be at our side always, instructed to guard and guide us,"* was transformed into a relentless determination. When Dr. John Lilly, whose work with dolphins is world famous, tells us quite simply in his autobiography that he encountered his guardian Angel as a child and conversed with him, one may well pause for reflection. Similarly for Francoise Dolto, the celebrated child psychoanalyst, who has made no secret of the fact that she constantly asks her guardian Angel to watch over her. If these statements were made by unknowns, no one would pay any attention. But coming from John Lilly and Francoise Dolto, who had no reason whatever to talk nonsense, they can be explained only by unforgettable experiences. During an interview at his home in Malibu, California, Dr. Lilly—who had dealt more than once with these "beings," always in dramatic circumstances—told me, *"I called them Angels, but that's a hangover from my Catholic education. Today it would be more accurate to*

5. That was in 1989–92.

6. Albin Michel, *Les Anges et les Hommes* a collection, 1978, p. 139.

*say, 'Being from a higher plane than ours.'"*
And it doesn't bother the old scientist at all that people may question his mental processes; after his work for the U.S. Air Force and the U.S. Department of Health, and above all after his observations on dolphins' systems of cerebral communication, he has nothing to prove to himself, and even less to prove to others, for what emerges from the whole of his experience is the sense that he is protected, a feeling perfectly translated by the expression "born under a lucky star." Well, is that just an accident? Nineteenth century engravings always depict the guardian Angel with a star shining from his forehead.


But what does it mean to be born under a lucky star? Simply to be fortunate, to win at gambling or avoid accidents regularly, to emerge unhurt from a terrible crash or to survive an attempted assassination? How can we explain those absolutely unpremeditated actions that save one's life, those inner voices that warn us suddenly, that premonitory dream, that insane series of coincidences causing a friend or a total stranger who had no business being on the spot at the crucial moment, to intervene and head off a catastrophe? A chance premonition, a stroke of luck, a coincidence? In French we often say, *"Something tells me that"* . . . But what is this something? Is it someone?

No one is prepared to offer a natural and objective explanation of these phenomena. And once we accept so much as premonition, we open the door to other realities. And we cannot deny experiences lived by millions of people on the grounds that we cannot explain them materially and scientifically. Those who have lived such an experience are forever marked by that "help" surging up from nowhere, of which the most elegant explanation (as there is none more logical) can be summed up as a very real intervention by what is called a guardian Angel.

But, to start with, do these Angels really exist? The answer is negative considering that we do not see them. On the other hand as soon as we collect data among the sick, or the victims of accidents, whose hearts have actually ceased to beat, the answer becomes positive. As we shall discover, the extremely vast and all perfectly documented domain of Near Death Experiences permits no doubt, because it was not charted by clergy or cultists, but indeed by some of the most serious doctors and academics of our era.

# CHAPTER 2

# Of Angels in the Tunnels

SINCE THE PUBLICATION OF DR. RAYMOND MOODY'S BOOK *LIFE AFTER LIFE* it may be said that death, once draped in a skeletal costume and armed with a scythe, will be clothed from now on by Paco Rabanne. It no longer presents a horrible face, because in a short period of time two major events combined to produce the most important discovery of this century's waning years, the topography of death and its journey. It was in 1975 that microprocessors were first used in cardiac monitoring and also that Raymond Moody published, almost entirely at his own expense, his *Life after Life*. How are the two connected? Microprocessors in instruments of medical mensuration allowed physicians to follow the heart's action in real time. Formerly when a patient's heart stopped beating after surgery, the staff discovered the cadaver in the morning, or at best ten minutes after death. Today the least fluctuation is signaled by the synthetic sounds of a video game, triggering an immediate rush of on-duty doctors and nurses to the dying man's room to bring him back to life, whether at four in the morning or five in the evening. And then the progressive miniaturization of chips doubled the microprocessors' calculating powers every year. Nowadays unstable patients are covered by electrodes connected to a central computer that detects the slightest problem in a hundredth of a second. It is not as easy as it was to die of cardiac arrest. One consequence is simple: the number of resuscitated patients rose exponentially. That technological evolution will be very useful to us in understanding the work of cardiologists Michael Sabom and Maurice Rawlings, and why they found so many NDEs.

And now back to Raymond Moody. Well before the dawn of the computer revolution, in 1965, he is still a student, not even of medicine but of philosophy. One day he meets George Ritchie, a teaching physician and psychiatrist at Charlottesville, who tells him how he "died" in 1943, when he was an army private in a barracks in Texas. Moody listens, interested but only moderately. Following a strenuous and intense basic training, Private Ritchie came down with pneumonia. His fever mounted so high that at 3:10 on December 20 he collapsed unconscious in the arms of a nurse, Lieutenant Retta Irvine. A few hours later the young man wakes up, leaps out of bed and tries to find someone who can tell him what time it is, because he doesn't want to miss the train for his Christmas furlough. He dashes along the hospital corridors and discovers suddenly that no one seems to see him, no one hears him, and worse yet that people are passing right through him without so much as a blink (exactly as in the film "Ghost"). Uncomprehending, the soldier returns to his room stunned, and sees a body lying in a bed—a body he identifies as his own because of a ring. At the same instant he notices a strange, tiny light, which begins to intensify noticeably: *"All the light bulbs in the ward couldn't give off that much light. All the bulbs in the world couldn't,"* he says.[1] More and more the young man is able to discern a human form in that luminous halo, even as he tells himself that the intense luminosity should have destroyed his retina within seconds. *"For now I saw that it was not light but a* Man *who had entered the room, or rather, a* Man *made out of lights. . . . I got to my feet, and as I did came the stupendous certainty* "you are in the presence of *the Son of God."* He then observes Him and becomes aware that *"this was the most totally male Being"* that he has ever seen. The only problem is that his face bears no resemblance to the face in the books of catechism:

> . . . *this was not the Jesus of my Sunday School books. That Jesus was gentle, kind, understanding—and probably a little bit of a weakling. This Person was power itself, older than time and yet more modern than anyone I had ever met. Above all, with that same mysterious inner certainty, I knew that this Man loved me. Far more even that power, what emanated from this Presence was unconditional love. As astonishing love. A love beyond my wildest imagining.*

1. *Return from Tomorrow,* Chosen Books, New York, 1978.

And as these reflections take expression, he discovers in the same way that He knows all about him, knows his life in its finest details. At the same moment George Ritchie sees his past life, his twenty years, pass in a second, from his mother's labor pains right up to this encounter, by way of the sexual explorations of his puberty. Ritchie specified in his second book, *My Life after Dying*[2] that he was horribly embarrassed as these manual "explorations" passed in review before Him, but that *"did not shake my Lord a bit."* Then Christ asks him, *"What have you done with your life?"* The boy tries hard to show off a few good moments from his childhood, and then gives up, thinking that he has nothing to show Him because he is too young to die. Christ dismisses his objection: *"No one is too young to die, for physical death is only of the body and a temporary doorway to another reality through which you just passed."* And immediately he takes the young man to visit five of these realities, which Ritchie will later believe may have been different zones of what we call Hell, Purgatory and Paradise. After the journey Ritchie wishes never to leave His presence, but sinks back into unconsciousness. The doctors have no slightest inkling that the dying man they have been trying to resuscitate has been strolling about somewhere in Heaven with a Being of Light. His heart has stopped beating and he has been pronounced dead a first time. They leave him. Eight or nine minutes pass, and they examine him again to be certain. This time Ritchie is declared officially and administratively dead. They draw up the sheet and leave him again. But a young intern, just Ritchie's age, upset *for reasons he cannot explain*, decides to check a third time, and administers an injection directly into the heart. Surprise: it begins to beat again. Private Ritchie has returned. And when he opens his eyes, it is to hear Lieutenant Irvine entering his room to say to him, *"Good to have you back with us, Private Ritchie."* *"What day is it?"* he asks, thinking of the train to his Christmas furlough. *"Dec. 24, Xmas Eve,"* she answers. *"You've been unconscious for four days."*

Moody was impressed as much by the account as by the doctor seated across from him. Ritchie does not seem eccentric or scatterbrained, rather a man with a good head on his shoulders, extremely likable, endowed with a solid sense of humor. And then Moody forgets about it, takes his Ph.D., and becomes a professor at the University of North Carolina. One day in 1970 he decides to

2. Norfolk, Virginia, Hampton Roads, 1991.

explore the *Phaedo*, a work in which Plato takes up the immortality of the soul. After the classroom discussion one of his students tells him in private of his grandmother's experience. Immediately Moody establishes a connection between that account and Ritchie's. A few days later he tells both stories in class, and asks his students for comments. Surprise—a student raises his hand and offers his sister's story: she was at the point of death, she passed through the tunnel, saw her whole life flash by as if on film in Panavision, and encountered a Light beside which the sun paled to a forty-watt bulb.

At this point Moody begins to ask himself serious questions, and decides to conduct a small investigation. Little by little he collects other stories, always the same, and files them away. In the meantime his teaching career becomes boring, and he decides to train as a doctor. He moves to Georgia and enrolls in medical school, where he will take his degree. In his third year there, one of his acquaintances invites him to talk about his "tunnels" before the membership of a local club of young doctors. Moody delivers a lucid account, and to his great surprise some young doctors, once he has finished, rise to report that they have experienced similar cases. Moody's address book fills up. A reporter does a story on him in the local daily, an article that crosses the desk of a publisher named John Egle, who asks to meet Moody with a view to eventual publication of his accounts. Moody accepts, and harnesses himself to the task, interrogating a great number of people there at the hospital where he studies and works. He turns up impressive examples, a hundred and fifty altogether, perfectly documented, with proof that the subject had been well and truly dead for some minutes. He discovers also that no one else has worked in this area except for another doctor, Elisabeth Kübler-Ross, to whom he sends his manuscript and a request that she write a preface.

His book *Life after Life* appears in 1975 during his fourth year of medical school. And while his publisher hardly expects to sell the two thousand copies of the first run (to local readers and friends of friends), he finds himself with a colossal success on his hands: to date almost ten million copies in fifteen languages. So much success that it became a nightmare for Moody: he lived permanently haunted by the idea that all his stories of ineffable love at the end of the tunnel would give his readers an itch to commit suicide. He commences immediate research into suicides (attempted, by definition) and publishes a second book, *New Light on Life after Life*.

Moody has laid the cornerstone. In his first book he identifies fourteen common characteristics among patients who have returned from "it." In a way he has drawn up the first Guide Michelin to the final destination of all human beings, death itself:

1. Subject always states that what he has experienced cannot be expressed in human language.

2. Subject hears himself declared dead, or everything seems quite strange to him; he feels "dead."

3. Subject no longer feels any pain and is perfectly relaxed and calm.

4. He hears a nearby bell ringing.

5. Subject leaves body and observes what is happening around him. He floats.

6. Subject is sucked into a sort of tunnel.

7. Deceased members of his family appear in the tunnel and help him.

8. Subject perceives a brilliant light.

9. He relives his life in its smallest details.

10. Subject comes up against a kind of "frontier."

11. He suddenly finds himself back in his body.

12. Subject wants to tell his story, but they take him for a madman. He closes up like a clamshell and decides that he is the only person in the world to have experienced such a thing.

13. He begins to read in an effort to understand.

14. He is no longer terrified by death.

The object of our inquiries, Angels, Moody treats with a certain restraint, not to say great caution, in Chapter 7, "Contact with

Others," of his first book: *"In a very few instances people have come to believe that the beings they encountered were their 'guardian spirits.' One man was told by such a spirit that, 'I have helped you through this stage of your existence, but now I am going to turn you over to others.' A woman told me that as she was leaving her body she detected the presence of two other spiritual beings there, and that they identified themselves as her 'spiritual helpers.'"*[3] he writes. Moody was cautious. He had no wish to rush into details that might have discredited his work, already bordering on the supernatural. His book conduces to the supposition that life after death exists, which was already an inconceivable audacity. Moody was to suffer vicious attacks, and looked forward to one thing: a scientific investigation initiated by a serious academician. Two years after his first book came out, a ranking cardiologist published a work confirming Moody's conclusions. The little doctor from Charlottesville was no longer alone. The work of Dr. Maurice Rawlings, a noted cardiologist, a solid and serious man, was to comfort him in his arguments.

Dr. Rawlings is a true Cartesian, hard-nosed and skeptical, formerly on the staff of the 97th General Hospital, the public health unit of American forces based in Frankfurt. His specialty? Wartime surgery—in other words, chests torn apart by bullets or exploding grenades. He serves for four years there and leaves the army for the U.S. Navy, where he serves as cardiologist with the rank of captain. Maurice Rawlings will end his military career brilliantly, at the Pentagon in Washington, the holy of holies. Back in civilian life, he sets up practice in Chattanooga, a quiet city in Tennessee. We can assume that after ten years in the army and navy there is little of the poet about Maurice Rawlings. He is, rather, a man thoroughly trained to grope in bloody bodies and try to glue the pieces together without blinking. It is not surprising, with such a profile, that for this military doctor religion represents nothing more than *"hocuspocus,"* in other words, a practice for superstitious Sicilians. *"I had never set foot in a church,"* he states to me, *"because I was absolutely not a believer. Religion was not for me."*

Outside the closed world of cardiologists, no one would ever have heard of this doctor with a crooner's handsome face if, one day when he was fifty-seven, a man who had come in for a consultation had not collapsed in the waiting room at the hospital, victim of a heart attack. It could not have come at a better time:

---

3. *Life after Life*, Moody, p. 57.

his heart had chosen a good time and a good place to go into arrest. Doctor Rawlings leapt to the man immediately and administered strenuous cardiac massage. Maurice Rawlings is a husky man, and his massage techniques would not have displeased a burly catcher. He went on massaging the chest, automatically checking the dying man's face: almost fifty, a farmhand, white, black hair, average size. Ordinary, but suddenly, in the middle of "manual" resuscitation, the man clutched the doctor's jacket as if to pull it off him, and demanded that he not stop. *"His body turned blue,"* writes Maurice Rawlings in his book *Beyond Death's Door:*[4]

> *While I started external heart massage by pushing in on his chest, one nurse initiated mouth-to-mouth breathing. Still another nurse brought the emergency cart containing pacemaker equipment. Unfortunately, the heart would not maintain its own beat. A complete heart block had occurred. The pacemaker was needed to overcome the block and increase the heart rate from thirty-five beats per minute to eighty or one hundred per minute.*
>
> *I had to insert a pacemaker wire into the large vein beneath the collarbone which leads directly to the heart. One end of this electric wire was manipulated through the venous system and left dangling inside the heart. The other end was attached to a small battery-powered gadget that regulates the heartbeat and overcomes the heart block.*
>
> *The patient began "coming to." But whenever I would reach for instruments or otherwise interrupt my compression of his chest, the patient would again lose consciousness, roll his eyes upward, arch his back in mild convulsion, stop breathing, and die once more.*
>
> *Each time he regained heartbeat and respiration, the patient screamed, "I am in hell!" He was terrified and pleaded with me to help him. I was scared to death. In fact, this episode literally scared the hell out of me! It terrified me enough to write this book.*
>
> *He then issued a very strange plea: "Don't stop!" You see, the first thing most patients I resuscitate tell me, as soon as they recover consciousness, is "Take your hands off*

4. New York, Bantam Books, p. 2.

*my chest; you're hurting me!" I am big and my method of external heart massage sometimes fractures ribs. But this patient was telling me, "Don't stop!"*

*Then I noticed a genuinely alarmed look on his face. He had a terrified look worse than the expression seen in death! This patient had a grotesque grimace express-ing sheer horror! His pupils were dilated, and he was perspiring and trembling—he looked as if his hair was "on end."*

*Then still another strange thing happened. He said, "Don't you understand? I am in hell. Each time you quit I go back to hell! Don't let me go back to hell!"*

*Being accustomed to patients under this kind of emo-tional stress, I dismissed his complaint and told him to keep his "hell" to himself. I remember telling him, "I'm busy. Don't bother me about your hell until I finish getting this pacemaker in to place."*

*But the man was serious, and it finally occurred to me that he was indeed in trouble. He was in a panic like I had never seen before. As a result, I started working fever-ishly and rapidly. By this time the patient had experienced three or four episodes of complete uncon-sciousness and clinical death from cessation of both heartbeat and breathing.*

*After several death episodes he finally asked me, "How do I say out of hell?" I told him I guessed it was the same principle learned in Sunday School—that I guessed Jesus Christ would be the one whom you would ask to save you.*

*Then he said, "I don't know how. Pray for me."*

*Pray for him! What nerve! I told him I was a doctor, not a preacher.*

*"Pray for me!" he repeated.*

*I knew I had no choice. It was a dying man's request. So I had him repeat the words after me as we worked— right there on the floor. It was a very simple prayer because I did not know much about praying. It went something like this:*

*Lord Jesus, I ask you to keep me out of hell. Forgive my sins.*

Completely shaken by what he had just been through, Maurice Rawlings went home in a more than pensive mood. For though he had heard about the stories of NDE circulated in Moody's book, he had never paid the least attention to them. You don't spend ten years in the army to come out believing in this kind of "stupidity." But there in his armchair, with the man's face still dancing before his very eyes, he wanted to know what Hell was like, and he went off to find a Bible in his library. He reflected; he decided this story deserved fuller investigation. So the military cardiologist made a thorough job of it: he systematically interrogated all his patients face to face, after their operations, which only a surgeon could do. And what he discovered sent chills up his spine: the out-of-body experiences, the tunnels, the dead relatives, Angels, the inexpressible Light, etc.

Like Raymond Moody, Dr. Maurice Rawlings found himself obliged to acknowledge that strange things sometimes happened to his surgical patients. One doesn't lie to oneself. He also came to the conclusion that life did not cease at the moment of the body's death. He gathered together his patients' testimonies and published his book in 1978. But curiously, Dr. Rawlings was rejected by the scientific community of NDE researchers, who could not forgive him for having written of his own personal conversion, in a book collecting his patients' testimonies. For that reason, he will be ignored and rarely quoted by later researchers. Yet his book adds one more exhibit to the heap of proofs of the existence of life after death, because his cases were "at first hand": unlike Moody, he could question his patients immediately after their post-operative return to consciousness. And if that privilege was denied to Kenneth Ring too, it was nevertheless this professor who would supply the scientific and academic context that NDE required to become common currency.

In 1977 Ken Ring was going through a period of depression, and was reading whatever he could find that would cheer him up. He came across Moody's book and devoured it. He wanted a truly original topic for research, and he had just found it. A professor of psychology at the University of Connecticut, he immediately set about finding "survivors," with a view to a truly scientific investigation. He wrote to hospitals, churches and doctors, and even inserted want ads in the local newspapers to find new cases. After several months of research he chose—in the most rigorous manner, conforming to scientific criteria—102 people[5] who had made a

5. Fifty-two "died" after a serious illness, 26 in accidents and 24 in attempted suicides; 37 were Catholic, 34 Protestant, 21 without religion, 7 atheists and 3 assort-

short journey into the hereafter; and he decided to interview them for as long as it took to collect their complete impressions. For these interviews he set up a battery of precise questions designed to create a detailed computer analysis that would establish the psychological implications of a NDE and identify its different stages. He spent thirteen months at that. And if his results scarcely differed from Moody's or Rawlings's, Ring nevertheless retained only five major stages:

1. A sensation of peace and serenity (60 percent)

2. Separation from the physical body (37 percent)

3. Entering the darkness of the tunnel (23 percent)

4. Vision of the Light (16 percent)

5. Fusion with the Light (10 percent).

Still, like Moody, Ring noticed no guardian Angels in his sample, except in one case, flawed for our purposes, in which the subject fell into the "5th stage" group, comprising those who had the immense privilege of melting into the Light, while the others had to settle for observing it, a bit like window-shoppers. This man flirted with death at the dentist's, where he was to have a molar extracted. He never got over it:

*"I took a trip to heaven. I saw the most beautiful lakes. Angels—they were floating around like you see seagulls. Everything was white. The most beautiful flowers. Nobody on this earth ever saw the beautiful flowers that I saw there. . . . I don't believe there is a color on this earth that wasn't included in that color situation that I saw. Everything, everything. Of course, I was so impressed with the beauty of everything there that I couldn't pinpoint any one thing. . . . Everything was bright. The lakes were blue, light blue. Everything about the angels was pure white,"* he told Ken Ring. *"Tell me what the angels looked like."*

*"I can't."* [6]

---

ed; 97 were white, 5 black; 45 men, 57 women; age range 18–84; average age at time of interview 43 years 1 month; average age at time of NDE 37 years 8 months; elapsed time between NDE and interview, less than 1 year, 37, 1–2 years 23, 2–5 years 17, 5–10 years 11, over 10 years, 16.

6. *Life at Death*, New York, Quill, 1982, pp. 61–62.

Once finished, the study at the University of Connecticut was to provoke a new explosion, for it validated the medical student's discovery. Moody's adversaries had rightly held that his cases were not perfectly confirmed by a scientific analysis and that consequently they were worthless. When Professor Ring published his study in 1982 under the title *Life at Death*, the number of opponents of NDE fell by half. It fell because two other books dealing with the same topic appeared almost at the same time, *Recollections of Death*[7] by Michael Sabom, a Florida cardiologist, and *Adventures in Immortality*, written by George Gallup, Jr., heir to the famous polling organization. The two professionals, complete strangers the one to the other (who could be more varied than a cardiologist and a pollster?), arrived at the same conclusions in regard to experiences at the frontiers of death. As if everybody was passing the word . . .

Indeed, George Gallup, son of George H. Gallup, was a kind of outsider, popping out of the imposing polling institute founded by his father like a rabbit out of a hat. But he was not much interested in polls. Scion of a family of Protestants, he had planned to enter the ministry and took a degree in religion at Princeton. But finally he decided to succeed his father. *"I had developed an interest in near death experiences,"* he explained to me in an interview, *"after several people close to me told me about their experiences. Then I read Raymond Moody's book and Elisabeth Kübler-Ross's and I confess they fascinated me. I was 52 at the time. Afterward I wondered, 'Why not do a poll on this, with simple clear questions, as long as I'm running a polling institute?' And what we found really astonished me: between 5% and 15% of the American people had gone through some exceptional experience (out of body, near death, etc.). The polls were conducted from 1980 through September 1981. The first enabled us to spot cases of NDE and the second refined the data because we concentrated on people who had reported extraordinary experiences. I think we must have found 500 specific cases in America, of which a quarter were out of body experiences. But you know, what impressed me most about the NDE was the fact that these people knew they were dead and felt enveloped by unconditional love."*

*"Were you much criticized when your book came out?"* I asked him.

*"No, not at all. In any case, I wasn't trying to prove anything."*

*"Then you, George Gallup, a Protestant, believe in life after death,*

7. Harper Row, New York, 1982.

*after these polls?"*

He burst into laughter. *"Yes, of course, and all that only rein-forced my faith in a scientific way. Now I believe definitively in life after death, and I find that very encouraging for the future."*

George Gallup's book impressed me by the sheer gigantic work it represented: hundreds of interviewers fanning out to question people all over the United States. When I realized that France fits easily into the state of Texas, I better appreciated the difficulty of that task. And then Gallup's commentaries were original and some-times even funny, which explains why his book is one of the best in the field. But because he is a professional pollster, his work never enjoyed the response we might have expected in the scientific com-munity, which accepts only the work of its peers. For that, we needed Sabom's detailed inquiries.

Michael Sabom was to hammer home the final nail in a mas-terly fashion after five years of meticulous research. Sabom is a true scientist, a member of the "high-tech" generation of cardiolo-gists, working with information systems and fiber optics. Above all, he belongs to an elite group of the best doctors in the United States. But unlike Dr. Rawlings, Dr. Sabom attended the Methodist Church with his wife, even if he customarily paid little heed—except on that Sunday in 1976 when a social worker asked the faithful if they would like to hear a talk on Moody's book. The parishioners agreed, and the young woman asked the cardiologist if he was interested in this or had an opinion on the topic. Sabom let her down gently, explaining that he had resuscitated many people and no one had ever mentioned any such things to him. The young woman asked him to help her with a documented exploration. He accepted reluctantly, knowing the result in advance because Moody's book was only an invention of the tabloid press.

At the hospital he riffled through his files looking for patients whose hearts had stopped during an operation. Sabom scribbled their names on a pad and shortly payed each a visit. He questions them gently, without stating his primary interest. The two first cases produced nothing. But after a few minutes with the third, the NDE popped up unexpectedly. And Sarah Kreuziger, the social worker, found a case in her dialysis ward. The cardiologist did not understand, feeling that there was an element lacking in this story. He went on hunting but found nothing more. Then Sabom decided to lance the abscess and conduct a scientific investigation himself to settle the question in his own mind. His inquiry took inventory of patients who had been declared dead by surgical teams during an operation. No Angels in Sabom's findings, but an infinite variety of tunnels with that inexpressible Light at the end. Reluctantly, unwillingly, the doctor reached the same conclusions as Dr. Rawlings and Kenneth Ring. An entertaining anecdote: after the publication of his book in 1982, during one of his meetings, a fellow cardiologist, livid with rage, rose to deliver a scorching rebuke, saying that in his whole career he had never come across one patient who passed along twaddle of that kind. Before Sabom could even open his mouth to defend himself, a man in the audience came to his feet and said loudly to the troublemaker, *"Doctor, I'm one of the patients whose lives you saved, and I thank you for it. But I can tell you one thing: you're the last man I'd tell about my experiences."*

What persuaded Sabom that NDEs were authentic were the descriptions of what he calls "autoscopic" survival. At first, even when the testimony of dozens of witnesses lay before his very eyes, he draped himself in his scientist's integrity, not hesitating to say that the states described by these patients derived from a chemical magma (endorphins, anesthetics, etc.) provoked by the brain at the moment of death. And if he had plunged into this investigation, it was to prove Moody wrong.

The explanation by chemical magma would have stood up perfectly, and everyone would have accepted it without argument, if there had not also been testimonies of discorporation as staggering as they were real, and above all confirmed. This stunned certain surgeons. How could a farmhand, or a child of four, who had never been near an operating room prior to their accidents, describe with a precision worthy of a medical student the various steps in the operation (buttons the surgeons pressed, flasks—their color and shape—taken up by the assistants, the resuscitation in fine detail, the nurse's beauty mark just beside her chignon, etc.)?

Let's be honest. Is it really possible to imagine that a patient, stretched out on an operating table, *eyes shut*, naked, the body sliced open by strokes of the scalpel, comatose for the most part or under deep anesthesia, could explain how he was saved, transported and operated on, as soon as he regained consciousness? And the very first reaction of these *"survivors"* was to rebuke the doctors fiercely and even insult them, and the angry question, *"Why did you bring me back? I was so happy there!"* shocked more than one anesthesiologist. Sabom says nothing about the possibility of life after death, but his book confounded skeptics all the more for that. From then on, those who claimed that NDE was only a tissue of falsehoods did so at their own risk.

Various doctors and researchers working independently confirmed, at about the same time or a bit later, the reality of NDE. Among them were Russel Noyes, Stanislas Grof, Phyllis Atwater, the Englishwoman Margot Grey, the French doctor Devawrin, Craig Lundhal, Bruce Greyson, John Audette, George Gallup, Jr., Arvin Gibson, the Frenchwomen Evelyne-Sarah Mercier, etc. Today books about NDE are accumulating like a long series of proofs, testimony which, in a judicial context, would easily have sufficed to convict the traditional image of death ten thousand times over for imposture.

Considering the universality of NDE, it is now truly impossible to ignore them, because the overlapping results of all the international investigations converge in the same direction: *"something"* exists after physical death, and *"yes, you can leave your own body."* Erlendur Haraldsson and Karl Osis even completed a rigorous inquiry among several hundred doctors and nurses, first in India and then in the United States, to determine the effect of religious beliefs and culture context on these experiences. The result of their investigation: the testimonies were strictly identical, and the two researchers realized—the evidence was conclusive—that their discoveries had filled them with hope, because the accounts were *"based on observations by more than a thousand doctors and nurses, bearing on the question of postmortem survival. To anticipate our conclusions, we will state here that this evidence strongly suggests life after death—more strongly than any alternative hypothesis can explain the data."* [8]

Besides, it was hard for them to imagine that these men and women, their eyes barely open, could all be lying. If that were so IT WOULD BE THE FIRST UNIVERSAL LIE, because the circumstances were not at all favorable to a conspiracy of coincidence. Nobody lying half-conscious on a table tells lies to the people bringing him back to life.

And it would be hard to imagine that these highly conservative doctors would lend their names and above all their reputations to these stories of resurrection if there were not that intimate conviction, that absolute certainty, that leaves no lingering doubts about the accuracy of the patient's testimony.

These doctors operated on them, and saw the cardiac monitor display a flat line, saw the electro-encephalogram display a flat line, saw the body turn blue. It was they who used the defibrillator

8. *At the Hour of Death,* Osis and Haraldsson, New York, Hastings House, 1977.

and felt the heart beat again after five, ten, sometimes sixty seconds of inaction. And what can we say about those clinically dead for over ten minutes, who later described to them their resurrection, in detail?

With resuscitating apparatus transformed into computers, detecting the slightest cardiac, or cerebral, or vascular fluctuation, the number of those restored to life grows daily. In operating wings "bringing a patient back" has become an event as frequent as it is clearly identified and followed on screens by millionths of a second. Difficult childbirths, surgical operations that go wrong, and heart attacks are the principal occasions during which a patient "takes off" easily, landing first in a corner of the ceiling before plunging into the famous tunnel *"at-the-end-of-which-a-golden-light-attracts-them-irre-si-sti-bly."* We now know with relative certainty the various stages of a voyage to the frontiers of death, one-way or return, since all testimonials agree. The nationality, age, race, sex and religion of the patient count for nothing:

- The subject suddenly finds himself outside his body, floats up to the ceiling and observes what is happening around his physical envelope. This seems perfectly reasonable to him, and he feels no pain. If the patient is afflicted by some physical infirmity (myopia, for example), it disappears. In general the patient does not understand what is happening to him, above all when he discovers that he can pass through walls or when he tries to explain to the doctors that he is not dead.

- After this observation period, he feels himself sucked at extraordinary speed into a tunnel (drain, pipeline, shaft, tube, canal, etc.) at the end of which he sees a light beckoning him on. The closer he comes to it, the more he wishes to merge with it. That light is described as being stronger than a thousand suns at their zenith.

- After having traveled through the tunnel, the subject may meet near and dear ones who died earlier.

- Fusion with the light, which seems like a living being made of light, overflowing with an unconditional love for the subject. His whole life passes before him like a film, in the space of ten seconds, but in three dimensions, with the effects of his actions and words experienced by others.

- A dialogue (not aloud but in thought) with the Light being, who ends the encounter by saying: "Your hour has not come; you must return and finish your job." Sometimes the subject is asked, "Do you wish to stay here or return?"

- Return to the body. Just chance? These descriptions (the tunnel, Angels, Light, etc.) correspond with perfection to "The Ascension, to Heavenly Paradise" a picture painted by Hieronymus Bosch in the fifteenth century.[9]

The NDE movement started involuntarily by Moody has spread so far and wide that it has become almost a "classic" of movie production. More than any television program or article in the press, two major films are spreading the idea of life after death to the four corners of the world. Hollywood studios brought out two worldwide successes: "Ghost" with Whoopi Goldberg and Patrick Swayze, and "Flatliners," from Joel Schumacher with Julia Roberts and Kiefer Sutherland. The first portrayed the murder of a man who, once out of his body, did not realize that he was dead by assassination. The second explored precisely Near Death Experiences. "Flatliners" showed five medical students who decide to put themselves on the "other side" after several accounts by their patients in terminal states. While one of the interns injects himself with a fatal dose of anesthetic, the four others must wait for a full minute of cardiac flat line before starting the resuscitation procedure.

But the last fireworks exploded on the West Coast of the United States, in Seattle. Dr. Melvin Morse's investigations would definitely confirm the NDE, well beyond all we have seen so far. With *Closer to the Light*,[10] the story of NDE in infancy, Melvin Morse will confer "letters patent of nobility" on experiences at the frontiers of death. Thanks to this young doctor, LIFE magazine devoted its cover story in March 1992 to visions of life after death!

What relationship is there between the guardian Angel and the defibrillator? The investigation conducted in 1984 at Children's Hospital in Seattle by pediatrician Melvin Morse, with the collaboration of Dr. Don Tyler, anesthesiologist, Dr. Jerrold Mil-

9. Oil on wood, Doge's Palace, Venice.
10. Melvin Morse and Paul Perry, New York, Ivy Books, 1990.

stein, director of the department of child neurology at the University of Washington, and Dr. Bruce Greyson, head of the hospital psychiatric service at the University of Connecticut, showed that even children, of whatever age, social condition or parental religion, described sensations and emotions identical to those of adults. Dr. Morse acknowledged that he was particularly intrigued by his first case of child NDE, that of 7 year old Krystel Merzlock, dead by drowning, who gave no signs of cardiac or cerebral activity for more than 19 minutes! *"When I saw her arrive at the emergency room in 1982, I told myself there was 'no hope',"* he remembers. *"Finally we succeeded in reviving her and I still wonder how. After three days in a coma, she recovered from death with no consequences, even though her brain received no oxygen for twenty minutes."* This is utterly improbable by medical teaching, which states that three conditions must occur at once to declare clinical death: heart stoppage, a flat electro-encephalogram, and respiratory arrest. This clinical death, which nevertheless remains briefly reversible, triggers the slower biological death. Within ten to thirty seconds of stoppage, the subject still has a chance. And if the heart restarts, the rest follows, more less well, but it follows. On the other hand, after one, then two, then three minutes of clinical death, the process is irreversible because the brain cells cease to function one after another for lack of oxygen. Even if the heart restarts the brain suffers more or less serious lesions which cause amnesias, paralysis, etc., a little as if one erased random areas on a computer hard disk. Even if you can determine the area affected, whole swatches of the disk are gone, bringing about paralysis of the software. Within ten minutes of clinical death, large areas of the brain are turned into sieves. But this young girl survived almost twenty minutes of clinical death!!!

During a routine visit several days later, Melvin Morse asked her if she remembered her accident. No one really knew how Krystel fell into the swimming pool. No, she didn't remember the circumstances. But she remembered very well that she felt fine afterwards because Elizabeth had kindly sent her to see the Holy Father and Christ. Dr. Morse was upset. Without a doubt, the lack of oxygen had destroyed areas of her brain. But he was a pediatrician and he played the game: *"Tell me Krystel, who is Elizabeth?"* The little girl looked around her and said, very softly, *"She is my guardian Angel."* Then she told him about her journey with the Angel. Melvin Morse stroked his beard. She told how the Eternal Father had asked her if she would like to stay with Him or return to her parents. Krystel had looked at her mother (still from above) and decided to stay with Him. However, He showed her a "vision" of her brothers and sisters playing, and at that she changed her mind and wanted to return home. Without further formalities, she found herself back in her body. To general surprise her heart took up its normal rhythm. The doctors had only one word, "miracle," to account for her resuscitation. After 19 minutes of clinical death, biological death had had plenty of time to start its process of destruction. But no. She recovered like a flower, with no after-effects.

Melvin Morse was not easily taken in: a pediatrician could hardly let himself be persuaded by a seven-year-old girl, so he decided to conduct an inquiry among the parents, to see if they had perhaps spoken to the girl about a tunnel, a white light, guardian Angels, etc. *"When Krystel arrived in the emergency room on a stretcher, I was twenty-seven years old and had only been practicing for two years,"* Melvin Morse explained to me. *"I had never read a single book on the subject, I had never even heard of NDE. When Krystel spoke of her meeting with the Heavenly Father, I didn't think for very long that she might be out of her mind from lack of oxygen, because she offered absolutely astounding descriptions, with exact details of what happened to her during the episode, for example her resuscitation. I was impressed. Normally patients don't remember coming back, and I was intrigued that she did. But she was too sincere, and her experience was too living, too detailed. One little detail proved to me that she wasn't lying: the tube we had inserted in her nose. I consider that detail irrefutable proof because most doctors don't intubate in that manner. It didn't come from television, where sick people or victims are intubated by the mouth, simply because actors have no wish to take a tube up the nose. And quite innocently Krystel said to me, 'I saw you put a tube in my nose.' This I found stupefying, because at that moment she was completely unconscious—in fact, dead. She might have said, 'I felt you put something in my nose.' But no: she said, 'I saw you put in a tube.' And when she recovered consciousness three days later, that tube was no longer in her nose. Besides, there was no way physically that she could have known, perceived, felt in any way that I was putting a tube in her nose at the moment of the procedure."*

Though truly amazed by his little patient's descriptions, Melvin Morse remained skeptical, and gave no credit to religious tales of resurrection: *"My mother was Jewish, and I received a Jewish education. But there was no real religious enthusiasm in my parents. I think they were probably unbelievers. The only holidays we celebrated were the 'social' holidays like Passover or Yom Kippur. I never set foot in a synagogue myself. You can imagine how I felt when Krystel's parents took their places at her bedside to pray. I decided it was doubtless that which explained the whole phenomenon, because the little girl was deeply religious. You realize that her family was praying at her bedside? I really thought she was making it all up. That she was repeating little snatches of what she'd heard, you see. Then I told myself that 'she wasn't properly anesthetized,' etc. Up to that point, my reason won out. But when she told me she'd seen me insert a tube in her nose, that floored me. And afterward her description of the doctors, the equipment, what we were saying in the operating room. I even asked her mother how they had explained death to her, and she said they'd told her death was like coming to a river bank, and stepping into a boat, and crossing the river. But her mother did not believe in guardian Angels. The deeper I investigated, the more I realized that this was not make-believe."*

The bearded young pediatrician was ready to store this case away forever in a corner of his mind when, a month later, he came across a second case of childhood NDE. *"I was really fascinated,"* Dr. Morse began, with more gleams of excitement in his eyes. *"At that time I was looking for a project because I wanted to conduct a study of my own. So I had joined together with some other doctors, and after talking it over we agreed that NDEs were provoked by pharmacological mixes. More exactly, and after reading Moody's book, we had two hypotheses:*

1) *It consisted of a combined reaction to a variety of medicines.*

2) *The patient had not received appropriate care (one had not been given enough Valium and other anesthetics).*

*"We thought for example that the subject was perfectly conscious during her resuscitation, which could explain how she could have understood everything. We had even thought of studying the effects of Ketamine. So we told ourselves that we would prove scientifically that Raymond Moody was wrong and that in reality all those people had simply not been anesthetized correctly."* After a complete dissection of Krystel's medical history,

11. Vol. 137, October 1983, pp. 959–961.

Melvin Morse wrote an article and published it in *The American Journal of Diseases of Children.*[11] Then he patiently observed his young patients. He even established two independent groups, the first composed of children resuscitated where there had been heart stoppage and the second of children in intensive care who had not suffered cardiac arrest. In 200 interviews with children aged three to sixteen, Dr. Morse obtained exactly 33 descriptions of the NDE type. And they all came from the first group. Paralleling the work of Dr. Morse, in 1985 another pediatrician, Dr. David Herzog of Massachusetts General Hospital, in his turn presented two cases of infant NDE in the magazine *Critical Care Medicine.*[12] This reassured the young pediatrician, who had wondered if he was the only doctor interested in NDE children.

In the end Dr. Morse's team established scientifically that:

1. to experience an NDE, the subject must undergo an extremely close brush with death.

2. this experience can in no case be tied to a pharmacological overdose (anti-depressants, tranquilizers, anesthesia, etc.).

But the more he worked on the subject, the more he encountered the role of the brain, which, according to him, operated selectively: *"Certain patients remembered nothing,"* he explained, *"But how could a patient, sometimes in a coma for a week, remember his or her NDE and not recall anything else? Normally, he or she shouldn't remember anything, seeing that certain medicines, like Valium, render the subjects amnesiac. And some don't even remember their stay in the hospital! How can memory retain only the one aspect? We know that there exists in the right temple a zone that activates out of body experiences, in a way the software of NDE. But even if we isolate this zone more exactly, that won't enlighten us as to what the patient saw during his out of body trip, or how he saw it. Some have seen their entire lives pass in minute detail and told us later that it lasted much longer than the life they lived. And yet the cardiac arrest had lasted only two or three seconds!"*

The results of his four years of inquiry were gathered together in a book that stayed at the top of the *New York Times*

12. Vol. 13, no. 12, p. 1074.

best-seller list for three months, and the direct origin of that volume was a guardian Angel, Elizabeth. *"When my book came out,"* Melvin Morse recounted, *"people came to me saying, 'Thank you, I thought I'd gone crazy.' Colleagues said 'You know, I had other cases like that but I didn't know what to make of them.' Nurses, too, and others. It opened a whole new world to me. I might have spent a whole career knowing nothing of these NDE. And I wasn't attacked by other pediatricians. Dr. Moody was attacked, but mostly because he's a psychiatrist. That's not my case. I see very sick people. I treat people's bodies, not their minds. Ken Ring and Phyllis Atwater don't have the chance to hear these stories at patients' bedsides like Dr. Sabom or Dr. Rawlings. So I did what the medical community's ethics demand of a doctor, and published the results of my researches in a medical journal first. I did that three times. And that's what validated my work conclusively."*

But Krystel is not the only case of a guardian Angel in an NDE. A fraction—true, a small fraction—of those who have lived through such an experience have felt a presence, sometimes invisible yet perceptible, sometimes perfectly clear, but always distinct and separate from the being of Light at the end of the tunnel, the central character in all NDE. In the various testimonies published and in those obtained during my own investigations, leaving aside the meetings with recently deceased near and dear ones or with the central being of Light, we can distinguish two types of meetings with the Angel, or "spiritual being" or "entity" or "guide":

Type 1: a vision just before the last breath.

Type 2: an encounter after the tunnel.

How does an NDE differ from a deathbed vision? According to Dr. Morse they are about the same, though there is a fundamental divergence: *"The former happens to patients whom we bring back from the dead, while the latter happens to people in the process of dying. The distinction is important. Let's say for example that the NDE constitute the sequel to a resuscitation, that we're really talking about a hallucination, an intoxication, that sort of thing. Then how do we explain pre-death visions? These visions become inexplicable because they occur among patients in clinically good health. Moreover, these visions occur to subjects who were gravely ill and registered a sudden and inexplicable clinical improvement just before dying. It is an odd thing, but it's just then that they have their visions, at the moment when the family is convinced that the patient is recovering because he seems to be clearly getting better. So let's say that pre-death visions are caused by a mix of medications. Once again, it doesn't hold water. It won't do, because if it were true patients would go through extended periods of delirium and visions. But that's not how it happens. They have these visions as if by chance some seconds or minutes before dying."* Melvin Morse strokes his beard again, as if his thinking aloud led him always to the same conclusion. *"A vision is different from an NDE and we don't really know what an NDE is. On the other hand, when they die, they all, invariably, describe the same thing. And all the confusion becomes quite clear and explains itself if you say, 'This is what happens when you die.' We just ran a similar inquiry on Japanese kids, and their results are the same as ours. Isn't that amazing?"*

Indeed, pre-death visions are well known. But the sick patient is delirious. Besides, it can't be anything else, since he or she says that there's an Angel at his bedside. They give him a tranquilizer before the delirium worsens. But the nurse hasn't enough time to make him swallow pills. The old man retired from the railroad is on his way, as if on tracks, without a cry or a whimper. His face is serene, while during the two months he has occupied this bed he has constantly fretted at the idea of death. Curious. A typical case of pre-death vision, immediately categorized by the doctors or his relatives as delirium. "She's ninety-two, you know, and in a second childhood." Sometimes the effects of a pre-death vision are prodigiously moving to the nearest and dearest, mainly to the women, above all at the bedside of a brother or sister, "I see Mama, she's right there, she's come for me." Then those keeping bedside vigil will dissolve in tears, as if the bonds of blood allowed them to share the emotion of that vision. As we shall see, the ratio of Angels in pre-death visions is equivalent to that in NDE—from four to eight cases in a hundred, a figure that proves that the patients are not as delirious as all that, otherwise they would all claim to see Angels. In fact, the Angel seems to manifest himself when the patient has no recently deceased near and dear ones to come for him!

## TYPE 1
## VISIONS BEFORE THE LAST BREATH

### 1) Angels on the Stairs

A patient suffering from a pulmonary tuberculosis in his last moments. Testimony of a nurse at the hospital recorded by Osis and Haraldsson[13] during their research:

> *He was unsedated, fully conscious and had a low temperature. He was a rather religious person and believed in life after death. We expected him to die and he probably did too as he was asking us to pray for him. In the room where he was lying, there was a staircase leading to the second floor. Suddenly he exclaimed, "See, the angels are coming down the stairs. The glass has fallen and broken." All of us in the room looked towards the staircase where a drinking glass had been placed on one of the steps. As we looked, we saw the glass break into a thousand pieces without any apparent cause. It did not fall; it simply exploded. The angels, of course, we did not see. A happy and peaceful expression came over the patient's face and the next moment he expired. Even after his death the serene, peaceful expression remained on his face.*

It is indeed interesting to note that this vision is corroborated by a material datum, a glass set on the stairs by which the Angels descended to the subject, and which broke for no apparent reason. The glass did not fall.

### 2) A Concert of Angels

In the LIFE magazine piece, "Life after Death?"[14] the reporter describes the death of a young girl in the arms of her parents, as observed by Dr. Diane Komp:

> *Early in her medical career, Komp sat with a family beside their seven-year-old girl, who was in the last stages of leukemia. "She had the final energy to sit up and say, 'The angels—they're so beautiful! Mommy, can you see them? Do you hear their singing? I've never heard such beautiful*

13. *At the Hour of Death,* Osis and Haraldsson, op. cit.
14. March 1992, p. 68.

*singing.'" Then the child died. "The word that most closely
describes what I felt is 'gift.'" says Komp. "It wasn't just that
the child was given the gift of peace in the moment of her
death, but that this was a gift to her parents.*

The child, her strength failing, departs this earth hearing the
songs of Angels come for her. At the very moment when she hears
the celestial melody, life leaves her. Is that by chance? Moreover,
can one suspect the parents, crucified by the loss of their seven-
year-old daughter, of inventing idiotic fantasies? No one lies in the
face of death, in the grip of the most violent emotions.

### 3) AN ANGEL WITH ME

The case of Ralph Wilkerson: A man, victim of a serious accident
while visiting a construction site, is rushed to the hospital. At the
hospital, the doctors discover a fractured arm and a broken neck.
They warn his wife that if she wants to see him one last time she
had better hurry, because her husband will not last three days.
Immediately she rushes to the hospital and hurries to her husband's room. After muttering a couple of phrases, he sinks into
unconsciousness. The doctors dare not even move him. It is the
end. The next morning, a nurse enters the dying man's room with a
hypo and discovers that he has awakened:[15]

> *"What are you doing awake?" she scolded gently.
> "Nurse, I have had a bright light in this room, and an
> angel has been with me all through the night."
> "Oh yes."*

The patient went home against the advice of the doctors, who
made him sign every imaginable release. But he truly and inexplicably recovered without a trace of paralysis or any setback. Put
yourself in his place for an instant: you have the arm and neck
broken. The arm is not very serious. The neck on the other hand
immobilizes you, and the doctors state that there is no hope. This
can only be a supernatural vision, that of an Angel at the foot of
your bed who can assure you absolutely that you are going to
recover from that nasty fracture, since he told you so. You would
never take the risk of leaving the hospital without that absolute
conviction. And even if you felt better, you'd stay "under observation." Well, once more this is of course all by chance.

---

15. *Beyond and Back,* Melodyland Publishers, 1977, Anaheim, California, p. 99.

## 4) Someone with Me

The case of nurses Maggie Callahan and Patricia Henley, who took care of a young woman of twenty-five, hospitalized with a melanoma that had progressed to the point where she had absolutely no chance of surviving. Angela knew she was condemned to die and did not want anyone to pity her fate. She had even warned the hospital personnel by saying to them, "I don't want any spiritual assistance, no prayer, no priest. That's not my way. I'm an atheist. I don't believe in God or heaven." The team of nurses accepts that, and agrees. Yet one gray morning in February, when the call bell rang constantly, the duty nurse rushed to Angela's room. Angela's mother, who slept in a bed at her side, was making it up, her eyes still full of sleep:[16]

> "Hi, Angela, what can I do for you?" I said.
>
> "Did someone come in here to see me?" she said.
>
> "I don't think so. I didn't see anyone. It's not even dawn yet, and there's no one around." I said. "Why do you ask?"
>
> "I saw an angel."
>
> I sat on the bed.
>
> "Tell me what happened," I said.
>
> "When I woke up there was an angel sitting in the light from the window," Angela said, with a smile on her face. She described feeling very drawn toward this being, who exuded warmth, love, and caring.
>
> Her mother jumped off the cot.
>
> "Angela, it's a sign from God!" she said.
>
> "Mother, I don't believe in God!" Angela said, now exasperated.
>
> "That doesn't matter," her mother said. "You've seen God, or at least a messenger from God!"
>
> "Does it matter who it is?" Angela snapped. "Isn't it enough to know that there's someone so loving and caring waiting for me?"
>
> "Angela, what do you think it means?" I asked.
>
> "I don't believe in angels or God, but someone was here with me. Whoever it was loves me and is waiting for me. So it means I won't die alone."

16. *Final Gifts*, New York, Simon & Schuster, 1992, pp. 90–91.

Even atheists are not spared by the Angels. In this case, the subject had experienced a presence that she called an Angel, as no other word could better define what she felt. She also became certain that she would not die "alone."

## 5) An Angel in a Hurry!

This case was passed along to me by Edouard Adamis, former CEO for United Artists record company in France. Here we have a typical deathbed vision:

> *My brother—he must have been fourteen or fifteen— had injured his foot, and gangrene set in. This happened in 1925 or 1926, I can't remember exactly, in Beirut, and for some reason I can't remember either, he was not properly cared for. My parents had made him comfortable in his room, and my mother was at his bedside constantly. Again, I can't explain how the infection developed or why he was not under a doctor's care; at any rate one day he asked my mother for some colored crayons and some paper. First my brother sketched a cypress, then a tomb, and finally my parents standing before the grave. Afraid, my mother asked him why he had sketched his own tomb. And Gerard answered: "I know very well that I am going to die, Mother."*
>
> *My mother did not pursue the matter, told him to forget it, and closed the door to the room. A few minutes later she heard him talking with someone. After five minutes of that curiosity overcame her, and she burst into the room, but she saw no one. "Who were you talking to, my son?"*
>
> *My brother answered, "With an Angel. He told me that it was time I went along with him. But I refused, because I want to see Dad again. So he told me that I'd come along after I saw Dad."*
>
> *My mother was sure that he was delirious or out of his head, but was astonished by his calm. My father, who knew nothing of all this, arrived at about eleven o'clock, went into the room to give him a hug, and had barely left the room when my brother died.*
>
> *My mother talked about that for a long time, because she was deeply shocked by the incident. And you know very well that no mother would make up tall stories about the death of her own son.*

Once more, although the subject seemed to be doing well and is in possession of all his mental faculties (the premonitory sketch), he announces to his mother that his Angel has given him permission to wait for his father, doubtless for a final farewell. From the materialistic point of view this can only be, again, a coincidence. On the other hand, from the point of view of "deathbed visions" we are in the presence of a clinical, and typical, case, which proves again that the Angel has a tendency to materialize only—exclusively—when the subject has arrived at the last gasp. Manifestly, this Luminous Being accompanied the boy to his new existence.

## TYPE 2
## MEETING AFTER THE TUNNEL
## OR ANGELS IN NEAR DEATH EXPERIENCES

Here, we enter directly into the famous tunnel at the end of which burns a light indescribable in human terms. Given the subject of this book, the light itself is not of primary interest to us. On the other hand, what happens during the passage through this tunnel and afterwards is our primary field of investigation, because one may say that it is in the tunnel, curiously enough, or at the exit of the tunnel, that one has the best chance of meeting an Angel. Indeed, after leaving his own body, the subject is sometimes accompanied by beings identified as guardian Angels, or guides, or spiritual beings. They are perfectly distinct from the central Light and the subject never confuses the two. However, according to statistics, of every one hundred clinical deaths, only 10 percent will have the "privilege" of merging with that Light. If we push the analysis further, we find also that only 10 percent will discover a presence at their sides. It is important to emphasize that finding an NDE with Angels as a hallmark is not an easy thing. In general, the subject is welcomed by the recently dead or else hears a voice that orders him to return. In questioning about a hundred NDE survivors, I recorded several cases where the subject held a conversation with one or more of these presences, and I have grouped them with NDE experiences of the "Angel Type" that I was able to find in various works edited by the most serious researchers (Morse, Moody, Ring, Rawlings, Gallup, Sorenson, Gibson, Ritchie). Kenneth Ring has told me of three magnificent cases that he has not published in his books. Kimberley Sharp has sent me a handsome present and Dr. Melvin Morse has also shared several cases with me and allowed me to search for Angels in his case histories. I warmly thank them here for their collaboration and their help. Without them, I would still be working a crossword puzzle ("can float" in five letters).

## 1) WE ARE NOT ANGELS

Intelligent, blond, slender, a typical California girl with a "Venice Beach" tan, Nancy Meier passes easily for thirty-five. She is very pretty and very feminine; she could be an ex-model. When you approach her, you'd rather ask her to dinner than talk with her about tunnels and other lights. Yet she has reached her 49th spring. And when people ask her, "What is your secret?," she won't answer. But her secret is her experience at the brink of death, which occurred in her garden in St. Louis one day in 1975 when she was trying to prune the highest branch on a tree. Suddenly she lost her balance. Today, Nancy explains very simply that that was the most important moment of her life. Nancy belongs to that minority of survivors who encounter spiritual beings at the end of the tunnel, perfectly distinct from the being of the Central Light. Here is the account of her experience:

> *I was on the top step of the ladder and I wanted to cut a branch when suddenly I lost my balance and fell. During my fall I said to myself: "This won't be very serious." As I hit the ground violently, the ladder fell on top of me, right on my stomach. My entire life passed in front of me like a movie. That was all. I got back up a trifle groggy and told myself that just in case, I should go to the hospital and make sure nothing was broken. At St. John's Hospital, the x-rays were negative, but because I didn't feel very well, the doctor kept my under observation. As time passed I felt worse, without knowing exactly what was wrong. After two days I was worse. The doctor took more x-rays and finally discovered that my liver had ruptured and gangrene had devastated not only my liver but also my intestines. There was a mad rush. I was hurried to surgery where my stomach was immediately opened for a thorough cleaning. The surgeons weren't sure I'd survive. For three days I went up and down ceaselessly in the tunnel at the end of which I saw that Light. The first time, it all seemed very strange because I saw myself suddenly . . . from the ceiling. I saw my body stretched out on the bed in my room and my mother seated at my side. I said to myself: "This is crazy, because I'm in the bed and up here at the same time." Then I turned away and traveled through that tunnel at an unbelievable speed. There was a very shrill sound.*

*When I reached the end, I met three Beings of Light. I under-
stood nothing, but I was trying—how do I say this?—to
stabilize myself in their presence. When I had done that I said
to myself: "O.K., I'm dead, where are the Angels?" They
answered me by thought: "For you, we don't need to look like
Angels because you don't believe in Angels." And I laughed
because I knew in my heart that they were Angels, in truth. It
was like a thought, a certainty that they had transmitted to
me. "Looking" at them, I had the impression that they constituted a welcoming committee. They resembled candlelights.
But I also felt that each of them possessed his own personality, that they were quite distinct one from another. I did not
see their faces but I felt their personalities, the essence of their
being. We did not speak; everything happened through telepathy. And I knew that these were Angels or more precisely
Beings of Light with their own consciousness, just like ours.
Then I found myself really in the White Light, that everybody
talks about, that envelops you with infinite love so every
atom of your being quivers with passionate love. To melt in
that light is a little like coming home, falling in unconditional
love. That was my experience of God. My life began to run in
three dimensions. It was as real as talking to you right now.
To feel the effects of your actions on others makes you realize
what you really are. Then I asked the question: "Nancy, what
do you want? Stay here or return?" I had two daughters and
a young son but I did not want to return. I wanted to remain.
Can you imagine such a thing? To abandon my children?
But it was so marvelous. Words can't express what I felt.
Than I asked, "If I go back, will it make a difference to my
family?" and He said to me, "Yes, to your son." So I came
back for him.*

Like all survivors, Nancy Meier was transformed by her experi-
ence. And if the existence of Angels had never struck her before her
NDE, henceforth it was a certainty. Note in this case that the three
Angels do indeed constitute the welcoming committee at the end of
the tunnel and that they possess a sense of humor: "We are not
Angels because you do not believe in Angels," and at the same time
they convey to her the absolute certainty that they are indeed
Angels. We note also that they resemble flames.[17]

17. A video tape "The Glimpse of Forever" of her experience is available. Write to:
   PO Box 9373, Marina del Rey, CA 90295.

## 2) THE SKY IS NIFTY

This is the case that fascinated Dr. Melvin Morse and inspired him to take an interest in children's stories of tunnels, with the results we have noted. He published Krystel's experience as an article in the *The American Journal of Diseases of Children*, Volume 137, pages 959, 961[18] and specified that the child, seven years old, had refused to allow him to record the conversation until he had seen the drawings she wanted to show him, illustrating her experience:

> *The patient said that the first memory she had of her near-drowning was "being in the water." She stated, "I was dead. Then I was in a tunnel. It was dark and I was scared. I couldn't walk." A woman named Elizabeth appeared, and the tunnel became bright. The woman was tall, with bright yellow hair. Together they walked to heaven. She stated that "heaven was fun. It was bright and there were lots of flowers." She said that there was a border around heaven that she could not see past. She said that she met many people, including her dead grandparents, her dead maternal aunt, and Heather and Melissa, two adults waiting to be reborn. She then met the "heavenly Father and Jesus," who asked her if she wanted to return to earth. She replied "no." Elizabeth then asked her if she wanted to see her mother. She said yes and woke up in the hospital. Finally, she claimed to remember seeing me in the emergency room, but could not supply any other details of the three-day period during which she was comatose.*

This case is fascinating: a seven-year-old girl (clinically dead for 19 minutes!) who states quite simply and without malice that she has met the Eternal Father and Jesus, while all around the world tens of thousands of monks and nuns, more or less cloistered, spend their whole lives awaiting that experience. Isn't that strange?[19] Here is a young girl to whom the guardian Angel

---

18. Reprinted by Dr. Moody in 1988 in *The Light Beyond*, p. 76.

19. This confirms perfectly the parable of the "greatest" in Matthew 18:1–4, in Christ's response to the disciple who asked him, "Who is the greatest in the kingdom of heaven? And Jesus called a little child unto him, and set him in the midst of them, and said: Verily I saw unto you, except you be converted, and become as little children, ye shall not enter into the kingdom of heaven. Whosoever therefore shall humble himself as this little child, the same is greatest in the kingdom of heaven."

appeared immediately as she drowned, a girl who straightaway goes to play in God's garden. *"Do you want to go back?"* the Eternal Father asks her. Her answer, imagine, is, *"Noooooo, I doooon't want tooo."* The simplicity of children is often disarming, even for the gods.

In his book *Closer to the Light*,[20] Dr. Morse gives more details of his impressions when the child's body arrived on the stretcher:

> *I stood over Katie's lifeless body in the intensive care unit and wondered whether this little girl could be saved . . .*
>
> *I didn't really expect to find out what had happened. The machines to which she was not hooked up told a grim story. An emergency CAT scan showed massive swelling of the brain. She had no gag reflex. An artificial lung machine was breathing for her. In the blunt jargon of emergency room physicians, she was a train wreck. Looking back even now, I would guess that she had only a ten percent chance of surviving. . . .*
>
> *One episode with Katie remains vivid in my mind even today. I was trying to thread a small catheter into one of her arteries so we could get an exact reading of the oxygen in her blood. The procedure, called arterial catheterization, is particularly difficult and bloody since an incision into an artery is required . . .*
>
> *Three days later she made a full recovery.*
>
> *Her case was one of those medical mysteries that demonstrate the power of the human organism to rebound . . .*
>
> *Her eyes revealed an intelligence that hadn't been dimmed by the deprivation of oxygen to the brain that always accompanies drowning. There was nothing abnormal in her walk or mannerisms. She was just another nine-year-old kid.*

Nothing abnormal after 19 minutes of clinical death! This is utterly unreasonable, a true miracle that has not been explained and never will be. The brain, with no oxygen available during this lapse of time, should have been totally destroyed. In similar cases, when doctors succeeded in "bringing back" a patient, after even a minute of clinical death, they start speculating on the patient's degree of paralysis once they revive. But this seven-year-old child

20. A "must read" book.

recovers like a flower. Another coincidence. Opening a book on the Angels at random, I found this quote: *"Take heed that ye despise not one of these little ones; for I say unto you, That in heaven their angels do always behold the face of my Father which is in Heaven."* [21]

### 3) ROBES OF LIGHT

A case from Dr. Raymond Moody: Jason, eleven years old, had just received a bicycle for his birthday. The next day, impatient to try it out, he jumped on and hurtled down his normally quiet little street. But this day, so happy aboard his new toy, he failed to see the car coming straight at him. The ambulance, the hospital, a little therapy and all seems in order. He had tried to talk to his mother about his experience but she did not want to hear about it. So he tucked the memory away immediately in a corner of his secret garden. But three years later one of his fellow students died of leukemia. The teacher discussed this event in class, and a light went on in Jason's mind. He raised his hand and explained to his young friends that in fact when we die, we do not die! Dead silence, prolonged. Even the teacher was stunned: *"Jason, what do you mean by that?"* Then he told them of his own experience, assuring them, *"Well, death isn't too serious."* [22]

> *I don't remember getting hit but suddenly I was looking down at myself. I saw my body under the bike and my leg was broken and bleeding. I remember looking and seeing my eyes closed. I was above. . . .*
>
> *The ambulance drove off and I tried to follow it. I was above the ambulance following it. I thought I was dead. I looked around and then I was in a tunnel with a bright light at the end. The tunnel seemed to go up and up. I came out on the other side of the tunnel. . . .*
>
> *When I was going up in the tunnel two people were helping me. I saw them as they got out into the light. They were with me the whole way.*
>
> *Then they told me I had to go back. I went back through the tunnel where I ended up back in the hospital where two doctors were working on me. They said, "Jason, Jason." I saw my body on this table and it looked blue. I knew I was going to go back because the people in the light told me.*

21. Matthew 18:10.
22. *The Light from Beyond*, p. 70.

*The doctors were worried, but I was trying to tell them I
was all right. One doctor put paddles on my chest and my
body bounced up. . . .*

*Moody: Jason, did you notice anything about the
people in the tunnel with you?*

*Jason: The two people with me in the tunnel helped me
as soon as I got there. I didn't know where I was exactly
but I wanted to get to that light at the end. They told me I
would be okay and they would take me into the light. I
could feel love from them. I didn't see their faces, just
shapes in the tunnel. When we got into the light I could see
their faces. This is hard to explain because this is very different from life in the world. I don't have any word for it. It
was like they were wearing very white robes. Everything
was lighted.*

*Moody: You said they talked to you. What did they say?*

*Jason: No. I could tell what they were thinking and they
could tell what I was thinking.*

As with Krystel, Dr. Moody noted that despite the seriousness of
his accident, Jason recovered without the slightest cerebral
damage or any sequelae, which is close to miraculous. Here the
subject distinguishes two forms radiating love, who comfort him
during his passage through the tunnel. Jason could not distinguish
them until he had left the tunnel. Communication was telepathic.

## 4) Hand in Hand with the Angel

A case kindly conveyed to me by Ken Ring and published later in
the *Journal of Near Death Experiences*, Volume 10, #1, Fall 1991,
pages 11-29. This is a story of considerable interest because it
reflects all the elements of Hieronymus Bosch's painting *Ascension
to Heavenly Paradise*. Beverly was reared in a conservative but non-
practicing Jewish family in Philadelphia *in a "materialistic and
claustrophobic atmosphere. In high school the girls were judged by
the clothes they wore and their beauty.* Despite her excellent grades,
Beverly was frightened by the school and her vision of the future,
and her adolescent crisis was exacerbated by her father's death.
After he died, her mother fell into a deep depression, and utterly
appalled by life, Beverly ran away from home. *"Since learning, in
very muted terms, of the Holocaust at age eight I had turned angrily
against any early belief in God. How could God exist and permit such
a thing to occur? The secularism of my public school education and
the lack of any religious training added fuel to my beliefs."*

She leaves Philadelphia for the eternal sunshine of California, and arrives in Los Angeles at high tide of the hippie years. The next day, to celebrate her arrival, a friend suggests a spin on his motorcycle. Far from the oppressive atmosphere of her home, she finally feels happy and carefree, and hops onto the passenger seat. The ride through the California desert ends badly. On a narrow road baking in the heat a drunk driver smashes into the bike, and Beverly, without a helmet, is flung clear, finally crashing to the ground head first and sliding several yards, leaving behind the skin of half her face. She spends two weeks in the hospital, full of anesthetics and tranquilizers to help her stand the pain of her fractures. Finally she is released from the hospital. She goes back to her little temporary apartment, sets down her bag, and opens the bathroom door. She switches on the light and for the first time takes a good look at herself in the mirror. She is disfigured. Her face is the face of a mutant. She realizes suddenly that with a face like that no man will ever look twice at her again. That thought becomes an obsession, a nightmare. She collapses in tears. She weeps, weeps as she has never wept before. After the loss of her father, this accident is the straw that breaks the camel's back. She reaches the depths of despair. And for the first time in her life, like so many people, she turns to God, the only hypothetical friend she has left, and prays to him, begs him to carry her off once and for all:

> *I could not live another day. At 20 I had no goals but to enjoy life and find someone to share it with. The pain was unbearable: no man would ever love me; there was, for me, no reason to continue living.*
>
> *Somehow an unexpected peace descended upon me. I found myself floating on the ceiling over the bed looking down at my unconscious body. I barely had time to realize the glorious strangeness of the situation—that I was me but not in my body—when I was joined by a radiant being bathed in a shimmering white glow. Like myself, this being flew but had no wings. I felt a reverent awe when I turned to him: this was no ordinary angel or spirit, but he had been sent to deliver me. Such love and gentleness emanated from his being that I felt that I was in the presence of the messiah.*
>
> *Whoever he was, his presence deepened my serenity and awakened a feeling of joy as I recognized by companion. Gently he took my hand and we flew right through the window. I felt no surprise at my ability to do this. In this*

*wondrous presence, everything was as it should be.*

*Beneath us lay the beautiful Pacific Ocean, over which I had excitedly watched the sun set when I had first arrived. But my attention was now directed upward, where there was a large opening leading to a circular path. Although it seemed to be deep and far to the end, a white light shone through and poured out into the gloom to the other side where the opening beckoned. It was the most brilliant light I had ever seen, although I didn't realize how much of its glory was veiled from the outside. The path was angled upward, obliquely, to the right. Now, still hand in hand with the angel, I was led into the opening of the small dark passageway.*

*I then remember traveling a long distance upward toward the light. I believe that I was moving very fast, but this entire realm seemed to be outside of time. Finally, I reached my destination. It was only when I emerged from the other end that I realized that I was no longer accompanied by the being who had brought me there. But I wasn't alone. There, before me, was the living presence of the Light. Within it I sensed an all-pervading intelligence, wisdom, compassion, love and truth. there was neither form nor sex to this perfect Being. It, which I shall in the future call He, in keeping with our commonly accepted syntax, contained everything, as white light contains all the colors of a rainbow when penetrating a prism. And deep within me came an instant and wondrous recognition: I, even I, was facing God.*

*I immediately lashed out at Him with all the questions I had ever wondered about, all the injustices I had seen in the physical world. I don't know if I did this deliberately, but I discovered that God know all your thoughts immediately and responds telepathically. My mind was naked; in fact, I became pure mind. The ethereal body which I had traveled in through the tunnel seemed to be no more. It was just my personal intelligence confronting that Universal Mind which clothed itself in a glorious, living light that was more felt than seen since no eye could absorb its splendor.*

*I don't recall the exact content of our discussion; in the process of return the insights that came so clearly and fully in Heaven were not brought back with me to Earth. I'm sure that I asked the question that had been plaguing me*

*since childhood about the sufferings of my people. I do
remember this: there was a reason for everything that happened, no matter how awful it appeared in the physical
realm. And within myself, as I was given the answer, my
own awakening mind now responded in the same manner:
"Of course," I would think, "I already know that. How
could I ever have forgotten!" Indeed it appears that all that
happens is for a purpose, and that purpose is already
known to our eternal self.*

    *In time the questions ceased, because I suddenly was
filled with all the Being's wisdom. I was given more than
just the answers to my questions; all knowledge unfolded
to me, like the instant blossoming of an infinite number of
flowers all at once. I was filled with God's knowledge,
and in that precious aspect of his Beingness, I was one
with him.*

This is not what we call a typical NDE, as there is no accident or
physical death at the time of the experience. But all the ingredients
are present. The common factor, intense emotion and despair mingled with a sudden appeal to God, provoked this voyage outside the
subject's body, the passage through the tunnel with the help of a
radiant Being of Light, a marvelous presence who takes her hand.
Here, the guide helps her enter the tunnel and then disappears. He
does not identify himself.

## 5) MY GUARDIAN

A case reported by the brilliant Mormon researcher Arvin Gibson,[23]
who tracked down and interviewed some hundred survivors. Ann's
account struck him so forcefully that he used it on his book's cover.
Ann is nine years old. As usual in the evening, her mother tucks her
in, without noticing this time that the child is pale and listless.
(Doctors had diagnosed an incipient leukemia.) She kisses the
child and says good night, turns off the light and leaves the room,
closing the door gently behind her. Ann feels strange and lies sleep-
less, when a sense of light makes her open her eyes. Then she
perceives a brilliant golden light that seems to emanate from the
wall to her left and spread gently over the room:

    *I sat up and watched the light grow. It grew rapidly in
both size and brightness. In fact the light got so bright that it*

23. *Glimpses of Eternity*, Bountiful, Utah, Horizon Publishers, 1991, pp. 52–54.

*seemed to me that the whole world was lit by it. I could see*
*someone inside the light. There was this beautiful woman,*
*and she was part of the light: in fact she glowed. . . .*

*It seemed as if she were a pure crystal filled with light.*
*Even her robe glowed with light as if by itself. The robe was*
*white, long-sleeved, and full length. She had a golden belt*
*around her waist and her feet were bare. Not that she*
*needed anything on her feet since she stood a couple of feet*
*off the floor. . . .*

*I had never seen such kindness and gentle love on*
*anyone's face such as I saw in this person. She called me*
*by name and held out her hand to me. She told me to*
*come to her—her voice was soft and gentle but . . . it was*
*more in my mind. Communication was easier than when*
*you verbalize thoughts. At the time I thought of it as*
*"mind talk."*

*I asked her who she was and she explained that she*
*was my guardian and had been sent to take me to a place*
*where I could rest in peace. The love emanating from her*
*washed over me so that I didn't hesitate to put my hand*
*in hers.*

*As soon as I was standing beside her we moved through*
*a short darkness to a beautiful, even brighter light. . . .*

*I asked my guardian why she took me to this place. She*
*said that I needed the rest because life had become too hard*
*for me to live.*

Ann was on a hillside in a radiant park, with other children who were playing with toys, and she joined them, wholly "immersed in this new world which breathed love, peace and joy." The luminous Being left her in the park and returned later. She grasped its hand again, as it explained that they must leave now, which enraged the little girl. She did not want "to go back." Then the Angel explained gently that from now on her life on earth would be easier. At that moment, Ann returned to her bed. Afterward the doctors found no trace of leukemia.

## 6) I Was Enveloped

The following case was sent to me by Evelyne-Sarah Mercier, president of the French branch of IANDS, the International Association for Near Death Studies. On December 6, 1983, while she was driving around suburban Paris, Madame B.'s car skidded on some gravel on the narrow road. After a wild spin the car smashed into a light pole, and finally came to rest, after a series of rolls, at the bottom of a hill. The consequences of this accident were terrible: fractured pelvis, spinal column crushed, and a leg driven up into the lower abdomen. But when she should have been screaming or passing out from the pain, Madame B felt a strange sensation come over her, as if she were leaving her body. . . .

> I was elevated (out of my body) and found myself in something blue. Everything was blue, including my car down below. I did not know why, or what had happened. And there in the blue stood a Luminous Being. He did not have a human form, but was rather a mass of light. One might describe him/her as a very large, long, luminous cloak observing everything about him.
>
> Even stranger, beside this Luminous Being was another being, this one invisible, I don't know how to explain this, whose breath I could sense on the left side of my face. My feeling is that this was a man, I don't know why. Beyond them and to the right was a line of trees. Light was everywhere, and was beginning to envelop my abdomen. Even more amazing, it was not a blinding light painful to the eyes. I felt it as I would feel love. . . .
>
> In fact, at that place and in the presence of that light, the dreadful state of my body was no longer of importance. But my descent was terrible, and I had the impression that I was traveling thousands of kilometers at frightening speed to re-enter my body.

A typical out of body experience at a moment of imminent death. And given Madame B.'s condition just after the crash, it could not have been a pretty sight. She leaves her body and finds herself, beyond any doubt, before the "Central Being of Light," which is not unusual in the domain of NDEs. On the other hand we note that He was accompanied by another Being of Light, this one invisible—though perceptible—standing behind her, as if to reassure her or sustain her, to the point where she uses the startling phrase, "I felt his breath on the left side of my face."

Here too, "It is not your moment" seems to come into play. Another interesting phenomenon, the Central Being of Light "envelops" her lower abdomen as if He were healing internal wounds.

## 7) A Beautiful Woman

Reported by Dr. Raymond Moody in his book *The Light Beyond,*[24] is this case of a little girl, five years old, whose heart gave out during an appendectomy. As soon as the cardiac monitor signaled no pulse, the doctors set about the resuscitation procedure. Nina's account:

> *I heard them say my heart had stopped but I was up at the ceiling watching. I could see everything from up there. I was floating close to the ceiling, so when I saw my body I didn't know it was me. Then I knew because I recognized it. I went out in the hall and I saw my mother crying. I asked her why she was crying but she couldn't hear me. The doctors thought I was dead.*
>
> *Then a pretty lady came up and helped me because she knew I was scared. We went through a tunnel and went into heaven. There are beautiful flowers there. I was with God and Jesus. They said I had to go back to be with my mother because she was upset. They said I had to finish my life. So I went back and I woke up.*
>
> *The tunnel I went through was long and very dark. I went through it real fast. There was light at the end. When we saw the light I was very happy. I wanted to go back for a long time. I still want to go back to the light when I die.*

This is our third case of NDE in female childhood, and here too it is a "very beautiful woman" who comes searching for Nina, because once out of her body she wanders about like a phantom. This account would turn any doctor of theology green with envy. The five-year-old girl meets the Eternal Father and Jesus, which is rather surprising in itself because even for adults the distinction between them is not obvious. A majority of Christians believe that the Father and Son are consubstantial, the same thing, without even mentioning the Holy Spirit, who completes the confusion; and their understanding is far from the theologians', who differentiate them by explaining that they are three Persons in one. . . . (Quick! An Aspirin!) But this child has no idea what she is talking about, except that for her the Father and Son were as real as her toys. As Dr. Moody interprets it, *"The child has not yet been jaded by the world around her, and has no idea what an NDE is like. Because children are less culturally conditioned than adults, their testimony*

24. New York, Bantam Books, 1988.

*reinforces the validity of the description of the basic NDE."* [25]

## 8) ANGEL AIRLINES

The account of a patient of the cardiologist Maurice Rawlings.[26] The man realizes that his pacemaker is not functioning properly. This is not the kind of electronics that we can leave malfunctioning while we wait for warranty service. So he decides to go back to the hospital immediately for a standard replacement, an extremely complex operation necessitating a stay of several days. At the time of the event, the patient is in his room chatting with his wife and brother-in-law. Suddenly he feels his heart begin to race. He hardly has time to ask his wife to call a nurse before he passes out.

> *I remember someone shouting "Code 99, Code 99." But I wasn't in the room after that. A nurse, it seemed, had grasped me from behind, encircling my waist with her arms, and took me out of there. We started flying out of the city, going faster and faster. The first time I knew it was not a nurse was when I looked down toward my feet and saw the tips of some white wings moving behind me. I am sure now it was an angel!*
>
> *After soaring for a while, she (the angel) sat me down on a street in a fabulous city of buildings made of glittering gold and silver and beautiful trees. A beautiful light was everywhere—glowing but not bright enough to make me squint my eyes. On this street I met my mother, my father and my brother, all of whom had died previously.*
>
> *"Here comes Paul" I heard my mother say. As I walked to greet them, however, this same angel picked me up by the waist again and took me off into the sky. I didn't know why they wouldn't let me stay.*
>
> *In the distance we were approaching the skyline. I could recognize the buildings. I saw the hospital where I had been sent as a patient. The angel descended and put me back in the very room where I had been located and I looked up and saw the faces of the doctors working on me. I was back in the body. I will never forget the experience. I don't think anyone could be an atheist if he had an experience like mine.*

25. Ibid. p. 65.
26. *Beyond Death's Door,* p. 78.

Now we are at the heart of the matter. The patient is an atheist. He dies. According to a Catholic priest, as an atheist he ought logically to land on Hell's runway with Satan himself in the control tower. What is marvelous about NDEs is that all the threats of this kind offered by brainless priests vanish in a puff of smoke.[27] The patient feels himself lifted by a nurse. But he discovers that it is not a nurse, but an Angel all in white, with wings! And that it is not his physical body raised up, but his ethereal body. In short, after a flight "through the air" he is set down in a city which we now recognize, considering the number of NDEs reported throughout the world that describe it in the same detail. He encounters his deceased parents, and just as he goes about to embrace them the Angel surges from nowhere, swoops down on him like an eagle, and restores him to the hospital. His cardiac arrest lasted fifteen seconds.

## 9) Two Sublime Girls

The following case is of interest because it comes to us from Yugoslavia, a Communist country at the time of these events. In 1956 the soldier Petar, twenty years old, has finished ten months of his service in the JNA, the Yugoslav people's army.

> *In '56 Tito was still living in fear of a Russian invasion, which translated to rigorous training exercises in the Slovene mountains. I was assigned to the Pivka Kaserna. One afternoon following a very long march at the double with full field pack, I grew dizzy, my chest tightened and my legs grew heavy. I couldn't walk. They had to take me on a stretcher to the barracks, where the doctor auscultated me and rushed me to the Domzale military hospital in Ljubljana. There the doctors diagnosed a heart fibrillation. I was in critical condition. I remember a sinister emergency room which I shared with an old colonel in no better shape than I was. Despite the tons of medicine they made me swallow, I felt no better; on the contrary. After a month in*

27. Dr. Raymond Moody ran across a preacher who, before his NDE, talked only about hell, fire, sulfur, souls in torment, etc., terrorizing the faithful by telling them that if they did not cease to sin, they would burn in hell for all eternity. Who hasn't heard this sort of sermon at least once? In a nutshell, accident, NDE: The preacher encounters the Luminous being, who shows him how he is poisoning his flock's daily lives. The religious man, profoundly affected by this experience, thenceforth speaks of love and of only love.

*the hospital I felt myself weakening faster and faster. One night I opened my eyes suddenly, and to my great surprise two sublime girls stood before me in almost sparkling white robes. Before I go on, I should specify that these were not hospital nurses. Nurses in Yugoslavian hospitals, and military hospitals especially, bore no resemblance to models; far from it. Especially in 1956. Those I knew were large swarthy matrons with hairy legs[28] and often mustaches, women with all the grace of a thermometer. Nothing at all comparable to these two superb blondes who seemed to be nineteen or twenty and who were smiling at me. They seemed to exist in a kind of fog, and I don't know how to explain that. But at the same time I could distinguish them clearly. So I wanted to see them closer up, as you can imagine. . . . And inexplicably I had the feeling that strength was invading me, enough for me to rise out of the bed and approach them. I wanted to join them. . . . But once I was on my feet, I saw no one in the room. That lasted no more than ten or fifteen seconds. I didn't understand all this too well, and thirty-seven years later I still think about it often. The fact remains that my health started to improve, and a month and a half later I left the hospital. During the last days I remember surprising two doctors who were murmuring together, saying, "Tough luck for this boy. So young, and he hasn't long to live." And indeed I've had some cardiac problems since because of my feeble constitution. But I've survived, and I tell myself that if they are what I will meet after death, I have nothing to fear.*

That is an NDE strangely similar to a "deathbed" vision, and one we can compare to Angela's case (page 38). Here, two "Angels" restore strength to the subject, apparently so that he may go on living. And we inevitably fall back on that unspoken sentence, *"Go back; your time has not come."* Incidentally, when I spoke to him about Angels he showed no interest, though he was polite. Only when I mentioned "deathbed" visions and NDEs did the subject connect, and tell me his story. *"In my mind, Angels had wings. But all I saw was two breathtakingly beautiful girls all in white. Ten seconds more and I'd have fallen madly in love. How could you expect me to make the connection?"* he explained, laughing.

28. In (ex)Yugoslavia for some mysterious reason it was considered chic by women to let the hair on their legs grow out and be seen!

## 10) An Angel beside Me

This absolutely mind-boggling testimony was passed on to me by Kenneth Ring,[29] and I will never be able to thank him enough. It concerns Bob H., hospitalized in 1979 for surgery on his leg, which had been badly damaged in an auto accident. It is the exceptional account of a survivor who had never imagined he would explore these regions. And the guardian Angel is at the very heart of the story. And we realize that all NDEs are not alike. Sometimes there are so many differences between one NDE and another that we wonder what criteria the Great Organizer uses, offering this one just a glimpse of the dark tunnel and others a complete panorama with a guided tour of the mysteries of Heaven. Let's return to Robert H., who feels himself depart right in the middle of the operation:

> *I was in a tunnel, traveling at enormous speed toward a light, which was incidental at this point. I had flown frequently on business, and participated in automobile racing at one time, and I was aware that the speed I was traveling was far in excess of anything I had ever experienced, and it was increasing all the time. The walls of the tunnel were a blur, but as I looked more carefully I came to the realization that this tunnel through which I was traveling at such unbelievable speed was composed of planets: individual solid masses blurred together by speed and distance. Incredibly, I seemed to be hurtling through the universe!*
>
> *There was tremendous sound, too. It was as if all the great orchestras in the world were playing at once; no special melody, and very loud, powerful but somehow soothing. It was a rushing, moving sound, unlike anything I could remember, but familiar, just on the edge of my memory.*
>
> *I was suddenly frightened. I had no idea where I was bound at such speed, nor had anything in my life prepared me for this adventure. As soon as I realized I was afraid, a presence reached out to me; not physically, but telepathically. It was a calming, gentle presence and a voice, which said, "Take it easy. Everything is O.K. Relax," and this thought transference immediately induced a soothing effect on me, far more powerful than*

29 Published in the *Journal of Near Death Experiences*, volume 10, #1, Fall 1991, pages 11–29, op. cit.

*anything within the experience of my stressful life.*

*I had been traveling toward the tremendous light at the end of the tunnel; but just as I was about to enter it, everything went black. When I close my eyes in a dark room, I still have the sensation of sight. I also retain a sense of touch and feeling, of having a body. The black of which I speak was total, absent of any sensation. My consciousness simply WAS. I existed, but without any senses whatsoever. It was absolutely terrifying. This lasted but a moment, as had the entire journey. Then sensations began slowly to return, and I understood that these were positive only. There was no longer pain in my leg, nor any physical or mental discomfort or unrest, where before there had been chaos. There was instead peace and joy and harmony and light. Oh, what a Light it was! As I became increasingly aware of it, it was gold and silver and green and full of love. As the sensations solidified, and this seemed timeless because there was no hurry in this place, I became aware of a being sitting beside me. He wore a white robe, and exuded peace. He was the one who had comforted me during the latter stages of my voyage, I knew instinctively. He was comforting me still. I knew he would be all the friends I never had, and all the guides and teachers I would ever need. I knew that he would be there if ever I needed him, but that there were others for him to look out for, so I needed to care for myself as much as I reasonably could.*

*We sat side by side on a rock, overlooking the most beautiful landscape I had ever seen. The colors were outside my experience, vivid beyond my dreams, the composition exceptional. It was exquisitely pleasant and there was no pressure, for my friend knew me and loved me more than I could ever know or love myself. I had never felt such radiance and peace. "It's really something, isn't it?" exclaimed my friend, referring to the view. I sat comfortably with him and admired it, uncharacteristically silent. He said, "We thought we'd lost you for a while.". . .While I was thinking about this remarkable fellow, we relocated again, INSTANTLY. . . .*

*This time we were audience to a choir of angels singing. Angels were totally outside my reality at the time, yet somehow I knew these beautiful beings to be angelic. They sang the most lovely and extraordinary music I had ever heard. They were identical, each equally beautiful. When their song was over, one of their number came forward to greet me. She was exquisite and I was mightily attracted, but I then realized my admiration could only be expressed in a wholly non-physical manner, as to a little child. I was embarrassed by my error, but it did not matter. All was forgiven in this wonderful place.*

*The feeling I must leave had grown into certainty and dread. My apprehension was confirmed when my guide told me plainly that it was time for me to go, but I should remember that this was always my home, and I would return some day soon. I told him it was impossible for me to go back to the life I knew after this experience, but he said there was no choice, I had work yet to do. I protested, saying the circumstances of my life were such that I could not continue, and I was filled with consternation at the thought of facing the mental and physical pain I feared would lie ahead. I was asked to be more specific, and I recalled an area of my life in which I had experienced difficulty. Instantly I was filled with an overpowering sense of that specific emotion. It was almost unbearable. Then, with no more than a gesture, the pain was made to vanish, to be replaced by a glorious sense of well being and love. This process was repeated several times, with specific areas of my life where I had been experiencing difficulty. My friend then pointed out that I could perform this astonishing feat myself.*

*I was given to understand that there was to be no argument about returning. Rules were rules, and I must abide by them without fail. There were to be no exceptions made for me, and self-pity was not an acceptable form of expression.*

*In an instant, it all vanished, and I found myself in the recovery room, wondering aloud what it was I was to remember. The experience might have lasted 5 minutes or 5 hours.*

This is unquestionably one of the most splendid testimonials of a guardian Angel in an NDE. An account rendered with surgical precision, which offers us a certain number of cross-checks. The subject travels through a tunnel as if outside of time, and at the moment he first feels fear he finds a presence beside him speaking to him, whose words, or more exactly thoughts, produce an absolute sense of peace, and above all of security: *"This thought transference immediately induced a soothing effect on me, far more powerful than anything within the experience of my stressful life."* This sense of security is one of the common factors in "angelic" NDE. First Act. Second Act: the subject floats in absolute blackness, and confirms his existence only by the fact that he is thinking (which flings us straight into Descartes' arms, with his famous "I think, therefore I am").

The darkness dissipates and the subject is seated on a rock with the "presence" from the tunnel beside him draped in a white robe, radiating a contagious serenity. A new certainty rises in his mind: It could hardly be clearer, and we shall see further on in this book how wonderfully precise are these similar definitions of the guardian Angel. Still, the subject never used the word "Angel," but always "Being." This very powerful description plunges us directly into the mystery of the Angel's function. It is a pure marvel, and among the many books I have read on the subject, not one gives as simple, brief and dazzling an explanation. And then the Being says a mysterious thing to him: *"We thought we'd lost you for a while."* Who is this "we?" Remember that in this account the word "God" was never spoken. But after the boulder and the town, the subject was instantaneously transported before a choir of Angels by the Being. Here he does use the word Angel. He observes them carefully: each is more beautiful than others, and in the end an Angel, a real "female" Angel, comes to welcome him. The Angel is so beautiful, so attractive, that our subject feels himself, in old phrase, growing wings, and discovers with a certain embarrassment that his *"admiration could only be expressed in a wholly non-physical manner."* [30] Let us emphasize that it is the choir of Angels, recalling Fra Angelico's *Dance of the Elect,* which places Bob H.'s account in a divine setting.

## 11) I REALIZED THAT I WAS NOT WALKING ALONE

At 3:30 A.M. one morning in June, 1959, Glenn Perkins wakes suddenly, after dreaming that his daughter, gravely ill and in the hospital, has need of him. He dresses, hurriedly wolfs a bite, finally takes the wheel at about 4:15 and heads for the hospital. He arrives at about 5 A.M. At just that moment, in room 336 at Union Hospital of Indiana in Terre Haute, the doctor notes Betty's demise and declares her officially dead. A gangrenous appendix, coupled with pneumonia, had destroyed her stomach and ovaries before attacking the rest of her body. The nurse pulls the bedsheet over her face

30. This passage makes me think of Gabriella Light, the character in Andrew Greeley's novel *Angel Fire* (Tor Books).

and leaves quietly to tell the relatives. While she telephones and fills out the necessary death forms, Glenn Perkins climbs the steps three at a time, bolts into the room and sees the sheet covering his daughter's face. Stunned, he flings himself on the bed and prays, wailing "Jesus, Jesus." Betty, meanwhile, finds herself "on the other side." The experience so overwhelmed her that in 1977 she published her account in great detail.[31] What is still remarkable about her story is that she did not remember having passed through a tunnel:

> *The transition was serene and peaceful. I was walking up a beautiful green hill. It was steep, but my leg motion was effortless and a deep ecstasy flooded my body. . . .*
>
> *All around me was a magnificent deep blue sky, unobscured by clouds. Looking about, I realized that there was no road or path. Yet I seemed to know where to go.*
>
> *Then I realized I was not walking alone. To the left, and a little behind me, strode a tall, masculine-looking figure in a robe. I wondered if he were an angel and tried to see if he had wings. But he was facing me and I could not see his back. I sensed, however, that he could go anywhere he wanted and very quickly.*
>
> *We did not speak to each other. Somehow it didn't seem necessary, for we were both going in the same direction. Then I became aware that he was not a stranger. He knew me and I felt a strange kinship with him. Where had we met? Had we always known each other? It seemed we had. Where were we now going?*
>
> *As we walked together I saw no sun—but light was everywhere. . . .*
>
> *Just as we crested the top of the hill, I heard my father's voice calling, "Jesus, Jesus, Jesus." His voice was a long distance away. I thought about turning back to find him. I did not because I knew my destination was ahead. . . .*
>
> *I sensed we could go wherever we willed ourselves to go and be there instantly. Communication between us was through the projection of thoughts. . . .*
>
> *The angel stepped forward and put the palm of his hand upon a gate which I had not noticed before. . . .*
>
> *Inside I saw what appeared to be a street of golden color with an overlay of glass or water. The yellow light that appeared was dazzling. There is no way to describe it. I saw*

31. Betty Malz, *My Glimpse of Eternity,* New York, Chosen Books, 1977.

*no figure, yet I was conscious of a Person. Suddenly I knew that the light was Jesus, the Person was Jesus.*

*I did not have to move. The light was all about me. There seemed to be some heat in it as if I were standing in sunlight; my body began to glow. Every part of me was absorbing the light. I felt bathed by the rays of a powerful, penetrating, loving energy.*

*The angel looked at me and communicated the thought: "Would you like to go in and join them?"*

*I longed with all my being to go inside, yet I hesitated. Did I have a choice? Then I remembered my father's voice. Perhaps I should go find him.*

*"I would like to stay and sing a little longer, then go back down the hill!" I finally answered. I started to say something more. But it was too late.*

*The gates slowly melted into one sheet of pearl again and we began walking back down the same beautiful hill. This time the jeweled wall was on my left and the angel walked on my right.*

Betty returned to her body and bed with verses of the Gospel dancing before her eyes. It was her father, still at the foot of her bed, who discerned a movement under the sheet and called the nurses. No one in the hospital understood how she was able to "come back," since she was clinically dead. Wasted after weeks of intensive medical treatment and almost no nourishment, Betty wanted to eat immediately, to the great horror of the hospital personnel, who positively forbade it. She paid no attention to them. By coincidence a plate of food not intended for her wound up in her room just after her return from the "hillside." By chance? She cleaned it up in two bites. No disastrous consequences. Her doctor warned her: her ovaries, attacked by massive infection, would never again function properly. He advised her to have them removed, and before that operation to "use protection" in her sexual relationships and avoid conceiving a deformed child. Several days later, she left the hospital in good health, made love in due course, and became pregnant. She suffered absolutely no sequelae to her illness and her child was perfect. We can call that a documented miracle.

Back to the NDE. She wakes after her "death" and walks in one specific direction as if it were customary. Suddenly she turns around and discovers that she is not alone. A creature of masculine aspect, clothed in a white robe, was behind her. Betty Malz would write in 1986, in a second book, that she could never have imagined a Being endowed with such beauty, such power and such assurance.[32] She uses the word Angel immediately, and looks to see if it has wings! No, he has none, but all the same she seems to have known him a long time, and senses that he could go wherever he wanted in just a fraction of a second: *"He recognized me and I felt a strange complicity. Where had we met before? Had we always known each other? It seemed so."* This reminded me of Gitta Mallasz's book, *Talking with Angels*, when the Angel asked Gitta if she knew him. Gitta was deeply touched by the words and knew with *"an inexplicable certainty that he is her inner Master: it is at the edge of her memory, and she tries with all her might to remember him. In vain."*[33] The two women had exactly the same reaction: *"I know him well, but where did I meet him?"* After a brief glimpse of this new "Jerusalem," Betty is led gently to the famous pseudo-choice *"Do you want to go back?"* She tries to work out a compromise but cannot. Return to her body, accompanied by her guide. In regaining her physical self, Betty Malz could not imagine that this "waking dream" would change her whole life.

## 12) A Voice Accompanied Me

Here is another French case. It concerns Marie d'Y., a young student, seventeen at the time of these events, who has like so many others heard about ether. After a disappointment in love, she decides one evening to saturate a wad of cotton, lie down and clamp it over her nostrils. The effect is immediate. Her body goes slack, then grows heavy, everything seems distant, sounds came to her echoing and she is surprised to discover that her body seems to be spinning faster and faster on its axis, like a top. Just as she is about to panic, a reassuring voice makes itself heard in her mind, and she feels herself being snatched up on high. She leaves her body and sees her room from above for a moment, before melting very rapidly down a tunnel made *"of dark arches and lighted arches."* The voice guides her gently and she lands in an *"atmosphere white, luminous, almost golden"*:

> *It was an adult voice. I didn't recognize it. It seemed masculine to me and I think I had heard it once when I was ten years old and fearful in a strange house. I emerge*

32. *Angels Watching Over Me*, New York, Chosen Books, p. 15.
33. *Talking with Angels*, Daimon Verlag (see the complete reference at the end of book).

*from the tunnel and that voice becomes several voices. In fact, I have encountered other beings. I don't really see them, I sense them. This is difficult to explain but that's the way it way. Afterward, I saw something even more luminous. And these telepathic voices were saying, "But what's she doing here? This is not her time. My girl, this is not your time, what are you doing here?" These Beings are full of love, like Angels, but without body or shape, like spheres of light, indescribable. Then I wandered in a fog, which was very disagreeable, always with the sense that I was hovering over something. Then I descended still lower and saw grayish forms. I saw them and they showed me their wrists. They were very gentle and kindly, and the voice told me "These are suicides," even as it made me understand that suicide was not a solution, that it served no purpose and everything would only have to start all over again. They had botched something and it was a serious matter. Rising again, I met an indescribable luminous form, whose seriousness and profundity greatly impressed me. The form asked me who I was. I was struck dumb. And my life began to pass before my eyes. It was crazy because I became all those with whom I had had relations, reliving my actions with them. It was terrible. One feels stupid afterwards, very stupid. The voice had changed, it was more impressive, different from the "Angels" I had seen at the exit from the tunnel. I cannot describe them. It was only a luminous form. It is impossible to describe because one "saw" and "felt" at the same time. During the review of my life, this Angel seemed amused that I was upset, reliving my actions. Obviously he had a keen sense of humor. My amazement, my jealousy, my egoism, etc., amused him greatly. After the review, I felt filthy, but also relieved.*

Marie's NDE does not end there. She melts into the cosmos, becomes a point of light, and feels like a grain of sand in the cosmic infinity, in which gleams a triangular shape that seems to be at the origin of everything. She does not remember returning, only her mother's face, weeping great tears at her daughter's attempted suicide. Marie explains that after this experience she gave up all notions of suicide, because what she had lived through altered her whole conception of the world, its values, human and material relations: *"Deep inside I was certain of life after death and the existence of a supreme light-energy that we may call God."*

Only too often do we encounter adolescents who attempt suicide because of a bad love affair. Here the Beings are perfectly "visible," or at least perceptible, and show her the gray eternity of suicides. If there are no white robes and golden cinctures, we find on the other hand the "luminous sphere" or the feeling that Angels are composed of a finely woven web of light.

## 13) THE ANGEL OF DEATH

The case of Dr. Phillip Swihart, reported by Dr. Maurice Rawlings. The patient was attacked in the street and beaten unconscious one Friday night in February 1967. He was hospitalized, and the doctor on duty decided to keep him under observation overnight so the morning team could explore the abdominal area. The patient's account:[34]

> *While in the operating room awaiting surgery, I felt the presence of some thing or some power and I thought, "this is it." Next, blackness. Time became of no more importance.*
>
> *I had no idea how long I was without any sensation in that darkness. Then it was light. I awoke and I knew it was real. In front of me, I watched my whole life pass by. Every thought, word and every movement I had made in my life since the time I knew that Jesus was real. I was very young when I took Christ as my Savior. I saw things I had done which I had forgotten but remembered as I watched them pass before me. This experience was, to say the least, unbelievable. Every detail, right up to the present time. It all took place in what seemed just a fraction of a second, and yet it was all very vivid.*
>
> *All the time I was watching my life go by, I felt the presence of some sort of power but I didn't see it.*
>
> *I asked the power who I and who he or it was. Communication was not by talking but through a flow of energy. He answered that he was the Angel of Death. I believed him. The Angel went on to say that my life was not as it should be, that he could take me on but that I would be given a second chance, and that I was to go back. He promised me I would not die in 1967.*
>
> *The next thing I remember I was in the recovery room, back in my body. I was so taken in by this experience that I did not notice what kind of body I had, nor how much time*

34. In *Beyond Death's Door*, pages 98–99, op. cit.

*had elapsed, it was so real—I believed it.*

*Later in 1967, a car ran over my neck and shoulders.
Still later in that year, I was in a car wreck in which both
cars were totaled and in both accidents I came out almost
completely unhurt. In neither accident was I at fault.*

*I did not tell many people about my experience; I did
not want to be considered crazy. But the encounter was
very real to me, and I still believe I was with the Angel of
Death.*

It had to come up: the Angel of Death, cruelly missing so far in
our study, manifests himself in an extremely serious NDE, when
the subject was badly beaten by a gang of hoodlums. This NDE
conforms nicely to the classical criteria, namely leaving the body,
the passage through the tunnel and the life passing in review. And
immediately after that, like a theatrical entrance, the Angel of
Death arrives, or at least a spiritual Being, a "presence," who
appears in his official capacity. In the end I find this Angel rather
droll. As in a Greek tragedy, the Angel announces (telepathically):
*"Your life is not as it should be."* He might have put it in verse, say
Alexandrines, but the Angel of Death is short on humor. . . . We can
imagine the soul suddenly frozen in terror, especially after a complete review of one's life. But the Angel is magnanimous and
permits the subject to return. Even better, he promises him that he
will not die that year. The subject returns to his body, overwhelmed
by the reality of what he has just passed through. And the Angel of
Death keeps his promise to the letter. Twice the subject lives
through accidents that would normally have killed him—a car runs
right over him! Which gives us a very precise notion of an Angel's
protective powers. This is truly thought-provoking.

## 14) I Have Not Forgotten You

The experience of Leonard Spade, now a Californian of fifty, shows
certain similarities to the preceding account, as we shall discover.
It happened in Brooklyn, New York, in February 1969, when he
was twenty-five years old. An ordinary case of grippe developed
complications, and the doctors identified a virus against which
they had no antidote. His suffering was so bad that Leonard prayed
to God to die:

*I was in my mother's house in Brooklyn when I sud-
denly felt awful. I was visiting her, and I went to lie down
in the room that had been mine as a child. It was New*

*Year's Day. Two months later I was still there, and I remember it clearly because a strange phenomenon occurred on my birthday, February 26th. That day I suddenly found myself floating high up in the room, gazing down at my body. Then I saw myself in a sort of vestibule or antechamber, and I heard a voice telling me, "I haven't forgotten you. I know that you called to me." And indeed, in my utter despair I had prayed for death, because the pain was so intense; I wanted to die, and for days I had prayed for it. I had prayed but not to anyone in particular, because I was really not at all religious. When you suffer so much, that's all you have left, your last resort. I prayed constantly. The voice resounded again: "I heard you, but you should know that it is not yet time for you to die." Then a tunnel appeared; it was more like a hole about forty feet deep than a tunnel. At the bottom I saw this brilliant and incredible white light. I could make out shadows moving within the light, and I knew—I'm not sure how— that they were the shades of people I had known, already dead, who loved me and were waiting to see me again. Then I felt love and compassion. And then I peered again into that recess and made out the silhouette of a tall man, quite tall, powerful and magnificently proportioned. I went closer and saw that he had immense wings, like an Archangel's, with that indefinable metallic black-gray color. I was very intrigued by this Being, but I never asked him who or what he was. But the more I looked at him the more I realized that he bore a feminine aspect. Then it all became confused, because in the end he was without gender. His wing feathers were black. His body expressed the strength of metal and at the same time a certain sweetness. He told me to be sure I had finished all I had to do here, because if I went on there would be no returning. Then my life passed before me and I thought I was truly finished. I considered my relations with my nearest and dearest, and discovered that they could survive perfectly well without me. Then I realized that I had spent my whole life reacting against my father, and that I no longer liked my life. At the same time I felt that to move toward that light was to move toward the light of God, and I did not feel ready, such as I was, to present myself before God. He was ready for me, ready to accept me without reproach. But I did not want to make the journey as I was. I felt that*

*all we did here on earth was without importance in view*
*of that love, that compassion. Yet I was not content,*
*because I felt that I had promised to make something of*
*my life and left that promise unfulfilled. Then I understood*
*that I must go back, and that I could not proceed toward*
*Absolute Love. I gazed down at my body and it seemed a*
*broken thing to me. I returned to it, rather disturbed. I*
*don't know if that was an Angel, my "superego," or who*
*knows what else, but it was certainly real.*

With this account we refer back to the case of Beverly B., who, discovering herself disfigured, prayed to God for the first time in her life, asking for death. A true paradox, with symbols telescoping. Leonard Spade prays to escape his suffering. The two "beggars for death" pass through a period of intense emotion. And in both cases the prayers are granted with variations after the subjects leave their bodies: Beverly is taken by an Angel into the Light of God and taken on a grand tour, while Leonard finds himself before a strange Being, endowed with wings (the first word he used to describe the Being is "Archangel"!), who first says, *"I have not forgotten you. I know that you called to me,"* and then, *"I have heard your call, but you should know that your time has not come."* Can we deduce that this is the Angel of Death? These two answers are important, because they show clearly that the prayers have been heard. Which means in turn that the act of prayer is truly effective. The prayer is heard every time by those "on high." Even more startling, they answer. In studying Angels, we eventually learn a great many things.

## 15) A LADDER OF ANGELS

The heir to the famous Gallup Poll, George Gallup, Jr., read Moody's books and developed a passion for the subject so strong that he conducted an investigation of NDE on a national scale, which—given the size of the United States—constituted a real first. The results of this poll astonished him, and he decided to analyze them in depth. His book *Adventures in Immortality*[35] is inspiring because it draws an exact picture of what happens after death, and most of all—because it confirms the testimonies gathered by his pollsters—of what we may discover in heaven. In all respects his conclusions confirm those of Moody and Ring. Among the accounts we find one truly far from the norm: a

35. New York, McGraw Hill, 1982, pp. 68–69.

woman from Pennsylvania, seventy years old when interviewed, a former nurse, who gave the interviewers a detailed description of what she had undergone fifty-three years earlier, when she decided to give birth at home.

The family doctor, noting complications at the time of birth, had to use forceps, which resulted in more complications, these internal. A week after the delivery, the doctor examines her again and decides to send her straight to the hospital. She is there for three days before they decide to operate. But her husband refused to authorize the operation, which risks irreparable intimate damages.

> *I was so ill that I was not able to sit up in bed. It was a Sunday afternoon. He took a taxi and had to carry me in his arms like a baby.*
>
> *By the time I got home, it seemed that I got strength—where from, I do not know. But I got out of the cab and walked into the house, up to our third-floor apartment. I changed the bed the way I wanted it. I then undressed and got into bed. I felt wonderful. I had never had a feeling like that before, and never since.*
>
> *My family and neighbors were all there because they were dumbfounded to see the miraculous change that had come over me. Then, just as though there was someone talking to me, a voice told me that I was going to die and that I should let my husband and family know.*
>
> *So I called them all together in the room. I held my husband's hand and said to them, 'You must all prepare to meet your God because I am now going to meet mine.'*
>
> *I felt so peaceful, I didn't have a pain. And when I left the hospital only about three hours before, I was racked with pain. It seemed that I went off in a trance of some kind. While I was in this state, I had a vision.*
>
> *It seemed that all these angels came from heaven and, holding hands, they formed a stairway reaching all the way up to heaven. It seemed that as I ascended these stairs up to heaven, I knew everything that was going on in my home. My family and neighbors were crying and my husband was kneeling at the bed, begging God to please spare me for the baby's sake.*
>
> *I kept going up this stair of angels' hands until I reached heaven. When I reached the top, there was a great mist before the door, and an angel said to me, "That mist is*

*your family's prayers for your return. Why don't you ask the*
*Lord to let you come back to raise your child?"*

*When I went through the mist, I could see this person*
*sitting on a throne, surrounded by this mist. I said, "Lord,*
*please let me go back and raise my child." He did not reply*
*but took my hand and turned me around and led me back*
*to the stairs to descend. In the meantime, I was out so long*
*that the family was making plans for the undertaker and*
*sending telegrams. When I came to, shouting and singing, I*
*am sure you can imagine what kind of a day that was.*
*Well, I was seventeen years old. I am seventy now, and I*
*only had the one child.*

A very curious case, because a voice warns the subject that she is
going to die, and asks that she inform her family. Up to now we have
encountered no such warning, though of course a guardian Angel is
quite capable of it. The angel does not seem to have shown himself
visually to his protégé, but his place is taken by a throng of Angels
surging out of the sky and, forming a ladder of their hands to help
the subject rise to God's Throne. This seems crazy. The problem is
that, considering the area of exploration into which we are trying to
venture without going mad, this case is atypical. We might call it a
hallucination. But the patient was clinically dead: her family had
begun to send telegrams. Besides, this subject uses the word "vision"
exactly as the great mystics do, as we shall see in a later chapter. Furthermore, her vision reminds us of Genesis 28, where Jacob, asleep
among the rocks, dreams of a ladder with Angels rising to and
descending from Heaven. Our subject finally reaches the top of that
strange ladder, where another Angel awaits her amid a fog, which is
*"your family's prayers for your return."* The helpful role of the Angel is
clear: he whispers the answer to the soul arrived for judgment. Even
if all this seems quite allegoric to us, this account is no more supernatural than all the testimonies that preceded it.

## 16) MICHAEL, THE ARCHANGEL

And here is a case passed on to me by Kimberly Sharp, president of
the Seattle branch of IANDS. Richard Philips experienced this in
March 1969 on an old farm in Minnesota, near the Canadian
border. He was fourteen when he came down with Hong Kong flu
and chicken pox at the same time. His parents had made him comfortable on the living-room couch and were watching over him, the
family immobilized by a violent blizzard. It was the coldest winter
in twenty years, with temperatures almost constantly below zero.

With the arctic cold freezing even his bones, the chicken pox and flu worsened. Feverishly, in the presence of his parents, Richard saw himself suddenly leave his own body:

*My hands and arms were transparent. I found myself on a glittering white plateau, at the same level as the ceiling of my house. Rising, I felt myself enveloped by a force, an agreeable influence, as if an Angel were repulsing the malevolent spirits around me. I looked down and saw my parents weeping over my sick body. I was sad for them; and then I realized that I knew everything about everything. There were no limits to my knowledge. In that white place I saw a wall, also white. A stranger over six feet tall advanced toward me. He told me he was the Archangel Michael. He walked with me and showed me the surroundings. I met a dozen near and dear ones, like my dead grandfather, who was only in his twenties here and no longer afflicted by an invalid's body. He seemed very happy. I met my future brother, who was to be born four years later. And other brothers and sisters dead long before my own birth. I had not known that my parents had children before me. Then I wanted to meet God, to tell Him that I was too young to die and was very happy with my family. God appeared to me in a white light. I could not look Him in the face, but His voice still resonates in my mind as if it were yesterday; it was all understanding, even wisdom, and it made me feel all His love for me. I asked Him why He was letting the world slide toward destruction, and He replied that He had given us all free will, and whether we maintained or destroyed life on earth was for us to decide. He said this because He has His own will, just like us, His creatures. At that moment Christ set his hands on my shoulders. I saw marks on his wrists. I remember spending some time with Christ, but I don't remember what we did. I asked God to let me go, so I could have a wife and a little girl in His honor before I was thirty, after which I would die happy. Or to let me live past thirty if I had no child. That's what I proposed to Him. I remember God being extremely attentive and understanding what I was asking Him for. Before I came back, I saw the Devil passing by and was surprised to discover that he was magnificent. When I returned from the white plateau I tried to describe my experience to my parents. They were so frightened that they rushed to the doctor. It transpired that the white corpuscles had destroyed my body's red corpuscles. The condition required immediate treatment, and I could not have been cared for if my parents had not hurried me to the hospital. And they would never have taken me to the hospital in such dangerous weather if I had not told them about my experience. In other words, my NDE saved my life.*

This NDE is a handsome addition to our panorama, considering the nature of our book. In this case, "an unknown, about six feet six," Archangel Michael himself, comes to seek out the boy and shelters him with supernatural protection: "Going up I felt myself surrounded by a power, a friendly power like an Angel's, repelling the hostile powers around me." Keeping up his reputation as a guide, the Archangel accompanied the boy, who obviously had no clear idea who this Angel was, showing him the "neighborhood." The boy converses with God, and when he returns he encounters another Angel, who is "magnificent. . . ."

## 17) I AM YOUR GUARDIAN ANGEL

To show that stories of NDEs existed long before anyone thought to give them that name, here is a case reported by Peter Johnson in 1920[36] and unearthed by Craig Lundahl, who holds down a chair in sociology at Western New Mexico University and who was kind enough to sent it on to me. Felled by yellow fever, Johnson lies in bed, burning with fever, and watched over by more than anxious nurses.

> *Soon after that, my spirit left the body; just how I cannot tell. But I perceived myself standing some four or five feet in the air, and saw my body lying on the bed. I felt perfectly natural, but as this was a new condition I began to make observations. I turned my head, shrugged my shoulders, felt with my hands, and realized that it was I myself. I also knew that my body was lying, lifeless, on the bed. While I was in a new environment, it did not seem strange, for I realized everything that was going on, and perceived that I was the same in the spirit as I had been in the body. While contemplating this new condition, something attracted my attention, and on turning around I beheld a personage, who said: "You did not know that I was here."*
> *I replied: "No, but I see you are. Who are you?"*

36. "A Testimony," *The Relief Society Magazine*, volume 3, no. 8, August 1920, p. 451.

*"I am your guardian angel; I have been following you constantly while on earth."*

*I asked, "What will you do now?"*

*He replied: "I am to report your presence, and you will remain here until I return."*

*He informed me, on returning, that we should wait there, as my sister desired to see me, but was busy just at that time. Presently she came.*

Cases in which the Angel identifies himself as a Guardian are quite rare. He even says specifically that he has followed him all his days on earth, which tends to prove that Angels accompany us from our very first day. These cases let us imagine that in this "elsewhere" time exists in some other mode.

## 18) I Have Heard Voices Ever Since

The accident, or more exactly the death, of Chuck Griswold, which occurred on January 25, 1959 during a rafting run down a river, changed his life entirely. This case is interesting because it concerns a marine engineer who was not, at the time, receptive to spiritual matters:

*We were running rapids on the Skykomish in Washington state, near a small town called Index. The river was icy cold; it was midwinter. There were twenty-three of us on an inflatable raft, and for an hour we maneuvered, rowed and slalomed among the boulders. Everything went just fine, and it was truly exciting to be swept along by such powerful rapids. The icy water didn't bother us because we were wearing protective neoprene outfits. And then suddenly, the unimaginable: a fall, not indicated on the chart, of about thirty yards. I felt tons of water pressing on my body, my contact lenses were washed away, my whole body scraped along boulders as big as cars, until I found myself swimming in the main current. But I realized that the raft was below me, which really did not seem normal. And it all became quite dramatic, for I had no doubt that I was dead, because I was floating above the whole scene. I was dead, all right. And then everything grew calm and tranquil, and at that moment I was dragged into a tunnel, at the end of which shone a dazzling golden light, which seemed to give off an unconditional and unlimited love. At the same time I felt two "presences" beside me, to my left and right, which by alternate thoughts, what we call telepathy, explained to me that everything was all right and I had no need to worry. I relaxed immediately and felt fine. I looked down and saw how they were trying to retrieve my body from the water. The sheriff, later I learned that it was Sheriff Twitchell, said to someone that it was hardly worth worrying about that one, about me, because he was dead. He was talking about my corpse. But they gave me artificial respiration anyway. Other members of the group were also in rough shape. I watched it all with my "guardians." I sensed them more in a telepathic way than a physical way. What struck me was that the personage to my left was a mechanical type, pragmatic, and the one on my right more ethereal, more angelic, as if his point of view of was God's. And at the same time I saw the sky and the sheriff's face above me. I could hear but not speak. I had returned to my body when I asked my two guardians to see how my friends were doing. Now they were giving me oxygen and I came to on the stretcher. But the difference was that my two guides stayed with me afterward.*

*I saw them again long after this accident, during surgery about fifteen years ago, in 1977, when I was one of the first to survive an operation for an abcessed liver. My guardians were there, and they told me, "Yes, you are on the right road," or, "No, avoid doing that." It was always in the evening, before going to sleep, that I made contact with them. They are why, for example, I don't drive any more. From the time I was twenty-four I always felt uneasy at the wheel of a car; after my NDE my guardians warned me strictly that I should not drive for any reason. So I only pilot boats. Once I told my wife I was going shopping. But behind the wheel I was paralyzed, I could barely move. I'm fifty-seven now, and I can tell you that my guardian Angels have saved my life many times. For example, I was asked to show up for work at a shipyard once, and my voices told me, "No No, Not a chance!" So I refused, and the man who took my place was killed that very morning. Another employer asked me if I'd sign on with a work team because of my expertise in demolition, and my guardians told me, "Absolutely Not." Three weeks later, five friends who had agreed to go to work on that project were killed in an accidental explosion. Since my NDE, I have what they call more highly developed senses, like premonition, mind reading and so forth.*

This case is a perfect illustration of the after effects of NDE, in particular the refinement of psychic senses to the point where the subject hears his Angels, something like Joan of Arc. He is not alone in this, even if he is one of rare subjects to converse with his guide. Others read people's minds like an open book, heal by the laying of hands or even "see" the future. It is extremely curious. Every researcher sooner or later stumbles on a similar case, which gives him the intimate conviction that during NDEs much more occurs than a simple round trip. Well after his NDE, Chuck Griswold saved his life twice by rejecting jobs at bad sites, and like John Lilly, he saw his guides while being operated on. We may well wonder why some are gratified by such a gift, and others not.

### 19) She Was Very Beautiful

A case from Arvin Gibson.[37] Kim, an adolescent girl of fifteen, goes into the hospital in Salt Lake City in June of 1990 for an operation on her leg for a twisted tibia. The operation proceeds without incident but a few days later a violent pain paralyzes her leg. She goes back to the hospital, and after various injections the pain seems to go away. But it comes back the next day, worse than ever, to the point where she wants to scream But no sound emerges from her lips, and her surroundings vanish. She does not see her bed, or her mother, or the electrocardiogram falling flat, or the doctors and nurses rushing into her room. She was clinically dead.

> I still don't know how to explain it, it was just blackness all around, kind of like being in a tunnel. It wasn't really a tunnel, but that's the best way I can describe it.
>
> I was standing there, and I saw this brilliant light—not like heat-warmth, more peace-warmth. I got curious, and I started going toward it. I heard somebody call my name; I turned to look, and there was this lady.
>
> She was dressed all in white. Her hair was white, and it was flowing down her back—it came to about her knees. She was really pretty, she was glowing not just from the light in the distance but from herself. She called me by name name and said: "It's not your time." I didn't quite understand, and she repeated the message; that it wasn't my time, and that I had to go back.
>
> When she told me, the second time, that I had to go back I remembered the pain, and everything, and I didn't want to

37. *Glimpses of Eternity*, Bountiful, Utah, Horizon Publishers, 1991, pp. 104–5.

*go. I wanted to go toward the light; I felt so good, I felt so happy. She repeated the message again telling me that it wasn't my time, and I must go back. She said everything would be okay. Finally, I agreed and turned around to return. Then I woke and it was a haze.*

Her heart stopped beating for some moments, while the doctors administered oxygen. After her "return" they injected her with sedatives, and as the Being promised, the pain in her leg disappears for good.

## 20) They Are My Guardians

This experience by Dr. John Lilly at the frontier of death took place in a Chicago hotel where he had to wait over six hours, most of the time in a coma, before an ambulance came for him. In great pain, he decided to inject himself with a dose of antibiotics to restore his strength and health. What is more natural than a doctor treating himself? But the needle, badly cleaned, still bore some residual detergent, which was immediately disseminated throughout his body, damaging some of the vital cerebral functions. Blasted by pain, he wondered what was happening to him: he could hardly think, and then the visual cortex ceased to function. Almost immediately he fell into a coma. A bit later he came to, picked up the phone and pressed 0. The house detective came immediately, and asked if he had a friend in the hotel. In an almost total fog, Lilly managed to give a name, and then passed out again. If he cannot remember the rest, he recalls perfectly what happened immediately afterward:

*Suddenly in the distance appear two similar points of consciousness, sources of radiance, of love, of warmth. I feel their presence, I see their presence, without eyes, without a body. I know they are there, so they are there. As they move toward me, I feel more and more of each of them, interpenetrating my very being. They transmit comforting, reverential, awesome thoughts. I realize that they are beings far greater than I. They begin to teach me. They tell me I can stay in this place, that I have left my body, but that I can return to it if I wish. They then show me what would happen if I left my body back there—an alternative path for me to take. They also show me where I can go if I stay in this place. They tell me that it is not yet time for me to leave my body permanently, that I still have an option to* go back to it. . . .

*As they move closer, I find less and less of me and more and more of them in my being. They stop at a critical distance and say to me that at this time I have developed only to the point where I can stand their presence at this particular distance. If they came any closer, they would overwhelm me, and I would lose myself as a cognitive entity, merging with them. They further say that I separated them into two, because that is my way of perceiving them, but that in reality they are one in the space in which I found myself. They say that I insist on still being an individual, forcing a projection onto them, as if they were two. They further communicate to me that if I go back to my body as I developed further, I eventually would perceive the oneness of them and of me, and of many others.*

*They say that they are my guardians, that they have been with me before at critical times and that in fact they are with me always, but that I am not usually in a state to perceive them. I am in a state to perceive them when I am close to the death of the body. In this state, there is no time. There is an immediate perception of the past, present, and future as if in the present moment.*[38]

John Lilly awoke in his body just as someone injected something into the arteries at the level of his neck. When he regained full consciousness in the hospital, he discovered that he had been blinded by a non-specific lesion of the brain. But just as his "guardians" had predicted, his eyes reacted better and better to visual stimuli after a few days. After two months of convalescence, they reacted normally.

This account is basic and essential because it comes to us from a scientist who is also a doctor of medicine. Dr. Lilly's description is impressive for its precision and clarity. It's a detailed description of what he felt and saw when he left his body. For him the Angels took the form of two luminous points, *"two similar points of consciousness appear in the distance, sources of radiance, of love, of consciousness, of warmth."* So we invariably find the radiance of love, reassuring and comforting the subject and entreating him from afar not to be afraid. Instinctively he also felt that these presences were "superior" to him, and, as we have noted before and will note again, he saw them "without seeing." That is the faculty

38. *The Center of the Cyclone,* pp. 23–24.

survivors have so much trouble explaining once back on earth; how they were able to see without seeing and yet perceive a precise image of presences.

We note in passing that unlike other survivors Lilly does not roam verdant hillsides or flowering landscapes with lakes of a blue that do not exist on earth, etc. He is simply floating in a zone. Out of respect for the mathematician, the Beings then show him what would happen if he decided not to return to his body, the "alternative" road, the tangent. And then we note the phenomenon of a fusion that the subject attempts to avoid, under pain of losing his own identity. Even more, the Beings explain that in fact they are not two, but one. Here are revelations that ask far more questions than they answer. How was Lilly able to separate them into two? And why, if he approached them, would they become one again? Truly curious. But inevitably we return to what we set forth previously about Betty Malz, who felt strangely attracted by the Being she sensed behind her. It may lead us to believe that part of our memory is disconnected when we come to earth.

## 21) AN INSTRUCTOR I DID NOT KNOW

The anecdotal but official testimony of Sir Auckland Gedee, a doctor, given February 26, 1927, before the members of the Royal Society of Medicine of London. It is interesting because this subject of Her Gracious Majesty had what they will later call an NDE, and he explained to his colleagues what he felt at the time of his "death" and what happened afterwards. We can imagine the faces of these bearded gentlemen when their illustrious colleague talks to them about the sensation of floating:

> Little by little I realized that I could see not only my body and the bed on which I lay, but also everything that was in the house and garden. . . . I learned from an instructor I did not know, whom I now call my mentor, that I was completely free in a temporal dimension of space where "now" corresponded in some measure to "here" in traditional three dimensional space.[39]

A doctor trying to explain his "death" and his Guardian Angel to the audience of an academy of medicine: now there's something unusual, especially since it happened in 1927!

39. Johann Hampe, *Sterben ist doch ganz anders*, Stuttgart, Kreuz Verlag, 1977, cited by Father Brune.

## 22) AN ANGEL IN THE FAMILY?

This is a question I am often asked: "Can a guardian Angel perhaps be one of our recently deceased dear ones, father, mother or grandparents?" To be absolutely frank, I have no idea! But here is what may be a typically angelic way of answering, knowing as we do that Angels always express themselves by what we call coincidence.

About a year ago I was lunching in Paris with Gabriel Milesi, chief editor of Radio Europe 2. We were on a terrace close to the Champs-Elysées, chez Andre. While we waited for an aperitif, he asked me the same question: *"Can the dead be our guardian Angels?"* He had hardly finished asking the question when our attention was drawn to a feather swaying gently in the air just above our heads, descending gently and calmly before landing delicately in . . . his plate! We stared at each other incredulous, and since Gabriel said nothing I had only one reflection: "One might say you just had your answer."

Still, the idea that a spirit we may call "familial" may "watch over" us is not entirely senseless—witness the following case of Ray Sanghavi, a travel agent whom I met "by chance" in New York at "Maharajah Travels," where he turned up a New York to Paris air ticket at the last minute for two hundred dollars! Ray was sixty-two, and his story unfolded in Bombay, in May or June of 1976. Beneath the dreadful heat of an Indian noon, our man's heart decided to seek shade, and he crumpled in the middle of the street.

> *I remember a sense of well-being, floating above my body for several moments, and then spinning very rapidly into a kind of tunnel at the end of which was a terribly attractive light. I had no time to think of anything at all, because suddenly I found myself, how shall I say this, at the other end of the tunnel, and my mother was there! But my mother died when I was six years old, and I had never seen her except in a wheelchair! But there she was, in perfect health, quite beautiful, in her thirties, wearing a sari, and she simply asked me, "What are you doing here?"*
>
> *To me it seemed quite natural to be there, and that she was there. Then my grandfather appeared, and he even bantered a little, complaining that I was still playing my schoolboy's tricks. I answered, laughing, that I was married and the father of two children, but just then, without waiting for his response, my mother said to me, "It is not your time. You must go back."*
>
> *I was immediately, how shall I explain this, sucked*

*down; I opened my eyes and pain crushed my chest. People were leaning over me, and far off I heard a police siren or an ambulance, I don't know which. I never forgot that. Thanks to that experience I have no fear of death, because I've lived through it. Strangest of all is that sense of protection I felt in her presence, and, I still don't know how to explain this, I still feel. Ever since then I've felt she was watching over me.*

And there it is. Generally when a man of forty is felled by a heart attack the pain is so great that he can think of nothing else. But Ray finds himself outside of his body, spins through the tunnel—the Angels ought to set up a speed-limit sign—and emerges at the other end. Surprise, what he least expected, his mother, whom he has not seen since early childhood, welcomes him and then sends him right back, as if he had been caught with his hand in the cookie jar. If the encounter was not long—no time even for a cup of tea—our subject leaves with two certainties:

1) that death is not death and

2) that he is guarded, somehow protected by his mother, even though she died when he was six.

When I talked to Ray I saw tears in his eyes when he tried to tell me how he had talked with his mother, his young mother, at the other end of the tunnel.

## 23) ANGELS TRYING TO HELP

It is impossible not to examine the NDE of Dr. George Ritchie, since he is, as we have seen, at the origin of the birth of modern NDE, presented by Dr. Raymond Moody. It was in 1978 that the psychiatrist from Charlottesville decided to publish his story, which we find on library shelves a year later. Since then, his work *Return From Tomorrow*[40] has been translated into fourteen languages including Hungarian, Japanese, and Czech. It is indeed not easy to find a trip to death's door in which the subject has Christ as guide. His book deserves to be read in one sitting, especially since it is quite short, less than 100 pages. Though brief, it is nevertheless a most disturb-

---

40. Tarrytown, New York, Fleming H. Revell Company. I also recommend reading his second book, *My Life After Dying*, Norfolk, Virginia, Hampton Road Publishing, 1991.

ing story, which plunges us directly into the mystery of death. Everything is there merged in the true sense of the terms: life, death, and God, and we might indeed classify it in the department of hallucinations if George Ritchie had not been in military hospital where he was twice declared officially dead before many witnesses.

Back to his NDE: he gets up, goes into the corridor to find out what time it is, discovers that he is passing clear through the medical personnel he meets along the way, returns to his room troubled, perceives a brilliant light and suddenly finds himself in the presence of Christ, made of this light. Instantly, his life passes before him in minute detail, and when the panorama ends, Christ asks him: "What have you done with your life?" After several moments, the young man rebels and answers that he is too young to die. The Manifested Light transports him through several levels of existence and their voyage becomes a true tour of what we commonly call hell, purgatory and paradise, even though Ritchie in fact wrote of five different levels:

1. The beginning of the voyage is an out of body exploration of diverse zones of the Earth and is practically identical to Robert Monroe's experience, which we will take up later.

2. Ritchie is not at all sure what to call this second astral reality. He thinks it involves a sort of reception area where souls arrive in a deep sleep. He notes that as this is happening in the middle of World War II, he saw innumerable young souls land at this spot, to be welcomed by what he believes are Angels. His description proves that even if he had Christ at his side, the reality of the Angels seemed to surpass him:

   > Here were what I would call angels working with them trying to arouse them and help them realize God is truly a God of the living and that they did not have to lie around sleeping until Gabriel or someone came along blowing on a horn. Maybe this is the realm Jesus referred to as paradise when he spoke to the thief on the cross.[41]

3. If George Ritchie was not sure how to characterize that second level, he had no problem at all with the third, given the sights he saw. It was not a matter of imps with pitch-

41. *My Life After Dying,* page 24.

forks boiling damned souls, but only of areas where those souls went on fighting and raping among themselves. He noted that this place was worse than hell because no trace of love could be found:

> *What I saw horrified me more than anything I have ever seen in life. Since you could tell what the beings of this place thought, you knew they were filled with hate, deceit, lies, self-righteousness bordering on megalomania, and lewd sexual aggressiveness that were causing them to carry out all kinds of abominable acts on each other. This was breaking the heart of the Son of God standing beside me. Even here were angels trying to get them to change their thoughts. Since they could not admit there were beings greater than themselves, they could not see or hear them.* [42]

4. They leave this place, also described by Robert Monroe in his book, *Far Journeys,* to visit zones of "knowledge," where, as he saw things, human knowledge was organized.

5. The last stage of this voyage with Christ is the Crystal City (the New Jerusalem?) which we have already seen in preceding experiences. Ritchie returned to his body the evening of December 24, 1943.

This account deserves further attention because here we have practical information rather than a theological supposition. For example, the Church tells you that your guardian Angel accompanies you to purgatory but leaves you as you are destined to burn in hell. According to George Ritchie's experience, this is not the case since even in that zone reserved for the violent and the aggressive, the Angels stay with them trying hard to *"change their thoughts."* In conversation Ritchie confirmed to me that what he had seen was indeed *"what one could call the Angels trying to help these lost souls, but without great success."* I asked him if he believed in Guardian Angels after that experience. His answer was curious, as though in spite of his NDE, he was not certain that he could possess a Guardian Angel, simply because all that was so far beyond his scientific belief, despite his experience. *"Listen, Pierre, I don't know if I have a Guardian Angel, even less if there are Guardian Angels; frankly*

42. Ibid., p. 25

*I know nothing about them. I remember simply all the angelic points of light, and I can no longer tell you what I wrote in my book. Believe me, what I saw is simply beyond me."*

Our doctor had noted in his first book that if he had not paid much attention to these lights in the beginning, in the end he realized that they were everywhere, in all the places Christ had shown him.

*In fact, now that I had become aware of the bright presences, I realized with bewilderment that I'd been seeing them all along, without ever consciously registering the fact, as though Jesus could show me at any moment only so much as I was ready to see. Angels had crowded the living cities and towns we had visited. They had been present in the streets, the factories, the homes, even in that raucous bar, where nobody had been any more conscious of their existence than I myself had.*[43]

## 24) A PRIEST'S NDE

By dint of researching and reading about the experiences of those at death's door, I arrived at the same conclusion as Dr. Moody and Ken Ring: atheists and believers tell the same story. The believers have a tendency to identify the central Being of Light as Christ; the atheists are content to speak of a Being of Light. And if there exist different interpretations, there is none concerning the Angels or the spiritual Beings that accompany them in the tunnel or that welcome them. But I noticed a gap; no one had succeeded in finding an NDE of a . . . contemporary Roman Catholic priest. And I said to myself that it would be fantastic to find a young priest, thirty or forty years old, who had passed through the tunnel or melted into the Light, and to understand the effects on his psyche, and even better on his calling. I took up my laptop computer and sent a mailing to a hundred or so churches scattered about America. I received no response, not even a negative response. Nothing.[44] I abandoned the idea. But as always it happened when least expected: I fell upon a priest, a true Roman Catholic in sombre robes and Roman collar, a large, sprightly man about six feet tall with a chubby face. When he began to talk to me about his experi-

43. Page 67 in *Return from Tomorrow*, Tarrytown, New York, Fleming H. Revell Company, 1978.
44. In fact, yes, one, from a French Buddhist Monk in San Francisco!!

ence, I did not immediately establish the connection because I was interviewing him about an entirely different subject, the stigmata, and his experience did not present the traditional features of a "Moodyesque" or "Ringian" NDE. Father Stephen Schneir represents the only case of an ecclesiastical NDE that we can examine, in the sense that his medical dossier proves point by point the events he relates. And if he recited them coldly, one might say, Good, he was hallucinating and that's all. But when Father Schneir talks of his NDE, his voice thickens and breaks, and one feels that this great man is trying to hold back his tears, trying to control the emotion common to those who melt into the Light. Ken Ring would have classed him with the NDEs of the fifth stage. I was prodigiously impressed by this giant's trembling voice because we accept the idea of women crying, but are less used to men, and even less to a large man six feet tall who ought to be armored against sentimentality by his profession, especially since he had been ordained a priest in 1973.

One day in October 1985 Stephen Schneir is driving his Thunderbird down a road in Kansas. It is four in the afternoon. He is behind another car and after a few minutes decides to pass it. He remembers nothing after that. According to the reconstruction, he pulled out without looking just another car was approaching from the other direction. An inevitable head-on collision. Nothing was left of his car but a heap of scrap metal. The other car was a pickup with three passengers who all survived with no serious injuries. An ambulance rushes the comatose priest to the nearest hospital. But that lacks the equipment to treat his two neck fractures, one of which is the second cervical vertebra. Immediately, the doctors call for a helicopter to transfer him as quickly as possible to the emergency room of Westley at Wichita, as his life hangs by a thread. His neck is broken at the C2 in surgeons' talk, otherwise known as "Hangman's Break," which inevitably causes paralysis. He is going to spend the rest of his life on a board with some sort of artificial respiration. In fact, considering the violence of the crash, he should have died instantly.

> I was there from October 18, 1985, until December 3, 1986. I don't really remember my hospitalization and even less the accident, as if they had never occurred. But somehow I recovered in record time even though I had not had spinal surgery. Finally, after more than a year in the hospital, the doctors allowed me to go home. I was happy to go back to my parish. Mechanically, I took up the Bible and

*opened it at random; my eyes fell on the parable of the tree that bears no fruit and invites pruning:*

*"A certain man had a fig tree planted in his vineyard; and he came and sought fruit thereon and found none. "Then said he unto the dresser of his vineyard, Behold, these three years I come seeking fruit on this fig tree, and find none: cut it down; why cumbereth it the ground? And he answering said unto him, Lord, let it alone this year also, till I shall dig about it, and dung it: and if it bear fruit, well and if not, then after that thou shalt cut it down." (Luke 13:6–9, Authorized Version)*

*At that moment I literally had a flash. The words seemed to have come alive, as if they had jumped off the page. And then, everything came back to me. I was paralyzed by fear. I was sweating. My pulse must have hit 200. I remembered everything. And that was not pleasant, it was terrifying, it was unbelievable because I felt all the emotion I had suppressed. I was trembling. I saw myself just after the accident, transported I don't know how before the throne of Christ. And He was judging me. He was judging me as a priest. I did not have a tunnel, nor light, nor my entire life passing before me in three dimensions. I knew simply that I was at that moment before Him and that there was no argument nor discussion possible. I was naked. He said: "This man has been a priest for twelve years for himself, not for Me. He will go where he deserves." Then I heard the voice of His Mother. I cannot say that I saw as one sees with one's eyes but their voices rang clearly in my head. She said: "My Son, spare his life." Christ heard her before replying: "My Mother, for twelve years he has been the priest of Steve Schneir instead of My priest. Let Me exercise My divine justice." But Mary insisted: "My Son, let Us pardon him much, and see if he bears fruit in the future and returns to You. If not, Your will be done." There was a brief pause and then Jesus answered, "My Mother, it shall be as You say." And I knew that She had saved me from my fate. I don't know what that fate was to be but I did know in the depths of my soul that it was the last place I wanted to go. This wasn't a dream because you don't relive a dream like that. What I relived was real, as real as my sitting here in front of you.*

*The doctors say that I'm a living miracle because a part of my brain was entirely crushed during the accident*

*and there wasn't the slightest possibility that it could
come back; it was physically crushed. That's surely one of
the pardons the Virgin Mary spoke of. And I did not have
a single sequel to the accident, like headaches or back-
aches. From a medical viewpoint, it's inexplicable. I
won't even mention paralysis, the classic result of such
accidents. It will soon be seven years, and I am in perfect
health; there have been no sequelae. You know, I am the
living proof that hell exists because I have felt it; and I
know now that priests risk ending up there even more
than common mortals because they're supposed to carry
His word. I know that my mission now consists of witnessing before the greatest number of people possible, to
convince them that there is a life after this one and it
depends on what we do with this one. People don't
believe in hell, the devil, etc., including some priests,
because they say "God is Love, God is Peace." I say, "Yes,
He is Love and Peace, and He is also Divine Justice." And
today I am a product of His justice and, since His Mother
intervened, of His mercy. I am also living proof of His
Mother's strong power of intercession, because there I
acquired the personal conviction that He could not say
"No" to Her.*

*This was not a dream. God, no! I was there. All that
happened converted me completely. I was converted as a
priest because now I know. My priesthood has changed
entirely since then and today I only regret one thing, all
those years of my ministry wasted in busying myself with
matters that did not concern God or His faithful. I felt
that I was on my own road to Damascus, and that He
broke my neck only to attract my attention. [His voice
breaks and his eyes brim with tears that he tries to hold
back by swallowing several times.] Before that accident,
my ministry was professional and nothing more, without
too much fervor, without too many prayers, without
real devotion. It was for Steve Schneir. But now . . . in
that accident I really learned how I should love Him and
serve Him.*

Since then Father Schneir has crisscrossed the country bearing
witness at large meetings. He has no hesitation in telling his story,
whereas most survivors do hesitate, afraid people will take them
for crazies. This big fellow who might have made a good quarter-

back is convinced, probably more than any other priest, of God's existence, for which he does "public relations."

There are no celestial Beings in Stephen Schneir's experience but when we ask him if he believes in Angels, it is as though we asked him if Paris existed. *"If He exists, then they exist,"* he replies empirically. We note that the priest does not know how to explain the fact that he saw them: *"I cannot say that I saw as one sees with one's eyes, but their voices rang clearly in my head."*

If we compare this to Dr. John Lilly's statement, we find a common characteristic, when the doctor spoke of his "guardians": *"I see their presence without eyes, without body. I know that they are there, thus they are there."* That ability to "see without seeing" comes only when out of body and the subject, on returning to earth, never really manages to describe that very disconcerting sensation. But Stephen Schneir was far from the explorations of Dr. Lilly, who scrutinized his trips as thoroughly as a paleontologist examines bone deposits. The effects of the NDE were greater with Father Schneir. We note for example his thoughts on the priesthood before and after the accident. His vocation before his NDE was flat, like that of thousands of priests throughout the world who might just as well have become businessmen. Without faith, a priesthood is always flat, a bit like a flower without scent, and the flock very quickly becomes aware that their shepherd has become a priest without knowing why. By extension, a priest who does not believe in God cannot hold his parish. Not everyone can have the talents of a Padre Pio. And so the churches empty, as the statistics (and the finances) of the Vatican reveal.

Nevertheless, with the NDE, priests hold an unbeatable weapon, even more formidable as it has been scientifically documented by doctors and universities. Instead of taking advantage of it, an ecclesiastic from Rome, Monsignor Corrado Balducci, explains that it is out of the question:

> *"They cannot be considered proof of the hereafter because proof of the hereafter comes to us only from the word of God. We might consider them the grace of God. But we should not look for them. God wants faith from us. If some one believes in an afterlife simply because he had such an experience,"* he adds, *"he is making a big mistake."* [45]

45. *LIFE* magazine, March 1992, p. 71.

I see those "ghosts" bent double laughing. And I think back to the businessman I met one evening who told me how he had smashed his Ferrari into a tree driving at 150 m.p.h.:

> *And then I was roaring through a tunnel like a missile, streaking toward the Light. I exploded in Him. I knew that it was He, that it was the ETERNAL and that I was one with Him. His voice held the power, the force, of a hundred thousand thunders. It was so strong. . . . I can't explain. I didn't want to leave Him but He said to me, "I AM EVERY-WHERE AND NOWHERE ALWAYS AND NEVER, FOR ETERNITY." And then I woke up in the hospital. Now I drive even faster. I know that He is there, and above all that there is life after death.*

He had solved his problem with death in his Ferrari—and I said to myself that it must be truly sad to die somewhere in a Ford Pinto—and he doesn't care at all what the priest had to say; since in any case he never went to church.[46] Remember that a good number of religious organizations have accused Dr. Moody, Dr. Sabom, or Ken Ring of being hellhounds, creatures of Satan, because the Lighted Being at the end of the tunnel could only be the Devil. Why not? Well, the trouble is that the Devil gives off no love; if he did we would have known about it long ago. And yet a problem remains, a very serious problem.

The reason the church is so distrustful of this groundswell is the absence of bad experiences. It is impossible in their eyes, abominable sinners that we are, that we could have access to God

1. without being confessed,

2. without first passing through purgatory, or, better, hell.

That does not conform to dogma. And from this point of view, the church may be right, not by the absence of confession, but

---

46. In her book *Coming Back to Life* (New York, Ballantine Books, 1989), Phyllis Atwater tells an even stranger story of a patient anesthetized by a dentist. He suddenly felt as if he were out of his body, swimming in a fog. Then his soul alerts him to the presence of God, even though he had never believed in His existence. Suddenly, these words echo in his spirit: *"I have led you. I have guided you. Never again will you sin, nor will you weep, nor will you complain since henceforth you have seen Me."*

simply by the absence of bad NDE. The NDE literature that talks only of positive cases tends to make you believe that after death, all is forgiven and we live in a permanent nirvana. The church explains that there is a hell, a purgatory and a paradise, a paradise that seems always to be the destination of these "ghosts." As if to confirm the church's belief, the community of NDE researchers unanimously reject the cases of cardiologist Maurice Rawlings. Professor Carol Zaleski, author of a comparison between medieval and modern NDE, remarks:

> *Only in explicitly polemical Christian near-death narratives, such as Maurice Rawlings's* Beyond Death's Door *and the account published by Jess E. Weiss called "I Was An Atheist—Until I Died," is there an effort to promote a specific doctrinal message.*[47]

These works are judged controversial by this community simply because they touch upon hell and bad NDE. Yet they push the reader toward God. That community forgets too easily that it is thanks precisely to the NDE experienced by George Ritchie with Christ that they are all working on this subject.

Let us review the most important common characteristics established by all the researchers in the field of NDE (Moody, Sabom, Ring, Greyson, Grey, Morse, etc.) when the subject relives his life in three dimensions, he is *invariably* judged by the love he has brought/given to others. Period. He relives each of his actions and words as well as their effect on others. If he has slapped someone in the face, he relives the slap as though he has given it to himself, experiencing it in the other's place. If we accept this reasoning, we may logically deduce that it applies to all of us, including the most abominable of criminals. Believe me, I would not like to be in a criminal's shoes when he relives his life. . . . And here it is Father Schneir who sums up the situation perfectly: *"Yes, He is Love and Peace, but He is also Divine Justice."* We can guess that those who have had a bad NDE are not going to broadcast it from the rooftops, with a few rare exceptions. To relive a slap is not a major problem. To kill or torture someone again will certainly create serious problems after that passage through the tunnel. Take another case, the Serbian soldiers who, during the night of June 16/17, 1992, turned up at the convent located at Nova Topola, close to the industrial city of Banja Luka, and raped several nuns, the

47. In *Otherworld Journeys*, New York, Oxford University Press, 1987.

youngest obviously.[48] We may wonder what the guardian Angels intended for the sisters, but aside from that we can imagine what these barbarians are going to relive after their passage through the tunnel. Will they merge with that magnificent Light which never dazzles the eye?

## 25) A MESSENGER

And consider the case of a soldier telling about his "death" in Libya during World War II. He explains how he was trying to go on fighting when he discovered suddenly that no one could see him and that others soldiers were passing right through. He looks over the battlefield and sees other "dead" comrades. The situation seems quite bizarre, and he started to ask questions, when he discovers a newcomer who seems different:

> *This stranger was not wearing a uniform, and for several seconds I wondered how a civilian had wandered into this. He seemed vaguely Arab. When he turned and gazed at me, I felt as if he had recreated me. I knelt and murmured, "The Christ," with all the reverence of a child.*
>
> *"No, not Christ, but one of His messengers," said the man I had knelt before. "He wants you."*
>
> *"He wants me?"*
>
> *He lifted his gaze to the others, but all I could see was a glorious light. It filled my head, and burned away the last bond holding me in that place.*

There's a textbook case: a battlefield in World War II. The subject tries to go on fighting but passes right through objects, the enemy, etc. Classic. This account, every bit as fascinating as the previous twenty-four we have just examined, differs not at all from NDE. Nothing very unusual. But the story, turned up by Louis Pauwels and Guy Breton,[49] *is* unusual, because the soldier did *not* return from the other side. He is indeed "dead" to us. The wife of Colonel Gascoigne (an English officer at the battle of Khartoum, known also as a friend of Cecil Rhodes), possessed a medium's powers and received this message by automatic writing. I would carefully refrain from venturing into the paranormal, which I

---

48. Object of a telegram "Open Letter" from Pope Jean-Paul II to the bishop of the region, Franjo Komarica, June 20, 1992.

49. *Nouvelles Histoires Extraordinaires*, p. 126. Pauwels is famous as the editor of *Le Figaro*.

detest, especially communication with the dead, but this testimony is oddly similar to the previous accounts of survivors' NDE. Better still, it confirms them all.


## CONCLUSION

### WE CAN DIE EASY IN OUR MINDS, FEMALE ANGELS EXIST

### OR

### IS GABRIEL A BETTER TRUMPET-PLAYER THAN MILES DAVIS?

They certainly come from somewhere, these immaterial beings. . . . Many people are intently studying experiences at death's door, but it is still true that none of these students have experienced the discrete presence of Angels themselves. Yet they exist; they are there, these guides, guardians, presences, friends, companions, in that dark tunnel which leads the subject toward the Light: one must be dead or close to death to first become aware of their presence. And why do some people have a single guardian while others discover several presences? And finally, more curious still, they are all generally clad in a belted white robe, radiating serenity, wreathed in light, reassuring and comforting the subjects. In averaging various cases, the first word that comes to the mind of the subject when he retells his story is *Angel* (twelve times), an overwhelming majority, followed far back by *Being* (four times), *Presence* (three times), *Guardian*, *Someone*, and *Woman* (two times). After that one finds *Entity*, *Power*, *Instructor*, etc. Children speak of a *Lady* or a *Gentleman*, always *very kind*. We note also that it is not the children, but the adults, who use the term Angel. Another datum: the Angels rarely possess wings. They appear shining, with a body, arms, and legs, and a splendid head of hair like you and me, though I would love to hear that someone talked to an Angel with a tonsure. In other cases, the subject does not see them but feels them at his side, a feeling indescribable in human terms, as they say. They know that someone is accompanying them.

Oddly enough, the Angels identify themselves in only a third of the cases: *"I am he who is always with you"* or *"I am your guardian"* or even *"I am he who watches over you."* Never do they introduce themselves immediately with *"I am your guardian Angel,"* as if this term would stun the subject, already quite disturbed. Another detail: the Angels generally make themselves known to their protégés after the tunnel, and only in a third of the cases before the tunnel; and when they appear before the tunnel it is generally to seek out children floating above their bodies. In 60 percent of circumstances, they speak with the subject, and always by telepathy (100 percent). An extremely significant detail: less than a third of NDEs with Angels include a complete review of the life lived—as if their presence dispensed with that requirement.

Let us now deal with the delicate subject of the Angels' sex. We noted in our sample that, yes, the Angels are sexed, as in several cases it is a feminine Angel that materializes to prop up the devastated soul. It would seem that these Angels are blonde, though we have seen a case where "she" had beautiful white hair. No redheads or brunettes, at least not in our sample, but I have not given up hope. In contrast the male Angels are blond and brunette; no matter, I am more interested in Angels of the so-called "weaker sex." Then again, it seems that neither male nor female Angels play the harp, contrary to Baroque representations that make us think of Paradise as little more than a music conservatory. The idea that we do not necessarily have to appear before an Archangel Michael dressed for chemical warfare is frankly reassuring. Another observation: they are often humorous, as if their domain is only a series of drolleries, perhaps like a good Jewish joke. One thing is certain, there are no chubby cherubs with powdered bottoms and plump arms. Instead, there are "powers" with the faces of handsome young men, or supernatural beauties that move with the speed of thought and radiate an immeasurable power that no one can resist, as the painter William Bouguereau seems to have guessed on the jacket of this book. Their favorite color is white. No Angel in these NDEs is clothed like Gabriella Light (though we regret it), heroine of the novel by Father Andrew Greeley,[50] or by Yves Saint Laurent, Montana, or Christian Dior. They all seem to frequent the same designer of white robes and golden belts. We are told of a *shining woman with blonde hair,* *shiny white robes,* of a *radiant being, bathed in a shimmering white light,* of *a being made of light, dressed in a long white robe glistening with white light and wearing a golden belt around his waist. His bare feet do not touch the ground,* or again of a guardian Angel with *golden hair, two meters tall, dressed in a long white robe, held on by a belt,* of *a belted white robe,* of *an Angel of light,* of a very beautiful lady *dressed*

50. *Angel Fire*, New York, Tor Books, 1988.

*in white with white hair,"* of *"glowing material,"* of *"brilliant points of light,"* etc.

To put it plainly, they seem to be made of light. An Angel, and I suppose, a female Angel even more, holds a powerful attraction for the subject, but the moment the subject perceives the Light, he forgets his companion. That is another constant. I very sincerely hope that my guardian Angel is a ravishing divine beauty who would make any Vogue supermodel green with envy. On this matter I quote from my honorable colleague Malcolm Godwin, author of the delightful *Angels, An Endangered Species,*[51] in reference to the sex of Angels: he affirms on page 43 that the Archangel Gabriel is the only Angel of the feminine gender in that celestial male or androgynous population. As we will see in the chapter "Mystics and Angels," the Archangel Gabriel seems to be exactly what we call an Angel; we will also see in this connection that certain mystics present indisputable supernatural guarantees.


Back to the subject of Angels in NDE. They exist; that is absolutely certain. If a priest had told me *"Angels exist,"* I would never have believed him, even though priests who believe in Angels are an endangered species. But in all these experiences at the frontiers of death, the presence of Angels simply demolishes any theological hesitation. The more so because even when the survivor's religion (Mormon, Jew, Catholic, Protestant, Hindu, Lutheran, etc., or atheist) affects the central character—the Light—we find few or no differences among these "presences" who sometimes accompany the subject in the tunnel.

The guardian Angel, the guide, the Beloved presence, the watcher, is assuredly there. And more than ever the NDEs make me think of the black holes discovered by astrophysicists: an NDE is like a black hole, except that at the end of the tunnel we find the Light and the Angels. That discovery moved Dr. Raymond Moody with great force, which explains why we read on the first page of his book:

> *To George Ritchie, M.D.*
> *and, through him, to the*
> *One whom he suggested.*

For his part, Dr. William Serdahely, professor of medicine at Montana State University, was so struck by his patients' NDEs that

51. New York, Simon & Schuster, 1990.

he launched an in-depth study of eighty cases, a study that he published in the *Journal of Near Death Studies*.[52] and he discovered that there is help at our disposal, loving, warm, and thoughtful help from the "other side." He too found guardian Angels, bright lights, inexplicable and complete cures of cases condemned to death by the medical technology of the 1990s. One of the cases that struck me most forcibly, and that recalls many aspects of Beverly B's NDE (Case #4), is that of a young woman of twenty-seven who committed suicide. She remembers her screams when she found herself in the tunnel, and also her last thought, which was *"My God, tell me if You forgive me, before I die."* She did not then know, as her request proves, that we do not die. She had scarcely finished the thought when, as she explained to Dr. Serdahely, two immense hands emerged from the Light and a voice full of love, compassion, and joy too resounded, saying to her in effect, *"I forgive you. I forgive you. I offer you a second chance."* God does not condemn as casually as certain priests tend to.

The conclusion of this chapter, which the facts oblige us to accept, is that God exists and so do His Angels. It is just that they do not appear to us in the awful guise that some claim for them. In fact, the question is no longer whether Angels exist, but rather whether the Archangel Gabriel is a better trumpet player than Miles Davis.

52. Human Sciences Press, 10 (3), Spring 1992, pp. 171–182.

CHAPTER 3

# Of Supernatural Interventions

"**S**UPERNATURAL" INTERVENTIONS MAKE UP A CATEGORY THAT COMPRISES examples of inexplicable facts. "Is it possible to escape an inevitable, ineluctable accident?" In his 1977 work *Life after Life*, on page 59, Dr. Raymond Moody had already noticed that in certain of the accounts he collected, the subjects *"were saved from physical death by the interposition of some spiritual agent or being. In each case, the person involved found himself (knowingly or unknowingly) in a potentially fatal accident or set of circumstances from which it was beyond his own powers to escape. He may eventually reach the stage of resignation, of accepting death. Just then, however, a voice or a light appears, which comes to his aid at the very last moment."*

And indeed, if you ask the question in your family circle, you are bound to come across at least one case of an accident avoided "by a miracle," in the time-honored phrase. As we saw in the last chapter, "Of Angels in the Tunnels," the human being is accompanied by a spiritual being which only seems to manifest itself only when the body is at the point of death. That guardian Angel helps its protégé pass through the tunnel, or reassures him about future events. Since we find them in the tunnel of death, we may conclude that on the one hand they are always with us and on the other hand they may intervene to save us from death in a dramatic situation. In the majority of the cases we have seen, the subject has heard the words, *"It is not your time,"* and though he often resists returning to his earthly body, the Being urges him back to it. That's a constant. We have also noticed that in certain NDE the subject, declared dead or dying by emergency staff or by surgeons, recovers inexplicably when by all logic (I am thinking of a brain deprived of oxygen for over ten minutes), he should never have

95

come back to life(!), or should certainly have been paralyzed for the rest of his days. To put it plainly, when we look closely at these NDEs it seems that:

1. We cannot die except at the time foreseen in the divine program.

2. Accidents do happen, and it is the Angels' job to see that nothing out of order occurs. I am thinking particularly to that young woman who returned to the hospital after an operation on her leg and there, blasted by pain, left her body suddenly: immediately a "woman" caught her by the neck as the last moment, as she was plunging into the tunnel, and sent her back, telling her that it was *"not her time."*

3. All this can be modified by prayer!

Even if it becomes a bit complicated, a hard look at various testimonies of unforeseen and inexplicable help has established that these "supernatural" intercessions can be divided into five major groups reflecting more or less their supernatural aspect:

A) Angel/Being arrives and vanishes supernaturally.

B) Inexplicable intercession at a dramatic moment:
   1. An audible voice within.
   2. An unexplained gesture forestalling the tragedy.
   3. Time suspended, giving the subject the impression that he alone can determine the proper decision.

C) Help that arrives and vanishes in a human manner, premonitory and warning dreams, synchronicities.

## CATEGORY A
## ARRIVES AND VANISHES SUPERNATURALLY

### A BOMB IS GOING TO EXPLODE

It is May 16, 1986, at an elementary school in the heart of the United States, at Cokeville, Wyoming. A madman named David Young, accompanied by members of his family (as crazy as he is), invades the school and takes 156 children hostage. The maniac explains to the police that he will execute the children by rifle fire, but as madmen so often do, he changes his mind and brings out a bomb; he primes it, and a few moments later, to the horror of all the police and spectators outside, the school implodes, as if in a movie.[1]

Firemen rush into the ruins, sure that they can only gather up the remains of the devastated little bodies. But there is no one killed or even wounded among the school children! The school children explain that "voices" or "beings of light" told them how to avoid the explosion. And bomb disposal expert Richard Haskell tells the press that nor even the word "miracle" can explain why not one child was killed. The case was first taken up by Judene Wixon in her book *Trial by Terror.*[2] A little girl's statement: *"They [the people of light] were standing there above us. There was a mother and a father and a lady holding a tiny baby and a little girl with long hair. There was a family of people. The women told us that a bomb was going off soon and to listen to our brother. She said to be sure we did what he told us. They were dressed in white, bright like bulbs, but brighter around the face. The Women made me feel good. I knew she loved me."* But not all the children saw that family which *"was dressed in white, bright like bulbs."* Some of them only heard voices. A boy's statement: *"I didn't see anything. I just heard a voice tell me to find my little sisters and take them over the window, and keep them there."* Afterward, the child identified one of the people in a photo album as a member of the family he had not known.

So here again we come across a truly classic element of "angelic" NDE, namely Beings *"dressed in white"* who shine like light bulbs.

Question: how these "lights" know that the bomb will explode?

---

1. See also: *San Jose Mercury News*, Monday, May 19, 1986, *School Hostages* or *Los Angeles Times*, Saturday 5/17/86.
2. Horizon Publishers, Bountiful, Utah.

## CATEGORY B 1
## AUDIBLE VOICES IN A NORMAL SITUATION

### JOAN OF ARC

Strange "voices" coming from somewhere are not uncommon, and the most famous of them all is the voice that instructed Joan of Arc to take up a mission absolutely inconceivable from a strictly human point of view. But the power of that "voice" is such that the one who hears it, at first highly distrustful, soon feels obliged to obey it whatever happens and whatever people say to her. To understand fully what befell Joan of Arc, let's briefly transpose the events of her lifetime into our own, and since shepherdesses no longer exist, let's imagine in her place a black girl of sixteen, virgin, cashier in a supermarket, a practicing Catholic, named Joan Arrow.

Joan hears an interior voice explaining to her that she must go to the White House to meet the President. There she must ask him for a body of police officers to help her fight drug traffickers. By a run of unlikely coincidences, Joan makes her way to Washington without a penny in her pocket, meets the President while he is out jogging, and speaks to him. In the end she persuades him, and his advisers as well, to give her two or three special anti-gang units to cleanse the country of drug dealers. At the heading of these forces she, who has never set foot in a police station or an academy, still aided by her "voices," cleans up Atlanta, New York, Detroit and Miami in a few months. The traffickers, terrified of her power, buy off the administration of Los Angeles for several million dollars just as she begins a massive clean-up there.

Arrested by the Los Angeles Police for speeding, she is beaten, raped and tortured by a dozen patrolmen before being delivered to the psychiatrists, who decide to keep her locked up because she claims to hear the Archangel Michael's voice. In the asylum, one day during exercise hour, the real mental defectives bind her and burn her at the stake to "see what it's like." The end.

This seems an altogether idiotic scenario, but it is just about what happened to Joan of Arc, called "the Maid of Orléans," a daughter of laborers, five centuries ago; she remains today one of history's great enigmas, accompanied by ten thousand books and papers about her, which might make us think that her military campaigns must have lasted at least thirty years.

Yet her career lasted only two years (from 1429 to May 30, 1431), which lends a certain weight to the theory of the supposed voices, who ostensibly directed her crusade against the English.

Historian Régine Pernoud remarks in her *Petite Vie de Jeanne d'Arc*[3] that those who condemned her *"did not suspect that they were preparing the most remarkable historical document: the text of her trial and conviction (1431), with their questions and Jeanne's answers, supplies a testimony about her all the more convincing because prepared by her adversaries determined to send her to the stake. Then eighteen years later, when Charles VII of France succeeded in driving the enemy from Rouen, begins another trial called a 'rehabilitation.': they interrogate everyone who knew the heroine to determine whether or not her conviction as a heretic was or was not justified; some hundred and fifteen witnesses testify, recount their memories, tell all they know about her: magnificent source material, telling us 'live' what impression she made."*

Armed with her "voices" and the innocence of her seventeen years, Joan never doubted herself, and with unfaltering determination succeeded in making her way into the presence of the Dauphin, whom she recognized immediately, though he had mingled with the crowd to see if she were well and truly sent by God, as she claimed. When she came in she went straight toward him, though a courtier, dressed in royal robes, had taken the Dauphin's place on the throne. *"When the king and those with him saw that sign,"* Joan recounts, *"I asked the king if he believed now, and he said yes. And then I left and I went on to a small chapel nearby, and I heard that after I left, over three hundred people saw the sign. The Angel left me in the little chapel. I was very angry that he left, and I wept, and would willingly have gone with him, to appease my soul."*

And never did she claim even a single military victory for herself. When she was not yet eighteen she fought the English at the head of a rag-tag army raised by the Dauphin, and she liberated Orleans, Patay, Auxerre, Troyes and Reims. She invented the "Blitzkrieg" (the siege of Orléans lasted seven months, but it only took her seven days to raise it), which clears out a given area in the space of a few days. Considering all the political, geographical, military, and historical implications, it is quite clear that the accomplishments of that young girl (being seventeen in that era was not at all what it is today) remain a complete mystery if we refuse to admit that she did indeed hear voices. She proved herself a peerless strategist, forcing the admiration and respect of the old captains who had at first refused even to look at her. To obey a woman in that era . . . what heresy!

But if we admit the authenticity of her "voices" and of her

3. Desclée de Brouwer, p. 9.

visions, then the mystery clears up as if by a miracle. *"When I was about thirteen,"* she explained, *"I heard the voice of God telling me how to behave properly. And the first time, I was very afraid. And that voice came, during the summer, in my father's garden, around noon. . . . I heard the voice from my right, toward the church. And rarely do I hear it without a radiance. That radiance comes from the same area as the voice. It is commonly a great radiance. . . . I heard that voice three times, and understood that it was the voice of an Angel. . . . The first time, I much doubted it if was the Saint Michael who came to me, and that first time I was much afraid. And I saw him later several times before knowing that it was Saint Michael. I saw Saint Michael and the Angels with my own eyes as well as I see you. And when they left me, I cried and I wished that they had taken me with them. . . . I replied to the voice that I was a poor girl who knew neither how to ride nor how to make war."*

Captured (her mission seemed to be finished) by the English and the Burgundians and flung into prison, Joan never allowed herself to be intimidated by the impressive judiciary apparatus mounted against her. Nor did the bursts of involved questions that fell on her concerning her "voices," asked by eminent theologians, disconcert her; she even retorted to her inquisitors:

> *"I am more afraid of sinning by saying something that would displease my voices than I am of answering you."*

The judge Jean Beaupère left us a marvelous question concerning the nature of the Archangel Michael:

> *"In what form was Saint Michael when he appeared to you? Was he naked?"* (An allusion to the centuries of theological debate on the sex of angels).
>
> *"Do you think God had nothing to dress him in?"*
>
> *"Did he have hair?"* (The judge was no doubt bald; a problem.)
>
> *"Why would they cut it?"* answers Joan, unperturbed.
>
> *"When you saw the voice that came to you, was there light?"*
>
> *"There was much light, as is fitting. There is not as much about you!"*

Not only did Joan of Arc hear the voices, but she possessed a sharp sense of humor, which makes that young nineteen year old martyr even more sympathetic. Thanks to her, the phenomenon of the "voices" is anchored in historical memory. Considering their effect on all of France, it is difficult not to take them seriously, especially with the even more common cases that follow.

## CHANGING LANES

Those "voices" are heard far more often than one would think and not especially for a cause as noble and warlike as Joan of Arc's. We shall see in several accounts to follow that their sudden appearance is particularly intended to save a person who is hurtling towards death. Take the almost banal case of Elizabeth Klein, which took place at the end of 1991 in Los Angeles:

> About a month ago I was in my car, driving down highway 101 in the middle lane. I was approaching the slope that goes down toward Malibu Canyon exit, when very distinctly I heard a voice echoing in my head telling me, "Get into the left lane." I don't know why, but I instinctively obeyed. A few seconds later, the flow of vehicles slowed abruptly because of an accident and the truck that had been right behind me a few seconds earlier (we were going downhill) braked suddenly; but his momentum was too great, and he crashed into the car in front of him, and there was a real pileup in the lane I had occupied a few seconds before. Without that voice, I don't think I'd still be here. That must have been my guide or my guardian Angel, I don't know.

As we shall see, a change of direction represents one of the most frequent cases in this set. People don't usually talk openly about it. Just like that, they obey a "voice," and afterward, when they discover that they have narrowly escaped death, it marks them for life. They do not understand what has happened; knowing that a "voice" has saved them, but as time passes they minimize that intercession to the point of denying it several months later. It is an hallucination, or a dream. In time it seems so foolish that they deny it and act as if it had not happened, in the secret garden where we hide everything we never want to remember. So we can say that the less visible an intercession is, the less people believe it was supernatural. These cases are quite frequent, and in the case above, the subject had instinctively obeyed, avoiding a great crash of sheet metal. But many people, though they hear the warning, hesitate, as we will see further along.

## A MARVELOUS PRESENCE

A case recorded by Dr. Raymond Moody[4] of a soldier during World
War II:

> *This was during World War II . . . and I was serving in*
> *the infantry in Europe. I had an experience I won't ever*
> *forget. . . . I saw an enemy plane diving toward the building*
> *we were in, and it had opened fire on us. . . . The dust from*
> *the bullets was headed in a path right toward us. I was very*
> *scared and thought we would all be killed.*
>
> *I didn't see a thing, but I felt a wonderful, comforting*
> *presence there with me, and a kind, gentle voice said, "I'm*
> *here with you, Reid. Your time has not come yet." I was so*
> *relaxed and comfortable in that presence. . . . Since that*
> *day, I have not been one bit afraid of death.*

Unlike the preceding case, where the subject did not know that
she was in danger, here the soldier saw the plane swoop down on
him and wondered what chance he had to survive. At that moment,
he heard a voice, accompanied by a physically comforting impression impossible to describe. The subject felt calm and could even
face all the enemy planes in the world since that strange voice, "I
am with you," somehow guaranteed that his hour had not come.
So! Here we are back among the cases of NDE where invariably the
subjects found themselves sent back with the admonition, "Too
early, it is not yet time."

## MARTIN CAIDIN'S "VOICE"

Martin Caidin is a seasoned pilot. He must be one of the rare
people left who have flown an authentic German Messerschmidt.
Aside from his passion for flying, he is also the best-known American writer in his field, author of thirty-some books like *The History
of the Boeing 707, Pilot's Manual for the ME-109, The Zero, Aeronau-
tical Medicine, The Flying Fortress*, etc. A real flying fool. After forty
years of talking with pilots of all nationalities (it was he who put a
Mickey Mouse hat on Russian engineer Mikoyan's head when he
visited Disney World in Florida) Martin decided that all these
"strange" stories that circulated only among pilots, merited more
attention. It intrigued him all the more because he remembered
surviving a strange adventure that neither he nor his copilot, and
even less the navigator, had been able to explain. The date: Septem-

4. *Reflections on Life After Life*, page 25.

ber 13, 1964. Flight plan: Florida to Las Vegas. Aircraft: a Piper Aztec, N5 196Y. Profile of pilot Eddie Keyes: ballistic engineer for IBM. Profile of navigator Zack Strickland: engineer for NASA. Martin Caidin sits in the copilot's seat. At the time of the incident, the two pilots are scanning for the frequency of the tower at Wichita just after flying over Dodge City:

> *I reached above and behind me for the ceiling-mounted cabin light. I never had a chance to move the switch.*
>
> *"What?" Eddie asked.*
>
> *"What what?" I shot back.*
>
> *"You just said something."*
>
> *"Didn't say a thing. You said give me some light, and then you said turn right."*
>
> *"No, I didn't."*
>
> *"You asked for the cabin light?"*
>
> *"Yep. But that's all. You said to turn right."*
>
> *"I didn't say anything," I told him.*
>
> *We looked at one another, we both glanced back at Strickland, who snored away blissfully, we looked again at one another, and Eddie said, very quietly, "Holy shit."*
>
> *Everything else seemed the result of long practice; we both did the same thing at the same moment and with perfect timing. Neither one of us had said to turn right. Someone said it, and it wasn't us, and sure as hell it wasn't Zack, so—*
>
> *We both tramped right rudder and banged the yokes over to the right and hauled the yokes back in our stomachs, and as Eddie hit the props for flat pitch, I shoved the throttles forward, and the Aztec sounded like she screamed, and we hauled around in a wicked right turn under full bore. Zack was bounced about in the back and came awake with the side of his face mashed against a window, and it took him several seconds to realize the horizon was a vertical line, and then it rolled back to an even keel and seemed to raise up a bit as Eddie and I dropped the nose a bit for some extra speed, for what, we didn't know. But we were doing it.*
>
> *That voice said to turn right, and we by God turned right.*
>
> *Then a glow appeared about the airplane. A golden glow that spread to the interior of the cabin through the windows. A gorgeous pure golden light in a huge bowl about us. And the light stretched from the southern horizon*

*to the north as, right where we would have been had we continued on our course, a huge flaming object hurtled down from the sky and plunged into the earth far below.*

*Right were we would have been . . .*

*Eddie and I didn't need a guidebook to tell us what was coming next. We chopped power and raised the nose to bleed off our speed, and the shock wave hit us like a truck, and the airplane calmed down and trembled a bit like a dog shaking off water, and we looked down, and that golden light was gone, and we came in with power and turned back on course.*

*"You see it good?" Eddie asked.*

*"Yeah," I said.*

*"What the hell's going on? Why'd we turn? What the hell was that thing?" The questions poured from Zack like nickels from a slot-machine jackpot. We ignored him.*

*"You thinking what I'm thinking?" Eddie asked.*

*"Uh-huh. That was no meteorite."*

*"You got it. Meteorites don't burn with a yellow-orange carbon flame," Eddie said.*

*"You see that solid flat surface?" I asked. "Looked like burning metal."*

*"It was," Eddie replied.*

*Something had come out of space. Most likely it was something very big that had been boosted into orbit either by us or the Russians, and we were right there at reentry.*

*I called Dodge City radio, identified ourselves, and announced a pilot report. "Go ahead," Dodge told me.*

*"We were pretty close to a flaming object a few minutes ago. We're just east of Dodge at thirteen thousand. Shook us up a bit with the shock wave."*

*"You guys just pass directly over the city?"*

*"That's affirmative."*

*"We're sure glad to talk to you. The way your course looked, it was coming down straight through you."*

*"Yeah," I said. "You get any other pilot reports?"*

*"Mister, that thing was seen in fourteen states, from Canada all the way down to Mexico. We got a call from NORAD flashed to all stations in this area. Meteorite."*

*"Thanks. We're going on to Wichita, landing there."*

*"Have a good flight. And watch out for rocks. Dodge out."*

*"Meteorite, hell," Eddie said.*

*"I know," I answered.*

*"Who the hell told you guys to turn before that thing came down?" Zack shouted from behind us.*

*Eddie never could pass up an opportunity. Not to tweak is to Eddie an unpardonable sin.*

*"I think it was Mrs. God," he said.*

*By the time I landed at Wichita, Zack had already wiped out half a bottle of scotch he yanked from his luggage. He was creamed. We couldn't blame him.*

*Postscript, I suppose, is called for.*

*What was that voice? Where did it come from? Who said to turn right? Three people in the Aztec; none of us said it. The radios were turned down, so that source was eliminated. That left only a voice from somewhere. Neither Eddie nor I could swear whether we heard the instruction "Turn right," as a spoken signal, or if we'd heard the words within our heads. We just don't know.*

*But we do know that if we hadn't made that turn, that was the end of the trip for all of us forever.*

Martin Caidin told that story in his moving book *Ghost in the Air.*[5] The three men are not bubbleheads, far from it, and anyway when you fly an airplane there is no room for fantasy. On a boat you may possibly jump overboard with a life jacket or into a lifeboat. That's hard, from an airplane. . . . The copilot asks the pilot *"What?"* Neither of them remembers saying to the other "Turn right." They almost argued but didn't have the time.

This case is extremely valuable because the subject did not obey the voice, and turn right as instructed. Then, to change their course definitively, a "marvelous" (when have we seen a "marvelous" light before?) white light appeared before the plane, forcing them to dive, to avoid that "marvelous" obstacle. At the same instant as the manifestation of that "marvelous" light, a meteorite, not "marvelous" at all, all aglow, fell from the sky and passed precisely where they would have been. Isn't that a "marvelous" coincidence, as materialists would say?

## George Ritchie's "Voice"

Now let's take up another change of direction because of a voice, the remarkable case of the soldier George Ritchie, whom we met in "Of Angels in the Tunnels." Recovered from his NDE and complet-

5. New York, Bantam Books, 1991, p. 47.

ing another training assignment, Ritchie lands in France with the rest of the U.S. Army, as a medical corpsman. The war goes on, bombardments, mines, confrontations, and we are still a long way from the Battle of Bastogne:

> *From Camp Lucky Strike we moved to the first place where we became operational. It was an estate called Arnicourt outside of Rethel, France. While we were waiting for our equipment to arrive, we were given one-day passes to go to Rheims. I had talked two buddies into joining me.*
>
> *This particular morning I had arisen early to write Marguerite a letter before I left. When the weapons carriers arrived that were going to carry us, I climbed into the back of one and took my seat on one side between my two friends noticing there were twelve of us in the carrier. We were waiting for the other carrier to fill when something deep inside of me placed the thought in my mind,*
>
> *"Get off of this carrier and go write Marguerite a letter."*
>
> *"This is absolutely ridiculous. I have just written her a letter. I have fought too hard to get this pass into Rheims and besides, what will my friends, who I have talked into going with me, think?"*
>
> *Again the voice deep within me: "I said, get off and go write Marguerite a letter."*
>
> *But I wanted to see the Cathedral of Rheims and I ignored the second warning. The third repeat order was so loud in my mind I was afraid my friends could hear it. Looking utterly confused and surprising them when I arose, I tried to make some plausible explanation as I was leaving the truck. If they could not understand, the top sergeant was even more surprised when I handed him my pass.*
>
> *The young soldier picked by the Sergeant to fill my place took my seat between my two buddies. The carrier had not gone eight miles from the hospital when it hit a land mine that the Germans had planted in the road. It blew the carrier over, instantly killing the soldier who took my place and causing severe injuries to my buddies, sending them to England and then to the United States.[6]*

We cannot rejoice in this change of course, because here

6. *My Life After Dying*, p. 39.

another human being is killed in the place of the course-changer. This brief account alone could be the subject of a thesis in philosophy, because life and death did a flip-flop in the space of a minute, and a die was cast. Ritchie hears the voice instructing him to go write a letter to his fiancee. He refuses. As in the previous case, he rejects the "voice." But the latter insists, and let us note that it does not tell him, *"Get out because this troop carrier is going to blow up,"* but *"go write to your girl friend."* So you might say that Angels can "lie." What would have happened if the voice had told him to *"Get out of there, the truck's going to blow up?"* In all logic, Ritchie would have told his two friends to get out along with him. But this was not foreseen in the Divine plan: those two were supposed to be wounded and shipped home (this opens infinite perspectives). In other words, they *were intended* to be wounded and the soldier who took George Ritchie's place *was intended* to die. And why did that soldier's guardian Angel not shout in his head, *"No, no, no, don't get into that truck,"* or even *"go write your will?"* The chapter "Of Angels and Tunnels" taught us that his time had apparently come. We also note that the "voice" intervened strongly three times in a row before he decided to get out of the truck, which may lead us to believe that this "voice" will hammer away at you until you obey it.

## CATEGORY B 2

## FORESTALLING TRAGEDY

## *"QUOD NESCIS QUOMODO FIAT, HOC NON FACIS."*

## *(IF YOU DON'T KNOW HOW YOU DID SOMETHING, IT WASN'T YOU WHO DID IT.)*

### THE SHOT RANG OUT; I WAS ON MY FEET

This account is a variation that indirectly roused my interest in guardian Angels. Catherine Leroy,[7] a reporter-photographer, was working for *Time* Magazine and the Gamma press agency, and was in Beirut in the middle of the civil war. This category of "unexplained gesture" is interesting because it seems less "supernatural" than the previous one, but its effect is no less salutary for the sub-

---

7. Catherine was a very famous reporter; she even got the cover of *American Photographer* (December 1988).

ject, who *not knowing why*, moved a tenth of a second before the tense event. Let's be clear about this: it's certainly not like someone telling you, "If I'd gone forward one more yard the truck would have hit me." Not at all; I would even say it was the opposite. In effect, the subject is in a calm, serene situation, sometimes without a shadow of danger on the horizon, when suddenly he jumps up without knowing why. It is inexplicable behavior. You don't fling yourself suddenly toward your driver, as I did in Silicon Valley, at the risk of scaring him and even causing an accident by this abrupt and unforeseen movement. Let's look at this reporter's similar adventure:

> It was in Beirut in 1976, in the quarter where the lavish hotels are, between the Phenicia and the Saint-Georges. A cameraman from Visnews came along with me from barricade to barricade. We had stopped at one of them to talk with some soldiers. A Palestinian soldier was at my right and we were chatting. It was a very quiet moment at about three or four in the afternoon. I was sitting on a sort of stool or sandbag, I can't remember which. The Palestinian was seated too, and he'd laid his Kalashnikov across his knees, with the barrel at about the level of my legs. We were drinking hot coffee. On a sudden impulse I shot up like a rocket, and at that same moment the Kalashnikov fired a round. We never understood why I hopped up so suddenly, and even less why the rifle fired. The soldier was not playing with his AK. As far as we could see he had not set the safety. I don't know why, but when it fired I was on my feet. I didn't think much about it at the time, because that sort of thing had happened to me several times. Each time, by a sudden impulse, I escaped a bad situation. One day a friend reproached me sharply for being too impulsive. And I said, "You know, if I'm still alive it's because I'm impulsive. Otherwise, I'd have been dead long ago, for sure." The cameraman, like the soldiers, saw what had happened. There were three of us, the Palestinian, Noel the cameraman and myself, and it was as if the whole thing hadn't happened. Otherwise I'd have had my legs badly shot up. We didn't think any more about it. That night I told myself that it had been a really close call. At the time, it didn't seem like a significant memory, only one more incident in a crowded day, but when I thought about it later, it was pretty terrifying. And certainly if we

*have guardian Angels, I've worn out more than one. . . .*

That is a typical example of intercession by impulse. It would be impossible to explain this kind of case otherwise. Could it be that the subject is more receptive to divine intercession, and doesn't need an audible manifestation like a "voice"? Here too we enter an area that seems to obey totally strange laws.

## I Hit the Brakes Without Knowing Why

Let's leave the battlefield and come back to everyday life. You might think that this kind of impulse occurs only in very special circumstances. Not at all. Here's the story of another photographer, for example, this time from the Sipa agency, who has never understood why he braked "suddenly":

> *One night in October 1991 in Los Angeles, I was following a friend's car, and we stopped for a red light at the intersection of Robertson on Burton. The light turns green, the car in front of me starts up and turns left. I had taken my foot off the brake and my car started forward, but—and I don't know why—I stopped when I had absolutely no reason to. One second later a car came barreling up from my right like a rocket, doing maybe sixty, carried off my bumper in a screech of torn metal, did a 180, rolled over, smashed into a parked car to its right and came to rest upside-down. If I'd made the turn I was about to make, with that car coming on at that speed, I'd unquestionably have been gravely injured or killed. I have no idea why my foot hit the brake, as if by instinct, when I had no reason to stop, none at all, and I was already in the intersection. And I hadn't seen or heard anything.*

Here we find again *"I don't know why, there was no reason,"* the subject seems to be excusing himself for braking or moving, as if for a few seconds he had lost his mind, as if he were behaving like a mental case. No one brakes while in an intersection, no one jumps up in the air like a gangly marionette for no reason at all. The subjects cannot understand how they could do such a thing without the action being planned and ordered by their brains. It is as if, for several seconds, someone else had acted in their place.

## CATEGORY B 3
## TIME IN SUSPENSION

### MARY FRAMPTON

Mary Frampton is a retired photographer for the *Los Angeles Times*. Her husband, a reporter and editorial writer for the same daily, dead at 57, was still alive at the time of the following events. In June 1979 they were aboard a sailboat at sea near the Santa Cruz Islands, on a story for the newspaper. The weather was clear and the Pacific was rippling calmly when the boat began to roll gently in the first gusts of a squall. Mary Frampton had her Rolleiflex in both hands and was leaning outboard to photograph a Bombard carrying divers, when she heard a ripping sound:

> *I realized instantly that a cleat had torn clear out and was shooting toward me like a missile. But at the same time I saw the whole scene in slow motion, as in a film, frame by frame, without really understanding. I had the impression that I had all the time in the world to come to a decision. But I felt myself pulled backward by someone, and the aluminum protective band around my camera seemed to absorb the shock, bending like plastic. I didn't understand at all, because there was no one behind me, and my husband, who had seen it all, was sure I would come out of it disfigured for life. The Rolleiflex was at the height of my chin, and I saw the ring bend in slow motion. I've carefully preserved it, because that object saved my life. Considering the weight and speed of the cleat, my camera should have been smashed and I should have been disfigured. But I don't know what pulled me backward or how I could have seen the whole thing in slow motion at the same time.*

This time we've plunged into science fiction. Time suspended! It isn't possible. And yet whoever has been through an accident can recall that sensation of seeing the collision "in slow motion." This "slow motion" seems to unroll at varying speeds. There's the "slow-down" that never ends, as if the subject had suddenly popped out of physical reality and life was passing at 20 percent or 30 percent of natural speed. A motorcycling friend of mine explained to me once that he remembered his flight through the air in perfect slow motion when a car hit his bike at full speed. In Mary Frampton's case, not only did she see the cleat streaking toward her in slow motion, but she also felt tugged backward by someone, when there was no one near her. Two strange events that defy our sense of logic.

## A GIRL WITH BLONDE HAIR

At the age of four, Wes Chandler was playing with some friends in treehouse when, for reasons only known to the children, they pushed him off the house. It seems like an ordinary childhood accident, but in retrospect his experience during the fall was not. As we are about to see, there comes a guardian Angel in all his splendor, not only sparing his life but also, at the least, a broken neck and the implied paralysis:

> As I fell through the air, I saw my playmates' faces; they expressed something like "Oh oh." At the same time I knew I was falling and was going to hurt myself. I tried to look at the ground but couldn't see it. And then I realized that I was falling very slowly. Then I saw a lady dressed in white with blonde hair who was saying, "Don't look down, don't look down." At the sight of her I was comforted. She repeated, "Don't look down, or you'll be hurt, it's important, keep looking at me, only at me." That took a long time and I remember not understanding why I still hadn't hit the ground. She said to me, "Everything will be all right, everything is O.K.," and just as she went to touch me, I touched the ground. Where I had just been, time did not exist. I believe that without her I would doubtless have broken my neck, but I had only a broken rib.

There is an accident which, without intercession by that "lady" with blonde hair, would have become a fatal drama. It is interesting to note that this "lady," appearing out of nowhere, wore a white robe and slowed time. The boy did not understand why his fall did not end. The Angel—there can be no possible doubt that she was a guardian Angel—warns him not to look at the ground during a modified space-time, thus altering the position of his body and avoiding a fatal fall for him. Time that is frozen, or at least seems "slowed down," is one of the most startling constants: in the NDE for example, when the subject relives his whole life—sometimes sixty years—we learn with astonishment that his heart stopped beating for only five seconds!! Time no longer exists, at least not as we normally perceive it. Let's try to reconstruct the accident. The tree is about fifteen feet high. If you drop a forty-five pound weight, the elapsed time before it lands is no more than four seconds. And see what the child said: *"She repeated, 'Don't look down or you'll be hurt, it's important, keep looking at me, only at me.' That took a long time and I remember not understanding why I still hadn't hit the ground. She said to me, 'Everything will be all right, everything is O.K.,' and just as she went to touch me, I touched the ground."* But if we put a stopwatch on the time it takes to say, *"Don't look down or you'll be hurt, it's important, keep looking at me, only at me. Everything will be all right, everything is O.K.,"* it takes five to seven seconds. Wes Chandler adds that she repeated these phrases, we may suppose at least twice, which makes it 10 to 14 seconds. About 300% of the time of the fall, even telepathically.

## The Rocket Lands on Me

Let's look at another witness to "O time, suspend thy flight,"[8] and see how a reporter, a war correspondent for the Sygma Agency and then for Gamma, interprets an event.

> *I was in Beirut with my assistant, with a Shiite in the streets. He was carrying a mortar and he stopped regularly to fire a round. Usually with this kind of weapon you only fire twice, and immediately evacuate the position, because the enemy home in on your position right away and return fire pretty accurately. No doubt to "shot off" he fired a third round, and a couple of seconds later we heard the characteristic sound of a mortar shell coming straight at us. We hit the deck and cross our arms over our heads. This time we didn't have a chance. And very clearly I saw the rocket coming, as in a slow motion film; I could even make out its little wings describing a pretty curve to land just a meter from my nose, in a sandbag. I tensed myself, waiting for the explosion, knowing that it was the end. I don't know why, but miraculously, the rocket did not explode.*

Again we find the mysterious phenomenon of time "slowed down."

## I Saw the Accident

Fred is a businessman who has created a very successful enterprise in the computer industry. He's in his sixties and has a sporting air about him, also a real passion for American cars. One evening after dinner in Paris we were chatting about one thing and another, and I don't know why but I mentioned my deep interest in NDE. He lis-

---

8. From Lamartine's idyll, *Le Lac.*

tened to me almost gravely, and at the end he said in a confidential tone, *"Pierre, I'm going to tell you something I've never told anyone because it's too crazy."* I pricked up my ears, expecting some far-fetched NDE, but I never imagined that his story would upset all my preconceived notions of the topic. His experience is unique because it comprises, all in one story, all the aspects we've broached in these chapters. It's like a resume, a sort of digest:

> *I was in Morocco, back in 1954. I was twenty-four or twenty-five years old. I came out of the movies with a friend. At that time I owned a big American car that I loved to drive; I blasted along at about fifty. You couldn't really call it a highway, just a road, not even paved. At one point headlights lit up a small truck in front of us. I drifted out of my lane to see if anyone was coming and, seeing no one, I accelerated to pass the truck. At that exact moment my eyes registered an oncoming truck, running with no headlights. I don't know what happened. But I saw the crash and the monstrous heap of crushed metal. I left my body and observed the mutilated corpses. Then I saw the announce-ment of my death to my mother and the repercussions in my family. I saw the funeral preparations, the newspaper article detailing the fatal accident and, above all, above all, I attended my own funeral. I remember particularly exam-ining all the faces of those present at my burial. I watched it all from outside.*
>
> *At that moment, inexplicably, the steering wheel turned to the left and our car went off the road to end its trip in the desert. I saw and heard the truck pass as if nothing had happened. He didn't even try to brake. My car came to rest two hundred yards from the road and we sat there in the dark for over an hour in absolute silence, hardly breathing, not budging, totally paralyzed, stunned, trembling. I have never, never forgotten.*

After a story like that, comment is difficult. I have read and reread that story often, and each time I react oddly, as if this life were only a movie, only a dream, where each act and consequence could be modified in the space of a single second. There, we do not live in "slow motion" but just the opposite, "quick time." This story is really gripping. Everything is there: the possibility of a fatal out-come, leaving the body, life out of real time, watching time speed up, and then the "supernatural" intervention, the steering wheel that turns suddenly to the left, and everything reverts to normalcy. Yet there is certain similarity to Dr. John Lilly's NDE: *"They then show me what would happen if I left my body back there—an alternative path for me to take. They also show me where I can go if I stay in this place. They tell me that it is not yet time for me to leave my body permanently, that I still have an option to go back to it."* In Fred's case it was after he saw his "alternative" route that the steering wheel of his car "turned to the left." He did not make any decision, did not ask anything of anyone and did not pray to God. . . .

## His Face Was Shining

I owe the following case to Evelyn-Sarah Mercier, president of IANDS France, a case which she also used to introduce her book, *La Mort Transfigurée.*[9] It is an experience of the imminent death type that closely resembles the case we just considered. Here the subject saw a Being who seemed to control time! Evelyn received this letter from an inhabitant of the city of Béziers who explained departure from her body just as a car came bearing down on her:

> *My husband was driving. To our right there was a gully. A truck was getting ready to pass us. Suddenly, a car coming toward us pulled out to pass and headed straight for us at high speed. I thought: "Death." Immediately I rose out of my body. Below me I saw the vehicles closing. Their approach was infinitely slow. Time almost stopped. I saw that the collision was inevitable, and I saw my body inside the car. What was about to happen left me totally indifferent. I saw my husband at the wheel. I knew that his efforts were in vain. I turned away. Before me there was an immense Being, immobile and silent, like an Angel. His face was shining, but in the shadows. From him emanated a power, a knowledge, a love greater than anyone could imagine. He was coming for me. My joy was indescribable, also my impatience to follow him. Far away on the horizon, above a clouds, I saw my "brothers," whose existence I realized only at that moment. The were waiting for me. My exile was about to end, for I realized also that my place was with them. I was going to join them. My guide confirmed that it was time. Nevertheless, I noticed that he seemed surprised and that he hesitated. He remained silent and immobile. He was waiting for*

*something. But what? He was giving me time, and again I saw the vehicles below approaching each other. I knew that I had been given a delay in order to find something. He would not help me. It was as if I were suffering from amnesia. Suddenly I saw my daughter, far below, falling asleep in her room, my mother at her side. I felt immense sorrow. I fell to my knees before the Being and said to him, "I know what you do is right, but my daughter—so terrible a loss, both parents at the same time—is that just? Let my husband at least not die." Then I saw his face and heard his voice. He pushed me toward the earth, saying, "Since you ask nothing for yourself, go on back, it is not your time." I saw that he approved of me. His face was more brilliant than the sun, and his voice was an enormous vibration. I returned to my place in the car, and saw the headlights veer off. My husband and I sat at the roadside for a long while. He was aware that we should have died.*

If the disembodiment is perfectly classic, on the other hand this mysterious Being, "like an Angel," is less so. And indeed it is rare when a Being appears during disembodiment in the face of imminent death. Generally the subject gazes down in calm indifference and feels as if disjoined from his body, as if it had suddenly become completely alien to him. But here the Being plays the part of a professor during an oral exam, with the subject put to the test while time slows, as in a film. The purpose of that exam is to witness to love, sanctioned by the *"Since you ask nothing for yourself, go on back."*

## CATEGORY C

### UNEXPECTED HELP, DREAMS, AND SYNCHRONICITIES

It is a certainty that these Beings intervene in our physical reality to save us from accidents. Time standing still, audible voices coming out of nowhere, and the sudden appearance of a Being of light who indicates the way to proceed; these are the various aspects of their materialization. Yet the most frequent case is certainly the warning dream, the dream that does not go away, that you cannot forget. In the morning, the dream obsesses you and urges you to do something, to make a decision almost immediately. And "you don't know why." After a bit, you ask yourself why you have done such a thing, and perhaps two weeks, perhaps a year later you discover that the advice was good for you. It seems quite fantastic. This kind of dream is indelible, and even two years later you remember it. You cannot confuse it with the classic dream that is forgotten as soon as you get up. We will not give examples because we have all more or less experienced this kind of dream, and it compels us, obliges us, to follow its advice, even if it seems to contradict the present circumstances altogether.

Another classic phenomenon is unexpected help. For example, you run out of gas in the middle of the Arizona desert and your car, with its last gasp, stops beside a broken-down truck . . . at three o'clock in the morning! The closest gas station south of you is sixty miles away, and north seventy-five miles. This happened to one of my friends who, as they say, is no rocket scientist. The driver truck pumped several gallons of gas from his truck, plenty enough to reach the nearest station.

The last level of classic intercession is the totally weird synchronicity. You're driving along at midnight, dead tired and running way late, and you ask your Angel to find you a good hotel and confirm it with a sign. Toward midnight I tried one hotel; it was full. Ten minutes later I found a second, but it seemed so blah that I preferred keep driving. At the third one, I was exhausted, and stopped, saying to myself, *"This will have to do. I can't drive anymore in this condition."* I was registering at the desk when a couple came into the lobby of this Holiday Inn. The woman asked if there were any messages, and the employee asked her name. *"Mrs. Angel,"* the woman replied. I paused for a second and smiled. It was the "sign." I was in the right hotel at the right moment. In other words, I was *"on time."* And actually the hotel was perfect with a spacious room and a fine swimming pool.

Synchronicity was also in play with a Jungian psychiatrist whose patient had a tendency to think himself Christ. One afternoon, the patient came in for a consultation, got comfortable on the couch and declared, *"I am He who brought light and He who will put out the light."* He had just finished his announcement when a light fixture came undone from the ceiling for no known reason and fell on his head. The story does not say if he was cured but it is unquestionably a splendid case of synchronicity.

After this short examination of several types of supernatural intervention, we cannot help asking a few questions: why in one case does a Being of light materialize to help children avoid an explosion, and in other cases, of equally mortal danger, do certain people hear voices, experience sudden impulses, suspended time, or even benefit from terrible premonitory dreams? Why in a pileup of fifty cars do we notice one intact car, boxed in by accidents ahead of it and behind it? And in the same pileup, right after the crash, why does a woman decide to leave her Renault immediately and get out of there; five seconds later a truck pulverizes her car, and there is nothing left of it.

**Chapter 2:**
**Dr. George Ritchie,** dead and resurrected on December 20, 1943, at a barracks in Texas. He is the father of the modern NDEs, since he met Raymond Moody "by chance" and told him about that experience. Moody later took a serious interest in the subject, with results known to all: ten million copies of his books sold world-wide. (Photo courtesy of G. Ritchie)

**Kenneth Ring,** professor of psychology at the University of Connecticut. In a masterful demonstration, he set NDEs in the scientific and academic context they required for authenticity. (Photo: University of Connecticut)

**George Gallup** (left), heir to the famous Gallup Polls, who completed the first survey of NDEs in the United States, and **Dr. Maurice Rawlings** (right), army doctor, cardiologist at the Pentagon in Washington, who discovered NDEs among his patients in spite of himself. These two men's work confirmed Dr. Raymond Moody's NDEs. (Photos courtesy of G. Gallup and M. Rawlings)

**Dr. Melvin Morse,** intrigued by an "angelic" NDE and hoping to prove Dr. Moody mistaken, confirmed scientifically, with his Seattle study on infant NDEs, that (1) to undergo an NDE the subject had to come within an inch of death, and (2) and NDE was not caused by pharmacological overload. (Photo courtesy of M. Morse)

**Chapter 4:**
**Robert Monroe,** acoustical engineer, unrivalled specialist in "out of body" experiences and inventor of the "hemi-sync." *"Angels exist,"* he says, *"but they do not have wings,"* confirming the visions of mystics and NDEs. (Photo: Monroe Institute)

Chapter 6:
Elisabeth Kübler-Ross (above), doctor, professor, doctor honoris causa from fifteen universities. She invented "accompaniment of the dying," which has now become an independent medical specialty. *We could not even survive without our Guardian angels,"* she says. She was so impressed by the "angelic visions" of the dying that she installed a gigantic angel at her center (left) kneeling at the foot of the bed of a sick person in the "terminal phase." (Photo P.J.)

Chapter 8:
**Anne-Catherine Emmerich**, stigmatic and temporarily incorruptible, is a "Formula 1" saint, though her beatification has been put off. The young German woman moved about regularly in the company of her guardian Angel, of whom she gave a description to her biographer Clemens Brentano. (Photo: a religious image of the 19th century from the Bibliothèque Nationale in Paris)

Chapter 8:
The Angel diverting himself with *Teresa of Avila,* as seen by Bernini. Ecstacies, levitations, stigmata, incorruptibility, sweet scents, miracles, so many characteristics that qualify a soul for immortality. The Spanish nun is alone in having been transfixed by an Angel.

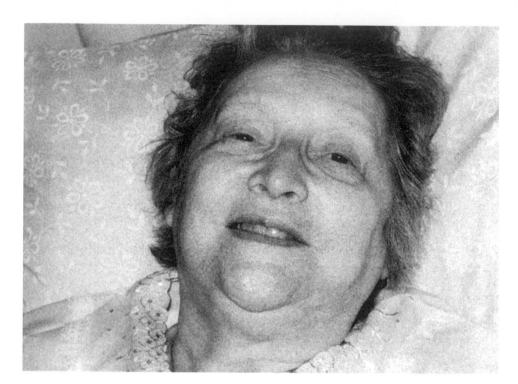

Chapter 9:
**Georgette Faniel** (above), the stigmatic of Montreal. Described by an English reporter as *"the most powerful of living stigmatics."* Her prayers of intercession have enabled many sick people, condemned by the medicine of the 1990s, to be cured instantly. Of her guardian Angel she says, *"He was wearing a white tunic. But you can't compare his beauty to human beauty."* (Photo: P.J.)

Chapter 9:
**Gemma Galgani** (left), the Marilyn Monroe of Catholic religious life, canonized in 1933 by reason of her ecstacies, her stigmata, and most of all her guardian Angel, who accompanied her all her short life. Considered by Italians, who are very demanding in these matters, as one of the most "efficacious" saints in the calendar. She is the oracle of the Passionists, an ultra-ascetic religious order. (Photo: Casa Generalizia Dei Passionisti, Rome)

**Chapter 9:**
Helene Kowalska (left), 1905–1938, a stigmatic bride of Christ to whom Teresa of Lisieux explained in 1930, in a dream, that she would become a "saint." Indeed beatified in 1993(!), Helene Kowalska had innumerable experiences with Angels, to which she paid no attention, living as she did with Christ.

**Chapter 9:**
Padre Pio (below), stigmatic and visionary, unquestionably the most famous priest in the world (d. 1968), with the seminarian Jean Derobert, who has since become chaplain of the Basilica du Sacré-Coeur. The seminarian took a slap in the face in the confessional because he was not praying to his guardian Angel, who Padre Pio saw just behind him! (Photo: Jean Derobert, Imar di Giuseppe Vinelli)

Chapter 11:
The body of **Jacinta Marto** (left), a "seer" of the Archangel Michael at Fatima, dead at 10 and discovered incorruptible on September 12, 1935, during a transfer of her remains. She was perfectly preserved, despite the "infernal" heat of that part of Portugal! There was no perceptible odor. The mystery is all the more significant because while the little girl's body was intact, her brother's had obeyed the laws of nature. (Photo: Vice-postulaçao dos Videntes, Fatima)

Chapter 12:
The biologist **John C. Lilly,** doctor, physicist, research director, deeply impressed by his meetings with this guardian Angel. John Lilly states, *"These are beings superior to us."* (Photo courtesy of Barbara Lilly, Human–Dolphin Foundation)

# CHAPTER 4

# Of Talking with the Angels

M Y OBSESSION WITH "ANGELS" BEGAN WITH A QUESTION: LISTENING TO Jean-Louis Murat's recording[1] I was humming the lyrics of "L'Ange Dechu" and, intrigued by the text, I wondered if I had a guardian Angel. It was a notion I found rather enticing without believing it for a second. About an hour later I left my apartment to go buy a few books and CDs in a store on the Champs-Elysées. At the bookstore I wandered down the aisles, opening books here and there and leafing through some until my hand fell on a stack of "Dialogues as I Have Experienced Them." I would have put the book down right away if my eye had not been caught by sentences written in capital letters—and in Hungarian. My grandmother was Hungarian, and I picked up the rudiments like a mother tongue. Interested now, I picked it up for a closer look, and great was my surprise to discover that it was an explanation of wordplay by Angels, and in Hungarian! A strange coincidence, considering that only an hour before I'd asked myself half in jest if I had a guardian Angel. I stopped right there, bought it, and went on home. The book kept me awake all night, and I was highly impatient for morning, so I could go out and buy the *Dialogues*[2] itself, the booklet I had being only a brief explanatory work.

And when I finally found it, after phone calls to several bookshops, I hurried home, drunk with sleeplessness and excitement. I read it, reread it, and read it again, discovering something new each time, an obscure passage suddenly leaping into clarity and overshadowing others, like violent incantations, ablaze with love and light. Those eighty-eight dialogues pounded at my spirit, and I

---

1. *Cheyenne Autumn*, Virgin Records.
2. In English *Talking with Angels* by Gitta Mallasz; see the bibliography.

119

could think of only one kind of music that might be a proper accompaniment, a sort of *Carmina Burana* played by the Orchestra of the Foreign Legion and sung by hysterical Red Army paratroopers—in other words the immortal work of Christian Vander of the band Magma, Mekanik Destruktiw Kommandoh.[3] Taking another look at the record sleeve, I was stunned to find this note by the composer, dated 1973!

> *They did not know death,*
> *And the angels and the Seraphim*
> *Bowed before them*
> *Cradling them like babies*
> *The whole universe vibrated in them*
> *Echoing with a thousand melodious and immaterial*
> *   voices*
> *And that sensation was so strong to human perception*
> *That they fainted away in space.*
> *The state of grace was achieved.*

I gave the book to some friends, and most of them tucked it away in their library, saying, *"Too violent."* True, it was violent and powerful, virulent, and corrosive, frenetic and furious at once (like Christian Vander's work), as opposed to the universal rendering of chubby-faced Angels firing arrows into young women's hearts. On every page, the *Dialogues* annihilate the amoretti, cherubim and other Angels with rosy bottoms and chubby arms. Certainly this is not the sort of dialogue we expect from alleged Angels; and we are disappointed, because these interviews constitute a torrent of lava, a magma of words teaching us in our deepest soul what the Word can be. These are unquestionably expressions of Beings not human; during his reading of the German version, Pierre Emmanuel of the Academie Française cried out, *"Where do these verses come from? It is impossible to duplicate their concision or their music."* These angelic verses scorch the soul. They are all flame. There is a fire on almost every page, which explains why there are no lukewarm opinions of the *Dialogues*. We love them or hate them. In them romanticism is altogether absent, banished, proscribed, like a "do not enter" in this mysterious hierarchy with its warlike accents, ready to brandish the divine sword and cut off heads. We finish reading the *Dialogues* as if leaving the prize ring,

3. This CD—Seventh Records—can be ordered for $21 postpaid from: Wayside, PO Box 8427, Silver Spring, MD 20907-8427.

our souls beaten to a pulp, our brows gashed and our lips split.

What is this all about? Together with three friends, Gitta Mallasz lived through a spiritual experience considered authentic, in Budapest in 1943. Let us recall the event: during the gloomy war years in Hungary, four friends (three of them Jewish; Hanna, Lili, Joseph, and one Catholic, Gitta) found themselves in the "presence" of what we customarily call "Angels" or "Beings of Light" while they were asking themselves some serious questions. Each Friday toward three in the afternoon, these beings "came down"— invisibly— and used the vocal cords of one or another of the four to answer their questions. The remarks—eighty-eight conversations in all—were scrupulously reproduced in small school notebooks, which waited thirty-three years to be published, the time it took Gitta Mallasz to flee the communist hell (the other three died, deported in 1944).

I saw Gitta Mallasz give a lecture at the Sorbonne. The auditorium was full, the aisles were jammed, and a crowd waited outside, waiting for a chance to slip into the packed house. Some of them held up omnidirectional microphones to record the lecture. Others stared at her with a gleam of envy in their eyes, as if she were a saint or an extraterrestrial. Her book was unaided by any publicity from its publisher, Aubier, but its impact was so powerful that it made its way alone by word of mouth, and was translated into a dozen languages. Works whose success crosses borders with more than ten translations are most rare, and can only be promoted by "word of mouth," a medium a hundred thousand times more powerful than any article in the press, or advertising, or television.

One might challenge the authenticity of the *Dialogues*. But curiously few have embarked on that course, because the reader senses an infinite power emanating from every sentence.

Still, before preparing my article for *Le Quotidien de Paris* I wanted to be clear in my mind about it, so I decided to go visit Gitta Mallasz in Lyons. I had foreseen everything except Philippe Tesson's reaction; he ran the newspaper, and when he read an outline of my proposed story, he wondered what it was all about. I hardly knew what to say to him, and preferred to explain simply that this lady had seen Angels, that her book was a great success, and that it would be interesting to know what she had to say. He sat there for a bit staring at me as if I were a madman, and then, after a moment of hesitation, he signed the expense voucher for my train ticket.

*"With the success she's had in the bookstores,"* I told myself, *"her royalties must be rolling in, and if her spirituality is a hoax, her way*

*of life will betray it."* When I reached her place I discovered a tiny little house, absolutely unpretentious, on a hillside overlooking some of the Lyons' vineyards. No swimming pool, no servants, no villa, no outward signs of wealth. The only evidence of modernity was a fax machine and a micro-computer. Nothing that would lead you to believe that you were in the home of an internationally successful author (or more exactly, "scribe"). That was the first indication. Another proof—psychologically irrefutable for a writer—was on the book-jacket itself: no trace of her name, on the front or back. But I know no author who would decline to see his name printed on the cover of a book, which he considers as his immortal creation, his child, and no reporter who would remove his name from an article he had written—the name is the incontestable seal on a literary creation or a piece of personal reportage. A book is oneself, a part of one's ego, and a bit of seeming immortality. On the first page of the *Dialogues* we read this warning:

> *I am not the author of the* Dialogues.
> *I am the scribe of the* Dialogues.

That profession of faith, added to the other indications and particularly Gitta Mallasz's refusal to set up as a guru or a "new age" star, proves her independence vis-à-vis the book's contents. She does not say *"I wrote this book"* with that pride so common to authors, journalists and others who turn out reports or editorials. With a girlish laugh she distances herself from all who would like to see her as a star or "the miraculous person" who has spoken with the Angels.

On my return to Paris, I wrote my article for the column, "Vivre Demain," a column essentially devoted to sciences of all kinds, and I handed it over to Henry Tricot, who was in charge of "selling" it at the conference for the morning edition, when all the heads of department gathered around Philippe Tesson. Publication of that article was postponed several times. One Thursday morning, for an 8:30 flight to Austria on an assignment, I went down to the taxi stand below my apartment at 7:15. Usually, four or five taxis were there waiting for fares. At that time of day twenty minutes was all it took to reach Charles DeGaulle airport. But that morning, no sign of a taxi. All those that passed were occupied. And in the grand old tradition of Paris taxis, some, empty, didn't stop even so. Prodigiously irritated and cursing all cab drivers, I finally found one at 7:40; he tore off for the airport and I arrived at 8:20, much delayed by Paris traffic. Rushing to the counter I asked the hostess for fast ticketing, and she explained to me, desolated, that the flight was closed. She nevertheless telephoned the "satellite" immediately, but was told that the plane was on its way to takeoff position.

All this was hardly believable because that morning most flights were either canceled because of an air-controllers' strike, which had begun at 6 A.M., or late because of rotten weather! And my flight left five minutes ahead of time! Stuck, I asked the hostess for a seat on the next flight for Vienna and she put me on an Air France flight at 1 or 2 P.M. Stymied, I decided to go to the newspaper offices in Neuilly while waiting. In the corridor I was quietly stupefied to hear Henry Tricot tell me, *"You're lucky. They okayed your piece on Angels, but I was about to cancel it altogether because I couldn't edit it in your place and you'd left for Vienna."* The article appeared in *Le Quotidien de Paris* Friday, June 15, 1990. A month later, the daily, *Liberation*, devoted three pages to *Dialogues*.[4] and much later the magazine *Elle* published a long article on the book in an edition that set a sales record because it covered the widowing of Caroline of Monaco. Coincidence.

Still, priests have doubted the authenticity of these Dialogues, which has anguished Gitta. Can we imagine a priest denying the existence of Angels? I suppose so. That's why she often said: *"Never talk about 'Dialogues' to a priest; they understand nothing and anyway they don't believe in Angels."* Nevertheless, it was a young seminarian, impressed by these texts, who visited her one day in 1978 and asked her: *"Do you know why the Angels only came on Fridays at three in the afternoon?"* Gitta had no idea and said so. *"Because Christ died on a Friday at 3 P.M."* he replied.

As if these Angels had decided to pay homage *"to a grand beauty, even though it does not conform to customary theological formulas"*—noted Father François Brune—to Him who came to teach long before them. Still, the way Gitta Mallasz presented these 'Dialogues' sets a small problem that must be solved. She said: *"No one has the right to teach about the contents of the 'Dialogues,' simply because no one has lived them. Because it is a personal experience, all comparison with known religions or other spiritual teachings is useless and out of place."*[5]

It is true: no explanation of *Dialogues* is possible because at each reading we discover something new. We might be tempted to say that if no one but her may comment on the *Dialogues* because it was a personal experience, it was not worth publishing them,

4. July 5, 1990.
5. *When the Angel Intercedes*, p. 122.

presuming these texts are an isolated gospel and that these Angels belong to a world unknown to all of us. Yet the Angels speak of Christ and the Father on almost every page. They simply do not speak with the Vatican's permission, and they express themselves much better than any earthly mystic, doubtless because they are infinitely closer to God. These Angels certainly come from a Christly sphere, and it is unthinkable to believe the contrary. They certainly belong to revealed religion, all we need do is read the note on page 16 of the French edition: *"The pronoun Ö, used by the Angels to designate the Divine, could mean God or Jesus equally— only a very subtle intonation allowing us to tell the difference. The written form HE, HIS has been adopted when it refers to God: He and His when it refers to Jesus."* A priori, since according to Gitta Mallasz *"all comparison with known religions or other spiritual teachings is useless and out of place,"* it seems to me thus that Christ belongs neither to the Buddhists nor to the Muslims nor to the Jews. Do we not read, for example, on page 241:[6]

> *The Seventh Heaven is just as near*
> *as the earth below where your feet rest.*
> *There He is King.*
> *Never again will He come to earth*
> *Blinding Light: sole reality.*
> *The King, eternal Being,*
> *dressed in white fire flaming up to Ö*
> *You are His servants. Serve Him:*
> *Him, the glorious Being of Light,*
> *too brilliant for the human eye.*
> *Him, the eternally unbelievable*
> *the only Source of belief!*
>
> *All of you: you are his blood.*
> *You are: JESUS.*
> *You are in His place.*
> *You act, you live, you become.*
> *And He is the Source, the Way, the Truth.*
> *He is Life.*

But happily, Catherine of Siena[7] never forbade anyone to comment or dilate on her *Dialogues*. And yet no one lived the *Dialogues*

---

6. Interview of March 24, 1944.

7. I do not compare Catherine of Siena with Gitta Mallasz; there is no comparison; I

in Catherine of Siena's place, and she could have announced that they were a personal experience, which is true, strictly speaking. She never did that, any more than Teresa of Avila, Hildegarde Von Bingen or Marie d'Agreda.

Another proof of the authenticity of the *Dialogues* is their power and their style. A reading of the various books of commentary "by" Gitta Mallasz reveals the difference in style and thought, which can be summed up with this: *"Isn't it nauseating to go into a bookstore?"* writes Gitta Mallasz. *"Tons of bookish knowledge! Rational thought conditions us like brainwashing. Doesn't this disproportionate intellectuality send us back to the natural measure of omniscience present in our cells?"*[8] Was she thinking of a bookstore that would sell only "proper" books, as in communist countries? Well, we can forgive Gitta Mallasz these little aberrations; it is thanks to her that these precious *Dialogues* have come to us. It is to some extent our own fault, after all, because we expected commentary and analysis from her on the level of the *Dialogues*. As we have seen, that is an flatly impossible, even for those who experienced them. And we come always to the same conclusion, that the *Dialogues with the Angels* are absolutely authentic. And as these *Dialogues* are authentic, we are going to try to examine, in the light of other angelic encounters, how Angels manifest themselves, under which circumstances they appear, and what messages they transmit.

A general finding is that the Angel appears when his protégé is undergoing a grave internal crisis, when he is *"at the end of his rope,"* or when he is honestly asking himself existential questions like *who am I, where am I going, what is the purpose of life*, etc. In these moments of stress the subject notes supernatural phenomena and remembers them perfectly, even thirty years later. The former Hollywood actress Earlyne Chaney, for example, remembers how she was awakened by a "voice." The "voice" was so loud that the adolescent girl feared it would wake her sisters, sleeping nearby. She went outside, and looked here and there, but found nothing, though the voice persisted in her head. That went on for several days, but it was only when she got used to the voice of this invisible presence that she was able to discover it truly on a night in June. At the time she was twelve years old. The voice woke her up, and as usual she stepped outside the house to sit in her customary place and observe the starry sky:

---

simply compare two women each of whom has transmitted *Dialogues* of great spiritual significance.

8. In *Les Dialogues ou le saut dans l'inconnu*, Paris, Aubier, p. 166. (*The Dialogues, or the Leap into the Unknown.*)

*Suddenly I felt a quiver over my body, similar to an electric current, and I knew without a doubt that someone stood behind me, not invisible this time. Panic filled me. My first thought was to flee, but I found that I could not rise. I was suddenly afraid to turn around and look. Yet I knew that he was no mortal.*

*And then I heard his voice. It was not like a human voice. I seemed to hear it inside my upper solar plexus instead of my ears. It was as if there was a sounding board inside my solar plexus, tuned in with a radio station which was picking up his voice.*

*The words came clear. "Be not afraid," he said. "I have been often with you." The fear instantly melted away, for though it was the first time I had consciously heard his voice. . . . Then I saw him. Although he stood just behind my left shoulder, I saw him as if he stood in front of me, as if his figure were reflected in a mirror before my eyes. . . .*

*I finally said to him, "Are you God?"*

*"No," came his answer. "I am someone who has watched over you a long time. Do not be afraid of me."*

*"Are you Jesus?" I asked.*

*"No," he answered, "but I am his disciple."*

*I tried to answer him, but the words would not come. I could only sit staring at him. He wore a long white robe, but over the robe, hanging from the shoulders down his back was a cloak of dark blue, almost purple. The cloak reached from his shoulders to his feet.*

*"Who are you?" I finally whispered.*

*"I am your Teacher," he answered. And the words melted into my brain like drops of water into a sponge. My brain felt as if there were a telephone inside with the receiver off. The voice seemed to drift between the radio receiving station in my solar plexus and the telephone inside my head.*

*Little by little the light began to dim and the shadowy, misty form began to recede into invisibility. "I will come again," he said.*[9]

The spiritual being disappeared bit by bit, leaving the little girl in an indescribable state, like a child suddenly abandoned by her

9. Earlyne Chaney, *Remembering*, La Canada, California, New Age Press, 1974, pp. 51–52.

parents. *"I wanted to follow him, I wanted him to take me with him,"* she explains in her autobiography. Just then she heard again the being's voice, telling her, *"I will never leave you; and you will see me again."* But Earlyne was not to see him for several years.

In Budapest it was Hanna who most often lent her vocal cords to the Angels. The first conversation took place on Friday, June 15, 1943, and the last on Friday, November 24, 1944. Over seventeen months the Angels accorded Gitta thirty-eight interviews, Lili thirty-five and Joseph four; beginning on March 24, 1944 (the eve of the Annunciation) they spoke only to the group as a whole, without distinguishing among them. The first conversation took place when the three friends were trying to answer grave interior questions. The Angels announced themselves with no warning, and Hanna barely had time to warn the others: *"Be careful, it's not me talking any more!"* And when Hanna asked Gitta in that other voice, *"Do you know me?"* Gitta could not remember, though she was certain that this presence was her "interior master."[10] When Earlyne Chaney asked that presence who he was, he replied, *"I am your Master,"* words that engraved themselves in her memory just like Hanna's and Gitta's, though these women had no way to know about their respective experiences, as Earlyne's took place during the thirties in the heart of the United States, and Gitta's in the forties in the heart of Europe. Earlyne published her book in 1974 and Gitta in 1977, and though their experiences differ, they have similar aspects at the beginning: the Beings do not identify themselves, or more exactly they do not materialize stating immediately, in energetic tones and to the accompaniment of trumpets, *"I am your guardian Angel, have no fear, I am here to protect you."* So in the *Dialogues* five months pass before the Beings use the word "Angel." In the meantime Hanna experiences every sensation of the Angels, their adoration, their annoyance and their anger; sometimes she is somehow consumed by the messenger's living word, overwhelmed by its heat. We will encounter that heat many times, for spiritual Beings find it difficult to translate themselves to our level, as the Angel will explain during the tenth dialogue in Budapest:

> *Angel: Let us give thanks! (with a radiant smile) It is good to be here.*
>
> *(Gitta): Hanna would tell me later that during the first dialogues she had often felt how difficult it was for my teacher to descend and be in our dense atmosphere. Now*

---

10. *Dialogues avec l'Ange*, p. 24.

*my joy makes it much easier. Pointing to the glass of water:*
*Angel: Water brings me closer to you. What water does*
*for me . . . fire does for you.*
*(Gitta): I understand that the more I burn in joy, the*
*nearer I come to my Angel . . . but the Angel's fire must cor-*
*respondingly be diminished with water, that I might*
*support it.* [11]

This difficulty in coming down to our "too dense" atmosphere
was also noted during an out-of-body exercise at the Monroe Institute. The student, a doctor, described his sensations to Robert
Monroe, and this recorded dialogue confirms what we have just
seen in the *Dialogues* of Gitta Mallasz. We note in the following
case that although contact is made outside the body, the entity still
experiences problems:

*55/she (psychiatric counselor) 1614 min #314*

*"Point of light. Other than that, I don't perceive any-*
*thing."*
*Monitor: "How does the light feel?"*
*"It feels like a star. When I focus on it, I begin to float."*
*Monitor: "Experiment with the light."* [12]
*"Now they are getting closer, now I am getting closer to*
*them."*
*(time lapse 2.55)*
*New Voice: "How are you?"*
*Monitor: "I am very glad to meet you. I am very thank-*
*ful that you came."*
*New Voice: "It is hard to get here."*
*Monitor: "What is the difficulty?"*
*New Voice: "There are many layers to penetrate."* [13]

Angels may encounter some difficulties in descending toward the
subject for a physical communication, but once they arrive the subject
feels a profound change, a joy as if he had suddenly found a missing
piece of himself, as we have already noticed in accounts of NDE. The
Catalan Capucin nun Marie-Angele Astorch (1592–1662) felt the
same happiness when she met her guardian Angel for the first time:

11. *Talking with Angels*, p. 59, Friday, August 27, 1943.
12. The "light" speaks through the out-of-body subject.
13. *Far Journeys*, pp. 44–45.

*From the moment I felt his presence, such a change was wrought in my spirit that one might have said I was living within myself and at the same time outside myself. It filled my senses with grand nobility, my heart with a very sweet comfort, and by a persistent work it strengthened my whole spirit. It left such an impression on me, a gratitude so humble and tender, that I no longer knew the weaknesses of fleshly existence, all passion having subsided; such a purity of consciousness and such a mortification of the senses that I had no further need to conquer them, thanks to the power of that divine mercy.*[14]

In all cases, the subject speaks of an indelible impression that is extremely difficult to describe in human terms. This is a constant we also find among those who experience episodes at death's door: unforgettable, indescribable, indelible. It was the same for John Lilly.[15] In writing his novel *The Day of the Dolphin* author Robert

14. G.Roxo, *Vida de la venerable Maria Angela Astorch*, Madrid, 1733, quoted by Vincent Klee, pp. 312–313.

15. At the age of eighteen he matriculated at Caltech, and graduated in 1938. John Lilly decided that physics was insufficient, and entered medical school at the University of Pennsylvania to complete his education. Granted an M.D. in 1942, he was enrolled immediately by the U.S. Air Force, which asked him to study pilots' blood pressure at high altitudes under anti-aircraft attack. Later this project served as a basis for his work in sensory deprivation; his work with dolphins made him famous, but he is even better known for his Isolation Tank, which he perfected in 1954, as part of his research at the National Institute of Mental Health in Maryland. At the time, it was believed that the brain could not relax beyond a certain point because the body's organs would keep sending it physical data—the hands, eyes, skull, legs, back, etc. Then Lilly had an idea: record the brain's reactions under sensory deprivation. For that he took over a completely soundproof chamber and pool the Navy used to study the metabolism of Navy frogmen. After several experiments Lilly found that at 93 degrees Fahrenheit the body was neither hot nor cold. The water he used in the chamber was like Dead Sea water, with a very high salt content plus certain chemical additives to support the body. Once a subject was enclosed in the chamber, information from the organs was neutralized, and one felt only one's thoughts. The body had in effect disappeared. The subject was no more than a soul, floating in the water. To his surprise, Lilly discovered that the brain had no need of external stimulation to stay awake. This finding impelled him to go further, and note his reactions after an hour, two hours, four hours in the chamber. Little by little he discovered that the chamber was a veritable "hole

Merle was inspired by the life of this famous American biologist,[16] who, in the 1950s and 1960s, succeeded in establishing methods of communication with dolphins. Two produced films were indirectly drawn from his life: Mike Nichols' *The Day of the Dolphin*, with the no less famous George C. Scott (once General Patton) in the role of Lilly; and Ken Russell's *Altered States*. It was also the basis of the television series "Flipper" from filmmaker Ivan Tors. Though he is still living, there are three biographical works, two written by John Lilly himself, *The Scientist* and *The Center of the Cyclone*, and the third, a definitive biography, by the California neurologist Francis Jeffrey, published in 1990 under the title *John Lilly, So Far . . .* The life of this American Jacques Cousteau is fascinating because we encounter everything in it: doctors, dolphins, soldiers, psychiatric studies, all forms of mystical experiences, illustrious friends and relations (Robert A. Millikan, winner of the Nobel Prize in Physics; Dr. Albert Hofmann, the inventor of LSD; novelists Aldous Huxley and Herman Wouk; Alan Watts; the pope of the 1970s Flower-Power movement, Timothy Leary); and above all, constant research into altered states of consciousness which allows us to "see" from here what there is . . . elsewhere. But at the base of this moving life, we find his infancy marked by a totally unexpected meeting with his guardian Angel in January, 1925. The boy was ten years old and consumed by a tubercular fever to the point where the doctors and his parents did not know if he would survive. But

---

in the universe," and that consciousness was naturally hospitable to other levels of existence, as if they were something innate but forgotten by the brain. Then he decided to go even further and investigate how the brain would react in complete sensory deprivation in a previously altered state of consciousness. So he placed himself in the chamber after a dose of LSD-25 (Lysergic Acid Diethylamide) from Sandoz Laboratories. (Ken Russell's film, *Altered States*, was inspired by this.) These experiments under LSD sometimes lasted twelve hours and more, during which time John Lilly lived through several out of body experiences at different levels, and it is astonishing to discover to what point his descriptions agree perfectly with Robert Monroe's. Furthermore, during his LSD experiments he sometimes met, to his great astonishment, guides—or Angels—who had visited him during his heart attack (see page 76). Later he fell into the habit of describing them not as Angels but as members of the "ECCO"—"Earth Coincidence Control Office," in other words, those in charge of luck or chance!

16. John Lilly was also father-in-law to the French singer Bernard Lavilliers, who married his adopted daughter, Lisa Lyon-Lilly, leading champion of the world of culture.

while they were watching him, the child, according to biographer, Francis Jeffrey, had an unforgettable experience:

> The Being came and said, "Do you want to go away with me or do you want to stay here?"
>
> "Where will we go?"
>
> "The choice is yours. You can stay here in this body and be the little boy or you can go back with me and join the other Beings."
>
> "Mommy said she didn't want me to die. If I go with you, do I die?"
>
> "That's what dying means, to go with me and leave this place, leave your mommy and daddy, leave Dick and David. Leave Jamey."
>
> "But I don't want to go away. I don't know what you mean, go to the other Beings. I want to get well and play."
>
> "The choice is yours. You will stay here for now and eventually you will go away with me."
>
> "Will you stay with me or are you going away?"
>
> "I will be with you always as long as you believe you will be able to meet with me." [17]

This experience was engraved in his spirit and the child grew ever closer to his guardian Angel. They met several times, always in dramatic or potentially dramatic circumstances. For example, when he lies trembling with fear on the operating table to have his tonsils removed: a nurse applied an ether mask to his face and John Lilly remembers leaving the operating theater immediately and landing directly on the wings of two Angels who comforted him during the whole operation. Another time, he is playing with his dog on a low wall, unaware that he is about to fall over the other side, into a ravine. The animal bites him and John turns quickly to hit him. But the Being decided to set matters straight, chatting with him a little later, leaving the boy quite thoughtful:

> The Being cut out of the body and looked at the little boy. The little boy saw the Being and said, "Are you my Guardian Angel?"
>
> The Being: "That's what your parents call me, that is not my real name, but it's good enough to use. I am available any time that you need me."

17. *The Scientist*, p. 39, and *John Lilly, So Far . . .* , p. 1.

*"But I needed you today when Jamey bit me."*
*"I was there. You were about to fall over the wall and I
instructed Jamey to pull you back."*
*"But I thought Jamey did it because he loved me."*
*"James loves you but could not understand that you
were in such danger. I had to make him do it."*
*"Will you always take care of me?"*
*The Being: "Yes, as long as you believe in me. Will you
always believe in me?"*
*"What do you mean, 'believe in?'"*
*"'To believe in' is to know, is to love, is to be with. I am.
You are. That is what 'believe in' means."*
*"I am. You are. I believe in me. I believe in you. Is that
what you mean?"*
*"Yes."* [18]

Now let's look into a fourth angelic encounter, that of Hawaiian
Pat Devlin, who is a living illustration of one of Christ's parables,
*"He that followeth me, shall not walk in darkness,"* because she has
been blind from birth. Patricia was born in 1952, premature by
three months. The obstetrician set her in an incubator where a
badly regulated flow of oxygen deprived her retinas of nourishment.[19] The baby is blind. This will be just the beginning of her
health problems. Her infancy is peppered by constant visits to various ophthalmologists who will even find an incipient cancerous
tumor. In short, on doctors' advice the parents decide to have her
operated on, in order to save her life, and Pat loses her eyes forever.
Her eyeballs will henceforth be empty. She gets used to her condition. She grows up, life goes on, she gives birth to twins, earns a
diploma in psychology and moves one day to Lubbock, Texas, a
city of two hundred thousand inhabitants where she holds down a
job as a marriage counselor. She moves into a small house where
she tries hard to forget her condition. For eight years, she suffers
Meniere's syndrome, a problem caused by bad drainage in an ear
that results in terrible headaches, nausea, loss of balance and
sometimes seizures. And Meniere's syndrome causes progressive
deafness.

In August 1988 she hears that the Virgin is going appear in the
church of Saint John Neumann of Lubbock. The news spreads
quickly, and is immediately denied by the ecclesiastical authorities.

18. *The Scientist,* p. 38; and *John Lilly, So Far . . .* , p. 1.
19. This also happened to singer Stevie Wonder.

No matter; a crowd estimated at twenty thousand people gathers around the church on August 15, 1988. Among them is our blind girl with the little computer she is never without, her Braille Speech. She is seated near a fountain. An outdoor Mass is being celebrated. Of course she sees nothing, but she hears people crying, "On your knees! Genuflect!" She doesn't understand. She hears people near her weeping. Pat Devlin asks the void, *"What's happening?"* Someone orders her to kneel. She still doesn't understand.

Finally a woman behind her enlightens her: *"The Virgin is ten feet above the font, and blessing it."* Pat Devlin wants to cry, not because it's the Virgin but because she can't see Her. In the depths of her soul she is full of anguish at not being able to see, at not having eyes like everyone else. A woman says to her, rather scornfully, *"Take off your glasses and pray,"* as if dark glasses were an insult to the apparition. The woman suggests that she ask God to restore her eyes so she can see what is taking place at the font. Patricia wants to shout, "Leave me alone!"[20] Five days later she realized that the symptoms of her syndrome had disappeared. She could hardly believe it, but there it was. The syndrome is diagnosed by an eye examination. But Pat no longer has her eyes. Consequently we cannot speak of a "miracle," as no scientific examination can be made. Only a detailed follow-up on the symptoms. From that point of view, she was indeed cured. No more nausea, no more loss of balance, no more seizures. It's over. On the other hand, this is the begining of a new "disease": *"I began to see bright lights,"* she explained to me. *"At first I thought I'd gone crazy. How could I see lights when I had no eyes? Then I thought I was seeing ghosts. But much later I realized that I was in touch with Angels. I could turn my head this way and that; the light stood still. And even if I put my hands over my eyes—where there are still optic nerves—I still see the light. It's magnificent, it's a magnificent light. My optic nerves don't react at all except in full sunlight, and then it's only the feeblest glimmer. But this light persisted, even at night. Later I began to hear voices emanating from the light. Then I really began to worry. And no one else could see that light or hear that voice."*

Her father, a civilian working for the military at Pearl Harbor, had a hard time believing her. He knows that his daughter has inexplicably been cured, he knows that she isn't crazy, but at the same time it isn't easy for him to accept her seeing lights.

*"Do you see Angels?"* I asked her.

___

20. The Church's official commission on Lubbock denied any supernatural phenomenon.

*"No, I've never seen an Angel or Angels. I only see lights. They speak to me. The first thing this shapeless light told me was to be cautious, and 'always to test the light,' and if I heard a voice, always to ask it if it was with Christ. . . ."* And on the spot she began to pray aloud to test the light she claimed to see behind me. In some way she was "testing" my light and doubtless my intentions. . . . All mystics think about the devil. A reporter, by definition a newsmonger, could only be an envoy from the Evil One. But after her prayer she was reassured, and she asked me to start up my tape recorder. My light must have been white and bright as a box of "Tide." Somewhere within, I too was agreeably reassured.

*"Can you give me a description of this light?"* The question was hardly out when I realized, with dread, my infinite stupidity.

*"Well, you understand that I don't know what colors are, or even what shapes and faces look like, so I can't describe them to you,"* she answered. Listening to the tape I hear myself saying several times, *"Yes, I see."* I had failed miserably in the area of tact.

*"Then you speak with this Angel?"* I asked, blundering on.

*"Oh yes, always, constantly. It was limited at first, and then our discussion grew more and more complex. Sometimes he was cross with me. Anyway he obeys God and not me. One day I was on the telephone with a friend, and my Angel asked me to tell him a certain number of things that meant nothing to me but astounded my friend. When I hung up I was trembling a bit, because it is very hard to translate what my Angel tells me into words. He reassured me right away, telling me that despite my doubts and fears he was quite happy with the way I had done what he asked. I carefully keep track of everything he tells me."* She hoped she wasn't talking too much about it. I wanted to know if she saw lights behind everyone. *"No, but I don't interpret that to indicate the absence of a guardian Angel. I don't see them, that's all. During the Mass, for example, I see lights around the altar, and the tabernacle, but not always. One day I asked my guardian Angel why I didn't always see these lights, and he told me that they were always there, but that my 'eyes' were not always open."*

I expected something similar to the *Dialogues* of Budapest. Not at all. I understood that Pat Devlin's Angels did not offer instruction. They simply comforted her or asked her to pray for their protégés. *"The Angels told me that I was not a messenger, but simply a chronicler,"* she insisted, *"and I asked, 'A blind chronicler?' "Yes, you write what you see,' and they began to laugh. Angels have a sense of humor, you know. Their voices are melodious, quite beautiful and always different. These voices, how shall I explain it, touch my soul, my heart, I hear them inside. On my birthday in 1990 I had no one to celebrate with, my daughters were off taking exams. I was very sad. Suddenly a choir of Angels sang for my birthday. It was the most beautiful gift in my whole life."*

Pat Devlin is the opposite of Gitta Mallasz. Where Gitta is full of life, with an abrasive sense of humor, Patricia is immersed in pain and sorrow. Normal. She is under the care of a spiritual advisor, a priest, Father Walsh.[21] But the latter explained to me that the only reliable book on Angels was written by Father Robert Fox, an active member of the international organization *Opus Sanctorum Angelorum*.[22] It is one of the most stupid books on Angels I have

21. He was her spiritual advisor at the moment of the interview. Pat Devlin published her own book in 1995, *The Light of Love*, Queenship Publishers.

22. This organization comprises priests and seminarians dedicated to the Angels; one of its principal leaders in the United States, Father Robert Fox, has published *The World and Work of the Holy Angels*, a book impressive for its intolerance. A true work of propaganda. Still its basis is a sound sentiment, the consecration of a soul to its guardian Angel. On the other hand, when we read (pp. 86–89) that most spiritual practices of Hindus, Buddhists, and Taoists, including Yoga and Zen, are only elaborate diabolical invocations, we can only gape in dismay. Hundreds of millions of people throughout the world are thus nothing more than satanists according to Father Fox. What contempt on the part of a priest of the Catholic Church, where it is said before all "Love one another!" To display such scorn for other human beings, on the pretext that they do not worship the same God he does himself, is sickening from a priest. The rest of his book is cast in the same mold, a sectarianism close to the extreme right. The only solution, according to Fox, if you do not want to fall under the influence of a fallen Angel: chastity, even between man and wife! He dared not talk of mortification, but he came very close. In a nutshell, that organization of sectarians in the end upset the Vatican, which is very hard to do. Rome's patience is legendary. You have to accumulate many rebukes before the Vatican hands down a serious warning, and many warnings before the Congregation for the Propogation of the Faith turns its attention to priests. But Opus Angelorum managed to catch their attention, and on June 19, 1992, the Congregation issued a decree forbidding its priests to go on with their "outside the faith" exorcisms, or to administer sacraments from afar, and above all to consecrate the faithful to Angels, a practice not sanctioned by any Scripture. Coming from Rome this is quite serious, because the real reasons are not all divulged. We can hardly imagine the Vatican issuing a press release on the real problems that could be exploited by secular newspapers. Simply put, when the powers are angered it is usually because a large number of slips and complaints have been registered by the faithful. So today we are left with three categories of priests: the first including fanatics like Fox, who would not have displeased the Ayatollah Khomeini;

ever read. Lost in thought, I watched her. She was holding her guide dog, Ghia, and seemed to be sizing me up. Very strange to be across from a blind person who "saw" Angels. Still, she did not have the air of a violent madwoman or a crank, but rather someone who has suddenly discovered God and lives in an interior world, a little like a Carmelite in strict retreat to the end of her days. To be blind and to believe in God is like being a cloistered nun cut off from the world. Pat Devlin has no need of locked gates because she sees nothing. And I asked her the question one does not ask.

"Have you ever held it against God that you're blind?"

She was not annoyed: *"No. On the other hand it hurt me to be treated like a second-class citizen. Apart from that, I've always thought that my blindness was a gift from God. Otherwise I would doubtless be quite superficial. Now I can concentrate on the spiritual, do you understand? I would never have been interested in God if I'd had my eyes, I'm almost sure. My life would certainly have been different."*

According to Pat Devlin's angelic conversations, the Angels are "the servants of our souls." But how to communicate with this invisible servant? It seemed to me that she might offer an interesting explanation. *"Very simple,"* explained Pat. *"All you have to do is talk to him, give him a name, Catholic if possible. They don't have first and last names like us, their names are descriptive and always related to an aspect of Christ. My Angel is called 'Joy in the love of God.'*[23] *You must constantly speak with your Angel. But if you say his name, then you understand the purpose of your life on earth; because his name is a summation of his protégé's mission. The Angel's name is directly linked to your task. We deviate more or less from the task God has assigned us. That's where our free will comes into play. When you pray, ask him to pray with you, and to deliver your prayer to the Creator. We have direct access to the Creator, but if your Angel and/or preferred saint should intercede for you it's even better; your prayer has a better chance of being granted. Keep asking him to help you approach God, to show you how He wants to see you, what it is He wants of you, and so forth. Approach him. It's not some magic*

the second including "progressives" for whom the Angels and sometimes even Christ are only fairy tales; and the third including humble priests, humanists, unassuming but quite engaging because they are true intermediaries between our physical world and the invisible world, like Stephen Schneir, Jean Derobert, Francois Brune, or Paul-Francis Spencer.

23. In the *Dialogues* of Budapest, one also finds "He who is radiant," "He who builds," "He who measures," "He who helps."

*formula; it's a construction, a relationship that you enrich every day."*

Yet Pat Devlin is disappointing, with her quite traditional attitude toward Christian dolorism. Her *"If you want to love God, you must suffer"* annoys me. Not with that sort of discourse will we convince people to rediscover God; far from it. But we find in her a similar attitude as in the Budapest *Dialogues,* where Angels lead their protégés into the arms of Ö, the Creator. Dominique Raoul-Duval justly remarked in his preface[24] that the Angels of Budapest were loath to use the word "God," preferring the pronoun "Ö": *". . . God, this word that generations of human beings have used, sullied, soiled,"* she writes, *"but to designate Him the Angels use the pronoun Ö—translated here as He—which, in the archaic language that Hungarian is, is neither masculine nor feminine but both at once, transcending that masculinity of the Divine which weighs so heavily on our revealed religions. Ö is the masculine and the feminine, the Father and the Mother, strength and wisdom, omnipotence and tenderness; and there is no need whatever to complete it by a feminine designation, since femininity is part of its very essence, and renders Him to us that much more precisely. . . ."* This Ö is the goal.

*Talkings with Angels* impresses us again as a spiritual maze or a cerebral job in the park. The more we read the more we lose ourselves in them and the less we want to find the exit. We want to stay with the Angels. But, exactly as Terry Taylor told me, they gently waft us away, into the presence of Ö, the Creator, Him, the Father. The Angels (of Budapest) were above all in the service of God, of the Creator, of the Eternal Father, call him what you will. They spoke regularly of Christ, but in fresh terms, as if freed of a certain dolorist weight, because in the end only HE is really important. They wanted only one thing: that the creature reconcile himself with his Creator, and for that the creature had to step onto the invisible bridge of faith.

But what is faith? The certainty that God and the Angels exist, or that our souls are immortal, or both? As we saw in experiences at death's door, the soul (or the spirit) leaves the patient's body and observes what is happening around it before entering the tunnel. And as some people have the gift of tongues, others (very rare, it is true) have received the gift of leaving their bodies with no difficulty. The phenomenon is not new since even in the most ancient times it was reported by Pliny, Socrates, Plotinus and even Plutarch and Plato, all of whom spoke of *"voyages of the soul."*

Rosemary Guiley notes in her remarkable *Harpers Encyclopedia*

---

24. *Dialogues with the Angel,* p. 11.

*of Mystical and Paranormal* that Marcel Forhan (1884–1917) explained his out-of-body experiences in his book *Pratique du voyage astral,* and also how he made it a habit to visit (incognito, of course) the room of a young woman (the rogue!) who later became his wife. He was persuaded that, like him, everyone could leave his body at will and all one had to do was concentrate. Across the Channel, the Englishman Whiteman said that he had made more than two thousand trips out of his body, experiences detailed in 1961 in his book *Mystical Life.* In the United States, Sylvan Muldoon published *The Projection of the Astral Body* in 1929, a collection of his journeys, a talent that came to him spontaneously at the age of twelve. In short, forerunners are not lacking. In 1958 the American Robert Monroe also found himself out of his body one day, and travelled in a very real way. On his return, he wondered honestly if he had not gone crazy. An acoustical engineer, businessman, owner of a chain of radio stations, he did not understand what had happened to him and consulted his doctor immediately, persuaded he had a brain tumor. As the phenomenon persisted for years, leaving him with dark circles under his eyes in the morning from lack of sleep, he decided in 1961 to liquidate his businesses and to devote himself exclusively to the study of his out of body trips, to the point of leaving New York and setting himself up in the middle of the country in Virginia, half an hour by car from Charlottesville,[25] where he founded a research center.

After more than ten years of "trips," in 1971 Monroe published *Journeys Out of Body,* a book retracing his nocturnal adventures. The volume, translated into several languages, was to establish him as the uncontested authority in the field. He explicated his rather fantastic journeys, and how he had experienced other levels of reality, and sometimes met bizarre beings or fought with others, and so on. In the end he grew weary of these excursions over the rooftops, and really expected that no more extraordinary events would occur. But one day he decided to try again, using a relaxation technique and praying ("I ask the help of all those more highly evolved than I"). When he left his body, Monroe experienced what a good number of people have discovered during an NDE, the impression that he was traveling at the speed of light, a sensation that went far beyond anything he had previously known. His research was about to take a new turn. From then on he held conversations with

25. It was somewhat disconcerting to learn that "everything" had started in the Shenandoah Valley in Virginia, the cradle of Elisabeth Kübler-Ross, Dr. Stevenson, Raymond Moody, George Ritchie, Robert Monroe, and Phyllis Atwater.

"beings," visited other dimensions and obtained information on other planes of existence. But an engineer is an engineer: an expert in acoustics, Monroe studied the element that allowed him to leave his body, a very low sound, and wanted to automate it, knowing that the brain was no more than a mass of electric circuits. He studied hard but learned no more than he already knew, namely the classic survey of the four electric brain states, each according to its function:

Beta waves (6 to 12 hertz) when wide awake;

Alpha waves (7 to 12 hertz) when relaxed;

Theta waves (4 to 7 hertz) just before sleep;

Delta waves (over 3.5 hertz) when asleep.

His experiments as a whole proved to him that his consciousness remained perfectly wakeful when his body was in deep sleep. All that remained was to find out how he could put his body to sleep while leaving his conciousness awake; he knew that the human ear cannot interpret waves at lower than 30 hertz, which hi-fi experts call "the extreme low." But in 1975 Robert Monroe would solve the problem thanks to stereo: when he beamed a sound to his left ear at 200 hertz and to his right ear at 208 hertz, he discovered that the brain made a subtraction. The left and right hemispheres canceled out the two frequencies and kept only the difference, namely 8 hertz. After various experiments, Monroe confirmed the concept: the brain set itself in tune (at 8 hertz, for example) and immediately programmed itself to relax. The ear did not interpret the sound, but heard it perfectly. He made up his first cassettes and tested them on students.

First you hear a steady tone in the left ear, joined by a steady tone in the right ear. When the brain traces out the difference, you have the impression that you're hearing sound waves. Combining the two, the brain undertakes its classic task, that is, it puts the body to sleep, as if normally; but on the other hand the mind remains wide awake, which translates into a body that feels numb.[26] From that point on, adventures, or more precisely openings toward other levels, could really commence. Invited as a

26. After twenty minutes of sound, I tried unsuccessfully to wiggle my fingers; they
    seemed altogether deadened.

speaker at the Esalen Institute at Big Sur, California, in 1977, Monroe decided to experiment with his patented invention, baptized Hemi-Sync, on about forty people. His success surpassed all his previous experiences and, as one thing led to another, the equipment came into general use. Even the U.S. Army[27] discovered that when recruits underwent several sessions, their performance during training improved astonishingly.

But Robert Monroe's most important work remains his insistent attempts to teach out of body journeys to all who had confidence in him. Since 1981, more than 8000 people have come and gone on the highly saline waterbeds of his soundproof chambers. If you are willing to enclose yourself in one of Robert Monroe's chambers and be guided by the operator as the brain absorbs alpha, beta, delta, and theta waves, nothing is easier than encountering your guardian Angel (or guide, or Being from another dimension, etc.) after a few training sessions. The subject is plastered with electrodes, on the fingers, the body and of course the head, all wired to a monitoring control tower that allows surveillance of the out-of-body "journey," and also allows an immediate return in case of excessively violent emotions. A reporter from *Newsweek* emerged from the chamber and wept for two hours, after an encounter with . . . Christ (I suggest reading the excellent piece written by Bob Ortega in the *Wall Street Journal* of September 9th, 1994, about Robert Monroe, titled "Research Institute Shows People a Way Out of Their Bodies").

Despite his seventy-seven years, Robert Monroe continues to help students and guide them in out-of-body journeys. We have gathered several commentaries by students. These are digests of "thoughts" sent by the entity to the student, who describes what he sees into his microphone. As we saw in near-death experiences, in these zones thought is no longer driven by speech: it becomes dynamic and conversations are mental. A curious fact: when these Beings use the vocal cords of the explorer for expression, his body and especially his brain show variations in voltage. Dave Wallis, director of research and development at the Institute, connected an NRS-24 electro-encephalogram to several subjects to monitor reactions in the two hemispheres. He found that at first the hemispheres reacted to the sounds from the Hemi-Sync and became synchronized, which normally is impossible. More interesting, when the spiritual being (which Dave Wallis named

27. At Fort Benjamin Harrison, Indiana.

I.S.H.—Inner Self Helper) expressed itself through the voice of its "protégé," the activity of the hemispheres, while perfectly synchronized, modified itself automatically and showed an unusual animation. All the neurologists who examined these printouts had the same reaction: there was no way the subject could transport himself into such a cerebral state, even in the most profound of meditations. And when the "conversation" ended, the hemispheres gradually returned to their previous desynchronized state. Here are two examples of "live" commentaries. The first is that of a social worker who on her out of body trip met a "green fellow":

> I am talking with my green man and practicing going up and down to where they are . . . and found out why he has this green robe. He said that he did not need it but that I needed it to make me more comfortable with him. And he said that I still have some fears, so he still wants me to feel more comfortable with going in and out of my body. . . . I want to sit and talk with him some more. . . . He just kind of sat down and talked about me and where I am. And he told me that he is kind of my overseer. And he is responsible, somewhat responsible for my growth and development. Overseer in that contact and responsibility. . . .
>
> I feel very comfortable here, like this is where I belong and I have felt like this before.[28]

The second extract is that of an engineer who, once out of his body, saw a living source of light and spoke with it:

> I recontacted the source and asked the source about his pointers and perspective and asked him if he was familiar with the earth and his reply was "Yes, that is my territory." I got the idea that the earth was sort of his assigned beat. I also got the idea that he and other entities are made available to us to help us maximize or get through our earth experience. I don't mean "get through" like "get it over with." I mean to help us get as much out of it as possible.[29]

In the first case, the entity confirms that "he told me that he is kind of my overseer and he is responsible, somewhat responsible, for my growth and development, overseer in that contact and responsi-

28. *Far Journeys*, p. 42.
29. Ibid., p. 43.

*bility. . . ."* In the second case, the entity explains (via thought) that it has been placed at the disposition of human beings to help them maximize or live out their existence on earth. Monroe noted with some surprise that the subjects permitted these "friendly" entities to take possession of their bodies and to use their vocal cords, and that sometimes the monitor, set up in the control room, could participate in the conversations. In analyzing the recordings, he has been able to establish four phases of an out of body meeting with a spiritual being:

1. These Beings radiate a love that immediately reassures the subjects.

2. Generally they present themselves with their faces hidden in shadow. When the subject grows accustomed to the Being, he sees only a light.

3. When this Being speaks, he is limited to the subject's vocabulary.

4. When a Being uses the voice of the subject, the body of the latter undergoes variations in voltage.

One of the conversations recorded by the Institute with one of these Beings of light illustrates perfectly the *sine qua non* for an interaction between an Angel and his protégé:

> . . . *Perhaps I can explain it by asking you to image seven of the circles, which would give you the forty-nine levels. The first three levels are physical matter as you know physical matter. They are your plants, your animals, your humans. The fourth circle is your bridge, your realm, your center for that overall plane. It is the time in which a consciousness can choose whether to go back into the lower levels or to transcend into the higher levels, and many consciousnesses do choose to go back into the lower levels in physical form. The upper three circles are the realm that in your consciousness is called the spiritual realm, and here much of the work is done. I could not help someone who was not on the eighteenth level very much because my plane, my vibrational rate would be different. This is why it is hard for me to help you with specific problems. I can give you ideas, but I cannot give you the direct guidance I*

*could if you were on level eighteen. Our planes do touch.*[30]

We understand that a good communication with an Angel/Being depends intimately on the spiritual level one has reached. As for Monroe himself, it took him about ten years of regular out-of-body trips to realize that he was being helped in his "explorations." But his out-of-body encounter with these Superior Beings, whom he has named INSPECS, corresponds perfectly to the descriptions given by Gitta Mallasz in her *Dialogues*. For Robert Monroe, the first rendezvous was to be followed by many others:

> . . . *began to feel warm, more so as I went until it became almost too uncomfortable and was at the point of turning back . . . when I rammed headlong into something and collapsed, shaken . . . I reached out and there was a barrier, smooth in texture, rigid, impenetrable. . . . Still very uncomfortable from the heat, I pulled myself together, knowing this was the end of the line. I might as well turn back to the physical . . . and a bright light, very intense, glowed in front of me, first ovate, reshaping into a tall humanoid form, so bright I cringed from it . . . for what seemed an eternity. I shrank back, trying to shield myself from the brightness . . . then I began to cool down until I was no longer uncomfortable, and I could tolerate the brightness.*
> 
> *(Is that better for you?)*
> 
> *"Better" was an understatement. Much longer, and I would have melted. . . . I was rapidly losing my sense of awe. It was replaced with a great feeling of warmth, of understanding, much on the order of old deep friendships, yet filled with intense respect, not the usual pattern of expected angels, if that is what they were.*
> 
> *(We can quickly grow some wings if you wish)*
> 
> *No, no, please, no wings. No halos either, although I got the clear percept, staring at my INSPEC—friend?*

What emerges from this altogether extraordinary description is that burning sensation on contact with the Being of Light, a burning that reminds us of a somewhat similar experience by Gitta Mallasz in the *Dialogues*:

30. Ibid., pp. 74–75.

*Now Hanna's body seems to lose its usual qualities and transform into an instrument serving totally, with nothing held back: her movements are simple, meaningful and dignified. Even her arm seems different to me. It radiates concentrated force, the muscles tense, and I am strongly reminded of Michelangelo sculptures. An abrupt gesture strikes like lightning. BURN!*

*I am struck, jolted, filled with wonder. But all this vanishes instantly when I notice that Hanna is shivering.*[31]

Is this a Seraph? Remember, the name Seraph means literally "burning." The most distinguished of all the angelologists and father of the specialty, Dionysius the Aeropagite[32] gives details about the inferno that a Seraph represents:[33]

*Those with a knowledge of Hebrew are aware that the holy name "seraphim" means "fire-makers," that is to say, "carriers of warmth." The name "cherubim" means "fullness of knowledge" or "outpouring of wisdom." (....) For the designation seraphim really teaches this—a perennial circling around the divine things, penetrating warmth, the overflowing heat of a movement which never falters and never fails, a capacity to stamp their own image on subordinates by arousing and uplifting in them too a like flame, the same warmth. It means also the power to purify by means of the lightning flash and the flame. It means the ability to hold unveiled and undiminished both the light they have and the illumination they give out.*

It doesn't matter whether Robert Monroe was dealing with Seraphim, Powers, Archangels or something else—at least we can be sure they weren't kites flying about. What matters is the similarity of experiences at the time: that same feeling of heat, burning at contact with a spiritual being. We can imagine that if the Seraphim are burning, so are the other Angels, to different degrees. During another

---

31. *Talking with Angels*, Friday, July 16, 1943, page 36.
32. Who inspired another remarkable modern angelologist, Gustav Davidson, author of the *Dictionary of Angels* (New York, The Free Press), a work of about four hundred pages in which he has compiled a registry of all the names of Angels, including the fallen Angels, mentioned in all religions.
33. Denys l'Aeropagite, *Mystical Theology and Celestial Hierarchies*, Mahwah, N.J., Paulist Press, pp. 161, 162.

out-of-body experience the American was granted a vision, which he calls a "ball of thought," describing roughly the role of these beings of light, a kind of celestial engineer who incidentally confirmed to him that there was no way they could be confused (as some maintained) with extraterrestrials: *"Those are a different type of manifestation."*

Hearing of such experiences, I had to meet Robert Monroe and ask him what he really thought of guardian Angels. So I went to see him in Virginia and was charmed by this seventy-seven-year-old man. No trace of megalomania or self-importance in him, as opposed to so many other proponents of the irrational who shout to the four winds that they are the only ones in possession of the absolute truth about God, the Angels, Christ, etc. I wanted to know who were these burning Beings, or INSPECS as he called them, whom he came up against. Monroe lit a cigarette, fixed his blue eyes upon me, and explained that his first meeting with these "entities" took place in 1981 or 1982: *"I never asked myself if they were Angels in the religious sense of the term because being an engineer, I have always tried to rid myself of any dogma that might influence my experiments,"* he told me. *"I wanted to go beyond these illusions because if you're Catholic it's a guardian Angel, but if you're Buddhist it's something else. I know now what my 'INSPECS' were, and if you want them to be Angels, fine. But from my point of view, Angels don't have wings. Yes, they are certainly figures of glory; yes, they possess knowledge and powers beyond ours. These Angels are quite real but with a fundamental difference: I know what they are, who they are and what they do. Still from my perspective, I also know what a Guardian Angel is, and it is not a messenger from God. It truly is not. You see, each of us has about two thousand previous lives within us. The experience acquired in each of these lives constitutes a separate Being, different. For me, your Guardian Angel is you yourself, the part of you that possesses the memory and experience of your previous lives. This group of previous lives contains considerable power and knowledge thanks to the combined set of experiences. So it can accomplish veritable miracles in physical life. He says for example: 'Pierre needs a miracle, let's give him one.'*

*"But you have it not because of prayer, but by the power of your emotion and your need. It is you who are helping yourself. No one else. People who have near death experiences and meet a light at the end of the tunnel meet only themselves.*[34] *But it's nice to know that all*

---

34. This declaration seemed too peremptory to me and I cannot confirm it by studying the NDEs. Indeed, we saw in Chapter 2 that the Being accompanies the subject toward the Light and that he is independent and autonomous.

*you have to do is lie down and breath deeply to meet all these Angels, Entities or whatever you like. On the other hand, if I held strong religious beliefs, an Angel—with wings—would have come to me and said 'Robert, it is time to do this and this'. And then, in that religion, I would have prostrated myself and said 'Yes, yes, anything you want.' I've gone beyond those games because I don't believe in them, and that's how I reach a point where I could say, 'Hello, I'm Bob, and you?' with no fear. And what you call an Angel said to me: 'Hello, happy to find someone enlightened at last.'"*

Listening to him I concluded that I was still unenlightened, and I wanted to know what "enlightened" meant from his point of view. *"To be enlightened,"* Monroe answered, *"is to be unafraid, to not fear. People in this world are afraid of death because they aren't sure what awaits them. But you have to understand that we don't die, we just change realities."* According to Robert Monroe, the Guardian Angel is no more than the true self that lives outside of time. That explanation bowled me over. Moreover, he inferred that God did not exist. But he offered a description of the Creator in his second book, *Far Journeys.* So I asked him if he accepted the principle of a sole Creator of the Universe. Robert Monroe acknowledged that initially he believed in neither a God nor a Creator: *"The desire to believe in a Creator was unknown to me before my experiences with the INSPECS. Then one day I came very close (to the Creator) but 'they' had not authorized me to go any farther. I won't hide it, I'd love to meet the fabulous and magnificent spirit who has created all this. When I approached the Creator at a great distance, approached that immense and extraordinary luminous being, I found myself in what we call a 'relay station,' that is, a place that transformed His energy to convey it to earth, and I could go no farther."*

So finally even Monroe was obliged to believe the evidence, God existed! Bravo, Mr. Monroe, you have won an out of body trip to Paris for two, all expenses paid. Even if some of Monroe's statements irritated me prodigiously, we invariably came to the same conclusion: New Agers, "out of body" specialists, Catholics, Jews, Hindus, etc., may disagree on a number of points, but there is at least one thing on which they agree, namely the existence of a guardian Angel. Certainly, the name varies, but the function remains. And as we are about to learn, if it is indisputable that we possess a superior level of awareness that notes all the details of our life, the guardian Angel is unique and totally disassociated from that part of our consciousness. It is LIVING and INDEPENDENT. The NDE have proved to us that the Angel who "watches over us" does not reveal himself, in 99 percent of the cases, until the moment of death or in particularly dramatic circumstances.

# CHAPTER 5

# *Elisabeth Kübler-Ross*

ELISABETH KÜBLER-ROSS, EKR, IS WHAT WE CALL A LIVING LEGEND. WE speak of Dr. Kübler-Ross in the world of thanatology as we speak of "La Callas" in the world of opera. She is an absolute and uncontested authority in her specialty. No one in the world, save perhaps Mother Teresa, has accompanied so many sick people up to their last breath. But no one, not even Mother Teresa, has done as much for those who have lost a dear one as Elisabeth Kübler-Ross, since it is she who *"invented"* the concept of accompanying the dying. Her numerous works have been translated throughout the world and even today she does not hesitate to emplane for Tokyo, Canada, or Paris to explain tirelessly how we should behave with the dying and what we can do to help them "live their death" better. Doctor, professor, doctor *honoris causa* of eighteen universities, Elisabeth Kübler-Ross was THE person I had to meet about a subject as "vertical" as the Angels. It took me six months of patience to set up a meeting, and in the airplane that took me to Washington, I was burning with the desire to see her. In all my interviews, I was invariably told, *"You know, you must meet Dr. Kübler-Ross."* In the end, it became an *idée fixe.* When thirty people, no matter who, all send you toward a single contact, you tell yourself that maybe your whole book is going to stand or fall by it.

When she began to talk about her patients' near death experiences, the medical community said that EKR spent more time with the dying than with the living and that she was mistaking their hallucinations for the real thing. But she paid no heed to her critics because these phenomena had become too repetitive.

*"In my opinion,"* she explained in an interview in a magazine, *"whoever sets down his discoveries and explains how he arrived at his conclusion is scientifically honest. They would be right to mis-*

147

*trust me and even accuse me of prostitution if I only published what pleased the public. It is no part of my intention to convince, much less convert, anyone. I consider that my work consists of the transmission of research. Those who are ready will believe me and those who are not will build arguments on rationalization and pedantry."*

Even Raymond Moody, when he finished his first book, *Life After Life*, asked her to round out his words with a preface. The Swiss doctor accepted and confirmed that she too had noted the same manifestation with her patients:

> *Since I have worked with terminally ill patients over the last two decades, I have become more and more preoccupied with looking into the phenomena of death itself. We have learned a lot about the process of dying, but we still have many questions with regard to the moment of death and to the experience our patients have when they are pronounced medically dead. . . .*
>
> *All of these patients have experienced a floating out of their physical bodies, associated with a great sense of peace and wholeness. Most were aware of another person who helped them in their transition to another plane of existence.*[1]

So it was obvious that I could not finish my inquiry in the field of NDEs without interviewing Dr. Kübler-Ross.

It took my three hours on the road from Charlottesville to reach the EKR Center, hidden away in George Washington National Forest. The sky was bright and sunny and I had the feeling I was acting in a movie: the Swiss flag waved over the wooden chalet, as if to remind us of that uncommon woman's nationality, and a little stream wound through the center, giving it all a bucolic, unquestionably "Made in Switzerland" air. It was a slight, gray-haired woman with a sharp Swiss-German accent who welcomed me. No need to tell me that this was the legend. It was "Dr. EKR" and now that I was before her, I hardly knew what to say, like a cub reporter face to face with his first big star.

*"Let's go into the house, it will be quieter there for the interview,"* she told me.

Arriving in front of her house, I thought I was hallucinating: a Saint Bernard, a real one, lacking only a small keg of rum and a stretcher, came to rub himself affectionately against my hip. No

1. Preface to *Life After Life* by Raymond Moody.

doubt about it, I was in Switzerland. All it needed were chocolates and a cuckoo clock to complete the illusion. Elisabeth Kübler-Ross headed for the kitchen, where she busied herself making tea while I tried to plug in my recorder.

*"Why are you so interested in Angels?"* she asked me.

*"I don't really know, but it has become a passion."*

*"Don't try to prove anything. Your job is not to prove. People who have their spiritual quadrant open will find their own verifications. Those who have nothing open say that you're crazy, that you're not scientific, or that you're a mystic. You will be mocked. You will convince no one, absolutely no one. That's what religious do who say, 'You will go to hell if you do not take Jesus as your savior.' If only they taught love, understanding, and compassion. . . . They ought to teach that life never ends, never, instead of making people feel guilty. They ought to teach that at our death, we will be responsible for each of our thoughts, each of our statements, and each of our deeds, that everything has its consequences. When you are in the Light, you will be accountable for everything, including your choices. Each person is entirely responsible. All that the Church should teach is that you are responsible for everything, absolutely everything. But the preachers only talk about hell, and they terrorize people instead of helping them."*

It was a powerful opening salvo, and it reminded me of Dr. Moody's comment about the preacher who had just described his NDE, during which he saw how he had poisoned the lives of his flock by talking to them of nothing but hell. I saw myself explaining to the "Light" why I had decided to write this book; to prove to myself that Angels did exist, and, I don't know why, I imagined a group of Angels bursting into laughter. . . .

Elisabeth brought out two cakes which she set down before me. "Eat." I told myself that it would be hard to eat and question her at the same time. My existential questions did not tally with chocolate cake. It was like talking about famine at the dinner table. But she insisted like an Italian mama. Just as I was framing my first question, the tea kettle emitted a strident whistle that recalled the sirens during an air raid.

*"After so many years of practice accompanying the dying, do you still believe in life after death?"* I ventured, timidly swallowing a piece of cake. She uttered a sort of groan, as if I had asked her if the earth was round.

*"I don't believe; I know. I know that life does not stop at death. That's all. It is not a question of 'believing something' but of 'knowing.'"*

*"How do you know it?"* Chocolate was sticky on my fingers.

*"Because I've tested it. There's not a shadow of a doubt. But you can't explain to people what there is afterwards, and it's not worthwhile trying to convince them. I know, that's all. Look at the pediatrician* [Melvin Morse] *who wrote the book on infantile NDE. He was skeptical too at the beginning. Excuse me, I'm going to fetch some needles. I want to knit. You eat. I can't sit there without doing something."*

Quickly I finished my cake. *"How many terminally ill patients have you accompanied in the course of your career?"*

*"I don't know. A lot. Perhaps twenty thousand people. I travel the entire world. But I don't keep count. I go see the patients and help them pass to the other side all over the world."* EKR was calmly knitting, like a grandmother. This interview was frankly startling.

*"What is your religion?"*

*"I have none. On paper I am Protestant. In my heart I believe like a Catholic, and I was married to a Jew for twenty-two years. Very ecumenical. That's of no importance at all, since we are all the children of a single God and one day we will eventually find Him. In the beginning, I was Protestant. But when patients began telling me about their experiences, everything changed."*

I wondered what she was knitting. *"Which is the NDE that influenced you the most?"*

*"It was a little boy who caught cold. The doctor gave him a shot, but he reacted very badly and was pronounced dead. The doctor did not understand. The mother went crazy and it took about an hour and a half to find the father on a construction site. And just a few minutes before his arrival at the clinic, the little boy suddenly opened his eyes and said to his mother: 'Mom, I was dead.' Profoundly shocked, she didn't want to hear about it, and every time the boy tried to tell her his story, she told him to be quiet. But in the end he told her his experience: 'Mom, I have to tell you, you know, because Mary and Jesus came to look for me and they told me that it wasn't my time. But I didn't want to leave and Mary took me by the hand and sent me down, saying to me, "You must save your mama from hell."' The mother was plunged into depression because she believed she was going to burn in hell and that it was her son who would save her, all because the Church teaches fear and guilt. Then I asked her, 'But how would you feel if Mary had not sent back your son?' and she said without even pausing for thought, 'My God, my life would have been hell.' At that moment she understood. In the 1960s no one was talking about NDE."*

*"And the Angels in these experiences, what do you think of them?"*

*"Normal, since each human being possesses a guardian Angel. You must know though that they don't always have wings. The Angel is a companion. In California they are called guides, I call them my 'spooks,' children call them their playmates, Catholics call them guardian Angels, there are different names for them throughout the world but everybody has one, even though everybody doesn't talk with his guardian Angel."*

*"Are you in touch with your Angels?"*

*"Yes, they help me, they guide me, they instruct me, they heal me when I have health problems. You couldn't survive in this world without your guardian Angel. Some people know that they have one, others don't. If you listen to little children talk with theirs when they go to bed . . . They have long conversations. And then the parents say 'Stop talking to yourself,' 'Don't believe those stories,' 'You're a big boy now,' and so on. Very very few people have maintained contact with their guardian Angel."*

*"When did you start talking with your Angels?"*

*"I don't know. Several years ago, about seven."*

*"Do you set down what they say to you?"*

*"No, it's here in my heart, and that's enough. You know, I've reached the point where I talk to them personally, just as you and I are chatting now. I talk to them for hours and hours. To see them is a very rare gift, because they seldom show themselves. When they do materialize they're like you and me, solid. But that's very very rare."*

*"And what have they taught you?"*

*"I've been talking with them for seven years, and I could talk to you for seven years without being able to explain a thousandth of what they've taught me."*

*"Is there a rule for allocating Angels?"*

*"That depends on your work and your mission in life. If your work is high risk, you have several, but even if you're not doing anything special, you have at least one from birth. Angels are more at home in the reality of NDEs than in out-of-body voyages."*

*"What have they taught you about suffering?"*

*"Suffering is like the Grand Canyon. If we said, 'It's so pretty, we must protect it from wind and storm,' it would never be sculpted by the wind and we would never appreciate its beauty. That is my answer in regard to suffering. If you don't suffer, you don't grow. You must experience sorrow, loss, tears and anger. Every time you go through those, you grow, you progress. There is nothing more important in life for your progress. No one will make progress if everything is presented to him on a silver platter. No one. Everything depends on what you have to do. Anyway, you know your guardian Angel before*

*you're born, you simply forget everything at birth. Your task is to find
the reason why you are on earth. One of my guides told me that if he
were reincarnated, it would be as an infant dying of hunger. And I
asked him why he wanted to do such a stupid thing. He replied that it
was to enlarge his sense of compassion."*

EKR's explanation accords quite well with what we saw in the
chapter "Angels in the Tunnels"—the subject feeling he has known
this Being for a long time.

*"Do you believe in chance, in coincidences?"*

*"No. No. Coincidences are only our divine manipulation. I don't
believe in coincidences. Everything, absolutely everything, makes
sense, has a reason."*

I wanted to know more about that. *"Then where is our free will,
if luck and coincidence don't exist?"*

*"Free will is the most beautiful gift we receive at birth. You your-
self choose your parents, your children, your wife before your
incarnation, and you cannot hold it against God if they present problems, because all the problems they present exist for positive reasons.
Life is full of challenge. If people examined their problems as a challenge intended to help them grow and not make them fear, it would
change a great many things. We are in this life to learn. Look at this
house, for example, that someone found for me. It's a magnificent
house, isn't it? People fire shots at my windows, they slash my tires
when I go to the airport, and since I adopted twenty children with
AIDS the Ku Klux Klan burns crosses on my grounds. Before that the
neighbors were charming and everything ran smoothly. When the
children arrived at the center, people tried to set fire to it. They put me
on their hit list, to make me the victim of an accident. At one point I
couldn't go anywhere without a police escort. I have to go through all
that to keep growing."*

It was the detachment of Catholic and Hindu mystics. *"Then it's
a kind of determinism?"*

*"It all depends on yourself. I could have become negative and
embittered, and said, 'To hell with these people and their AIDS,' and
set up housekeeping on the Riviera to live in luxury and forget about
my patients. But I see this situation as a challenge. If I can survive
here I can survive anywhere. There is a positive reason for everything."*

*"What is the purpose of our earthly existence?"*

*"To suffer, because that helps us grow, to proceed toward the
Light, to be like Christ. The only thing in life that counts is love. Fear
helps us to survive."*

EKR was as dolorist as the strictest of Jesuits or stigmatists.

Amazing. I never dreamed that the famous Kübler-Ross would deliver a speech even more dolorist than any mystic's. So then I wanted to know if she prayed as they did. *"Do you pray?"*

*"I pray when I'm gardening, when I feed my animals, always, when I cook, but I never meditate because I always have to be doing something. I always pray. Your whole life should be a prayer; no need to kneel in a church, you're much closer to God in your garden. You must ask things of God. We always receive what we need, but not always what we want."*

*"Do you realize that everything you've said is very close to Christ's teachings?"*

*"Yes. But when I look at today's Christians, I tell myself they're a long way from what Christ taught. It's just a matter of money. Listen to the evangelists on television: All they know how to say is 'Send money, send checks, send pennies.' What Christ gave us is marvelous. But what they do with it is something else."*

*"Yet you say that hell does not exist."*

*"I have the feeling that apparently I must explain to people that indeed hell does not exist, and that's the reason I started working on death."*

*"And the people who had bad NDEs?"*

*"My cases of bad NDEs were generally men between forty and fifty years old, fundamentalists, some of whom deceived their wives even as they told themselves that what they were doing was bad, or a sin. Then one day on a golf course they're victims of a heart attack and they see the Devil and I don't know what else, and it seems terribly real, when they ought to be concentrating on the Light at the end of the tunnel and going there right away to find love and compassion."*

*"But people who rape, or kill, or torture?"*

*"Once out of their bodies, they know what's waiting for them: They'll have to relive everything, in full, with all the consequences on their spouses, their families, and so on; and especially all that their victims suffered. Down to the last detail. That could last for thousands of years because on the other side time doesn't count, it is eternity. No one can relive in their place the negativity they've created, no one. I've thought often of Hitler. If you can forgive Hitler, then you will be forgiven. The only possibility for Hitler, in my fantasy, is that he be reincarnated and that he save as many lives as he destroyed. Millions. The only way he could redeem himself in one lifetime would be for example to develop a vaccine against AIDS. That is why I can imagine that he could erase his—I don't like this word—his sins."*

EKR affirmed that hell, the Catholic version, did not exist. But what she said about what awaited the violent was in the same vein,

perhaps worse. It may be that this is hell: a place where these individuals relive, out of time and thus eternally, what they have made
their victims suffer. Again, that clearly recalls the visions of George
Ritchie, the "father" of NDEs. It's just that the definition of the
word "hell" is not the same.

The "legend" knitted constantly, until I began to feel I'd been
there forever. It is curious what a calming influence a woman knitting is. . . . I tried to learn more about Angels from her, but EKR
obviously did not want to reveal too much of her spiritual life; she
had already told me a great deal about it, and in a way it was perfectly understandable. The spiritual life is an area even more taboo
than the sexual life. We do not tell others in detail how we pray, to
whom we pray or for whom we pray, or what we ask of God. My
interview with EKR had left me wanting more even as it confirmed
what I had discovered in the course of my researches, namely that
life doesn't stop at death and we really do have guardian Angels.
But hearing it from Kübler-Ross reassured and somehow comforted me. As she said, *"We would have a hard time surviving
without our guardian Angels."* But sometimes I told myself that I
was wasting my time with this book and that it might have at most
two or three thousand readers. In discussions with certain people,
however, I was surprised by their interest, at first veiled, as if they
did not wish to tell me right away that they shared my concerns,
and then eager to talk openly about it. But I was certainly more
sensitive to those who took me for a lunatic.

During dinner, a California architect asked what I was writing
about, and I answered *"people who die and see Angels."* There was a
moment of dead silence—an Angel passed overhead, as they say, in
a hearse—and the guest across from me upset a glass of wine,
clearly considering me a mental defective. Watching him leave
almost dead drunk behind the wheel of his car, I decided that all in
all I'd rather investigate Angels than get drunk like an idiot and risk
an automobile accident. But the conversation with EKR had made
me gloomy. The idea of living on this earth to suffer distressed me.
In the end wouldn't it be easier to get drunk? It couldn't be what
she said, or at least not totally. And why not live in a certain joy
with this Creator who created us all, whom we shall find at the end
of the tunnel? But how could I reproach EKR for this dolorism, her
who had seen so many infants die?

*"A child who dies in his parents' arms, what do you call that?"* I
asked her.

*"It is a lesson. Children return to where they came from. I've
noticed that a dying infant receives a sort of compensation for the*

*loss of his physical body: his spiritual quadrant opens altogether. He finds everything he had forgotten—for example his guardian Angel or his playmate. The child knows ahead of time that he is going to die, even if you've said nothing to him. Just look at his drawings. You absolutely cannot lie to a child; he knows. Children who die are our teachers."*

*"What you think of the typical NDE phrase 'It is not your time, you must return to your body' Is that determinism?"*

*"No, since before we are born we choose the parents, spouses and children we will need for our own progress. We have chosen all the important people in our lives ahead of time, for the qualities in them that we will need for our own development."*

*"They why do you pray?"*

*"Because we can correct everything, modify everything as we go along. We can repair everything, too. As I told you, We must ask God for what we need, but never for what we want."*[2]

2. See also the piece written by Johnathan Rosen in *The New York Times Magazine* "Rewriting the End," January 22, 1995.

## CHAPTER 6

# Where Are the Angels When Accidents Happen?

S O THEN: WHY DOES THIS DIVINE PROVIDENCE (THUS NAMED IN THE *Dialogues* of Catherine of Siena, who mentioned the arrival of Angels at crucial moments) manifest itself to some and not to others? Each day accidents occur, children die, pedestrians and drivers end up in wheel chairs, children are born paralytic without their guardian Angel showing up to save them at the last minute. Let us even admit that death may be programmed, and I am thinking of the almost unbelievable case of the driver speeding through the American desert on a perfectly straight, deserted road when his tires hit a jack forgotten at the roadside by someone. Flung up by the violence of the impact, the metal jack perforates the car's chassis and lodges directly in the driver's heart. His last reflex is to yank it out of his body. The police, shocked by their discovery, told themselves that his time had really come, like this rugby player struck down by lightning in the middle of a match one Saturday afternoon, before thousands of spectators in the south of France.

Then why in NDE do we regularly come across the question, *"Do you want to stay or go back?"* At first glance, the subject has a choice. But that's only an impression. Take the typical case, so typical that it is wonderful, of the victim of a motorcycle accident who told his story to Arvin Gibson.

In 1978 John Stirling rode over a hogback that threw his motorbike off kilter as he was climbing the side of a canyon. He tried as best he could to keep his balance, but under the weight of its passenger, the bike headed straight for a cliff. That forced him to jump, and a few seconds later the wheel slammed into a rock. The motorbike fell back on him, the rear view mirror striking his head (no helmet) before smashing up a hundred meters down the hill. John immediately found himself out of body, observing the scene,

157

and then beginning to pass through a tunnel at incredible speed. *"Like in the movie Star Wars,"* he said. Then he heard a voice asking him if he had finished. *"Certainly, I've finished. I don't want to go back. I don't ever want to go back."* The voice asked him again, *"Have you finished?"* and he again answered, *"Yes, I've finished, I don't want to go back there again."* A third time he gave the same answer. Then, as the voice said calmly, *"Good, let's take a look at your life,"* John instantly relived his life in three dimensions and in color, experiencing again every emotion he ever felt from birth to his accident. Watching the last day, he understood that he must return to raise and educate his son. Then he surrendered to the evidence and said, *"Yes, I want to go back."* The voice was not heard again and he immediately re-entered his body.[1]

But for Dr. Morse it is only a false choice, a false proposition: *"you know, it's like when my son is playing in the garden. If I say to him 'Come on, we're going in,' he refuses and wants to go on playing. But if I say to him 'Come on, Brett, let's go see what your mother's doing,' then he drops everything and comes running. I have rarely seen an NDE in which the subject wanted to come back all alone. He feels so good outside his body, it seems so natural to him, that he's ready to abandon everything; parents, wife, mistress, child, baby. Everything. It was Tom Sawyer, a mechanic crushed by a car he was repairing, who said he was ejected from Heaven by a kick in the pants because he didn't want to return to his body."* Presumably this false choice obliges the soul to study the subject's life and to understand that it has to stay and finish its job, because its time has not yet come. What else can we think, indeed, except that the hour of death is certainly fixed in advance? I asked Kenneth Ring about this: *"Do you think predestination exists?"* He played with his glasses for a few moments before answering, as if the question had never before been asked: *"Many survivors argue, but in some cases people return without the impression of having made a choice. But I think they are guided to make the better choice for themselves. The Light seems to know the subject's past and future perfectly."* Which bears a strong resemblance to some sort of predestination.

Nevertheless, a comment is in order: If the hour of death seems to be set in advance, it seems to me, after examining all the NDEs, that prayer, in other words the real dialogue between the creature and the Creator,[2] can modify the life of the subject.

---

1. In Arvin Gibson, *Glimpses of Eternity*, pp. 183–184.
2. I always think of this admonition about prayer: *"One must not mistake God for a waiter."*

But what do we discover in the studies of NDE? That in almost all cases, the subject does not want to return (to Earth) and that he is driven back either by an already deceased member of his family or by an Angel, or by the Light. who all say the same thing: *"Your time has not yet come; you still have things to do/to complete/to finish/etc."* Sometimes, when the subject answers, *"No, I don't want to go back,"* the Light says: *"Yes, but look at what you will miss,"* followed by a picture of the future. Then the subject agrees to go back. After the thousands of stories of NDE that I have heard or read, I have come inevitably and always to the same conclusion: *"The time of death is programmed like the activation of a virus in a computer."* I am absolutely convinced of it, together with the following consolation: *"which is of no importance anyway, since only the body dies. Not the spirit."*

But what good does suffering do? If we admit the existence of the Creator, we have the right to think that as our Father, He would not amuse Himself passing out wheelchairs, cancers, and horrible incurable illnesses to his creatures, much less to the very young. Before developing an interest in Angels, I had always thought that He certainly created us, but that for some incomprehensible reason lost all interest in his creation. The Creator forgot his creations. But that simplistic notion melts like snow in the sunshine with the stigmatics, whose wounds were sworn to by thousands of officials, and with the saints and their miracles, acknowledged very cautiously by the Church, and above all by those who underwent a genuine experience at death's door.

When I made Kenneth Ring's acquaintance at the University of Connecticut, I asked him about the effect of his research on his own beliefs, and also if he now believed in Angels. *"Yes, I believe we have a consciousness that survives physical death. I don't like the phrase 'life after death' but I believe we don't disappear when our body ceases to function. The guardian Angel is a concept I associate with Catholics. From my perspective, we each have one or more spiritual guides who seem to manifest themselves at the most critical moments of our life, like for example our death. The concept has real meaning, but the phrase maybe not. I believe in these Beings. I have many cases where they appear in NDE. And the survivors are sure from then on that they have a helper, that they're guided. As if it were a Higher Self, a Super-Me."* At this point in my work I was not about to quibble over a few words. Angel or Super-Me? The debate is open. But it doesn't matter; my inquiry has been confirmed again. I then asked him what this Super-Me was, according to him. *"We have an ego,"* he answered me in a sober voice, *"who belongs to a more important part of us and who helps us, who may not interfere in our lives but aids us and knows us perfectly from start to finish. And in crucial moments it manifests itself. The common factor in all that, guardian Angel, inner self, guide, is a benevolent aid that we learn about only at the moment of our death."*

And God in all that? *"Have you been struck by a connection between the NDE and the Resurrection in the New Testament?"* I asked him.

Kenneth Ring laid down his pen in the manner of a British lord and, still quite slowly, began to fiddle with a paper-clip.

*"Yes, that's obvious, not only in the Bible but also in all other religious texts. Saint Paul's experience on the road to Damascus shows a number of points in common with what we now call NDE. The NDE is like a code that sheds light on a great number of religious texts that seem obscure at first glance. I think people who have had an NDE have one way or another touched this transcendental reality. NDE people fall to prayer because they feel the presence of God. And since they have fused with the Light, when they come back they keep some within them. Which explains why they feel closer to God. But they don't feel the need to go to church or synagogue to find God. I would say that this Light is the visible, palpable emanation of God. His visible manifestation, His cognitive aspect. You could also say that in any case, the Light is God. All religions associate light with God and this Light represents one of His extensions."*

I was burning with curiosity to know if, after two major books on the subject, he had a spiritual life. *"What is the state of your own spiritual life after all these NDEs?"*

*"They've probably made me more spiritual. I'm Jewish but don't consider myself a practicing Jew. Religion is a doctrine, an institution where spiritual life is not put first. After the NDE many people become extremely spiritual but not religious. I certainly believe in God, but I'm not more religious."*

*"But since you first heard of that Light, haven't you wanted to discover it, to see it yourself?"* (The luckiest ones, who spoke with the Light during this communion, retain an indelible memory of it, as if branded on the forehead, because every atom of their soul vibrated at the same frequency as the Being of Light, bestowing upon them an incorruptible happiness beside which earthly sexual delights, even at the height of ecstasy, are like the ephemeral glow of a wooden match. They often say, *"I was bathed in light,"* or *"I was swimming in pure love,"* or even *"I was love."*)

*"Oh yes, I'm truly curious. After fifteen years of work on the subject, an NDE is still a moving experience. But for all that, I haven't*

*become religious."*

So Kenneth Ring was sure that God existed—he called it Light—and by extension "guides." But this does not explain the thoroughly inequitable distribution of suffering, which has exercised theologians and philosophers all through the ages, though they have never been able to offer a truly convincing explanation to a materialist. The American rabbi Harold Kushner has gone so far as to think that the Creator has been surpassed by his own creation! As a very young rabbi he was transferred to a suburb of Boston with his two sons; Aaron, three, and Ariel, a few months old. Examining the older boy during a medial checkup, the pediatrician discovered he was a victim of progeria, a disease which would keep him from growing: *"Your son will never grow hair, will never be more than about three feet tall, will look like an old man, and will die at the age of about ten."* Imagine the effect of these words on the poor rabbi.

> *There is the eternal question: "How could He do such a thing to me?" How does one handle news like that? I was a young, inexperienced rabbi, not as familiar with the process of grief as I would later come to be, and what I mostly felt that day was a deep, aching sense of unfairness. It didn't make sense. I had been a good person. I had tried to do what was right in the sight of God. More than that, I was living a more religiously committed life than most people I knew, people who had large, healthy families. I believe that I was following God's ways and doing His work. How could this be happening to my family? If God existed, if He was minimally fair, let alone loving and forgiving, how could He do this to me?[3]*

Catholic dolorists will say, *"You deserved it,"* or *"It's to test you."* Hindus will say, *"It's your karma."* And I've always wanted to ask them how they react when they see a blind man trying to take the subway: do they let him move forward until he falls to the tracks because it's God's will, or because it's his karma and he has to get on with it? That question leads to another: *"Where are the guardian Angels when accidents happen?"* Indeed, nothing is easier than writing a book full of anecdotes about people mysteriously saved, and saying, *"Angels exist."* All right. But take this case from 1992: an adolescent boy goes aside to pray. He takes his beads from his

3. Rabbi Harold Kushner, *When Bad Things Happen to Good People.*

pocket and begins a Rosary, which as we know is a prayer/litany to the Virgin. In circumstances still unclear, five other adolescents (from 14 to 17) see him, make fun of him and decide to strangle him. And they do strangle him! Strangled while he was telling his rosary! The *Los Angeles Times* ran the story in a front-page piece about violence among children. What was that poor boy's guardian Angel doing? Devout Catholics can hardly make an argument for an incident like that, because the victim was killed while at prayer. But if we look at it from the point of view of an NDE, we see clearly that:

1. his time had come.

2. we may imagine that it was the Virgin at the end of the tunnel, because in the rosary we find these words: *"Holy Mary, pray for us now and at the hour of our death."* It was more than fitting. . . .

But also, why, during a press junket, did one reporter oversleep and miss the plane; another cancel his ticket because of an emergency; and a third pick up a flat tire on his way to the airport, his first flat in twenty years of driving? And why did the other reporters board the plane, which was to crash a few hours later with no survivors? And how do you explain a one-year-old baby's fall from the eighteenth floor of a Paris apartment building with no bruises (dispatch from Agence France Presse), and the banal, but fatal, crossing of a street by Michel d'Ornano, the mayor of Normandy's Deauville? And why were there only three deaths when the Airbus A-320 crashed at Mulhouse and in the catastrophe in Strasbourg only eight survivors,[4] while just three weeks before, a Scandinavian SAS airliner crashed on Christmas day, right after takeoff, with full fuel tanks (!) without one victim? For them their Angels seem to have avoided a tragic end. But what about suffering?

Here is Rabbi Kushner's[5] answer to that question; for him human life is only a jungle:

> *I believe that God gives us strength and patience and hope, renewing our spiritual resources when they run dry . . . I believe in God. But I do not believe the same things*

4. Eighty-seven deaths.
5. Kushner, op. cit., pp. 127 and 134.

*about Him that I did years ago, when I was growing up or when I was a theological student. I recognize His limitations. He is limited in what He can do by laws of nature and by the evolution of human nature and human moral freedom. I no longer hold God responsible for illnesses, accidents, and natural disasters, because I realize that I gain little and I lose so much when I blame God for these things. I can worship a God who hates suffering but cannot eliminate it, more easily than I can worship a God who chooses to make children suffer and die, for whatever exalted reason.*

That is very curious reasoning. Personally, I see even less interest in being a priest/representative of an "incapable," "limited" God, sort of a doddering God, surpassed by His own creation and incapable of helping His creations. A paraphrase might go: *"Ah yes, absolutely, God exists, but you know, He is getting very old, He doesn't know what he's doing any more."* Paradoxically, it is in *Dialogues with the Angels*[6] that we find an answer inhuman in a real as well as a figurative sense:

> *A hard word:*
> *WAR IS GOOD.*
>
> *Take care!*
> *Falsely used force becomes destructive,*
> *becomes devastating;*
> *It would never come to a halt*
> *without the weak—the victim—who absorbs it.*
> *That belongs to the past. It had to be that way.*
> *Past wrongs cannot be righted.*
> *But the victim absorbs and extinguishes the horrors.*
> *If the persecutor finds the persecuted,*
> *death is satiated.*
> *The weak shall be glorified*
> *and no more lambs shall be slaughtered*
> *upon the altar.*
> *War was unavoidable.*
> *Now the bitter chalice is filled.*
> *Fear not! As full as it is of bitterness*
> *it is equally full of Divine Drink*
> *of Eternal Serenity.*

6. Friday, October 25, 1944, p. 436.

Still better, in the *Treatise on Divine Providence* by the inspired Catherine of Siena, we discover a very interesting chapter subtitle: *How divine providence seeks to torment us for the sake of our own salvation. On the unhappiness of those who repose their confidence in themselves. On the excellence of those who repose it in providence.* In this dialogue, He explains quite simply that if His providence is so used, it is to succor us, as it dashes all hope for this world and pushes us toward Him, who should be our only goal. He even clarifies the point:

*"Imagine, daughter, what they (man) would do if they found perfect pleasure and painless rest in the world!*

*"This is why in my providence I allow the world to bring forth so many troubles for them, both to prove their virtue and that I may have reason to reward them for their suffering and the violence they do themselves. So my providence has ordained and provided in all things with great wisdom. I have given because I am rich and I was and am able to give, and my wealth is infinite."*

Which amounts to saying again that all things, good and bad, come to us from Him. The Moslems say the same thing in a different way: "It is written," including suffering, which confirms Elisabeth Kübler-Ross' explanation that suffering is no more than a predetermined element, destined to make us grow, to help us progress, to help us evolve, even if it seems incomprehensible to us. Sometimes, on the other hand, it is He who appears, according to the findings of Kenneth Ring: *"Fusion with the Light was often offered to subjects who had had an unhappy childhood; to battered or raped children,"* he assured me. And I thought back to a nun I had met in Paris who said to me: *"You know, we have noticed that people do not turn to God sincerely until they have been devastated by an immense grief, a grief that leaves them only one hope, just one way out, God. Then they land in church, in tears, sit down in a pew and pray for the first time since childhood or perhaps in their life. God's call sometimes takes extremely dolorous ways. The problem is that they pray and pray, and once their prayers are answered, they forget that grace and return to their old ways."*

Does this seem to say that everything, absolutely everything, is predetermined? And if everything is predetermined, then where is the "free will" that allows each person to act and react according to his own unique conscience? And if all our steps are predetermined, then what is the interest of God who defines our relation to Him in advance? After five years of research on Angels, it seems to me that nothing is predetermined, because if it were, we would have no intercession by Angels in our lives; but at the same time, He sees all and knows in advance what we are going to do, what decisions we are going to make. As Kenneth Ring noted: *"The Light seems to know perfectly the past and the future of the subject."* This Light is timeless, and therefore possesses a vision of the past, present and future. For Dr. Kübler-Ross, once out of body, the subject is immediately confronted by the whole of his life with all the details; all his words, deeds and thoughts, even the most secret, with their effects on others. Dr. Morse was struck by the fact that some relive forty years of their life when the cardiac arrest lasted only three seconds. In that other reality, time, as the poet says, suspends its flight. Divine interventions take on their full meaning then: the war photographer who says, *"It's as if time were frozen,"* or the reporter who said it seemed *"that time slowed down, like in a movie."* So these interventions are better explained as constant surveillance, outside time, a kind of divine fine-tuning of our lives so that we stay on our destined tracks. The Englishwoman Margot Grey reports in her book *Return From Death*[7] the testimony of one of her subjects who had a profound near death experience, fusing with the Light at the end of the tunnel:

> *During my experience I became aware of everything that had ever happened and everything that was going to happen—all my past lives and all the future lives I would have. I was also shown events that are likely to happen in the near future, but was made to understand that nothing is absolutely fixed and that everything depends on how we choose to use our own free will, that even those events that are already predestined can be changed or modified by a change in our own way of relating to them*

So the grand lines of our life do seem to be established in advance—predestination—and only the life of this day depends on free will and, it seems, on the subject's spiritual life. On determinism, here is the opinion of Robert Monroe, who admits his ignorance in regard to that other level of existence, which is beyond him: *"Our physical life creates larger or smaller variables simply to divert, assist or create a change."* Monroe, in voyaging out of body, noted these words from a spiritual Being whom he was unable to approach because he was . . . burning, and who declared to him: *"Free will is vital in the experience of human*

7. Margot Grey, *Return From Death*, New York, Penguin Books, 1985, p. 123.

*knowledge. Deviations from the primary intention are frequent and calculated in advance, as you might say. These adjustments are nothing more than—the exact term escapes me—fine tuning. Yes, fine tuning."*[8]

Thus the appearance of an Angel in human life may be nothing more than an adjustment induced by the free will of the subject. And these adjustments are often answers to prayers. But Angels intercede by the interaction of several other factors, the most important being their spiritual relationship with their protégé, as that other entity explained during an out of body experience at the Monroe Institute: *"I cannot help you resolve your personal problems. I can convey ideas to you, but not the direct orientation that would be possible if you were on level 18. Our levels touch."* If the protégé does not believe in a guardian Angel (in the spiritual domain) and only discovers his existence later, the actions of that immortal being are more or less modified, yet ready to develop: the Angel awaits his protégé's awakening, as the German poet Christian Morgenstern guessed.[9] But if the subject does not believe in this, and will never believe, interaction is not impossible but will never be as effective as the subject who invoked it regularly. As that anonymous esoteric author[10] remarked, there is no worse tragedy in heaven than a guardian Angel deprived of "work," in other words an Angel laid off:

> *But —and this is the tragic aspect of Angelic existence—that brilliance* [of the Angel] *bursts forth only when man has need of it, when he inspires its lights to burn brightly once more. The Angel depends on man in its creative activity. It may then fall into a state of consciousness where all its creative genius remains potential and does not show at all. This is the state in which it vegetates, in which it muddles along, a state comparable to sleep among humans. An Angel who exists for no reason is a tragedy in the spiritual world.*

And who would have dreamed that this anonymous author's remarks would be echoed on May 12, 1992, on the first page of the *Wall Street Journal*, the New York financial newspaper, the most influential financial newspaper in the Western world!

8. Robert Monroe, *Far Journeys.*
9. See his poem that opens this volume.
10. *Méditations sur les 22 arcanes majeurs du tarot*, Paris, Aubier, 1980, p. 454.

LONG UNEMPOYED ANGELS NOW HAVE WORK

Journalist Gustav Niebuhr explained in his article that after three hundred years of neglect and even more of skepticism, Angels were making a comeback. The case of the "unemployed" Angel was well illustrated by young John Lilly's experience at the point of death:

> John: "Will you stay with me or are you going away?"
> Angel: "I will be with you always as long as you believe you will be able to meet with me."[11]

Or even more when the dog bit him to keep him from falling:

> John: "Will you always take care of me?"
> Angel: "Yes, as long as you believe in me. Will you always believe in me?"

A belief in Angels does seem to be the key to interaction between our visible material domain and his domain, invisible but just as material as ours, since it exists. We note again the importance of faith in the Angel, in the *Dialogues* of Budapest from Friday, November 26, 1943, when Lili asks him if everyone has a guide, an instructor Angel or a guardian Angel.

The answer was unequivocal:

> No.
> We consist of faith, purely of faith. TO THOSE WHO
> HAVE FAITH, WHO BELIEVE
>     WE ARE
>     AND FAITH IS THE FORCE OF THE DIVINE.
>     IF YOU BELIEVE THAT I HAVE A VOICE . . .
>     I CAN SPEAK.
>     IF YOU DO NOT BELIEVE IT . . . I AM MUTE.
>     IF YOU BELIEVE THAT I AM YOU . . . I BECOME
> YOU.(. . .)
>     BUT THROUGH YOUR BELIEF, WE DESCEND,
>     FOR BELIEF IS THE BRIDGE.[12]

---

11. *The Scientist*, p. 39.
12. *Talking with Angels*, Friday, November 26, 1943, p. 161.

This does not mean that some people don't have a guardian Angel, but just that the Angel cannot really intervene except through the faith of his protégé—by extension, faith in the Angel. And in the worst case, the "unemployed" Angel can only watch with folded arms as his protégé's life unfolds, as the director Wim Wenders has shown in his film *Wings of Desire*: a young man without hope (unemployed?) decides to commit suicide by throwing himself from a bridge. The Angel, played by the actor Bruno Ganz, tries to talk to him but the man does not "hear" him, in the intuitive sense.

On the other hand, if belief in the Angel does not stop growing, his power does not stop increasing, bringing on what Carl Jung called synchronicity—signs, coincidences, and strokes of luck making sense only to one person. Again, the best illumination has been supplied by the remarkable anonymous author of the Aubier edition:

> A guardian Angel defends his protégé as a mother defends her baby, whether he is good or bad. This is the mystery of maternal love that lives in the heart of a guardian Angel. All Angels are not guardian Angels; some have other missions. But the guardian Angels as such are the mothers of their protégés. Also, traditional art portrays them as winged women. And that is why the fourteenth mystery of the Tarot is clearly shown as a woman with wings, wearing a dress half blue, half red. That is why the Holy Virgin and Mother of God bears the liturgical title of "Queen of Angels." It is maternal love that she has in common with the guardian Angels, love which, outshining theirs, makes her their mother.[13]

In the same vein the Italian theologian Giovanni Sienna remarks quite poetically that an Angel loves his protégé unselfishly, and that his solicitude is inspired only by love:

> The guardian Angel loves us as a celestial creature can who burns with divine charity and who, in a closer image of God, is nearer to Him in his primary essence: Love. He loves us with a pure, unselfish love. His partiality to man rests on no ambition except to see us always happy with him and like him. . . . Moreover, being at the highest step

13. *Méditations sur les 22 arcanes majeurs du tarot*, p. 452.

*on the angelic scale, the guardian Angel lives in a close relationship with man and, as more than one doctor of the church affirms, bears a certain resemblance to him. Between man and his guardian Angel there is an affinity that binds them together and favors their relationship. . . . Would this be a soul mate? It would seem so. In any case, it is certain that the caring, solicitude, love of that celestial being surpass those of the sweetest and gentlest of mothers."[14]*

And yet we should allow him to explain himself, that celestial being. But how to go about it? There are not many ways to invite him closer to us. In talking to him, and praying to him, we are not really praying to the Angel but to God, even if the Angel intercedes for us far better than we might ourselves. As we have already seen, the simple act of believing in a guardian Angel puts you automatically in contact with divine reality. The Angel will take up the work of directing you, since you ask him to. But, and it is here that free will comes into play, if we ask for nothing, he will do nothing. The German mystic Theresa Neumann, during one of her numerous ecstasies, left us hopeful advice:

*The earth produces enough for the nourishment of all men. But, as they sigh only for worldly goods here below, the result is the oppression of some by the others; and thus they invite the scourge of extreme misery. And yet, as vast as that misery is, it is always in the power of the Father to remedy it, because he is All-powerful. He has created the world and sustains the Earth and the stars. Why could He not help man? Nevertheless, God desires men to love him and call upon his name, if they truly wish to be helped. Men do not sufficiently meditate on God's power, and they rely too much on their own strength."[15]*

We may be permitted to think that if God himself wants to be loved (like all of us), how much more must our Angel want contact with his protégé. . . .

And as we shall discover in the next chapter, the Angels mani-

---

14. *Padre Pio: voice l'heure des Anges (Father Pio: the Time of the Angels),* Editions Arcangelo, San Giovanni Rotondo, 1977, pp. 96–97.

15. Pascal Sanchez-Ventura, *Stigmatisés and apparitions (Stigmatics and Manifestations),* Nouvelles Editions Latines, Paris, 1967, pp. 124–125.

fest themselves to those who pray like Stakhanovites, otherwise called saints, as they do in near-death experiences. But be careful: those we shall discover in this chapter are truly predestined, and their greatest glory is precisely that they accepted the life that awaited them, a life that had nothing in common with our own quite comfortable lives.

# CHAPTER 7

# Mystics and Angels

AFTER TRACKING ANGELS THROUGH THE TUNNELS OF NEAR-DEATH experience, I was forced to acknowledge that the Divine Light the survivors spoke of was more than similar to the descriptions of mystics. Before, the religious texts had seemed to me like stories by old bearded men and old Holy Joes; but in the light of NDE, they took on an entirely different aspect. A little as if, with the NDE, I had found the key or the code to decipher a difficult article. At the newspaper they often criticized my pieces on computer science as incomprehensible, and I retorted that it was the same with financial articles. Whoever doesn't know what the Dow Jones is, or the CAC or the Nikkei index, cannot understand a stock market analysis on first reading. It requires a little explanation. The same for these texts. But in the glow of NDE the Light Saint John spoke of, and Saul on the road to Damascus, suddenly became clear. In fact I discovered that the Gospels often seem to touch on NDE. The resurrection? It is at the end of the tunnel. Hell? Those who relive their lives in three dimensions and who, after having tortured and killed, experience in a space WITHOUT TIME all that they have made their victims suffer.

The combination of NDE and Angels was to lead me directly into an even more fascinating area, that of the saints. According to the NDE, no one dies; but simply changes his reality. That means also that John of the Cross, Gemma Galgani, Thérèse de Lisieux and all the others are as alive as you and I. So I discovered the world of mystics like a child discovers Disneyland for the first time. For them, the "marvelous Light inexpressible in human terms" at the end of the tunnel is like a coupe of Dom Perignon before a gala dinner, because the fusions with the Light, the visions of Angels, the ecstasies, the beatitudes, the dialogues with the Light (which

Kenneth Ring immediately diagnosed as NDE of the fifth stage), the out of body trips, the seraphim and the visits to other realities, all constitute experiences I would dare to call trite among the saints. With the NDE we find ourselves at the gates of a reality that is out of our depth; with the mystics, we jump in with both feet!!!

Take the case of the German Carmelite Marie-Anne Lindmayr who explained how her soul left her body to visit other dimensions. She had never heard of NDE nor of Robert Monroe nor of John Lilly's "isolation tank," since all this happened in 1705 in Munich:

> *In the beginning, when I still had no experience of these three kinds of ecstasies, I prepared myself for death. In the course of these ecstasies, I received assurances (and the experience taught me) that the spirit or the soul went completely out of the body and left it entirely. This ecstasy always produced, as one consequence, such a force that it is impossible to describe. . . . But it is the body that is most sharply surprised when the soul reenters. Often for three whole days I could not get warm; my limbs were as swollen and useless as those of a dead body. . . . I prayed God to allow me to see the ecstasy occur with all my faculties still in play, as many of the dying remain fully conscious until the last moment. That boon was granted me by the intercession of Saint Teresa [of Avila]. I experienced the beginning, the climactic moment, and the end of that ecstasy in the following manner. I was seized by a great weakness. It was not the result of a natural weakness, but because God wanted to show me wonders. This weakness was accompanied and followed by an inexpressibly intense cold which, starting in the lower part of my body, spread slowly throughout my body, so that it became completely numb. . . . Before my soul left my body I felt that I was still there, but outwardly I was as if dead, absolutely insensible and cold as ice, feeling an icy breath upon me. In an instant, reason and spirit disappeared, and at the same instant I was led where the Lord wanted me to be. . . .*[1]

I plunged immediately into the accounts of the lives of the saints, in search of testimony about Angels. After all the accounts by survivors of near death, I had formed the intimate conviction

---

1. Marie-Anne Lindmayr, *Mes relations avec les âmes du purgatoire (My Contact with Souls in Purgatory)*, Christiana, pp. 17–18.

that guardian Angels were more than a product of the imagination, and that saints more than any other socio-cultural group must have left detailed descriptions of their angelic visions. If a little while ago anyone had told me that one day, sunk deep in a seat on a 747, I would be devouring the complete works of Marie d'Agreda, I would have burst into laughter. I could never have imagined that mere curiosity, transformed into an obsession, would have led me to such pious reading matter! And I was quite frankly taken aback to see how omnipresent these personalities are in our lives, without realizing it fully. They are everywhere: we bear their names, we observe their days, we cross their streets, we live on their avenues, in their plazas, on their mountains, in their villages and cities and even their megalopolises. Around the world are millions of people who live in cities bearing the name of a saint and sometimes of an Angel. It is so obvious that we don't even notice it, something like a Coca-Cola sign. Before setting to work on this book, I saw the saints, as a majority of people do, as almost mythical beings; perfect, chaste, and gentle as lambs (not to say altogether idiotic), who were canonized over the centuries for various reasons by popes just as visionary, gentle, chaste, etc.

After a plunge into the specialized literature, I had to admit that the saints had not been saints all their lives; some of them had even married and been parents, and others had not lived up to saintly standards by a long way. That was comforting. Then I discovered that as a general rule those close to a "saint" had no suspicion that he was about to become one. He was an unknown among unknowns. What struck me most forcefully during this research was the popes' reactions; they were just as distrustful as you and I of these saints and the supernatural air that sometimes surrounded them. In their lifetimes—with a few rare exceptions like Teresa of Avila, Catherine of Siena or Padre Pio—they attracted no attention at all, as they were often relegated to utter anonymity and assigned thankless tasks, like Catherine Laboure, Charbel Makhlouf, and Juan Capistrano.

So very few suspected that these servants of God were headed for canonization. Most amusing: I learned that when the documentation was being prepared, the Vatican used to request the deceased saint *prove his survival* by working some miracles, and this as a condition for continuing his case. Indeed, the Vatican, even more rigid in its beliefs than the rank and file, is reluctant to authenticate a miracle or a saint; if either proved unreliable it would discredit the whole Church. Consequently Rome found only one way to distinguish a true saint from a false: to demand that he manifest himself through miracles. So a candidate for sainthood has every reason to provide himself with a defense if he or she wants to sit enthroned in chapels one day. Here are some of the supernatural signs that matter during the process of beatification and canonization:

- The incorruptibility of the cadaver

- Flows of fluid from the mortal remains

- Supernatural manifestations of light

- Inexplicable medical healings of all kinds

- Fragrances of unknown origin

- Appearances before the faithful

- The stigmata, which, like the incorruptible flesh, are helpful in establishing the file but do not guarantee a positive outcome

Among these signs, the most spectacular—and utterly unexplained—is the incorruptibility of the flesh. In this very specific matter, it is not the owner of the body offering a sign, but God Himself: not only does the corpse remain perfectly preserved, but it also gives off an odor, in flat contradiction to "normal" cadavers. When we exhume a coffin two years, or twenty, or two hundred after the burial, we have a legitimate right to expect a skeleton— surely dusty but perfectly fleshless. Yet with the remains of certain men and women the laws of nature seem suspended: gravediggers will discover a body in good condition; supple, soft, clean, fragrant, as though it had just been buried. Cases utterly incredible yet attested, measured, weighed, examined are in good supply even nowadays. But no one talks about them.

Among the textbook cases, the remains of Charbel Makhlouf (1828–1898) are exemplary. This young man, born to poor Lebanese Maronites, left the family home one fine day in his twenty-third year, and retired to a monastery. After being ordained a priest, Makhlouf fell ill during a Mass, and decided after that incident to live as a hermit in his cell until his death. Eight years later he died, and his companions laid him in his grave directly, letting his monk's robe serve as shroud. There was nothing unusual about that, for all the monks of that order who had preceded him were laid to rest in the same Spartan manner. And like the memories of those others, the memory of the monk Makhlouf would have joined the cohort of nameless dead if a mysterious white light had not surrounded his tomb for forty-five consecutive nights after his burial. Four months after the burial, and solely because of that light, the superior of the monastery, with the agreement of the ecclesiastical authorities, decided to exhume the body in order to lay it in a more prominent grave, considering the "supernatural" events.

Upon exhumation before numerous witnesses, the body proved to be in perfect condition, showing no signs of decay and giving off no nauseous odor. Neighboring graves were opened to compare the remains, but nature had taken its course with the other bodies. To understand this kind of mystery (miracle), go to your neighborhood butcher shop, buy a freshly killed rabbit or chicken, bury it or place it in a hermetically sealed container. Leave it in your cellar for three or four months, and open it on some morning of your choice to observe the result. Even after only a few days, the animal's corpse will demand your attention. . . .

Another example, even more striking, is that of Bernadette Soubirous, who as a teenage girl saw the Virgin appear in a grotto at Lourdes eighteen times. You may decline to believe in these visions, as well as the miracles regularly attested to at Lourdes, but the incorruptibility of her cadaver is nevertheless quite real and tends to validate her Marian visions. But the life of Bernadette Soubirous is far from extraordinary beside those of the Curé d'Ars or Catherine of Siena or Teresa of Avila. At the age of twenty-two, the object of hysterical acts of devotion and attacked on all sides, Bernadette chose to retire to the Little Sisters of Nevers. She died at thirty-five and was buried behind her convent, after thirteen sickly years. In short, the very opposite of a Catholic star's life, like the life of the Curé d'Ars or Padre Pio, even if today's magazines would have bought photos of her and today's editors would have bought the rights to her memoirs.

But, according to the Most High she lived like a saint, and in 1909, thirty years after her death, her cadaver was exhumed in the presence of all constituent bodies, who discovered, stunned, that her face had remained intact. After washing and dressing her again in a clean habit, it was decided to replace her body in its tomb, and during a second exhumation ten years later, on April 3, 1919, her corpse, still impeccable, was placed in a shrine, after which her face was covered with a light waxen mask.

No forensic surgeon can find a way to explain the phenomenon of the body's incorruptibility, as the American Joan Carroll Cruz notes after five years of research:[2]

> It is regrettable however, that, with the exception of the physicians and men in science who examined individual remains of saints, the writer could find no one who, to any depth or degree, had made a study of any sort concerning this subject. We must rely, then, on the opinions of those physicians who, after careful examination of the saints' bodies in question, variously declared them to be unaccountably, mysteriously, or miraculously preserved.
>
> How else can the existence of these relics be explained when it is considered that many of these saints died of diseases and infirmities that so vigorously assaulted their bodies as to extinguish life? How else can we explain their existence when they were not embalmed and when their internal parts contained all manner of corruptible materials? How could some have resisted extreme dampness, which encourages dissolution, or burial without benefit of a coffin? How could they resist the countless bacteria which are attracted not only to living bodies but, especially, to those that are devoid of living forces to challenge them? If living flesh is so delicate and prone to infirmities, how can these bodies, which are unable to heal or restore themselves, endure throughout the centuries exposure to various climates, fluctuating levels of humidity and temperature, frequent reclothings, the taking of relics, and countless probings during periodic examinations? That some bodies which are now somewhat discolored exist at all, in spite of these factors, is no less a marvel. But what of those that are perfectly preserved!

Indeed, how do these bodies manage to stay in perfect condition, defying all the laws of nature? Helene Renard, a French reporter and author of several books, also goes into this matter in *Des prodiges et des hommes,*[3] and she came up against the same will in questioning Michele Rudler, professor of forensic medicine at the University of Paris Sorbonne: *"Red blood cells die as soon as they are deprived of oxygen. As for odor . . . bacteria, breaking down*

2. *The Incorruptibles*, Rockford, Illinois, Tan Books, 1977, p. 301.
3. Editions Philippe Lebaud, p. 212.

*proteins, free sulfuric gases, hydrogen or ammonium sulfide, methane, etc., and release a terrible stench. Then the putrefaction phase begins with a green stain at the abdomen, near the right iliac fossa, not far from the appendix, and a bloating of the large intestine, which is a very bacterial zone. The stain forms after forty-eight hours, and the putrefaction spreads throughout the abdomen."*

In short, if forensic specialists are perfectly capable of examining a corpse and determining more or less precisely the date, time, and causes of death, and the menu of its last restaurant, they still cannot explain the cases in which the body remains intact after three days. And even if the "fresh" red cells are placed in a freezer immediately, in the end they explode. Back to square "divine."

Of the 103 cases of "incorruptible" bodies listed by Joan Carroll Cruz, the ratio is fifty-nine men to forty-four women; her book ends with Maria Assunta Pallotta, dead in 1905, which might make us think that the phenomenon itself died at that time. Such is not the case. The French historian, Joachim Boufflet, in his astronomical and altogether exceptional book *Encyclopedie des Phénomènes extraordinaire de la vie mystique*[4] drew several more cases, not without interest, from the Vatican archives. Like Leonie Van Den Dyck, died 1949 and exhumed in June 1972, or Joachim-Marie Stevan, died 1949 and exhumed in the summer of 1951! In 1965, again in Italy, at Turin, twenty-five years after the death of Father Louis Orione his grave was opened in the presence of physicians and surgeons: his remains showed no sign of decay, and the complete file assembled by the medical corps can be examined at the Vatican.

In the light of these mysteries, we may wonder why ecclesiastical authorities do not proceed systematically to exhumations. To that the Vatican simply answers that it is impossible to open all the tombs of priests, monks and nuns dead since 1900 to determine their corporeal envelope, which may testify to their sanctity. That may explain why these "incorruptibles" are discovered only during transfers and shifts brought about either by material considerations (lack of space, floods) or by supernatural phenomena (lights, miracles, etc.). Otherwise only the proceedings of beatification require exhumation, with an autopsy in order.

But even an incorruptible body is not sufficient evidence for Rome to beatify or canonize a soul.

What's this got to do with guardian Angels? The perfect preservation of the bodies of men and women, for the most part anonymous in their own time, proves their existence (for those

---

4. Paris, Editions Oeil, 1992.

who affirm that the saints, like Christ, never existed), and above all
ratifies their writings, thus establishing for them a supplementary
and indisputable supernatural (divine?) dimension. Then, considering the number of supernatural signs, it is consequently out of
the question that in their lifetime these saints could mystify, exag-
gerate, or lie. So we may suppose that all these servants of God,
stating that they saw their guardian Angels or Archangels, were not
making up fantastic stories. But rest easy: that gift is no more
common among saints than among ordinary people. Among the
saints, those who had this privilege are fairly rare.

After an inventory of these angelic visions, we may classify
them in four different groups, according to the importance of the
supernatural signs that validated the person.

Group I:
• Stigmatic while alive.
• Miracles.
• Visions of Angels.
• Incorruptibility of the remains.

Group IIa:
• Stigmatic while alive.
• Miracles.
• Visions of Angels.

Group IIb:
• Miracles.
• Visions of Angels.
• Incorruptibility of the remains.

Group III:
• Visionaries.
• Miracles.
• Visions of Angels.

These men and women seem to have lived in another world. To
our eyes, their behavior is totally incomprehensible and confusing.
What are we to think of those women who, reliving the Passion,
regularly asked Christ to bring them more suffering, more pain,
and other tortures? This is altogether disconcerting. And all of
them, as if answering with one voice down the centuries, declare
that they want to alleviate His sufferings.

Are they really human, all these mystics who have briefly passed through earthly life, as if in relief of one another, as if passing along a torch of thorns? In their lifetimes considered by modern medicine[5] hysterics (Gemma Galgani, Marthe Robin), by the Vatican tricksters (Padre Pio), or simply unknown (Teresa Musco), the memories of these men and women have nevertheless come down through history by supernatural grace. But we must remember that every year tens of thousands of priests are ordained in this world, and still more men and women don religious garb, without being "marked" by the Most High, not before, not during, not after.

5. Which is absolutely incapable of explaining the psychic and physiological phenomenon of the stigmata.

# CHAPTER 8

# Super-Saints and Angels

L ET'S PLAY DEVIL'S ADVOCATE (DON'T FORGET THAT ACCORDING TO Scripture the Devil is none other than the most handsome Angel) and admit that nothing is more natural for a Cartesian mind than to doubt a person who says he has seen and spoken with an Angel. The Cartesian will say one of the following:

*"You've had a drop too much."*

*"You've been smoking a joint."*

*"You've overdone the Valium."*

or more flatly:

*"You're stark raving mad,"* which puts an end to any further discussion.

But then think of a young woman who, in addition to her angelic visions, contemplates Christ, works miracles, levitates, and relives the Passion every Friday, enduring the consequences in her own flesh through stigmata. And, as if these proofs were not enough, after her death her body is not decomposed by worms, nor by bacteria, nor by moisture and even less by time, all the while emitting a delicate fragrance of French perfume while the bodies in neighboring tombs were cleansed perfectly by nature, as if putrefaction were reserved for the plebeian herd. It is unnecessary to emphasize that those who have accumulated so many supernatural signs (all of them!) are very rare. Four cases meet our criteria:

Anne-Catherine Emmerich

Maria-Magdalena dei Pazzi

Teresa of Avila

Catherine of Siena

181

Four women, brides of Christ by an invisible marriage, who were filled with divine grace. Yet their lives seem to us to have been a veritable hell. And those graces that accompanied them throughout their lives permit us to believe that the *Dialogues* of Catherine of Siena with her "husband" are perfectly authentic and indisputable, and so are the ecstasies of Teresa d'Avila and the passions of Anne-Catherine Emmerich and Maria-Magdalena dei Pazzi. All lived with a Christ who sent them into invisible transports; a characteristic that remains a common factor, whether during Marian visions or divine betrothals, to the point that Maria-Magdalena dei Pazzi, who received dresses and jewels from Christ, walked about totally nude in her cloister, clothed in these invisible gifts.

A journey to the mystics, in company with the women of God and His Angels:

## ANNE-CATHERINE EMMERICH
### 1774–1824
#### (Group I: Stigmata, Miracles, Angels, Incorruptibility)
#### Germany

The Augustinian nun Anne-Catherine Emmerich (1774–1824) is known around the world. In the publishing field, her visions are regularly reprinted in different versions; as for example *The Passion* told by Sister Anne-Catherine or *The Life of Mary* according to the visions of Fräulein Emmerich. In that category, incontestably, she wins out over the other "chosen," including Teresa of Avila, which is no small thing. In her lifetime she was so captivating by her fragility and her material poverty, which contrasted so sharply with her life in the "other" reality, that a priest, Karl Schmöger, dedicated ten years of his life to writing her biography, a hefty tome of one thousand two hundred pages. The life of Anne-Catherine Emmerich is a jump into the supernatural where the Angels are the flight attendants during regular trips toward the Light. This poor girl's visions are astonishing, yet she was treated like the "Elephant Man" by Prussian doctors, by French doctors after the rise of Napoleon, and again by the Prussians after his defeat.

Born in Flamske in Westphalia on September 9, 1774, Anne-Catherine get her first visions at the age of nine; of her guardian Angel to start with, and later of Christ and Mary. After such promising beginnings she could only retire to a convent, which she did in 1802. In 1811, when the Prussian government decided to suppress religious institutions, the young girl found herself in the street and was taken in by a French priest, Father Lambert. She was thirty-eight years old. A year later the stigmata appeared on her body. Each Friday, Anne-Catherine relived and above all saw the Passion of Christ as if she were at his side with a camcorder in her hand. Like the stigmatic Frenchwoman Marthe Robin, she never ate, nourishing herself exclusively on communion hosts. That was the era when the wildest rumors about the virgin began to circulate in the general population.

The visions of Anne-Catherine, to which Paul Claudel owed his conversion to Catholicism, were very much like journalists' reports, a kind of live chronicle of the past. Those who came in contact with her never got over it: Anne-Catherine read their thoughts, levitated regularly, and was carried by her guardian Angel thousands of kilometers from her natal village, which enabled her to announce news well before it arrived in that out-of-the-way corner. Her confessor never got over one of her visions, describing the pope crowning a short man with a greenish face. Four years later the people learned that Napoleon Bonaparte had been raised to the rank of emperor by the sovereign pontiff. Years later, unable to break into the stigmatic's house, six French hussars went through her window and landed at the foot of the young woman's bed. Frightened by the light encircling her face, the soldiers, dumbfounded, were not sure what to do. Some fell to their knees asking forgiveness while others stared wildly at her, as if refusing to interpret the information conveyed by their eyes. And all of them left quietly through the doorway, like young boys caught stealing jam. With so many divine graces, Anne-Catherine Emmerich was accused of fraud and a preliminary inquiry was requested by members of the local clergy. The priests discovered no cheating and, prudent after all, wrote a circumspect report suggesting an independent civil inquiry. On August 7, 1819, a new commission, composed of the prefect, a State health officer, Doctor Zumbrink, chemists, scientific and civilian witnesses, all atheists or freemasons, attacked the young girl. *"On August 7,"* recounted Johannes Maria Hocht, *"the sick young woman was brutally dragged from her bed and, with the help of an unknown nurse, placed on a stretcher; this was taken in charge by four police officers, surrounded by a platoon of guards commanded by a lieutenant. Hundreds of neighbors, present at this spectacle, showed their distress by their tears. The sister was taken to an unknown house, where she was set down in the middle of a large room, where they could observe her from all angles.'*[1] The commission examined the young woman's body unceremoniously for several days: her hands were bandaged and sealed to be sure the wounds were not self-inflicted. "Stalinist" interrogations, the obligatory search of her cell for instruments or chemical products capable of helping her wound herself, cross-interrogations, etc.

Wasted effort.

The previous interrogation team, aware of results that were more than embarrassing, decided to install her in another house, hoping that the stigmata would disappear as a result of the move. That altered nothing, and the results of the various "examinations," some of them quite intimate, put the civil commission in a delicate position. Honest reports established *"the certain absence of fraud,"* while dishonest men, unable to explain her stigmata, accused her of *"lying,"* finding nothing else to fault her for. The German doctor Bahrens summed up their observations as follows, observations that had never convinced them that stigmata were involved, but rather *"animal magnetism!"*

> *The double cross on her chest bleeds regularly every Wednesday, the other gashes on Friday, the headband on her forehead even more during the week. The cross and the wound in the side appear on an area of skin without blemish otherwise, and the blood seeps out exactly like sweat through the pores. From Good Friday to Easter Sunday the blood flows freely and the stigmata cause her intense suffering. The wounds bandaged by force for seven days and seven nights remain in the same condition, getting no better or worse, and not suppurating. Same comment after 24 hours of plaster cast. . . . Almost every day she experiences ecstasies during which she lies as rigid as a log, her eyes shut fast, apparently dead. Her face remains the same color, and she displays an incomprehensible sensitivity to a priest's blessing or the presence of holy objects. Sometimes she shows a surprising knowledge of the future as far as she herself or her nearest and dearest are concerned. She seems to read the human heart. And last of all I ought to mention that the patient was observed continuously, night and day, for ten consecutive days, by trustworthy people, with the permission of the ecclesiastical authorities. These observers unanimously attested that nothing was done to*

1. Cited in *Stigmatics and Apparitions.*

*the wounds, that the patient imbibed nothing but water,*
*and that there was no bodily evacuation of any kind. That*
*last circumstance has been observed for the past four*
*months. . . . In the realm of medical and physical experi-*
*ence, the phenomena observed on the body of the young*
*nun, Miss Emmerich, are of so exceptional a character that*
*no known law of nature could explain them plausibly.*[2]

In short, nobody understood much about the case of this poor
girl, other than than the possibility that it was "animal magnetism"
that enabled her, nobody knew how, to bleed every Friday.

Now that we have established the setting in which Anne-Catherine's career unfolded, and seen how she was supervised by the
authorities, let us be more intimate and listen to what she has to
say to us about Angels. It is purely astounding. For example, her
own Angel was permanently visible to her, or almost so: *"The splendor emanating from her guardian Angel,"* the Abbé Schmöger tells
us, was unequalled except by his expression, *"a ray of light."* Anne-
Catherine said that the Angel called to her, and she followed him
from one place to another:

> *His head is uncovered, and his robe long and dazzlingly*
> *white like that of a priest. I address him freely, but I can*
> *never look him full in the face. I incline before him. He*
> *gives me all kinds of signs. I never ask him many ques-*
> *tions; the satisfaction I take in being near him prevents me.*
> *He is always very brief in his words. I see him also in my*
> *waking moments.*[3] *. . . One winter evening in a heavy storm*
> *of snow and rain I returned home over the fields to*
> *Flamske. I was frightened, and I began to cry to God. Sud-*
> *denly I saw a light like a flame on before me. It took the*
> *form of my guide in his robe. The ground under my feet*
> *became dry, it cleared overhead, neither rain nor snow fell*
> *upon me, and I reached home not even wet.*[4]

Anne-Catherine never spoke of wings, and in that sense what

2. Aimé Michel, *Metanoïa* , Paris, Editions Albin Michel, 1986, pp. 156–157.
3. We cannot help referring back to case no. 4 in Chapter 2 "Of Angels in the Tunnels." A journey at the speed of thought is a common factor in all NDE, and this
   statement by Anne-Catherine once more confirms that altogether amazing ability
   of the soul once out of body.
4. Carl Schmöger, *Life of Anne-Catherine Emmerich*, vol. 1, Tan Books, 1976, p. 72.

she tells us confirms perfectly and in all points the testimonies at death's door, the more so as she says, *"When my soul left my body . . ."* Here is the vision she leaves us of the Angels who appear mysteriously all along the road of Christ's calvary:

> *No human tongue can express the dread that filled our Savior's soul at the sight of these terrible expiations; for he saw not only the vast extent of the torments he was to undergo, but also the instruments of torture, the diabolical fury of those who had invented them, the cruelty of the executioners, and the anguish of all the victims, innocent or guilty. The horror of that vision was such that his whole body was covered with sweat: it was like drops of blood falling to the ground. While the Son of Man was thus plunged into sadness and despondency, I saw the Angels seized by compassion. It seemed to me that they desired ardently to console him, and that they were praying for him before the throne of God. . . . At the end of the visions of the Passion, Jesus fell on his face like a dying man. The Angels disappeared, the tableaux vanished; the bloody sweat flowed more abundantly, and I saw it run down his garments. A deep darkness lay upon the grotto. And then I saw an Angel descend beside Jesus. It was larger, more distinct and more like a man than those who had appeared in the preceding vision. It was garbed like a priest in a long flowing robe, and bore in its hands a little vase in the shape of a chalice. When this vase was opened, I saw an oval body about the size of a broadbean, radiating a reddish light. The Angel, still gliding, extended its right hand toward Jesus, and, when the Savior rose, set the shining body in his mouth, had him drink from the luminous chalice, and then disappeared.*[5]

In 1824 Anne-Catherine died at the age of fifty, imitating Christ; her last words, *"Let me die ignominiously with Jesus on the cross,"* testify to her detachment and indifference to all the doctors, curiosity-seekers, priests, and soldiers who thronged at her bedside to examine her like a farm animal at a fair, who was ravaged by the Passion every Friday. Six months after her burial, she was disinterred to make sure that no one had been inspired to "steal" a few "relics." Her body was still in perfect condition, supple and without

5. *Visions d'Anne-Catherine Emmerich,* Paris, Editions Téqui, quoted by Vincent Klee.

odor, with no trace of decomposition. Just the same, unlike Teresa of Avila and Catherine of Siena, Anne-Catherine Emmerich has not been canonized, for her visions were set down by the German poet Clemens Brentano, who is suspected of having added his own commentary to the young woman's visions.

Which proves that in the face of the slightest doubt, and despite authentic stigmata, the Vatican's finicky administration will not hesitate for a moment to cut short the process of beatification. Which means nothing to the faithful: the memory of Anne-Catherine Emmerich has more than survived Rome's neglect, and her *Visions* like Catherine of Siena's *Dialogues*, continue to shower blessings on publishers and convert many souls. And in the end, she may be beatified on a September 9, in the next few years.

## MARIA-MAGDALENA DEI PAZZI
## 1566–1607
### (Group I: Stigmata, Miracles, Angels, Incorruptibility)
### Italy

Her body is still there, perfectly preserved and in plain sight in the Church of the Carmelites in Florence, continuing to defy the laws of nature and to give off an agreeable odor of sanctity more than four hundred years after her death. Born in 1566, Catherine dei Pazzi was the daughter of one of the most prominent noble families of Florence (with the Medici), and was destined for a fruitful marriage of convenience. But at the age of ten Catherine decided that she would become a nun. And when her parents, having tried several times to marry her off, realized that there was no other solution, they yielded to her wishes and allowed her, at sixteen, to join the Carmelites of Our Lady of the Angels in Florence. Catherine changed her name to Maria-Magdalena and went on to distinguish her convent and her century by her frequent levitations,[6] her stigmata, her visions of Christ, her ecstasies, her miracles and, after her death in 1607, her incorruptible body.

During some of her transports, Catherine received teachings from Christ and from . . . Catherine of Siena, her model. Jean-Noel Vuarnet[7] finds her less interesting than the "grand" Catherine: *"The dialogues she held with Christ (Colloques d'Amour) during her ecstasies are often very tender. Jesus calls her 'My little girl . . . my*

6. Like Teresa of Avila and Joseph of Copertino, the "flying" monk.
7. *Extases feminines*, Editions Hatier.

*beloved . . . my dove . . . my little wife,' etc., and over the course of years offers her a certain number of garments and mystical jewels. Clothed in these gifts, she walks naked in the cloister. Jesus also allows Catherine to 'read his heart like an open book,' and, on a certain June 29, he made her aware of the pains of the Passion. Other times it was in the form of a vine that he appeared to her or sometimes as a fire that raged within her breast to the point where she had to roll in the snow to avoid being consumed by it."*

Catherine dei Pazzi spent her first five years of reclusion without any "miracle," and only in 1590 did she experience her first ecstasy. The content of her dialogues and visions was set down by the sisters of the convent and published well after her death, May 25, 1607. But, like the Cure d'Ars and Padre Pio later on, the Carmelite could read minds, cure the sick, and above all discern true postulants.[8] In her "Very Profound Contemplations on Divine Perfections," she has left us details on the nature of the love between man and Angel:

> *This love is far from equaling that of God. The Angels love human beings with an intense love, an expanding love, a love of truth and of regeneration. Intense love, which has its source in the heart of the Word, because they see in the Word the dignity of humanity, and the love it bears them; that love of the Angels is, so to speak, the superabundance of the love of the Word that they gather up and then communicate to the human in the most noble part of his being, that is to say the heart. Oh! If the human being only recognized that intense love of the Angels! . . . That love makes the soul wise and prudent: wise in the works that it does with firm intent for the greater glory of God; and prudent in guarding the virtues that produce all those loves which, united, make a precious ring for the bride's betrothal; the seraphim who have passed them along descend from heaven, take them with two of their wings, embellish them with two others, and carry them with the last two into the presence of the Groom. At that point, all the angelic choirs rise up, also wishing to do something for the bride; but not knowing what to do, they break out in her praise with all their heart, crying: "This one is worthy of receiving a new name," and, prostrating themselves—because in the bride, they honor the Groom—they render homage to her.*

8. This is a crucial problem for every convent superior.

Catherine/Maria-Magdalena dei Pazzi received the stigmata at the age of nineteen, and, desiring to deepen her sufferings even further, sometimes rolled in thorns, and among other things flogged herself several times a day with the "discipline": *"It was not enough that her body was tortured,"* Aimé Michel tells us in his *Metanoïa*, *"she wanted to be further humiliated and sickened. They saw her with a rope around her neck, eating on the ground like an animal, crawling on the paving stones of the refectory while the other nuns ate so she could kiss their feet under the table. She wanted to be flogged by the prioress before the other nuns, or even trampled by them. She tried to nurse the sick, especially when the care was tedious and difficult. They saw her licking the wounds of a sister suffering from a repulsive skin disease, a leg ulcer swimming with worms, and, in another case, of a leper."*

There were no limits to her excesses in all that might mortify her sensibilities. And the more excessive she became, the more she experienced ecstasies incomprehensible to the rest of the convent. At forty-two, Catherine dei Pazzi returned finally to the embrace of the Almighty, during sufferings of an atrocity we can only imagine, thin as a rail, toothless, her body covered with scabs, forbidding the sisters to ease her pain, even in her last moments.

She was buried in the church. The Carmelites noticed immediately that a pleasant odor rose from her tomb. One year after her death, in 1608, the convent obtained authorization to recover her relics (the sisters did not know that her body was incorruptible) and were surprised to discover, when the coffin was opened, a body in "perfect health," despite the humidity of the tomb which saturated the Carmelite's clothing. Later, the body was examined in 1612, in 1625 and in 1663, for purposes of beatification. Another phenomenon, a sort of oil oozing from her knees, lasted eight years. The remains were never embalmed.

## Teresa Of Avila
## 1515–1582
### (Group I: Stigmata, Miracles, Angels, Incorruptibility)
### Spain

The best known and surely most mysterious encounter of a human being with an Angel remains that of Teresa of Avila, one of the mystical brides of Christ. The meeting of the Angel and the Carmelite reformer and first female doctor of the Church (born March 28, 1515 and died October 4, 1582) has been immortalized by the sculpture of Bernini (1598–1680), called *The Ecstasy of Saint Teresa,* an angelic ecstasy narrated by the Carmelite:

> *The Lord wanted me while in this state to see some-times the following vision: I saw close to me toward my left side an angel in bodily form. I don't usually see angels in bodily form except on rare occasions; although many times angels appear to me, but without my seeing them, as in the intellectual vision I spoke about before. This time, though, the Lord desired that I see the vision in the following way: the angel was not large but small; he was very beautiful, and his face was so aflame that he seemed to be one of those very sublime angels that appear to be all afire. They must belong to those they call the cherubim, for they didn't tell me their names. But I see clearly that in heaven there is so much difference between some angels and others and between these latter and still others that I wouldn't know how to explain it. I saw in his hands a large golden dart and at the end of the iron tip there appeared to be a little fire. It seemed to me this angel plunged the dart several times into my heart and that it reached deep within me. When he drew it out, I thought he was carrying off with him the deepest part of me; and he left me all on fire with great love of God. The pain was so great that it made me moan, and the sweetness this greatest pain caused me was so superabundant that there is no desire capable of taking it away; nor is the soul content with less than God. The pain is not bodily but spiritual, although the body doesn't fail to share in some of it, and even a great deal. The loving exchange that takes place between the soul and God is so sweet that I beg Him in His goodness to give a taste of this love to anyone who thinks I am lying.*
>
> *On the days this lasted I went about as though stupe-fied. I desired neither to see nor to speak, but to clasp my suffering close to me, for to me it was greater glory than all creation.*[9]

The heart in question has been meticulously preserved and kept on display in the Carmelite Church of Alba de Tormes. That heart, transfixed by an Angel with an arrowhead symbolizing the love of

---

9. *The Collected Works of St. Teresa of Avila,* volume one, Washington, DC, I.C.S. Publications, translated by Kieran Kavanaugh and Otilio Rodriguez.

God possesses its own history, and seems to go on living independently of its owner: it swells, bursts into flame, and breaks its crystal container. After an extensive examination of this incorruptible bit of flesh, a surgeon, Dr. Manuel Sanchez, will provide in the late sixties a detailed description: *"A transverse opening or gash can be noticed in the upper anterior quarter of the heart; it is long, narrow and deep, and penetrates the very tissue of the organ, as well as the ventricles. The form of this opening allows us to guess that it was made with consummate artistry by a long, hard, very sharp instrument; and it is only in the interior of this opening that we can recognize indications of the action of a fire or the beginning of combustion. . . . All along the wound we can easily see traces of combustion. They are especially visible on the two gashes in the upper lip of the wound, which seem charred as if by the action of a hot coal or a red-hot iron."*[10]

Later on, other doctors from the University of Salamanca will note a perforation effected by the arrow previously mentioned by the saint herself. The three doctors will also certify on their honor that the preservation of this organ over three hundred years old could not possibly be effected by means of any chemical product, or in any other manner whatever, even natural!!!!

And the cadaver of this exceptional woman of destiny, whose heart was pierced by an Angel's arrow, had a destiny just as exceptional. *"The day after her death* [October 5, 1582]," recounts Sister Ana de San Bartolome, *"they buried her will all possible solemnity. Her corpse was placed in a coffin; but they weighed it down with so many stones, so much lime, so many bricks that the coffin collapsed under their weight, and they all tumbled into it. . . . But from the grave of Teresa of Jesus wafted a scent so delicious that the Carmelites desired to see again the body of their Mother."* On July 4, 1583, nine months after her death, the coffin was opened. Francisco de Ribera was there: *"We found the lid broken, half rotten and covered with mold, the odor of humidity was very strong. . . . Her habit had also rotted. The holy body was covered by the earth that had fallen into the coffin, that too was moldy, but was as healthy and whole as if she had been buried the night before."* Father Ribera, moved on more than one count, added, *"She was so intact that my companion, Father Cristóbal de San Alberto, and I left the area while they undressed her; they called me when she was covered by a sheet; uncovering her breasts, I was surprised to see them so full and firm."*

10. *Stigmatics and Apparitions*, 1967, p. 83.

Only a man could be fascinated by that detail, which we must admit is not lacking in charm, even when the bosom in question is a dead woman's, and she a saint. But her perfect body did not remain so for long, for exactly because of its condition and pleasant odor, various orders and churches literally tore away—in the literal meaning of the word—the limbs, which remained . . . in perfect condition, masterfully thumbing the nose at forensic surgeons and other scientists who challenge these phenomena.

In her beautiful *Vie de Sainte Thérèse d'Avila*,[11] Marcelle Auclair drew up an inventory of the veritable butchery of this body, which continues to give off an indefinable but pleasant odor, somewhat like that of fresh clover. *"The right foot and a portion of the upper jaw are in Rome, the left hand in Lisbon, the right hand, the left eye, the fingers, shreds of flesh all over Spain and doubtless all Christendom. Her right arm and her heart are in reliquaries at Alba de Tormes, as well as what remains of that perfect and incorruptible body."*

What barbaric madness swept over these priests, *a priori* perfectly normal mentally and representing the elite of the time, that they cut away an arm, a leg, a foot, a finger, from the saint, and even remove the heart and the eyes, if it was not the perfect authenticity of these encounters, attested to by thousands of witnesses? The provincial of the order, Jerome Garcian, relates, doubtless with pride, how he cut a finger off that hand to keep it about his person permanently. He even specifies that when he was captured by the Turks, he was able to ransom Saint Teresa's finger only by offering several gold rings and twenty reals. Try for a moment to imagine yourself going for a spin in your car one morning with a saint's finger or eye around your neck. . . .[12]

What madness if not the absolute certainty of touching God Himself through these bloody remnants of sanctity? But also what extraordinary proofs, fantastic to some, disturbing to others, of the presence of the Most High in these stigmatic or incorruptible bodies, a majority of whom have seen the mysteries of heaven.

11. Editions du Seuil, Paris, 1960, p. 462.

12. Readers will perhaps be as surprised as I was to learn that they can buy an official relic of their favorite saint. Apply to Monastero "Agostiniane S. Lucia," 82 Via in Selci, 00184 Roma, Italy, Tel 06, 482-76-32, which stocks the remains and legacies of about two thousand saints. The relics are classed by category. In other words, a "first choice" relic will be a fragment of bone; a "second choice" relic will be a patch of cloth from a garment worn by the saint; and a "third choice" relic will be a chunk of his or her tomb.

## CATHERINE OF SIENA
## 1347–1380
### (Group I: Stigmata, Miracles, Angels, Incorruptibility)
### Italy

Despite the passing time, Catherine of Siena (1347–1380) is a furiously modern mystic. She is for all time, doubtless because she lived outside time. Reread her *Dialogues* and her correspondence, and there she is, every time. We can't help finding her much more delicate, much more sensitive than Teresa of Avila, doubtless because she was more feminine. Catherine of Siena is our contemporary if we compare her writings to the prelates of the present New Age. Near-death experiences? She had one well before the birth of Raymond Moody, one which left her in tears for several days: *"I did not want to return to the prison of my body."* The awakening of what some call kundalini? They saw her levitate several times, in a full ecstasy that *"cannot be described in human words."* Catherine of Siena is eternal because she is one of the greatest mystics in the history of the Church, though the Church was far more misogynistic at that time than now. And she has left us her celebrated *Dialogues*[13] with the Creator and Christ, a real gem that has only one equivalent, *Talking with Angels.* Though she did not live long, only thirty-three years, her whole life was constantly steeped in the supernatural: stigmata, visions, ecstasies, levitations, incorruptibility, etc. She explained one day that she did not see the faces of people who visited her because she was gazing at their souls: sometimes, like the Curé d'Ars or Padre Pio much later, she recited an exhaustive list of his sins to some fellow she had never seen before, striking him dumb on the spot. At one time there had to be eight priests at her side constantly, for anyone who spoke with her was immediately transformed. So it is no accident that the memory of a soul like Catherine of Siena spans six centuries of history. A mystic among mystics, terribly feminine, with a piercing gaze (to judge from paintings and sculptures portraying her), she was devoted body and soul to Christ, her only love, her only lover, her only husband and her only God. God, whom she had begun to venerate at the age of six, irrefutable proof of a predestined soul.

We must study the life of this unique woman who, though almost illiterate, had a considerable influence on the political and religious life of her country, on the popes and really on her epoch's whole religious community, including the Franciscans and Domini-

---

13. Catherine of Siena, *The Dialogues*, Mahwah, N.J., Paulist Press, translated by Suzanne Noffke.

cans. Not because she was a devout woman but because her reputation crossed frontiers so rapidly. At prayer she once collapsed suddenly before the church congregation, pale, her body rigid, without a heartbeat, in ecstasy. She lay there for three or four hours, to the point where the priests, with the help of her "spiritual children," carried her out to the square in front of the church, no part of her body moving even a millimeter. A Dominican, persuaded that she was only pretending, waited treacherously in the church for one of her ecstasies so he could rush up to her and jab at her feet and body with a knife.[14] But Catherine Benincasa did not react at all to the cuts. On the other hand, "returning to earth," three hours later, not only did she complain violently about the attack but she suffered great pain from it, and a wound formed. One August Sunday in 1370, her body displayed all the aspects of death and, after several hours, her companions, persuaded that she had died, placed her in a coffin, left open for last respects. But Catherine finally opened her eyes, striking terror into the poor sisters who kept vigil.

"*What happened?*" her confessor Raymond of Capua asked her. "*Were you really dead?*"

"*My heart broke, burst, it split from top to bottom,*" she answered. "*My soul detached itself from my body.*"[15] *I don't know how long, the sisters say four hours. But I saw the mysteries of God. I did not see the divine essence itself, but I saw the glory of the saints, the agonies of sinners in hell, and souls purifying themselves in purgatory. My memories are not too clear. And then, I don't have words to explain such things. Ah, what sorrow to have come back here! But the Lord said to me: 'The salvation of many depends on your return to earth where you will henceforth no longer live as before, confined in a cell.'*" That didn't keep the young woman from weeping: she didn't want to return to her body. Another time, a priest tested her by offering her an unconsecrated host at communion. Furious, she stood up and violently rebuked him. Afterward, as we can imagine, no one had to jab at her feet, because at the start of some of her ecstasies she rose up slowly, like a feather, and without moving a muscle, was borne through the air in the arms of her Husband, invisible, of course. The faithful who participated in the Mass sat paralyzed with fear, which is understandable.

14. In our time, when children claim to see the Virgin, doctors rush to stick the children with a needle or pass the flame of a lighter beneath their hands and before their eyes to verify that it is not a fake.
15. Today New Age specialists would say that she had an out-of-body experience or an NDE.

Her marriage to Christ naturally gave Italian jewelers ideas. One evening in 1337, while she was lost in prayer, Christ appeared to her and spoke to her thus: *"Since, for love of Me, you have renounced all vanities, scorned the pleasures of the flesh and fixed all the delights of your heart in Me, and now that the rest of the house is diverting itself, I have decided to celebrate the nuptials of your soul and marry you in faith as I promised you."* Then, still according to her testimony, the apostle John, Mary, Saint Paul, and Saint Dominic materialized in the small cell to be witnesses. Mary took Catherine's hand and presented the young virgin to her Son, who placed a golden ring set with a diamond and four pearls on her finger. *"Here, I wed you to Myself in faith, I your Creator and your savior. Keep that faith stainless until you come to Me in heaven, to celebrate this eternal marriage. From this moment, my daughter, be firm and decisive in all that I shall ask you to do in my providence. Armed as you are in the power of faith, you will conquer all your enemies and you will be happy."* That ring remained invisible to all but Catherine who saw it always, except, she admitted blushing, when she had offended her Husband (after a confession in good order, everything returned to "normal!").

Curiously, we have few texts on the Angels from Catherine of Siena, except in one of her *Dialogues*, which have been constantly in print for six centuries. This section speaks of "Divine Providence," which some call chance, others coincidence, and still other synchronicity:[16]

> *But sometimes, for my great servants, I act directly, by myself alone, without any human intermediary, as you know from your own experience. And you have heard how your glorious father Dominic, in the early days of the Order, was once so in need that when it came time to eat, the brothers had nothing. My beloved servant Dominic, trusting by the light of faith that I would provide, said, "Sons, take your places at table." The brothers obeyed him, and at his word sat down. Then I who provide for those who trust in me sent two angels with the whitest of bread, so much that they had great plenty for several meals. This was an instance of providence worked by the Holy Spirit's mercy without any human intermediary.*[17]

16. Catherine of Siena was a tertiary Dominican.
17. A painting of that scene is in the Louvre: *The Repast of Saint Dominique Served by the Angels* by Fra Angelico.

Catherine of Siena felt the first pangs of the Passion in 1373 with the crown of thorns around her head, followed two years later by the marks of the five other wounds that appeared on her body, painful but invisible as she had asked of Him (on the other hand they appeared after her death). All her life Catherine destroyed herself ceaselessly to make room for Him: destroyed the physical needs of her body, overcame her need for sleep, suppressed her appetite, and above all annihilated her psychological reluctance so that nothing would stand between her and communion with Christ. On paper that may seem simple, but in practice, as we shall see, it is much less so, and it illustrates perfectly the difference between ordinary mortals (you, me) and almost all the mystics discussed in this chapter who have seen one or more Angels.

From adolescence, for example, Catherine mortified constantly with an undeviating discipline, to the point where her weeping mother pleaded with her to stop mutilating herself: *"My daughter, you are dying before my eyes. You're going to kill yourself. Pity, pity! But who will carry off my daughter, who brings me so much unhappiness? What have I done to God to deserve this,"* etc. She little knew how well she spoke. Upon that Catherine replied with a superb and unanswerable *"I do not want to see in you only the mother of my body but also the mother of my soul."* She was seventeen. Later, Cabriani, one of her faithful followers, described the lesions and wounds—results of her flagellations—as *"little roses"* and *"little flowers."*

Before going further, let us examine the inevitable but too hasty conclusion of sadomasochism. It is Aimé Michel who, after a profound study of the life of another great mystic, Catherine dei Pazzi, which we have just reviewed, gave the best analysis:

> *"All these phenomena,"* wrote Dingwall about the saint's mortifications, *"are well known to specialists in psychopathology, in particular those who are concerned with masochistic practices, in which sexual pleasure is experienced by means of certain mental and physical hurts inflicted preferably by a person of the opposite sex. In certain cases, especially among those vowed to the service of religion, this masochistic pleasure is distinct from all that might be called consciously sexual, and this variety of ascetic masochism must be clearly distinguished from the others."*
>
> But what do these *"specialists"* of whom Dingwall speaks know of asceticism? Nothing. Did they frequent the convents, interview saints? No. Dingwall, who has read

*extensively and who quotes an overwhelming bibliography on flagellation as a sexual practice, draws all his science (he says so himself) from books, and among those he cites is a high proportion of works of pure and simpe woman-baiting. It has always been good form to mock monks. The bawdy monk already leads the five hundred devils on Roman capitals and on sculptures in cathedrals. But when a nun flagellates herself, it is inevitably a masochistic fla-gellation. I will not go so far as to say that convents were the only places in the world where there were no sexual deviants. But here we are dealing with a particular and well-documented case, and that case alone: yes or no, were the flagellations and mortifications of Maria-Magdalena dei Pazzi intended (consciously or not) for sexual pleasure? I answer in the negative for the following reasons:*

*Masochists love not only the pain. They love a certain pain inflicted in very precise circumstances. I am waiting to be shown, with statistical support, that masochists are in the habit of pulling teeth without anesthesia, or flinging themselves in fires to save lives, that now they are lining up for jobs in leprosariums, and that in the army they auto-matically volunteer for work details. In fact the masochist is a backward creature: "Sadism and masochism . . . can always be found in young children at a certain stage of development;" in the adult, they are only a "survival." (Dr. R. R. Held)*

*The masochistic drive waxes and wanes with sexual drives: non-specific pain (that is, pain other than that demanded by the neurosis) extinguishes it, and so does sickness, and so, of course, does satisfaction. The masochist who is dying of hunger forgets about his masochism and feels only the desire to eat. By sexual drives we must obviously understand those of the imagination as well as those of the senses: an old man can be a masochist: always on the condition that he is not too hungry, too thirsty, or suffering from the toothache or a whitlow.*[18]

But in this area Catherine of Siena's practices go far beyond sadomasochism, and I defy anyone to do as much: she never hesi-tated, for example, to care for the very sick, with a predilection toward those whom no one else wanted to take care of, like Andrea,

---

18. *Metanoïa*, pp. 108–109.

stricken by a cancer so advanced and so nauseating that no one wanted to come near her. In undressing her to clean the wound in her chest, Catherine, turning pale at the sight of the ghastly wound, flinched so in disgust that she drew back with a strong desire to throw up. But that was all, for she had sworn to annihilate within herself everything that might still react, in order to make more room for Him. She got a grip on herself, and cleaned the wound, placing all the putrefying tissue and fluids in a bowl, and then . . . drank it up. Then she set her face upon the wound and licked it to clean it. We may speak of madness. But who would still dare speak of masochism?

The mystical bride died at thirty-three like her divine husband, on April 29, 1380; at that moment the stigmata appeared. Catherine of Siena's body, laid out in state for three days after her death, was viewed by thousands of the faithful, commoners and nobility, all drawn by her intimacy with God. Only five years later, in 1385, was her coffin opened during a transfer, to recover her bones—in other words, relics. The witnesses were thunderstruck to find her as intact as if time had stood still. And her body suffered the same fate as Teresa of Avila's. Her confessor Raymond of Capua tore out her heart and cut off her head (!) to send as a relic to the Church of Saint Dominic in Siena, which later inherited a hand as well. An arm reached the same city, and three fingers left for Venice. Rome kept most of her things and the other hand. Florence was satisfied with a rib; the finger bearing the invisible ring came to earth among the Carthusians of Pontiniano; in an act of great generosity, the teeth were distributed to the next of kin; and the Dominicans of Rome inherited . . . a shoulder.

A real butchery, perpetrated by religious men themselves, which can only be explained by the authenticity of this most uncommon woman. Better yet, on October 4, 1970, Pope Paul VI ordained Catherine of Siena a doctor of the church, as which her authenticity continues to haunt the spirit, thirsty for the Most High and the Angels, even after all this time.

# CHAPTER 9

# *Of Stigmatics and Angels (IIa)*

FOR A LONG TIME ANY MYSTIC HAS AUTOMATICALLY ROUSED ROME'S suspicions. Proofs of sainthood must be numerous, accompanied by incontestable miracles and a divine sign, the crowning glory, as it were. The *Newsweek* reporter Ken Woodward, in his fantastic book *Making Saints*, tells us how the all-powerful Cardinal John O'Connor of the New York archbishopric suffered a blunt refusal from the Vatican: the archbishop, at the request of Cardinal Theodore MacCarrick, initiated a process of beatification of his predecessor, Cardinal Terence Cooke, at Saint Patrick's Cathedral in New York, only five months after his death. Sure of their considerable influence (above all financial), the two American cardinals wanted to put pressure on the Congregation for the creation of saints. Rome's reply, not to be appealed: *We wait minimum fifty years to examine a dossier.*

The subtext understood is that if the memory of the deceased survives the time thanks to his or her miracles (generally unexplained cures), the dossier may be accepted in the first instance, that is, for preliminary discussions. Not before.[1] To put it plainly, absolutely no detail that may raise a doubt may be ignored, lest it discredit the other saints and, above all, Rome. That is an unacceptable risk considering the consequences, especially in an age as spiritually arid as this last bit of the twentieth century. Maria

---

1. The process of inquiry leading to canonization was established in 1910 by Canon Macken, an English priest. It breaks down to nine steps: (1) the prejuridicial phase, (2) the informative phase, (3) Judgment of orthodoxy, (4) Roman phase, (5) Historic section, (6) Examination of the remains, (7) Examination of the miracles, (8) Beatification, (9) Canonization. The whole thing may last from forty to four hundred years.

Simma, the Swiss visionary, summed up the reasons for the church's mistrust perfectly in her book *Les âmes du purgatoire m'ont dit:*[2] *"We often misunderstand the deep reserve displayed by the Catholic Church in regard to personal revelations. . . . It is better that the Church fail to recognize ten cases as authentic than that they recognize one as authentic which is not."*

So this Group IIa comprises only those stigmatics (wounds attested, verified and authenticated by the various civil, medical, and ecclesiastical authorities of the time) who had, among other things, angelic visions. In the same way as the incorruptibility of the flesh, the stigmata validate the supernatural relationship between the subject and divinity, their "visions," and, above all, give us clues to the nature of Angels.

Like the preceding group, this one includes illustrious names. In the case of Padre Pio, for example, who died in 1968, of course we have photos available, but also films and audio recordings, independently of the numerous expert medical opinions. All those who think these stigmatics have been stricken by mental illness are invited to meet whichever they prefer of several contemporary stigmatics like Jane Hunt, an Englishwoman born in 1957 (various reportages and interviews with the BBC are available), or Vera d'Agostino, an Italian woman from Pescara, born February 21, 1959, or, eventually, Father Jim Bruse of Lake Ridge, Virginia. To this day, despite the scientific methods available to doctors and biologists, no explanation of this mystery has been offered.

It is the American writer Michael Freze who has analyzed the common factors among all these stigmatics, in one of the most complete volumes on this phenomenon, *They Bore the Wounds of Christ.*[3] Seven major characteristics can be distinguished:

1. They are chosen by God (therefore predestined).

2. God always requests their consent before granting them this life of an expiatory victim.

3. The subject speaks of having visions from the age of four or five. Christ or the Father speaks to him.

2. *(What Souls in Purgatory Told Me).* This book has been highly successful throughout the world since its first printing; more than five hundred thousand copies have been sold in different translations.

3. Huntington, Indiana, OSV, 1989.

4. He loses his near and dear ones in childhood: that is, his family.

5. The subject is often felled by one or another paralysis, and the doctors search desperately for its causes.

6. The subject is all but destroyed, but his sufferings are compensated for by ecstasies which "cannot be described in human words."

7. The subject dies when the doctors least expect it.

To put it simply, if your little girl is playing with her Barbie doll and suddenly says to you, *"Mommy, Daddy, Jesus spoke to me, and said I'll marry Him"* you may indeed expect that she will become a nun or a stigmatic, or both. In any case her fate is sealed, and there is very little chance that she will refuse her role as victim to redeem our "sins."

Some psychiatrists hold that the stigmata are caused by auto-suggestion and offer as proof the fact that the wound of Christ's flank, whether right or left, is really an imitation of the crucifix before which the stigmatics pray. True, the Gospels do not specify on which side Christ suffered the spear. According to the Holy Shroud of Turin, the wound, elliptical, is on the right side. We might eventually be able to accept the hypothesis of auto-hypnosis if there were not also the total absence of alimentation (as we will see further along with Therese Neumann) with no consequences, pleasant scents emanating from the sores, wounds that are never infected, a manifestation most severe on Fridays, the gift of reading of souls (stripped naked), and sometimes after death an incorruptible body to plunge us back into the inexplicable.

## GEORGETTE FANIEL
## 1915–
### (Group IIa: Stigmata, Miracles, Angels)
### Canada

After months of total immersion with the stigmatists, researching their visions of Angels, I discovered that these people fascinated me as much as, or even more than, the celestial Beings. Catherine of Siena, Padre Pio, and Gemma Galgani literally captivated me. Then I imagined in a rather fantastic way that the *Quotidien de Paris* sent me to Italy with our photographer Salvatore Carambia to interview Gemma Galgani: *"Mademoiselle, you say that you see your guardian Angel. What is he like? What is his name? Does he read* Our Sunday Visitor *or* Rolling Stone? *Does he eat? Does he smoke some Raphael Gonzalez?*[4] *Does he go to Mass? Does he work for the Archangel Michael or for God? Is it true that he was on sick leave when you broke a leg?"* etc. During this time, Salvatore primed his "flash-umbrellas," his 400 ASA Ektachrome films and his Nikon to immortalize the young woman and his guardian Angel. In short, at my office on the rue Ancelle in Neuilly, I dreamed of meeting "a true stigmatic." But I discovered that their telephone numbers were as hard to come by as those of movie stars. I can still see Father René Laurentin, after all a fellow journalist, rather irritated when I asked him for the address of a stigmatic, and especially a visionary (they aren't all both). He gave me no address, obviously. As I was not a priest but a journalist, specializing in computer sciences, my intentions were inevitably unhealthy and certainly inspired by the Devil, that villain! That's one reason why I keep saying that if the priests had fewer blinkers and more humor, the churches would surely be less empty.

But Divine Providence was watching over me, and put me on the trail of the Canadian Georgette Faniel, of whom I had never heard even though she was perfectly "authenticated" by the church. Cardinal Leger of the archdiocese of Montreal had even authorized his spiritual director to celebrate Mass in her home. So this was a "legitimate" stigmatic. And all the questions I had dreamed of asking Catherine of Siena, Teresa of Avila, Anne-Catherine Emmerich, and Gemma Galgani came flooding back. I bought a ticket for Montreal immediately, and was quite surprised to receive a cordial welcome from Father Guy Girard, spiritual director of the woman I was ready to bombard with disrespectful questions like *"Why do you suffer like that?" "Does it serve any pur-*

---

4. A delicious Cuban cigar.

*pose?" "What was your guardian Angel doing when you fell down?"*
*"Did Christ give you a ring when you married Him?" "Have you ever*
*wanted a divorce? "Why do they give you medical care, since your ills*
*are imposed by God?"*

After having studied all these brides of Christ, to speak with one
of them represented a sort of success. It felt like meeting an extraterrestrial, for stigmatics seem to like living in a permanent state of
suffering. Worse, even while insisting that they were his "beloved,"
Christ "offered" them even more suffering and pain. This exaltation
of pain made me ill at ease. Moreover, these Christly declarations
were in flat contrast to experiences in the NDE, where the subjects
speak of an infinite and compassionate divine love.

So?

My meeting with the stigmatic of Montreal would clear up the
matter once and for all, especially when she told me that in 1947
she *"had passed through a tunnel with a magnificent light at the*
*end."* As I listened to her, the reason for those suffering became
clear, limpid, the more so as I was utterly convinced by the simplicity of that seventy-six-year-old lady with the innocent look of "a
consecrated virgin." As a reporter I had interviewed too many
people not to be convinced of her sincerity and above all her
authenticity. Her answers were clearer than those of any doctor of
comparative theology. She spoke from the heart and with a childlike simplicity because she never went beyond primary school,
felled by various illnesses from infancy, like Marthe Robin. No
trace of hysteria in her; and her first spiritual director, a Jesuit like
they used to make them, would have discovered any fakery early
on. *"Some people are afraid of me,"* she confided to me. *"A few days*
*ago, a woman recited a dozen rosaries before she climbed the stairs,*
*she was that frightened."* A true stigmatic indeed; even if she did not
always bear visible wounds, she caused fear.

The first contact was curious. In Montreal, I arrived a little
early at her apartment tucked away on the first floor of a building
in a little street near Rachel Avenue. Georgette Faniel's aide almost
didn't let me in because the priest was not with me. After an argument I finally penetrated the apartment. The decor and furniture
reminded me of the modest interiors in Eastern countries. All was
silent. Even the three parrots in their cages said not a word. Georgette Faniel was sleeping in a small white-walled room with a
crucifix hung above her bed.

Waiting for her spiritual director, I checked the batteries in my
tape recorder, readied the cassettes, tested the microphone and
also reread the list of questions I had prepared. Oddly enough, I

sensed no special atmosphere, when I had expected some sort of supernatural air. Nothing. The calm and peace of an old person's apartment. Then Father Girard came in and shook my hand vigorously, smiling at me. It was the first time I had seen a priest in a sky blue habit, indicating his membership in the priestly Society of Holy Apostles, and that was a pleasant change from the sinister black robes. *"So you write about Angels?"* he asked me. That was a change from *"Have you brought your butterfly net?"* Then in a few words he told me the story of Georgette Faniel. The daughter of a Belgian painter who emigrated to Canada, she began to hear inner voices starting at the age of six, and thought it was the same for everyone. Classic. At the age of five Catherine of Siena had also explained to her mother that she was talking with Jesus. In short, for nearly seventy years, Georgette Faniel talked with the Eternal Father, Christ, and Mary, and saw the Archangel Michael and her guardian Angel. Sometimes she bilocates and thus is in two places at once, but it is a subject that she does not broach. That is her "secret garden." And like other stigmatics, various illnesses immobilized her from a very early age. To regularize that divine union in suffering, she had been "consecrated" by her then spiritual director, Father Gamache, as "victim." Before that she had taken her vows of chastity and poverty. Today, if her sufferings are "normal" during the week (aside from the daily Mass), on Friday they become frightful.

Up to here Georgette Faniel's life corresponds point by point to the profile of Gemma Galgani. But the latter did not have to suffer very long, as she died at the age of twenty-five, while the stigmatic of Montreal has not left her home for more than fifty years. At the time of the interview, she was suffering from a fracture of the sternum. Her doctor does not abandon her and tries to ease her pain. But really, to what purpose are her sufferings? Father Guy Girard was not at all surprised by my question. *"You see, she regularly has transfixions or ecstasies,"* he explained to me. *"That is, a sudden torment, particularly brutal and painful, followed by a joy beside which all the other joys of the world are nothing. But recently, the Eternal Father has asked her to renounce even that joy to offer more to the world's salvation, and in particular for Medjugorje.[5] Her ecstasies are an act of love by the Father or Jesus proving all the affection They have for her, assuring her that she is a source of redemption for the world. That suffering is a source of salvation for millions and millions of souls who, without her, would not know of God. A*

5. At the time of the interview, the war between Serbs and Croats was raging.

*transfixion is like a coronary. The pain is terrible, as if someone had driven a knife into her heart. At those times, Georgette clutches her chest. She does not cry out, because after fifty years she has the courage not to cry out. She only repeats 'Lord, thy will be done, I offer all my suffering, for the dying, for the hungry children, for the wounded, for all those who will die today, for the church,' and so forth. When she suffers, she is praying and offering. She bears the sufferings of Christ in her feet, in her hands and on her forehead. But it is during the celebration of the Eucharist that she suffers the most."*

I could not help finding that horrible. But when the stigmatic explained, in her little girl's voice, the reason for her suffering, it became blindingly clear to me. And I have never been sure how she made me understand the grimmest aspect of this concept in the Catholic Church. Finally Father Girard invited me into the stigmatic's room. Georgette Faniel gazed at me with the eyes of a child, and I told myself that I must at no point grow sentimental.

*"Is offering your suffering the most important thing in God's eyes,"* I asked her.

*"Yes, because we are doing what he asks, bearing our cross. So suffering is for me part of the cross, physical as well as spiritual."*

I wondered why suffering rather than happiness.

*"Can't we offer Him our joy or our happiness instead of suffering?"*

*"It's hard to understand, but it was obvious. I feel the joy of knowing that I have done God's will, have accepted what He asks of me without protest."* She was silent for some moments. *"You must know that there are three degrees of suffering: we can expiate our sins, cooperate with Christ in the salvation of men, and also be deserving. No one can take that away from you. But there is no joy in suffering unless it is accepted. Our Father and Christ ask me regularly to suffer, and They bring it to me to redeem souls."*

*"What is the difference between the Father and Christ?"*

*"When the Father asks something of me, He asks firmly. Jesus is more like a husband. He brings himself to it gently, or takes a roundabout way sometimes to ask me this or that."* She laughs gently, as if she saw him but dared not ask him something. *"The Father asks much more than the Son. Christ is a husband, He is with us, He loves us, strengthens us in the Eucharist, while the Father makes much more difficult demands than the Son could. We sense a difference between the Father's demands and the Son's. The Father is much more direct but He always asks if I agree. He respects my freedom. But I am so habituated by the grace of God to complying with His wishes that I never refuse—when my doctor, for example, gives me painful treatments like this afternoon when he had to pierce my ster-*

*num with a needle. Instead of thinking that it was going to be very, very painful, I thought of Jesus on the cross who had nothing to alleviate His sufferings. Afterward, I make acts of Love, that is to say I thank the Father and I join my sufferings to those of Jesus and to Mary's burdens of personal poverty. It is not my suffering, but that which the Father has chosen for me."*

*"You are a mystical bride of Christ . . ."* (No time to finish the question.)

*"I don't like the word mystic, I'm allergic to it. I am a simple servant of God."*

*"But Christ certainly married you at some point?"* I showed surprise.

*"Yes, of course, I don't mean to deny that I am His bride."*

*"When was the wedding?"*

*"He was already my companion every day. The wedding took place February 22, 1953, when He asked me is I would agree to be His bride as well as taking up the cross to save souls with Him. He told me that He was Everything and I was nothing. Then he asked me to wear a ring, blessed by my confessor. So I consented, not really knowing what I was agreeing to, or for how long. I was hoping He would come for me soon. But I will soon be seventy-seven, with seventy-two years of sickness behind me. So . . ."* (she laughed).

*"Are you a bride of Christ and also of the Father?"* This point had escaped me altogether.

*"I am the bride of the Trinity."*

I thought back to the marriage of Catherine of Siena. *"How did the marriage come about? You had a vision, an ecstasy, a ring?"*

*"Yes, but it is invisible. There is a cross on it. It was placed on my right ring finger. On the left hand it would only show the engagement or marriage on the human level. On the spiritual level the ring goes on the right hand. Mary was present with the celestial court."*

*"The celestial court?"*

*"The Angels, the Archangels and all those who adore God and are present in His works."*

I had the sudden impression of dropping back into my childhood, to the time of my first catechism at the age of six. But this interview fascinated me more and more because, for the first time, the supernatural began to be palpable.

*"Well, what are the Angels like?"*

*"Of great splendor . . . the Archangels are the ones who have messages to transmit to the world; the others seem to be created for the adoration of God, for the service of God and to help us, like the guardian Angels."*

*"Have you seen your guardian Angel?"*
*"Yes, I've already seen him!"*
More and more I had the feeling of becoming a child again, or of being a blind person with a guide.
*"What was he like?"*
*"Very handsome."* (She laughed like a young girl whom a young man was courting.) *"He was wearing a white tunic. But you can't compare his beauty to human beauty. He is beyond all that, in his features, his face, in everything. I've never seen such a handsome man. I also see the Angels during the Eucharist. They are in a state of adoration, prostrate before the real presence of God in front of the altar. I don't see why people, and even priests, don't believe in the guardian Angel that's always with us."*
*"How can we talk with our guardian Angels?"*
*"First believe that you have an Angel that accompanies you until death, that intercedes for you, guards you and protects you. A guardian Angel never stops interceding for his protégé. I pray for him every day, and also for the Angel of everybody who lives in moral, physical, and spiritual suffering. You see, there is so much suffering wasted because people don't know they can offer their suffering to God."*
Georgette Faniel tries to find a more comfortable position in her bed, because her sternum is bothering her again.
*"Just what was your guardian Angel doing when you fell down?"*
*"I think it is God that permits any test or trial. I could have died, you see. After I fell and fractured my sternum, I heard the Eternal Father tell me, 'This is your first fall, my beloved, on the physical level. You will have two more, like my Son. The second will be worse because it will be on the spiritual plane. But the third fall will be in my arms.' I was hospitalized immediately afterward, and when the doctors looked at the x-rays, they asked me, 'But who hit you, Madame? You absolutely must turn him in; this is a crime.' I said, 'No, it's just a fall.' They didn't believe me."*
*"How have you been able to stand all these sufferings?"*
*"These days it's primarily the Eucharist that sustains me. It even cured me of a paralysis on the right side of my face. One afternoon I heard an inner voice tell me, 'My beloved, receive the body of Christ and you will be cured.' Father Girard had just come for a visit and I tried to signal him with my left hand, showing him the sky, the host, and my mouth, but he thought the window shade was too high and that he should lower it. When he came back toward me, I asked the Lord to make him understand that I wanted to take communion. I had made the signs but he hadn't understood. Before he left, I said to*

*God the Father, 'If You want me to remain paralyzed, Your will be done, I thank You for it. If not, if You want me to heal so I can bear witness, inspire Father Girard to give me communion.' Being a chaplain he always had the host with him. It was January twentieth. Just as he was leaving, he turned back to me and said 'Ah, I forgot to bless you.' Then, seeing my face, he added, 'And if I give you a bit of the host, do you think that would help?' Then he gave me the host, arose and got ready to leave. Just as he ended the benediction, I said 'Thank you' to him without thinking. He couldn't believe it. 'What? You're talking, you're moving, you're cured!' And he broke into sobs. I had never seen a man cry like that. It was the first time he'd been present at a miracle. When I called my doctor, he hung up on me, thinking it was a bad joke because he knew I couldn't speak. His nurse came to see me and saw that it was true. He couldn't get over it. Another time I was seriously ill, a terrible hemorrhage, and they were waiting for me in the emergency room at the hospital. I said to Father Girard, 'Give me the Eucharist, and I'm sure I'll feel better,' and indeed I was cured. I was sure that the Lord had wanted to test my faith. So I can't not have confidence in the Eucharist."*

"Then you're happy in your . . . divine marriage?" I did not want to use the word "mystic," which had annoyed her.

*"Yes. The only thing is, I don't want to displease God by forever accepting his will. But I try. We're only human. I never rebel against the suffering. I often pray for my guardian Angel to help me."*

"And he comes?"

*"Oh, yes, He does what I'm incapable of doing. The first time I met the celestial court I was working for the poor and I had to tie boxes and my fingers couldn't do it. So I asked the Lord to send my guardian Angel to help me and He said to me 'Yes, I am going to send you more than your guardian Angel, I am going to send you the celestial court.' 'Who?' I asked. 'The celestial court, to me?' I was stunned. 'Yes, to you, My beloved. If my Angels obey Me and you obey Me, then I am going to ask them to obey you and to help you.' And it was all done easily."*

"You speak often of the Archangel Michael. . . ."

*"Yes, because I prefer him, without wanting to offend the others, because I know he is there and because he protects me always."*

"But Father Girard explained to me that the Devil had tried to strangle you. He really protects you?" I was amazed.

*"Yes, he was just waiting for God's commands. The Angels can't decide these matters themselves; the Lord commands them and tells them I must pass through this or that trial. Then they agree, and intervene so I don't give in, so I don't get discouraged."*

*"Have you ever wanted to 'divorce' or just stop all this?"*

*"Yes, when I was seventeen. I had had enough of suffering and seeing everyone else have fun and run around when I was stuck in bed. Years after, I had even taken off His ring. One day I said to my then spiritual director that I had had it up to there with life. I asked myself, 'Why me?,' why did He choose me. Also why did people come to ask me for prayers so that Monsieur could have a car, so that Madame could have her health, so that they could make trips while I was stuck in a bed of pain. I found that revolting. Well he was upset, because he knew it was the Devil who made me say that. He prayed, he asked the Lord for forgiveness. Then he told me to buck up because the Lord had sent a trial for me. He wanted to know if yes or no I would accept the life that He had chosen for me in order to save souls. I answered that I was going to think about it. And then I said 'Yes.'*

*"'Mimi,' added my spiritual director, 'I'm going to do something that I have never done since I became a priest: I am going to offer you to the Lord in a special way. Do you accept?' I answered 'Yes.' He raised his hands and offered me to the Eternal Father as a sacrificial victim, a victim consecrated by His loving mercy. He prayed: 'Eternal Father, do what You will, she accepts.' At that moment I felt a sharp pain in my toes, as if someone were pulling them and twisting them. It was horrible. And it kept getting worse. At the same time, I felt an extraordinary joy in suffering, because God had accepted my offering. Inside myself I was saying that when the pain reached my heart, I would die and it would be all over. But it went on and on. I would have liked so much to die that way. It would have been so beautiful. But I still had a way to go."*

*"Have you visions, do you relive Christ's Passion?"*

*"During Communion and especially on Good Friday. I feel the wounds of Jesus again in the feet, the hands and especially the heart, His agony in the garden, and the wound on the shoulder, because He asked me to bear His cross."*

I felt as if I were going crazy. I was in Montreal, taping the words of a woman who was doubtless incapable of getting out of bed, and she was explaining to me very simply and most sincerely that she sometimes bore Christ's cross. Weird. I might have become accustomed to the existence of Angels and to their celestial jokes, but here I was left far behind when it came to the supernatural.

*"What other graces are you blessed with? I am thinking of bilocation, for example."*

*"People claim to have seen me in Rome and in Medjugorje in my blue robe. They say they've seen me three different times. So I asked them to take my picture so at least I could see myself."* She laughs.

*"In spirit I travel a lot, mainly in Yugoslavia. I asked the Virgin last January for a rampart of the celestial court around Medjugorje (Croatia) to keep the Serbs from entering the village. According to the latest news, no one there has been killed or wounded. A Serbian plane aimed at the church of Medjugorje and dropped four bombs, but they didn't explode."[6]*

*"What is 'ideal' conduct according to the Eternal Father?"*

*"It is to have faith and above all to accept His will and be convinced that He is omnipotent and that He created us. Whether we are believers or atheists, we return to the Father to be judged."[7]*

*"During your twenty-four different surgical operations since you were fifteen, has it ever happened that you lost consciousness and 'departed?'"*

*"Yes, during the time of Father Gamache.[8] They had just operated on my spinal column, and the doctor said I might die and told me I would never be able to move or walk again. I felt very bad. They moved me into my room and I was there all alone for about an hour, as the sisters [nurses] had left. I finally lost consciousness. They brought me around, but feeling worse and worse, I said to Father Gamache, 'Father, I think this is the end; give me extreme unction.' And he was shocked: 'You are at the point of death?' He gave me an unction and I 'departed.' I was in a large tunnel filled with an extraordinary Light. I felt fine. Oh, I was happy. And it lasted for a good while, but I didn't see anyone. The further I advanced, the greater the Light. When I came to, I looked around me at the nurses, the doctor, the priest, and I broke into tears. I was disappointed; I did not want to return. I was on my way to the brilliance that brought me so much joy, so much happiness, and when I realized that I was still alive, it was very painful. But the Lord consoled me, saying, 'You see, to save*

6. The Serbs, who try unrelentingly to bomb as many Croatian churches as they can, have failed to destroy this place, which they named "Our Lady of Foreign Currency," despite many attempts, which in itself constitutes a true miracle. One bomb exploded but only killed one ox. No, it was not the ox from the creche in Bethlehem.

7. I am inevitably reminded of all the NDE, and indeed believers and atheists both tell the same story, as we have seen: the tunnel, then that ineffable light they want to melt into. The Lord's judgment seems to be the judgment of the subject, who relives his live in three dimensions in one second, and the results of his acts on others. It is not God who judges them; he does not judge. It is the subject who discovers his own faults and shortcomings in a single unique area, Love.

8. Her first spiritual director, an extremely strict Jesuit who controlled her for twenty years.

souls I often ask people to offer their lives as a sacrifice; but the sacrifice I ask of you is to go on living to save as many souls as possible.' He was asking me just the opposite of what He asked the others. And I agree to drain that cup to the last drop."

"How did that happen?"

"According to the doctors I was apparently dead. The nurse checking my pulse found none. But Jesus told me, 'Don't worry; they think you're dead, but you're still with us here on earth to help us save souls.' That was what consoled me."[9]

"When was that?"

"In 1947, I think.[10] It must be written down somewhere in my spiritual diary for that period."

"Since you hear God and Christ, why do you need a spiritual director?"

"Because the Evil One would like to deceive me and make me believe false things. Sometimes he tells me that everything I live through is no use, and I'm wasting my time, and sometimes he plants a seed of doubt. But because I tell everything to my director of conscience, he can see what's happening."

"How can he identify what comes from the Evil One?"

"By the grace of his priesthood. It is a rare thing for a priest who is close to God and has faith to be wrong."

"A priest is never wrong?"

"Not if he has faith in his priesthood."

"Where is your free will, if God chose you to be a victim?"

"In accepting or refusing. Some accept what God presents to them, and others refuse."

Georgette Faniel was smiling. More, she seemed to take real pleasure in responding to this interrogation. Obviously she found me rather amusing with my stupid questions. I thought back to Angela de Foligno and her mystical unions. "What is a union with God?"

9. Her precision here would surely intrigue Drs. Maurice Rawlings, Raymond Moody, and Sabom. Moreover, I found three cases of apparent death in Catherine of Siena, Teresa of Avila, and Gemma Galgani, oddly enough all three stigmatics. In each case the observers found no heartbeat, to the point where after several hours with no sign of life, they reserved a burial plot. Teresa of Avila even had trouble opening her eyes, which had been sealed shut by candle wax.

10. Surprised by this story, Father Girard, chaplain at the hospital, explained that twice patients had taken him aside to describe similar experiences; but he had not the faintest notion that his "spiritual daughter" had lived through such an event.

*"Almost death, because the soul leaves the body altogether to join Him. So it's the perfect union of two souls. True Love. It cannot be described and does not depend on our will. The transfixion is as if God took an arrow, thrust it into the heart and pulled it out twisting and turning it. At that moment, knowing it comes from God, I feel a very great joy. It can't be explained, I can't compare it to any human joy, all the more because I've never in my life known anything else like it. But the Lord asked me to renounce even that joy. There remains only suffering, no consolations, only faith to sustain me."*

*"Let us go back to your stigmata. The number 'two' that was inscribed on your body—do you still have it?"*

*"Yes, for ten years now. It was on the feast of the Precious Blood. The Father made Himself manifest to bring me a terrible sorrow; He said to me, 'I have incised My signature in your flesh: "two" in one and the same flesh. By this union you will always be protected.' That is the union, inscribed on my skin, on my right side. The doctor came to examine it. While he was standing there with his head cocked, I heard a voice say to me, 'Ask him to kneel.' But I was uncomfortable asking my doctor to go to his knees. So I begged the Father: 'Enlighten him.' And in the end he knelt all by himself. What he saw filled him with wonder, without really being able to explain what was happening. He held a magnifying glass to it and said it resembled a neon light and he could see the blood circulating. The 'two' is made up of seven tiny points, symbolising the seven gifts of the Holy Ghost."[11] Jesus told me that it stood for the oneness of God with a soul in the sufferings of Christ crucified. The first time I felt the pain of the Passion was in 1950. The crown of thorns did not come until 1953, in April."*

*"With your testimony for Medjugorje[12] you revealed yourself. . . ."*

*"They did an autopsy on my soul. Everything, everything that I had hidden for thirty years was revealed in one stroke. And I had begged them to use 'Mademoiselle X or Y' instead of my name. But my spiritual director suggested that I ask the Eternal Father what He thought. So I prayed, and He said to me, 'Have you begun to blush at your baptismal name?' So I agreed against my will that my name*

11. The statement of Dr. Mishriki: "During a thorough examination I could see that this cutaneous lesion forming a perfect numeral two was composed of several red dots, perfectly integrated to the vascular system." For my part, I confess to utter surprise at this luminescent "two" whose seven dots seemed to be lit from within, a bit as if diodes were grafted under the skin. Amazing.

12. Guy Armand Girard, *Mary, Queen of Peace, Stay with Us, Testimonies in Favor of Medjugorje*, Montreal Editions Paulines. Also available in French.

*appear in the book. But the Lord promised me that no one will know all the sufferings I've been through until after my death."*

*"What was He like? Can you describe Him?"*

*"Very often I see Him veiled. I can't make out His features. But it's happened several times. They say that He is pure spirit. I don't think so. I don't think Mary and Jesus can see only a 'spirit.'"*

Then Georgette seemed to be suffering. I looked at my watch; I had been pressing questions upon her for nearly two hours. I asked if I could photograph her. She agreed, though it was difficult for her to hide her pain. I took two or three snapshots quickly, knowing they wouldn't be very good because she was stretched out in her bed. I could hardly ask her to pose. . . . But just as I started to focus my Fuji, Father Girard asked me if I would like him to take a picture of me with Georgette Faniel. I accepted and sat beside her so he could get the two of us. Soon he snapped the shutter. I was not aware that she was wide-eyed. And she said to me laughing, *"This is the first time in sixty years that a man has sat on my bed."*

I was truly reassured. Stigmatics, despite their sufferings, have a sense of humor.

Even though Georgette Faniel has not published her spiritual journals (we must wait until she "falls a third time"), this interview gives us a better insight into the psychology of the stigmatics who follow in these pages. Taken all in all, these souls show nothing in common with ours, in the sense that they are predestined to be expiatory victims. And that is comforting.

## PADRE PIO
## 1887–1968
### (Group IIa: Stigmata, Miracles, Angels)
### Italy

There is no question that when the tomb of Francesco Forgione, better known under the name of Padre Pio, is opened, it will reveal an incorruptible body, which will qualify him to enter group I (stigmatics/incorruptibles) with Catherine of Siena, Teresa of Avila, Anne-Catherine Emmerich, and Maria-Magdalena dei Pazzi.

In the history of the modern church, Padre Pio constitutes a special case, a unique case, sort of a combination of the Curé d'Ars and Catherine of Siena, since he was the first priest "marked by God" in two thousand years. We have seen nuns, monks, and even laypersons receive the stigmata over the centuries, but never a consecrated priest. Why? Only God knows. But the tens of thousands of stories reported about Padre Pio by so many trustworthy witnesses represent only a tiny part of this Italian's works. And when we read these testimonies trembling with faith, love, and supernatural tenderness for this old priest who was our contemporary, when we listen to those who knew him and those curiosity-seekers who went to see the "phenomenon" and came away shaken, there can exist no possible doubt.

Science fiction books and films are nothing beside the stories of Padre Pio, who lived every second of his life in the supernatural, in the impalpable, in the shadows of Christ and the Angels. Maria Winowska, author of a moving book on the stigmatic of San Giovanni Rotondo, concluded that *"the adventure of Padre Pio is just a link in the series of events that, over two thousand years, stud the life of the saints."*[13] As for the Lutheran pastor Bernard Ruffin, who in 1991 edited the most complete book on the Italian priest,[14] he notes that without ever publishing a single work or delivering a single university lecture, Padre Pio is, over twenty years after his death, more alive than ever.

With this man, you might say that He needed to send us regularly a kind of *living proof* of His Passion so that we could believe, like Thomas, in His existence and in His survival.

As if, through the stigmata of his servant, He was trying to say to us, *"Come now, I exist, I died for you and you still scorn me, while I love you with an unconditional Love* (as all those who have had a near-death experience would say) *that cannot exist on earth. Come to me through him."* You might say that He is a beggar for our souls and does not know how to draw us to Him. Padre Pio is also absolute and inarguable proof of the Church's mistrust of mystics, be they stigmatic, in levitation, or in bilocation, or appearing to thirty different people simultaneously. But most of all, he is to our knowledge the only one, with Gemma Galgani, in this twentieth century who spent his life conversing with his guardian Angel, an Angel that he saw as he saw those of others. He was incidentally in the habit of saying *"If you need me, send me your guardian Angel"* to all his spiritual children who, while ready to die for Padre Pio, did not believe in Angels at all.

Born in 1887, the eighth child in a family of poor Italians, Francesco Forgione followed his vocation at sixteen by joining the Capuchins, the most austere order of Franciscans, and studying with them for eight years before being ordained in 1910. The young

---

13. *Le Vrai visage du Padre Pio (The True Face of Padre Pio)*, Editions Fayard, p. 60.
14. *Padre Pio, the True Story*, revised and expanded, OSV.

priest was conscripted in 1916, and it was then that the young Padre Pio attracted the attention of military doctors for the first time. Shortly before being sent to the front, he fell gravely ill, which entitled him to go on "sick call," as the military say. During a routine auscultation the doctors noted a fever as high as 118.4 degrees Fahrenheit,[15] a level at which thermometers invariably exploded, a level that left the doctors gaping, quite sure that they had here a patient in the last throes of tuberculosis. Certain that the young man had only a few weeks to live, the medical authorities granted him a six-month leave on the spot, time enough to die someplace other than the hospital. Forewarned by his medical records, the Capuchins' father superior also decided to send him someplace calm and sunny, the monastery of San Giovanni Rotondo, so that he might end his days in serenity.

But once at the monastery the saint recovered suddenly; and shortly afterward, on September 20, 1918, Brother Arcangelo (!) found Padre Pio's hands bleeding copiously. The invisible stigmata that he had received in 1910 had come to light. The young Capuchin was about to alter life in the monastery for good.

He was immediately taken to his cell, and the father superior, before calling in a doctor for a detailed examination, insisted that the wounds be photographed immediately. Of course the village doctor found no natural explanation for the wounds, which should have either been infected or formed scars. Another surprising phenomenon: the blood did not coagulate, and gave off a pleasant smell.

These stigmata, which afflicted Padre Pio until his death in 1968, were not welcomed by the church: examinations, re-examinations, inquiries, and finally a formal interdiction to appear in public or to receive visitors. So doctors sent by the Vatican came one after another to Padre Pio's side, including Pope Benoit XV's personal physician, Dr. Luigi Romanelli, director of the city hospital of Baretta, who would physically torture him with tight dressings.[16]

15. 48 degrees centigrade. They used a thermometer from a boiler to take his temperature.

16. Here is an excerpt from Dr. Romanelli's report translated by Maria Winowska, p.82:

*"The lesions on Padre Pio's hands are covered by a thin membrane of reddish color. There are no bleeding spots, nor swelling, nor inflammatory reaction of the tissues.*

*"I have the conviction and even the certainty that these wounds are not superficial. On pressing them with my fingers I felt an emptiness through the whole thickness of the hand.*

*"I was not able to determine if, in pressing more strongly, my fingers would*

Dr. Amico Bignami, who held the chair in pathology at the University of Rome, set seals on the hands, and the next doctor, Dr. Festa, surgeon in a private clinic, was obliged like his two predecessors to acknowledge that these wounds, which were never infected nor healed, defied any medical explanation. The traces of blood on the bandages that the doctors took away more than once to analyze them in the lab never smelled . . . . when normally blood exposed to the air emits a fetid odor after a few hours. More, there emanated from these bandages an agreeable fragrance that could not be compared to any terrestrial perfume (which some commonly call "the odor of sanctity").[17] Despite all the opinions, the Vatican forbade him to show his stigmata to anyone, even a doctor, without its written permission.

Profoundly humble and respectful of his superiors' orders, Padre Pio always complied with good grace with these restrictions and the injunctions of his superiors. In the end everyone saw in him the successor to Francis of Assisi, the Church's first stigmatic.

---

*touch each other* [sic]*, as that experiment, as well as any pressure, provokes a sharp pain in the patient.*

*"Nevertheless, I subjected him to that painful test several times, morning and evening, and I must admit that each time I reached the same conclusion.*

*"The lesions in the feet present the same characteristics as those in his hands, but because of the thickness of the feet I was unable to make the same experiment as on his hands.*

*"The wound on his flank is a straight cut, parallel to the ribs, seven to eight centimeters long, cutting the soft tissues, of a depth difficult to verify and bleeding abundantly. This blood has all the characteristics of arterial blood and the lips of the wound show that it is not superficial.*

*"The tissues that surround the lesion present no inflammatory reaction and are painful at the least pressure. I visited Padre Pio five times in fifteen months and after having noted some modifications, I was unable to find a clinical formula that would allow me to classify these wounds."*

17. There exists a very curious exception to this divine rule of the odor of sanctity, that of Rita de Cascia (1381–1457), better known as Saint Rita, called upon for hopeless causes and whose body was stigmatized and found incorruptible (she left us no word on the Angels). Jo Lemoine tells in her biography of the saint (Editions Medispaul, Paris, p. 78) that the blood that oozed from the stigmata of Rita de Cascia emitted a dreadful odor while she was alive: *"But the other nuns' senses of sight and smell are soon offended by the proximity of that gaping wound, which is, perhaps—some still doubt it—of celestial origin, but which smells bad. Without hiding it, now, some draw away from her as from a plague victim. . . . She must eat alone, at the end of a bench, and pray apart from the others. . . ."*

And in the best tradition of certain war years, Padre Pio was denounced! He was denounced to the Vatican by the archbishop Pasquale Gagliardi of Manfredonia as a fraud, inflicting wounds on himself so as to be more interesting and to make money. Already in 1919 another priest, Don Giovanni Miscio, had written to the newspapers, to the archbishop, to the head of the Capuchins and to Rome to denounce the swindler. But most curious is the behavior of archbishop Gagliardi, a notorious homosexual, who also had a tendency to mix the Church's wealth with his own. So Bernard Ruffin recounts that in 1919 a statue of the Virgin particularly worshipped by the population of Viesta disappeared from the church. Knowing of his debauched life, the people were fed up, and went to the cathedral that same day, seized Gagliardi and literally beat him up. He owed his life—and his manhood—to the arrival of the police just as the women, knives in hand, were attempting to emasculate him! Despite the scandal, the Vatican said not a word. Ten years later in Rome, the same Archbishop Gagliardi swore with his hand on his pectoral cross that with his own eyes he had seen Padre Pio make up and perfume his wounds before celebrating Mass: *"He is possessed by the devil and the Capuchins who live in unbelievable luxury are nothing but a pack of thieves,"* he added. Then he asked all his priest friends, homosexuals like himself, to send letters of denunciation. Rome's reaction was not slow to come: in 1931 the Vatican stopped Padre Pio from celebrating Masses in public, from hearing confessions and from speaking with . . . women, and it lasted until 1933.

Worse, in October 1959 Father Emilio, his new superior, installed a microphone in the room of the sacristy where Padre Pio received confession, in the hope of hearing some spontaneous admissions, thus violating the sacred rule of secrecy. Father Luna was indignant and noted that *"thirty-seven tapes were thus recorded during the three months that this most unworthy profanation known to our history lasted."*[18]

We seem to be in a bad dream when we discover such behavior at the highest levels of religious authority. But that isn't all: on June 5, 1923, the Vatican had already published an apostolic act officially informing the public that the phenomena associated with the Capuchin brother Padre Pio had not been authenticated by Rome as supernatural. Then, books dedicated to the Capuchin brother were put on the Index!!! To be complete, our list lacks only an auto-da-fé. *Newsweek* journalist Ken Woodward determined that in

18. Jean Barber, *Trois Stigmatisés de notre temps*, p. 81–82.

the 1960s, eight years before the death of the priest, contacts between the faithful and Padre Pio were strictly limited by Cardinal Alfredo Ottaviani, in hopes of killing off this personality cult among the thousands of people who came to visit him from the four corners of the world.

But he didn't count on the Italians, who know better than anyone how to marry commerce and holiness. So they had to decide, in "high places," to silence the Padre by shifting him to another monastery, in hopes of calming the spirits of the faithful. As soon as the news got out, there was an insurrection in San Giovanni Rotondo: peasants, businessmen, hotelkeepers, and the mayor Morcaldi blocked all the exits from the monastery, armed with hatchets, scythes, and even hunting rifles, ready to chop up the first "monsignor" or Capuchin who tried to leave with the Padre. Nobody takes a saint away from the Italians, especially southerners, who didn't hesitate to sell chicken's blood to innocent pilgrims, claiming it was blood from the Padre's stigmata. Business was flourishing in the small town. All businesses. The Capuchins, for example, sent their habits to the laundries of the village, from which socks and linen stained with the Padre's blood never returned, replaced by new items. Why? because of the "scheme": all the Padre's bloody clothes were immediately cut into pieces and sold as relics. Some, with an especially refined business sense, had even cut pieces from the chair where he habitually sat. In short, the entire village knew that without the Padre, all the illicit and licit commerce would disappear. So the population rose up, but not always for spiritual reasons, as is too often claimed.

Helpless, especially after noting the people's reaction—the mayor himself announced that they would remove the Padre over his dead body—the "top brass" decided that it would be more prudent to leave him where he was. One day, in the middle of Mass, a madman with a pistol in his hand jumped on Padre Pio, taking him hostage and threatening to kill him if he left San Giovanni de Rotondo: *"Dead or alive, you will stay here with us,"* he cried to the priest!!

Never again did Padre Pio receive an order for transfer.

A certain number of cardinals, including the future Pope John Paul I, regarded him from the gilded roman panelling as a mystical clown, and put no faith in him at all. This despite the various investigating committees composed of general practitioners, dermatologists, and surgeons who established the authenticity of his wounds. Discovering no fault, no fraud, and above all no natural explanation for the stigmata, the Vatican finally raised its interdictions, but in name only, for if Padre Pio was once more authorized to celebrate a public Mass, it would have to take place . . . at five in the morning, almost clandestinely.[19]

But the people shrugged off that early morning hour, and waited patiently through the night for the opening of the church doors. Then the attacks came from elsewhere: finding no fault with the poor priest, certain spirits, though very Catholic, let it be known that the stigmatic took advantage of his feminine relations (*sic*) in the confessional, an accusation mingled with other equally elegant denunciations.

No mystic was ever victim of so many attacks by his peers or faced such hostility in the bosom of the church. It was the faithful who protected him by instituting "Padre Pio" prayer groups around the world, and who raised him to the level of saint. After his death, Padre Pio is more alive than ever, even though he has not even been beatified. What can the Vatican do against the *vox populi?* What can it do against the stigmatics, against the miracles brought about by his intercession and above all, against his legendary *"clairvoyance?"*

Like the Curé d'Ars, Gemma Galgani, and many others, Padre Pio read souls, baring them totally, knowing in advance what the penitent was going to tell him, confess to him, and especially hide from him. One day in 1947, a Polish priest, just ordained, who came to the monastery to make his confession to the already famous priest, heard him say: *"One day you will be Pope."* This explains why John Paul II showed himself more lenient with the Capuchin's file and prayed on his knees before his tomb. Attilio Crepas, an Italian reporter for *Stampa Sera*, was seated on a pew in the church, observing Padre Pio and pondering a lead for a feature article. The Padre, who did not know him, turned around, approached him and said, *"Why are you thinking of your office and your article? It's not nice to make noise around a priest at prayer."* The reporter never got over it.

And like Teresa of Avila and Catherine of Siena, Padre Pio made a name for himself by the true saintliness of his life, even before being recognized by the Church. The public was not mistaken: the faithful waited hours to be confessed by him, to the point where the Capuchins, to avoid queue jumpers, had to distribute num-bered tickets[20] and sometimes called the police to maintain order.

19. Finally it was Pope Paul VI who, shortly after his election, rebelled against the "criminal" measures taken toward Padre Pio. He cancelled them all on September 8, 1963.

20. Of course those tickets gave rise to scalpers, and it is rather a surprise that the Italians never printed false tickets to hasten their confessions to Padre Pio.

After all that, the Vatican inevitably seemed a cold and cynical administration,[21] a little like social security. Padre Pio's miracles number in the thousands, and some remain totally inexplicable from a medical point of view. A stigmatic, he was forced to wear gloves sewn especially for his hands, so the blood did not spot his sleeves or the altar cloth. His gait testified to the suffering of his feet, also nailed to the invisible cross that he was the only one to carry deep within his flesh. In the end he frequently spent twelve to fourteen hours daily in the confessional hearing and absolving the faithful who sometimes waited three days before seeing him. And like the hysterical fans who tore pieces out of Elvis Presley's shirt, pious Italian matrons came into the church with scissors and razor blades in their pockets, in the firm hope of snipping off a piece of the illustrious soutane.

In the tradition of all the "great" stigmatics, Padre Pio enjoyed all the divine graces: bilocation; distant vision; knowledge of the past, present, and future life of the faithful; reading of souls. . . . We can no longer keep count of those, condemned by orthodox medicine, whom he healed with just a prayer, nor of conversions as sudden as unexplained, nor of the stigmata. With so many divine gifts in exchange for his constant sufferings (try to walk and work with holes in your feet and hands), Padre Pio could hardly help seeing not only his own guardian Angel but also the guardian Angels of others. Alberto del Fante, reporter for *Italo Laica*, a freemason, was intending to drag him through the mud, calling him an impostor and using unflattering adjectives. One day he decided to confront him on the priest's own terrain and entered his confessional. The priest recited to him a complete list of his sins, tetanizing him with tears of emotion. You can guess the sequel: the journalist became his most faithful supporter, to the point of writing a book that gathered all the priest's miracles, testimonies from reliable sources, confirmed, verified, examined, and authenticated.

And yet I found the most astounding testimony of this book on Angels in altogether astonishing circumstances in Paris. It was, incidentally, the first time in my career as a reporter that I conducted an interview—with microphone and tape recorder—in a confessional . . . interrogating the chaplain of the basilica of Sacre-Coeur in Paris, the Abbé Derobert.

In 1955 Jean Derobert was a young seminarian in Rome and

---

21. Mother Teresa, for example, who has devoted her life to caring for the sick in Calcutta and who is considered a living saint by the entire world, will have to wait at least fifty years before a file on her beatification can be opened.

heard time and again about the case of Padre Pio. In very odd circumstances he was finally led to visit San Giovanni, so he boarded a train for Naples, convinced beforehand that he would be meeting, in his own phrase, a crank. Once in San Giovanni de Rotondo, the young Frenchman observed the conduct of southern Italians in church and was scandalized. *"It was October 2d,"* he recounts in his book *Padre Pio, temoin de Dieu,*[22] *"and they were preparing for Saint Francis of Assisi's feast day. So there was a ceremony with preaching, song, and telling the Rosary. I felt a curious sensation, one I had never felt before, a kind of scorn for this demonstration of faith. I had already seen and heard several ceremonies of this sort, but never had such a disdain swept over me toward these peasants from Gargano and these pilgrims. It was all the more bizarre because my position as an ecclesiastic contrasted somewhat with such a state of mind. There, in that church, I felt an allergy to the things of God."*

Taking advantage of his seminarian's robes, Jean Derobert had himself led to the loft, whence he hoped to observe matters. *"Then I noticed an empty seat in the first row. I went and sat down. My neighbor to the left was coughing, spitting, wiping his nose . . . and annoying me no little. I cast a furtive glance at him. 'I've seen that face somewhere before,' I said to myself. Suddenly the unknown Capuchin ran his hand along his head in what must have been a habitual gesture. That hand was gloved. . . . I found myself on my knees beside him whom I had dreaded meeting, Padre Pio himself! . . . It made a terrifying impression on me, like a kick in the belly. I could hardly stay upright on my knees. . . . I had to sit down, legs useless, no strength left in me. I did not take my eyes off him; I was fascinated by that face focused on a beyond I knew nothing of. I was experiencing the birth of a strong inner affection for this man who was visibly suffering to the extreme, an affection which by the way contrasted strangely with the scorn I felt for the crowd below who were listening to a Capuchin denounce communism, talk of the Madonna, and I don't know what else."*

The least we can say is that this first contact was paradoxical: Here is a future priest who, at the sight of religiosity carried to its Italian climax, is invaded by an intellectual contempt for all these people who know no restraint in their prayers, especially when they lament and pray aloud.

The sequel is even more surprising: next morning Jean Derobert, thanks to the custom that priests benefit by a priority, did not have to wait three days with a number to be confessed by the

22. *(Padre Pio, Witness for God),* Marquain, Belgium, Editions Jules Hovine, pp. 7–8.

Padre, and at seven in the morning he found himself fifth in the long line.

>*I waited with a certain anxiety. From time to time the Padre raised his voice, crying out, "How many times?" or "Why did you do that?" Now and then he drove a penitent away: "Out! Go look for another confessor!" "No, no, Padre." And so it went.*
>
>*I took my place in the confessional. "Father, I am French."*
>
>*"Well, what have you done?" he asked me in Latin.*
>
>*"Speak Italian, Father. I understand it."*
>
>*"Bene, cos'hai fatto?"*
>
>*"I don't know!" And then, losing my composure, I grew excited. I felt ridiculous because I didn't know what to say to him. The black hole. Only later did I learn that Padre Pio stripped the soul bare. During this brief time he was smiling. "Father, I did this . . . and that . . ."*
>
>*"Yes, that's true," he told me, "but that was forgiven last Friday."*
>
>*And that was the strict truth.*
>
>*"But you've forgotten this thing, and that thing . . . Two years ago, in such and such a place. Why did you do that? And that? True?"*
>
>*With tears in his eyes he showed me the seriousness of certain actions, a seriousness which, to tell you the truth, I had never thought of. But then and there, as they were explained by Padre Pio, they took on their true dimensions for me.*
>
>*"That's serious, that's serious!" And he started weeping and suffering.*
>
>*I was very ill at ease, the more so because everything he said was true. He even provided precise details that I'd forgotten. Sometimes we act by reflex, with no sense of guilt whatever. He gave me absolution. Then he said to me, "Do you believe in your guardian Angel?"*
>
>*"Uh, I've never seen him."*
>
>*Fixing his penetrating gaze upon me, he rebuked me with a couple of sharp slaps, and let these words fall: "Look carefully, he's there and he's very beautiful!"*
>
>*I turned and of course saw nothing, but he, Padre Pio, had the look on his face of someone who sees something. He was not staring off into space. "Your guardian Angel is*

*there and he's protecting you! Pray heartily to him, pray heartily to him!"*

*His eyes were luminous; they were reflecting the light of my Angel.*[23]

If I could keep only one story about Angels, that would be the one. Jean Derobert is a large and sturdy man, like a rugby player. To have slapped him twice could not have been easy. Only Padre Pio managed it, exasperated as he must have been by the reply of the seminarian kneeling before him, *"Uh, I've never seen him,"* which is a little like *"all he has to do is show me his wings."* And the young man was far from imagining that he was going to *"take two slaps in a confessional. . . ."* But the detail that could never be invented in the reflection of the Angel in the Padre's eyes. . . . That is angelic and at the same time terribly down-to-earth.

It is unnecessary to emphasize that from adolescence the Padre regularly experienced mystical ecstasies in the grandest tradition of John of the Cross or Angela de Foligno. How many times had he not been caught totally "out of it" by his brothers and even laymen! They could pinch him, pass a lighted candle in front of his eyes—which he kept open—or shout at him: He did not move, did not blink, felt nothing. On the other hand, if the witnesses heard him speaking with someone, or more than one, they did not understand the replies. Here is one example of his dialogues with his guardian Angel noted feverishly by the Capuchin brothers:

*"Angel of God, my Angel, Are you not my guardian? You were given to me by God.. . ."*
*". . ."*
*"Are you a creature or a creator?*
*". . ."*
*"You are a creator? No. Then you are a creature and there is one law and you must obey. You must stay beside me willy-nilly."*
*". . ."*
*"You're laughing!"*
*". . ."*
*"And what is there so funny?"*
*". . ."*

23. Father Derobert told me that in Padre Pio's church, the confessional was in a corner, with a prie-dieu about four feet wide facing a chair, so close that the confessor and the penitent practically touched heads, because there was no grille.

*"Tell me something . . . you must tell me. Who was that? Who was there yesterday morning?"*[24]

*" . . ."*

*"You're laughing."*

*" . . ."*

*"You must tell me."*

*" . . ."*

*"One or the other, the professor or the guardian? Go ahead, tell me."*

*" . . ."*

*"You're laughing. An Angel that laughs . . ."*

*" . . ."*

*"I will not let you go unless you tell me."*

*" . . ."*

(There follows an incomprehensible dialogue with Christ, after which the Angel finally tells him that it was Father Agostino).

The Italian priest seemed to see guardian Angels all the time. For that reason, he never neglected to ask his "spiritual children" to pray for their Angels, and, in case of need, to send them to San Giovanni Rotondo. Incidentally, we note this solicitude at the very beginning of his career, in a gracious letter dated April 20, 1915, addressed to Raffaelina Cerase, taken from the voluminous correspondence of Padre Pio assembled by Jean Derobert in 1987:[25]

> O Raffaelina, how consoling it is to know that we are always guarded by a celestial spirit who does not abandon us (admirable thing) even when we displease God. . . . Adopt up the fine habit of thinking of him always. That there is at our side a celestial spirit who from the cradle to the grave does not leave us for an instant, who guides us, who protects us like a friend, like a brother, who must also console us always, especially in the hours which are, for us, the saddest.
>
> Know, O Raffaelina, that this good Angel prays for you: he offers to God all the good works that you have done, your holy and pure desires. When it seems to you that you are alone and abandoned, never fear that you do not have a friend of the soul to whom you can open yourself and to

24. Padre Pio was upset because he thought that a layman had surprised him in full ecstasy.
25. Editions Hovine, p. 243.

*whom you can confide your sorrows; in charity, do not forget that invisible companion, always there to listen to you, always ready to console you. O delicious intimacy! O happy company . . .*

And there are weird stories of synchronicity, of Angels coming and going, which among others forged the legend of Padre Pio. In his lifetime, for example, one of his spiritual children, the English gentleman Cecil Humphrey-Smith, had a serious auto accident in Italy (indeed, what was his guardian Angel doing?) and in view of his condition one of his relatives went to the telegraph office to wire Padre Pio, asking his prayers for a rapid recovery. After filling out the form, the man handed it to the telegrapher for dispatch, but upon reading it the clerk immediately handed him a wire . . . from Padre Pio, addressed to Cecil Humphrey-Smith and assuring him of the Padre's prayers for his recovery. . . . Giovanni Sienna reports that one of his friends, Franco Rissone, asked Padre Pio one day if he really heard what was sent to him through the intermediary of his guardian Angel. The priest looked at him and said, *"Do you think I'm deaf?"*

But if Angels exist, the Angel brimming with beauty also exists, as ABSOLUTELY ALL the mystics, without exception, have discovered. Thus the Italian priest complained one day to his guardian Angel when the fallen Angel assailed him with unusual brutality. Padre Pio continued to invoke his "guardian" Angel but the Angel did not respond to his appeal. When he finally appeared toward morning, like a cat coming home after a night on the tiles, a furious Padre Pio would not say a word, and turned his back on him. The father did not forget that his "guardian" that night was a guardian in name only, and he recounted his misadventure to Father Augustino, his spiritual director, in a letter dated November 5, 1912:

*I scolded him severely for keeping me waiting so long, when I had been calling for his help constantly. To punish him, I did not want to look him in the eye, I wanted to get away, I wanted to flee from him, but he, the poor thing, rejoined me almost in tears. He grasped me until I raised my eyes, I looked him in the face and found him very angry. And then: "I am always near you, my dear child, I always surround you with the affection that gave birth to your gratitude to the beloved of your heart. The affection that I have for you will not end even when your life does. I know very well that your generous heart is always beating for our common beloved. You would climb all the mountains and cross all the deserts to find him, to see him again, to embrace him again in extreme moments, and to tell him to break the chain quickly that holds you to your body. . . . You must wait a little longer. . . ."[26]*

Indeed, more than once outside of Mass, the faithful could clearly see bruises on the Padre's face, a "black eye," etc. Here too we may legitimately ask, What was his guardian Angel doing?

Let us describe a Mass by Padre Pio: *"'I hear the sound of keys,' cries a young woman with a baby in her arms. Immediately, the human wave rolls toward the church. The portals open with a loud groaning of hinges. It is like a dike that breaks. Dumbfounded, jostled, trampled, manhandled, forced back, I remain far behind,"* reports the factual Maria Winowska, *"while these hairy furies howl, screech, swear, whine, shout in rage and use any means to push to the front. It is such a hullabaloo that even the sturdy sacristan has trouble making himself heard: 'Peasants! Rascals! Rogues! Wretches! Scoundrels! Wait! For pity's sake! Are you Christians or animals?'"* Padre Pio's Mass, in Latin, sometimes lasted two hours by the clock. All who attended these celebrations were nailed to the spot by the drama that unrolled at the altar, beside while a scene from the No theater would seem like a puppet show: *"From the first moment, violently, we were plunged into full mystery. Like blind people around someone who could see."[27]* The mystery of the Eucharist in the hands of the Padre was suddenly becoming clear, the supernatural was invading the church, and I imagine that the Angels too must have followed every gesture of the stigmatic, who, sometimes immobile for many minutes, as though mummified, gazed raptly at the host, his eyes shining with love. Even for the purely curious, it became much more than a simple piece of unleavened bread.

Furthermore, Padre Pio seems to appear where he was not expected. I can still remember an event that impressed me during a dinner in New York in March 1992 with the American philosopher Michael Grosso. We were eating quietly in an Italian restaurant, chatting about the after-death experiences turned up by Dr. Raymond Moody, when he asked me suddenly how I could consider tackling a topic as difficult as the Angels outside a theological con-

26. Jean Derobert, *Padre Pio témoin de Dieu*, Jules Hovine, 1986, p. 76.
27. *Le Vrai Visage de Padre Pio*, p. 18.

text. I explained to him that we had many cases of mystics whose stigmata were authentic, as, for example those of Padre Pio, who had been examined by Catholic, Protestant, Jewish, and even atheist doctors, and a priori these things eluded modern medicine. Moreover, these mystics, like Padre Pio, swam permanently in the supernatural and spoke often of Angels. At that moment Michael Grosso took his wallet from his jacket hanging on the back of his chair, opened it, and showed me a photo of the Italian priest. That had a startling effect on me because I absolutely did not expect it, above all from a real hair-splitter like Grosso. Giving me no time to ask questions, he told me, *"you know, I saw Padre Pio when I was in Italy. He was already very old and I couldn't approach him closely. But when he blessed the crowd from his balcony, something happened that touched me deeply. Since then, I always have this with me."*

A similar adventure befell the British journalist John Cornwell[28] in interviewing the novelist Graham Greene. What a surprise for the atheistic journalist when he caught the English gentleman *in flagrante* observing an Italian superstition: Graham Greene took two photos of Padre Pio from his wallet and explained how he had heard talk of this priest in 1949 and decided to go to San Giovanni Rotondo to take a closer look at him. Making a stop in Rome, he met a Vatican ecclesiastic who said to him apropos of Padre Pio: *"Oh, that holy fraud! You're wasting your time. He's a fake."* When he reaches Gargano he is warned about the length of the mass. But moved by curiosity Greene goes to the church at 5:00 A.M.. to attend the ceremony. *"He celebrated the mass in Latin,"* he told the journalist, *"and I thought thirty-five minutes had passed. But on leaving the church, I glanced at my watch and saw that it had been two hours. . . . I didn't know where the time had gone. And there, with that mystery, I recovered a little faith, because it seemed an extraordinary thing."* Had not the monsignor told him he would be wasting his time? And from that day on, Graham Greene always carried on him the two photographs of the Italian priest.

The incredible Padre Pio, even hearing what is said about him many kilometers away! So we can imagine his weariness after a mass. But, even though exhausted, he went on to the confessional where he spent hours with "sinners." During his rare moments of repose, he meditated in calm surroundings. He meditated only, because on this topic we have the testimony of Brother Alessio Parente, who accompanied him up to his last moment, to the point

---

28. *The Hiding Places of God,* Warner Books, 1991.

where the old priest called him his *"guardian Angel on earth"*:[29]

> One day I was sitting beside him [Padre Pio] on the
> veranda outside his room and it was about 2:30 P.M. As all
> the brothers had retired to their cells for the "siesta," the
> place was deserted. I saw Padre Pio pick up his rosary;
> there was such calm and peace around him that I felt
> encouraged to approach him to ask him a few questions.
> During all these years, I received quantities of letters from
> people who wanted advice from Padre Pio on all sorts of
> matters. I opened an envelope, and, turning toward Padre
> Pio, said: "My father, Madame B.R. would like you to give
> her advice on her work. She has a good job but another
> business is offering her a more interesting post with a
> better salary, which means an easier life for her. What do
> you think she should do?" Instead of an answer I received
> a reprimand, to my surprise: "Go away, my son, leave me
> alone, don't you see that I'm very busy?" "Strange," I told
> myself, "he's sitting there telling his rosary, and says he's
> busy." While I sat in silence thinking that he wasn't really
> busy, Padre Pio turned to me and said, "Don't you see all
> my spiritual children's guardian Angels coming and going,
> bringing me their messages?" Not really surprised, I
> answered him, "My father, I have never seen a single
> guardian Angel, but I believe you because every day you tell
> people to send you theirs."

This passage is more than disturbing, as it raises a new question, never before noted in the history of the church and its saints: the guardian Angels go to *Padre Pio* for instruction when a priori an Angel takes instruction only from God. Which sends us directly to Father Derobert's most audacious explanation; he wrote in his work *Padre Pio, Transparent de Dieu*, page 782:

> We are convinced, for our part, who knew the Padre
> well, that Jesus came back to relive his life and his Passion
> in Padre Pio. He became, for Jesus, an extraordinary and

29. Brother Alessio wrote and edited a small very interesting book, exclusively
devoted to the relationship between Padre Pio and the Angels. This work is available in English and Italian by order at the Padre Pio's monastery: *Send Me Your Guardian Angel*, by Fr. Alessio Parente; Notre-Dame de Grace—Capuchin Monastery, 71013 San Giovanni Rotondo, FG, Italy.

*superior human being, a perfect and docile instrument in the hands of God. Several times in these pages we have affirmed that the father was like the mystical incarnation of Jesus, the Lord having taken possession—in the full sense of the word—of the whole person of this humble monk. Through him, Jesus came to remind the world of the need for prayer, suffering, sacrifice, to expiate the sin that destroyed the Love of God. Through Padre Pio, Jesus came to call the world once more to conversion, to return to Him, and to Holiness. His mission was henceforth accomplished. . . . Padre Pio died, Jesus returned, as in his Resurrection, to the bosom of the Father, and there remained nothing here below but the remains of Francesco Forgione, who had never really walked the Earth. . . .*

And indeed, on the day of his death, to everybody's stupefaction, the stigmata disappeared, leaving a clear and immaculate skin. . . . We might think that Padre Pio winked an eye at Catherine of Siena: During her lifetime the stigmata were invisible. But on the day of her death they appeared.

## THERESA NEUMANN
## 1898–1962
### (Group IIa: Stigmata, Miracles, Angels)
### Germany

The German visionary Theresa Neumann, who died in 1962, represents a contemporary case, in the sense that she has been examined, she too, like a circus animal, by all the doctors, ecclesiastics, and civil authorities possible and imaginable. She was even put in quarantine for fifteen days in a hospital, because according to medical authorities a human being cannot live more than eleven days without eating or drinking (Theresa Neumann stopped taking nourishment on April 29, 1923, and continued thus until her death in 1962). In her lifetime seven hundred books were devoted entirely to her, and ten times as many articles in the press, all of which furnish excellent documentation on her.

Like all the stigmatic mystics, she was attacked principally by theologians (one is never better betrayed than by one's own). Michael Waldmann, professor of theology at Regensburg, stated that the blood running from her body was nothing but a trick, that in reality it came from her periods. The German journalist Anni

Spiegl, who was close to Theresa Neumann, reports that despite all these outrages, she kept her sense of humor to the end. A skeptic spoke to her of autosuggestion, and Theresa put her in her place:

> *"You imagined these stigmata so intensely that they appeared. . . ."*
> *"Obviously!" answered Theresa. "And if you in turn imagined that you wanted horns, they would probably spring up on your head."*[30]

Nothing was spared this young woman, who not only relived the Passion every Friday, but also was regularly dragged through the mud. That prompted her to submit one single time to secular scientific examinations. For example, a Communist magazine had stated that *"Theresa Neumann was the mistress of a prestidigitator to whom she gave a child,"* which was not without involuntary humor when one knew that she had a tendency to appear in various places without leaving her bed.

On the other hand, professional journalists who went to visit her simply testified to what they had seen, which also created troubles in certain publications. For example, in 1926 Dr. Fritz Gerlich, editor in chief of the *Munchener Neweste Nachrichten*,[31] rebelled on reading an article about Theresa's stigmata written by one of his colleagues, the Baron Erwein von Aretin. Johanes Steiner in his book *The Visions of Theresa Neumann*[32] reports that Gerlich did not believe a word of the article, which he felt was a disservice to the faith and prejudicial to the newspaper's reputation. Nevertheless, as a conscientious journalist he decided to check the story himself, and went to the little village of Konnersreuth where Theresa Neumann lived. He described his state of mind after his inquiries:

> *I came to Konnersreuth as a man of almost forty-five. Since my twenties I had actively engaged in the intellectual life of my country . . . . In this philosophy of life many of the things that I had experienced or investigated in the case of Therese Newmann had no place at all. This was only one more reason for making the most thorough  and painstak-*

30. Jean Barbier, *Trois Stigmatisés de notre temps (Three Stigmatics of Our Time)*, p. 10.
31. Fritz Gerlich was one of the rare journalists to commit his publication against the rise of the Third Reich. And on May 9, 1943, he paid with his life in the Dachau concentration camp.
32. Alba House, New York, 1975.

> *ing investigation possible. The following is my report of these investigations. How all this managed to harmonize with my philosophy of life is not the question here. The question here is simply the facts of Therese Neumann's life. Scientific investigation—so called objective or neutral scientific investigation—has, in my opinion, to be guided by one single thought, and that goal, for any individual philosophy of life, is one and the same: "Thou shalt not bear false witness."*

Unquestionably what he discovered there marked him for life. Moreover, he testified about what he had seen when a goodly number of priests stated immediately (without meeting her) that these visions were simple hallucinations and that the stigmata were autosuggested (how?). Going back to the quarantine: Theresa was kept in a hospital room from July 14 to July 28, 1927, surrounded by doctors and nurses, under twenty-four hour surveillance, in shifts. On her admission to the room she weighed 110 pounds. On her departure, she weighed . . . 110 pounds, with no other beverage or nourishment but three communion hosts of normal size, each weighing 13 grams, washed down by 3 cubic centimeters of water which enabled her to swallow them. This extract of the final report written by Doctors Otto Seidl and Ewald von Erlangen of the Waldassen sanatorium of Waldassen permits of no doubts:

> *NOURISHMENT INTAKE: The nourishment intake was the object of the greatest and most painstaking attention throughout the entire period of the observation. All the instructions, for washing, for water to rinse her mouth, etc., were most strictly adhered to. Despite this most painstaking observation, it was not once observed that Therese Neumann, who was never alone for a single second, ever ate anything or ever in any way attempted to eat anything. Not only ws the patient's bed subjected to a rigorous examination at the start of the observation, but it was made fresh every day—not by one of the staff, but by one of four nurses under oath. Neither I nor any of the sisters could possibly admit that any failure in observation could have occured with respect to the nourishment intake. Throughout the period of observation, only the following elements entered Therese's body:*
>     *a) At her daily Communion, she was given a small par-*

*ticle, about one-eighth of a normal host. Even if one were to compute that, in the time from July 14–28, about three entire hosts were thus consumed, the total combined weight still would be only thirty-nine grams.*

*b) In order to help her swallow the host, she was regularly given some water, in the measure of approximately three ccm; the combined volume of the water given to her from the morning of July 14 to the morning of July 28 would thus be about fifteen times three ccm—approximately forty-five ccm, or the volume of three teaspoons full of water.*

*c) As was carefully described in the instructions, whenever Therese wanted to rinse out her mouth, the nurse would give her a precisely measured volume of water; the water was afterward caught into a basin and carefully measured. The volume of water before and after was different only on two occasions: on July 16 there was a deficit of five ccm. The nurse mentions that when Therese spat out the water "some of it spilled on the floor." On July 17, in the evening, there was another deficit of five ccm. For all the others occasions, there was no measurable deficit observed.*

*WEIGHT: Therese's weight, in order to avoid any possibility of error, was always taken without shoes and wearing the same clothing. One Wednesday, July 13, she weighed 58 kg, and on Saturday, July 16, her weight had gone down to 51 kg. The weighing on July 20 shows 54 kg; on Saturday, July 23, 52.5 kg; on Thursday, July 25, 55 kg. The original weight on the first day of observation had been reached again. This is the most surprising element in the entire observation. The fact that the weight on the Saturday weighings showed a loss of 4 kg the first time and a loss of 1.5 kg the second time is to be explained by the activities of the preceding Friday: the elimination of urine, blood, vomit, the extraordinarily intensive metabolism during the ecstatic states, and the extensive perspiration which followed the ecstatic states. The fact, however, that Therese showed a gain in weight, 3 kg in the first case and 2.5 kg in the second case, withouts taking any nourishment or liquids, is to be explained by none of our physiological laws or experience. Now it is true, and clinical observations to this effect have been made available to me, that people who are starving often do not experience thirst, since when the albumen breaks down, enough water is released to support life. This would demand a considerable reduction in albumen, and this simply was not the case with Therese Neumann.*

The doctor noted that the personnel had taken an oath before the cardinal, who also wanted to be sure that Theresa Neumann was authentic. To understand the effects of a lack of nourishment and drink, we have only to read articles on Vietnamese or Cuban "boat people" who drifted for several weeks before being (the luckiest) rescued by a ship. Later, Anni Spiegl very accurately remarked that *"to eat and drink, and move one's bowels in hiding, all that for thirty-six years, while being closely watched by thousands of people, would be a marvel to equal that of her abstinence."*[33]

Theresa Neumann, like Catherine Emmerich and especially all those who preceded her, like Hildegarde Von Bingen Mechtilde von Hackenborn, or Mechtilde von Magdebourg, was not debilitated by undernourishment. More, when these women were not reliving the Passion, they were seeing the life of Christ as if they were traveling in time. There exists a stunning photo of Theresa taking communion from a priest. But instead of the priest, she "sees" Christ, and her face is completely illuminated, her eyes shining with beatitude. Her expression of beatitude seems to pierce the black and white photo. The photographers who were able to shoot her reliving the Passion left the house utterly transformed, all their preconceptions having suddenly collapsed.

Among the angelic "visions" of Theresa Neumann, one is of particular interest: her highly meaningful vision of the Annunciation. She spoke of that vision to one of her biographers, Johanes Steiner, who was at her side on March 25 at 9:12 A.M.:

> *Therese sees a young women, who appears to be almost still a girl, in a small house, praying. Suddenly a shining man is at her side; He did not enter, he is there. "With big wings?" I ask her, in an effort to lead her astray. She answered: "What are you thinking of? The shining man does not need any wings." The man bows down before the frightened maiden and says: "Shelam elich, Miriam, gaseta . . ."*[34]

33. Jean Barbier, op. cit., p. 20.

34. Dr. Wessley, an Austrian linguist and orientalist, confirmed that Theresa Newmann spoke good Aramaic during some of her visions.

> *And a few more words follow. I say: "Wait a moment, what*
> *comes after gaseta?" She thinks for a while and anwers:*
> *"You should have written it down faster; I don't know it*
> *anymore." It is the greeting of the angel Gabriel:*[35] *Hail,*
> *Mary, full of grace."*
>
> *Mary, still frightened, although, to judge from her*
> *expression, gaining confidence, is looking intently at the*
> *light vision, which resembles a man but shines by itself.*
> *The angel continues to speak something powerful. The*
> *maiden interrupts him to ask a question and the angel*
> *answers her. When he is finished, the virgin bows her head*
> *and says a few words. At that same moment Therese sees a*
> *mighty light from above enter into the virgin, while the*
> *angel, after bowing once again, disappears into the air.*

I am still amazed by the altogether extraordinary resemblance between that description of the Annunciation by Theresa Neumann and a painting of great originality by Dante Gabriel Rosetti (1828–1882) in the Tate Gallery in London: Mary is curled up on her bed and a little frightened or perhaps sullen. The Archangel Gabriel is there, without a hint of a wing, holding a lily branch with four flowers in his right hand. His feet are not touching the ground. Mary, prostrate, is staring at the Archangel's lily as if she did not comprehend what was happening. She seems so thin, so fragile, even sulky, like a young girl who is being lectured. The Archangel, as simple in his dress as in his attitude, implies by the lack of contact between his feet and the ground that he appeared in a fraction of a second and he is going to disappear just as quickly. Time is frozen. We might believe that Theresa had guided Gabriel Rosetti's hand, so prodigious is the similarity.

## MARIE-JULIE JAHENNY
### 1850–1941
#### (Group IIa: Stigmata, Miracles, Angels)
#### France

Who would have believed that one day the Archangel Michael, prince of warriors, supreme fighter, God's five-star general, and chief justice of the celestial armed forces' courts-martial, would

---

35. Steiner wrote Angel instead of Archangel, showing that he was not at all familiar
    with the Angels.

sometimes speak like a peasant? Well, it happened! And by the same token, Christ shows us that he does not choose a bride by her rank or education, but by the state of her soul. Marie-Julie Jahenny, a peasant from the Nantes countryside who had at most six months of schooling, and spoke not French but the local patois, is the best example of that. Without instruction, she nevertheless lived His Passion for sixty-seven years. Marie-Julie was one of the *"guinea-pigs"* of the celebrated Doctor Imbert-Gourbeyre, a university professor, who spent twenty-six years of his life investigating and examining stigmatics. His book *Stigmatization*, published in 1895, remains even today the definitive work in this field. Dr. Imbert-Gourbeyre came across more than one hysteric and, after twenty years, he could determine in a few days of observation whether he was dealing with a false stigmatization. He also studied and authenticated Louise Lateau, the famous Belgian stigmatic. Marie-Julie was also authentic, for false stigmatics did not flog themselves, did not sleep of beds of nettles, did not wear belts of nails whose points penetrated the flesh, and did not deny themselves nourishment. In the classic manner, the young girl devoted herself to Christ from her early childhood. She cherished the cross and never missed a Mass or communion. But that is not enough to receive stigmata. Besides, she did not even know the word and could only express herself in patois, so that during the bishop's visits he could only speak with through an interpreter.

Then, on January 6, 1873, she fell gravely ill. The local doctor diagnosed a cancer of the stomach and a scrofulous tumor. Nothing can be done. It is all over. Her condition deteriorates, and at the end of a month, seeing her at the point of death, the family asks the priest for extreme unction. She remains in a coma. But seven days later she opens her eyes and sits up, stiff and immobile, before lapsing into unconsciousness again. She had just seen the Virgin, who promised to look after her by bringing her suffering each day between two and three in the afternoon. But it was not until March 15, 1873, that She asked her if she would accept the five wounds of her Son. Marie-Julie accepts and the Virgin promises her the wounds for Friday, March 21, 1873.

The entire village gathers at the farmhouse. After "invisible" sufferings all morning long, the stigmata arrive before an incredulous crowd: she loses consciousness, a hand begins to bleed, then the other hand, and so on. The five wounds appear in the space of half an hour. The onlookers are stunned, not knowing that these are called the stigmata. It is 1873, in the deep countryside of France, in an era when the schoolmaster and the village priest were the most important people in town. Some months later she announces the date of her marriage with Christ to the priest who promises to attend though he doesn't believe a word of it. And on February 20, 1874, fourteen dumbfounded witnesses observe her ecstasy and above all her hand: The ring finger of her right hand swells, reddens, and begins to bleed until a ring appears.

Of all the stigmatics, this is the only case I know of a marriage to Christ before human and lay witnesses! That union would naturally be accompanied by a number of supernatural phenomena, as for example levitation or hierognosis.[36] On this topic the stigmatic's biographer, Pierre Roberdel, reports that on July 17, 1874, Monseigneur Jacques Fournier decides to visit the "saint," accompanied by the Jesuit superior and two of his ecclesiastical friends. He awaits the ecstasy in order to test it, and at the moment when her body is most rigid he sets on the young woman's chest a cross made from the bark of a hazelnut tree where Christ appeared in Paray-le-Monial. Marie-Julie then murmurs: "Marguerite-Marie . . ." Like Theresa Neumann, the stigmatic of the place called La Fraudais identified the origins of blessed objects!

Marie-Julie Jahenny did not leave us a book like Anne-Catherine Emmerich, but her friends had the presence of mind to set down descriptions of her ecstasies. One among them interests us because it consists of a dialogue with the Archangel Michael. And this discussion between the Archangel and the little peasant stigmatic, on the weight of souls and on what we find in Paradise, is not lacking in bite:

> *Michael:* "*Now the time is nigh when victims will close their mortal eyelids to go and sit enthroned with the Lord, in glory.*"
>
> "*Oh, Saint Michael,*" answers the ecstatic, "*what have we to offer that we could even think of so lofty a journey?*"
>
> "*All the merit of the trials, all the virtues won by suffering and renunciation.*"
>
> "*That is nothing, holy Archangel. I will borrow something from my friends that I can return when they rise to heaven.*"
>
> "*It is I who hold the scales.*"
>
> "*Yes, I think of that often. When you weigh our souls in the balance, be careful to rank the good and the bad justly.*"

36. The ability of a person to recognize a holy object.

> *"All, I think, I will introduce you to the celestial Jerusalem. . . ."*
>
> *"When will you judge?"*
>
> *"During the day; there is no night."*
>
> *"Who does the judging while you are here with us?"*
>
> *"I am there."*
>
> *"Ah, Saint Michael, you cannot be in two places!"*
>
> *"Eternal power is great."*
>
> *"How many souls do you judge each day?"*
>
> *"Sometimes ten thousand, sometimes less. . . ."*
>
> *"Is there a rosary in paradise?"*
>
> *"Yes, and books as well."*
>
> *"And books as well? And those who wish to read them will learn how? Then who teaches school there?"*
>
> *"Good Jesus, the Angels, the saints."*
>
> *"Are the letters scratched with a quill, or are they formed with great care?"*
>
> *"They are glorious letters that have nothing in common with those of the earth."*[37]

The Devil also came to visit from time to time, which brought her the nickname *"Quequet!"* She almost chased him away with a rolling pin. In short, she could be truculent despite her stigmata. On the other hand during her ecstasies she always broke into Latin, a language she obviously did not know, serving as mouthpiece for holy figures (today we would say she was channeling!), indeed for even the Holy Ghost. This is interesting because the tenor of her talk is very different from what the illiterate peasant Marie-July could say in her normal state. Her body became progressively rigid and the Holy Ghost spoke through her mouth, while leaving her awake. And that "spirit" expressed himself in a rich and perfect "aristocratic" French, very far from Marie-Julie's local dialect, and touched on subjects that she knew nothing about. For example this communication on the "holy novitiate," which would not displease Saint Augustine, was miles from any of Marie-Julie's concerns:

> *At the seventh stage, the path of union to God costs the body more than all suffering, more than the greatest of sorrows, because the union of God and the soul must enter all the different parts of the body. That is why the body revolts against the soul and its new life. It is because the body is a*

37. Marie-Julie Jahenny, Editions Resiac, pp. 161–162.

*cowardly, idle flesh, that does not like sacrifices. The body*
*rebels because it sees itself invited by God to submit to the*
*perfect light of the soul: it is a shattering, a suffering*
*beyond comparison, not to be described in words. One*
*might say that it is the death of the body, and that the parts,*
*broken, shattered and reduced to nothingness, are obliged*
*to savor that death.*[38]

## HELENE KOWALSKA
## 1905–1938
### (Group IIa: Stigmata, Miracles, Angels)
### Poland

At the age of five, Helene Kowalksa explained to her parents that
she had visited Heaven (!), and at fourteen she asked her mother to
let her enter a convent. There was immediate family opposition. At
eighteen she had not abandoned the ambition, and she made her
request again. Once more, a refusal. On the one hand, the family
would be deprived of revenue (Helene worked as a maid), and on
the other hand there wasn't much money in the house to start with,
so putting together a dowry was not possible. Helene accepted the
decision. But during a neighborhood dance, she had a vision of
Christ, who asked her *"How long must I wait for you?"*

Helene Kowalska was a predestined soul with a specific mission,
in the fashion of Marguerite-Marie Alacoque or Maria Droste zu
Vischering. As Christ Himself had instructed her, Helene became
His secretary. Thus she fled her home and, without a dowry, joined
the Sisters of Mercy in Warsaw, which in itself is already a small
miracle. From there on it was just a series of supernatural events:
out of body trips, Angels, divine dialogues, stigmata, and especially
a diary. In effect, under Christ's orders, Helene, having become a
Faustian sister, kept a diary almost up to her death. And it is
unquestionably the most stunning testimony we possess, a sort of
daily chronicle of her particularly rich spiritual life—*A History of a
Soul*, in Polish. During my reading of this seven-hundred-page
tome, I was struck by the similarities between the Foreign Legion
and a strict convent. In some ways there is no difference. In both
organizations, free will, the ego, the "I" of the individual is erased,
destroyed, annihilated, wiped out by a wide range of possible and
imaginable humiliations. It must not, it cannot survive. Insofar as

38. Op. cit., p. 159.

the soul has not submitted totally, surrendered unconditionally, to the superior will, it is not ready to wear the white kepi in the first instance, and the veil in the second. Only absolute submission, that is to say the disappearance of all self-love, permits one to survive. Afterward that, there is only a series of events to manage daily. Sister Faustine let herself be entirely controlled by Christ and did nothing that He did not tell her to do. "You are My bride forever," He said to her, "your purity must be purer than angelic, as I do not admit any Angel into such intimacy. The least act of My bride has an infinite value, and a pure soul before God has unbelievable strength." But the reward for these mortifications was countless graces. Here, for example, is an experience of Sister Faustine which would not displease Dr. Melvin Morse:

> . . . *the traces of past torment remained on my body: for two days my face was deathly pale and my eyes were blood-shot. Jesus alone knows what I suffered. What I have written is quite feeble in comparison to the reality. I do not know how to explain it, it seems to me that I have returned from beyond. I feel a distaste for all creation.*[39]

But the reason why this Polish nun's notoriety penetrated the Iron Curtain lies in the painting of Christ that He asked her to execute, saying *"I promise that the soul which worships this image will not perish. I also promise victory over his enemies, particularly at the hour of his death. I will defend him myself as My own glory."*

When she revealed this order to her superior on February 22, 1931, *"The Lord wants this picture to be painted and worshipped in our chapel first and then throughout the world,"* her superior was sure she was dealing with a madwoman, a crank.

We also cannot help noting how similar this matter of Christ is to the matter of the Virgin and Catherine Laboure. The two women were considered mad, but in both cases, the medal and the painting were finally created in curious circumstances despite the opposition of confessors and mother superiors. Here, on January 2, 1934, three years after her vision, that the young woman was authorized to leave her convent, accompanied by Sister Borgia, to go to the home of painter Eugene Kazimierowski of Vilna. The artist listened to the nun, took notes, made rough sketches, asked for details and went to work. The young woman visited him once a week to help him with shapes and colors. But, when five months

39. *Journal of Sister Faustine*, Editions Hovine, p. 78.

later he presented her with the finished work, Sister Faustine broke into tears because the painter had not succeeded in making Him as handsome as He really was. Once finished, the painting hung in a corridor at the Sisters' for over two years. Christ is angered! He demands that it be blessed, shown, and publicly worshipped. We can imagine the expressions on the faces of the ecclesiastics who met as a commission on April 1, 1937, to deal with this exceedingly weird request by this ordinary but possibly hysterical nun from a convent. The painting nevertheless won their support. But only during the war would that image streak about like a line of gunpowder, exactly like the miraculous medal of Catherine Laboure.

Angels were rare in Sister Faustine's life, and when one did appear, it was in the role of bodyguard. But the sister who experienced the love of God and saw Christ was not really interested in Angels. He was there and she knew it. From time to time she perceived him, a *"bright and radiant apparition,"* but we see no such profound attachment to the Angel as we shall see with Gemma Galgani. Nevertheless she saw them, as for example on the day she renewed her vows:

> And I saw the Angels take from each sister something which they put in a golden bowl, which had the shape of a censer. When they had made the round of all the sisters, they set the vase on the second dish of the balance, and its weight immediately overwhelmed the dish with the sword. Then a flame shot up from the censer and rose to utter brightness.

Very mystical, Helene Kowalska was not a sister to spend her life only in praying. She saw everything, and the little details of life were more touching to her than a great sermon. One evening, she examined the starry sky from the window of her cell and marveled like a child at this *"firmament seeded with stars and the moon":*

> Suddenly in my soul there rose an inconceivable flame of love for my Creator. Not knowing how to bear the yearning for Him that rose from my soul, I prostrated myself, humbling myself in the dust. I praised Him for all his creations. And when my heart could no longer bear what was happening in Him, I burst into sobs. Then my guardian Angel touched me and said, "The Lord tells you to rise." I obeyed immediately, but I was not consoled. The yearning

*for God invaded me again.*

*One day when I was lost in adoration, my spirit was as*
*if in agony and I could not hold back my tears; then I saw a*
*spirit of great beauty who said to me, "The Lord  says, do*
*not weep." After a moment I asked: "Who are you?" He said*
*to me: "I am one of the seven spirits who remain before the*
*throne of God night and day, and praise Him ceaselessly."*
*And yet even that spirit did not appease my yearning for*
*God, but only made it increase. The beauty of that spirit*
*came from his close union with God. It never left me for a*
*single moment, it accompanied me everywhere. During*
*Mass the next day, before the Elevation, he began to chant*
*the words, "Holy, holy, holy," and his voice resounded like*
*the voices of thousands; it is impossible to describe.*

We are going to meet this angelic spirit again, but much later, to
be precise on September 10, 1937, when Poland feels the first stir-
rings of future turbulence. The young woman is in charge of the
entry door of the convent:

*When I realised how dangerous it was in our day to be*
*near the entrance, because of the revolutionary discord,*
*and how many bad people hated convents, I had a conver-*
*sation with the Lord and asked Him to see to it that no evil*
*person dared approach the door. Then I heard these words:*
*"My daughter, the moment you were assigned this service, I*
*set a cherub there to guard you. Therefore do not be dis-*
*tressed." When I returned from my conversation with the*
*Lord, I saw a light white cloud and in the cloud a cherub,*
*hands clasped, whose glance was like a flash of lightning.*

Note that while at the time the portrait of a cherub was
inevitably a little angel of six or seven with chubby buttocks, there
is no such description by sister Faustine. A glance like lightning,
which makes us sense power and contained violence. The same
when she fell sick. In the sanatorium she was dying and could not
take communion. No problem. The Angels were there for that as
well. An Angel from the hierarchy of the seraphim (Sister Faustine
did not explain to us how they differed) appeared suddenly at the
foot of her bed:

*A great light surrounded this seraph, divinity and*
*divine love were reflected in him. He wore a gilded vest-*

*ment covered by a surplice and a transparent stole. The
chalice was of crystal and covered with a veil, also transparent. Once a certain doubt crept over me a little before
communion and the seraph appeared before me, accompanied by Jesus. I prayed to Jesus, and receiving no response,
I said to the seraph: "Can you not confess me?" He replied,
"No spirit in heaven has that power." At that very moment
the host was laid upon my lips.*[40]

From the very start of her religious life, Sister Faustine had
managed to overcome various pulmonary congestions of her tuberculosis, but in 1938 they became more and more serious. She died
at the age of . . . thirty-three, on October 5, 1938. That nun's soul
would surely have been forgotten—after all she was not the only
nun to keep a diary—but the distribution of the portrait of Christ
that she herself had commissioned became so widespread after the
war that in 1965 a certain Karol Wojtola, archbishop of Cracow,
examined her dossier and decided to open her cause of beatification. Today that portrait of Christ, like the miraculous medal, is to
be found in many churches, without any reference to or indication
of its origin. She was beatified on April 18, 1993 by John-Paul II.


# GEMMA GALGANI
## 1878–1903
### (Group IIa: Stigmata, Miracles, Angels)
### Italy

Gemma Galgani is a true diamond among the "Flower of the
Saints," a unique person in the Church because, like Marilyn
Monroe, her beauty has been made permanent by her death. She is
unquestionably the prettiest of all the saints in the calendar, for
"Divine Providence" gave her a dazzling, almost unreal beauty,
with the features of a noblewoman and a delicacy worthy of Carole
Bouquet when she starred in Buñuel's *That Obscure Object of
Desire.* Gemma Galgani is the aristocracy of discreet luxe, the
power of humility, voluntary victim of divine brutality. Gemma
Galgani is almost an illustration from the novel *The Angel of Fire,*[41]

40. *Journal of Sister Faustine,* p. 536.

41. Written by the Russian author Valery Brysov, her contemporary (1873–1924),
   *The Angel of Fire* served later at inspiration to the composer Sergei Prokofiev. His
   opera is, alas, so boring as to induce an NDE.

which tells how a young woman, Renata, looks for her guardian Angel, whom she was privileged to see constantly during her childhood, a little like the Brasilian nun Cecilia Cony. But Renata, unlike Cecilia Cony,[42] outraged her Angel, Maniel, when, attaining puberty, she asked him in all innocence to make love with her. The Angel left her promising at any rate to come back in human form when the time came. After that Renata, become a woman, never ceased to search for him and tried to discern in every man the presence of her Angel. This was a novel based on the relationship between the terrestrial and celestial worlds, where Angels, demons and humans are intermixed in a perpetual fight for souls, a perfect setting for Gemma Galgani. She spent her (short) life swimming in the supernatural as others did in music. Angels and demons waged daily battle for the soul of that young and magnificent virgin. We can understand that. I know some who would not hesitate for a second to confront Satan himself for her beautiful eyes.

Gemma Galgani's life is a synopsis of this permanent combat, of every soul's tribulations. Only with her, it was carried to extremes. A predestined soul, Gemma accepted her mission very early without really understanding what it was. But from the end of her adolescence she wanted to become a Passionist nun. And as usual, when she was twenty a paralysis of the legs—Pott's Disease—immobilized her. As if this were not enough, she was then felled by a tumor in her head coupled with a purulent ear infection.

The doctors operated on her several times, but, unable to cure her, finally decided to give up on her, decreeing that science could not save her from a quick death. Gemma did not give up hope. Her spiritual life was already prodigious and, bedridden, she started upon a novena to the Sacred Heart of Jesus and to Marguerite-Marie Alacoque. The morning of the ninth day, she inexplicably recovered from all her ills. It was Friday, March 3, 1899. From that day on, much more grateful to Christ than to the doctors, Gemma regularly observed the holy hour,[43] a habit which bore her toward constant devotion to Christ. And while praying before her crucifix on a Friday in March, 1901, she felt the flagellation of her flesh, like all stigmatics. Her adoptive mother found her lying on the ground, her back bloody and striped by the marks of a lash. Thenceforth Gemma Galgani would relive Christ's Passion every

---

42. Note her little book *Je dois raconter ma vie, Ange gardien mon ami (I Must Recount my Life, Guardian Angel My Friend)*, Editions Téqui, utterly insipid, it seems so "arranged."

43. Every Thursday from 11:00 P.M. to midnight.

Thursday from 10:00 P.M. to Friday at 3:00 P.M.

Theologians have a tendency to compare the saints among themselves and discuss their merits and respective powers (a little like sports cars), and we cannot help noting the marked similarities between Gemma Galgani (a Ferrari, of course) and Thérèsa of Lisieux. Both of them, with a simplicity and a candor that would make a hangman cry, scaled the steps of Saint Peter's of Rome at lightning speed: Gemma died at the age of twenty-five and Thérèsa at twenty-four (when Gemma was nineteen). The Carmelite did not bear the signature of Christ, but Gemma, although a laywoman, participated of her own will in the Passion, the open door to the most amazing graces. Other than levitation and communication at a distance, Gemma Galgani could also "see" her guardian Angel and talked regularly with him during her lifetime. Notes from her journal, 1895:

> One time, I remember very well, I was given a gift of a golden watch with a chain; ambitious as I was, I hastened to put it on and go out (my imagination ran away with me). So I went out, and when I came back I was about to undress when I saw an Angel (now I know that it was my Angel) who said to me very seriously: "Remember that precious jewels adorning the bride of a crucified king can only be thorns and the cross."
>
> I did not even repeat those words to my confessor; I am saying them today for the first time. Those words struck fear into me. So did the Angel; but a little later, reflecting on those words without understanding them, I made the following resolution: for Love for Jesus and to please Him, I will no longer wear nor speak of vanities.[44]

Some consider Gemma Galgani a minor mystic, doubtless because she "saw nothing" like Hildegarde von Bingen and because she was neither a gifted tertiary Dominican, nor a Carmelite in ecstasy, nor a troubled Franciscan, but simply a stigmatic laywoman. Yet in her memoirs we find passages that inevitably make us think of the more than disconcerting ecstasies of Marguerite-Marie Alacoque, of Angela de Foligno or of Maria-Magdalena dei Pazzi. We also discover sentences we could call classic, of Christly statements made to mystical brides condemned to live in suffering in exchange for His love:

---

44. *Writing of Gemma Galgani*, Editions Téqui, p. 52.

> *"I burn with desire to unite with you," Jesus repeated to me. "Hurry to me every morning. But you must know," he said to me, "that I am a father, a jealous husband. Will you be a daughter and faithful bride to me?"*

On her part, the conversations between Gemma and Christ did not lack spice as we shall see:

> *"You ask me constantly, Jesus, if I love You. You repeat, 'Gemma, do You love me?' I say No! You have given me so much grace, but You do not grant me the most necessary grace of all. Do I upset You? Well! When I have upset You enough (the Italian word saccato has here a friendly familiar sense), then You will say to me 'Yes I grant it to you!'"*
> *Jesus broke into a smile.*
> *And then she said: "Listen, Jesus. Will You grant me that grace? If not, this will end badly."*[45]

If Gemma's guardian Angel hovered on the second level, their entire relationship spoke of a "great love": the Angel watched over her, made coffee for her, explained the Mysteries to her, kissed her, but above all helped her as best she could to suffer for Christ. As for Gemma, she spoke to the celestial being, and more than once her close friends saw her walking, all the while chatting with an invisible companion:

> *The Angel was looking at me so affectionately! And when he was about to go away, and came closer to kiss me on the forehead, I begged him not to leave me again. But he said to me: "I must go."*
> *"Then go and greet Jesus."*
> *He gave me a last look, saying: "I do not want you to hold any conversations with anyone; when you want to talk, talk with Jesus and with your Angel."*
> *Next day at the same time, there he was again. He came close to me, he caressed me, and I could not keep from blurting, "My Angel, how I love you!"*[46]

Even though a laywoman, this splendid virgin was canonized

45. Thor Salviat, *Gemma Galgani, Vierge de Lucques*, Paris, Maison de la Bonne Press, 1936, pp. 118 and 120.
46. J.F. Villepelée, *La Folie de la Croix*, vol. 2, Editions Parvis, p. 165.

only thirty-seven years after her death. Because of various supernatural signs and inexplicable healings, Rome became interested
in her case in 1917 and she was proclaimed a saint on March 26,
1936. Since then, her face continues to fascinate multitudes, a bit
like the enigmatic Great Garbo's. Gemma Galgani is the mystery
of Mysteries, the Love of a virgin for the One who loved the
World, and their colloquy of sufferings seems to belong to an
absurd world. In learning to suffer as He suffered, in succeeding
in resisting temptation, and in achieving self-mortification to the
point of killing any desire that might have endangered her virginity, Gemma raised herself to His level and cleansed herself of all
stain. With such purity, seeing her guardian Angel was as natural
to her as for us to see the mailman every morning. But Gemma
never described her companion, for she saw her Angel as she saw
her mother-in-law or her confessor. To her its presence was not
in the least exceptional, and in her childlike simplicity she was
totally unaware that it would have fascinated thousands of
people. She moved among the Angels like a swan on a lake,
insensible to the beauty that surrounded her. Only Christ mat-
tered in her eyes. Even her confessor, the very strict Father
Germain, noted his surprise on hearing Gemma explain that her
Angel had said this or that, and he asked her to be prudent; is it
not written that the Devil can disguise himself as an Angel of
Light, and consequently reject all vision? Then Gemma, still with
her disarming naïveté, wrote to him a few days later that when
the Angel comes, they joke together and adore God. She even
asked him: *"Is that good? Tell me if I am being obedient?"* Even the
confessor no longer knew what to tell her. Nevertheless, she
finally "tested" the presence, obeying the orders of Father Germain to the letter, which allows us to state that this is the only
case in the annals of modern angeology where a protégé  spits at
his guardian Angel!!

> *One day when the guardian Angel presented himself,*
> *Gemma spat in his face, trying to sent him away. But the*
> *Angel did not move; more, there at the Angel's feet, where*
> *Gemma spat, appeared a white rose; on its petals was writ-*
> *ten in letters of gold "from Love we accept everything."*[47]

This detail is important—really, what an idea, wanting to spit at
an Angel! It is grotesque and very ugly, so ugly that clearly this

47. Ibid., p. 153.

cannot be a made-up story. But Father Germain doubtless feared that the Evil One would take advantage of Gemma's naïveté. Finally he decided to verify her experience for himself. We don't know exactly how he arrived at this conclusion, but he wrote that having observed *"the prayers and meditations of Gemma and her Angel several times personally, I was able to convince myself, solely by my own objective observations, of the reality of all the details she gave me later in her examinations of conscience."*

The objective observations of which the priest speaks are no less rigorous than what children who claimed to see the Virgin had to undergo:

> *Every time, he* [Father Germain] *remarked, that she raised her eyes to the Angel to listen or speak to him, even outside of prayer, she lost her senses. One could shake her, prick her, burn her, without awakening her sensitivities. But as soon as she averted her gaze from the Angel or ended the conversation, her relationship to our world was restored. This phenomenon invariably recurred at each of her communications with the blessed spirit, so close were they.*[48]

According to the priest, Gemma also sent him messages that her Angel gave her for him, even when he was in consultation in Rome. In his room he found letters from Gemma without stamps! That impressed him so much that he never again doubted the presence of Gemma Galgani's guardian Angel.

## MARGUERITE-MARIE ALACOQUE
## 1647–1690
### (Group IIa: Stigmata, Miracles, Angels)
#### France

France too had its Maria-Magdalena dei Pazzi in the person of Marguerite-Marie Alacoque. Alas, unlike to the "great" Pazzi, Marguerite-Marie was never authorized by her Divine Spouse to leave her convent of Paray-le-Monial. That is a shame. Happily all the contemporary documents have survived describing this other faithful "bride," born July 22, 1647, in Verosvres in Burgundy to the notary

---

48. Germano and Félix, *La Bienheureuse Gemma Galgani (The Blessed Gemma Galgani)*, Paris, Librairie Mignard, 1933, p. 231.

Claude Alacoque and Philiberte Lamyne. And yet Marguerite-Marie
is little known. Let us also emphasize that of all the "brides," Marguerite Alacoque's ecstasies and raptures "Alacoque" influenced the
Catholic community most, as we owe to her the universal worship of
the Sacred Heart, a concept totally nonexistent in her era. Without
her, no churches dedicated to Sacre-Coeur, no representations of
Christ with a bleeding heart, no nuns bearing that name, no basilica
in Paris,[49] in short, no cult dedicated to this organ of Christ which
would thenceforth not live a completely independent life of its own.
Marguerite was chosen to begin the worship of the Sacred Heart, as
formerly, in the 13th century, Sister Juliette du Mont-Cornillion was
chosen to begin the worship of the body of Christ (Corpus Christi).

But no saint lived as miserable an existence as Marguerite-
Marie. A true martyr of His Heart . . . why? From her adolescence,
during a vision, she had dedicated herself to Christ by taking a vow
of chastity. He accepted it and spoke to her thus:

> *I have chosen you for my Bride. We promised fidelity
> each to the other when you made a vow of chastity to Me.
> It is I who urged you to make it, before the world partook
> of your heart, because I wished it utterly pure and unsul-
> lied by earthly affections.*

At eighteen, when her mother wanted to marry her off, she
wavered, but not for long, because He intervened vigorously:

> *Constantly He reminds her of her vow, and one day
> after communion He shows her that He is the handsomest,
> the richest, the most powerful, the most perfect and accom-
> plished of lovers. He also threatens her also if she chooses
> someone other than Him.*[50]

Real scenes of jealousy. But no woman has resisted Him. Just
the idea of marrying a man and abandoning Him made her suffer
dramatic remorse. To strike that idea forever from her mind and to
beg His pardon, Marguerite did not take to lace-making; she
whipped herself with a scourge,[51] slept on a board, tied a knotted

---

49. Open night and day, it dominates Paris and is always at the top of the list among
    the three monuments most visited by tourists.
50. Jean Ladame, *La Sainte du Paray,* Editions Resiac, p. 33.
51. I would love to find an essay or a book on this subject some day, like *Memoirs of
    Convent Discipline over the Centuries.*

rope around her body, wrapped her arms in chains, etc. Finally, after some rough family squabbles, she entered the Convent of the Visitation in Paray-le-Monial as a novice at the age of twenty-four. On December 27, 1667, her visions of Christ became more and more intense: He informed the pretty virgin that He had chosen her as his instrument to establish the cult of His Sacred Heart. Then, showing her a cross covered with flowers, He warned her:

> *Here is the bed of My chaste brides where I will have you consummate the delights of my love. Little by little, these flowers will fall, there will remain only the thorns that these flowers hide because of your weakness; soon they will make you feel their points so sharply that you will need all the strength of My love to accept your martyrdom.*

Terrible words, that even seem dreadful to us, but which never dimmed the young bride's enthusiasm. Besides the sufferings imposed by the stigmata, Marguerite-Marie had also to stoically withstand the nuns of the convent, who humiliated her daily for years, as a pastime.[52] How far does mystical devotion go?

> *I was so delicate that the least filth made my heart leap. He (Christ) admonished me so strongly on that point that one time, wanting to clean up an invalid's vomit, I could not help doing it with my tongue. He had me take so much pleasure in the act that I would have liked to do the same every day. To repay me, the following night he held me two or three hours with my mouth pressed to his Sacred Heart. . . . Holding Marguerite-Marie's head to his heart, He said to her: "My heart is so full of love for all humanity and for you in particular that, unable to hold back the fires of its ardent charity, it must magnify them in you."*

Curiously, the biographers of *Flowers of the Saints* regularly forget to note that the individual was stigmatic or incorruptible and always tell a gilded story which we doubt immediately, not because the biography is false, but because the events are embellished, ornamented, scorning the details that do not conform to

---

52. Sister Jeanne-Marie Contois, forty-four years later, would testify to the court in 1715 that the mistresses, seeing Marguerite enter her novitiate with extraordinary joy and fervor, would make her rather than the others suffer a variety of mortifications and humiliations. Page 56 in *La Sainte de Paray.*

Christian "morality." But Marguerite-Marie Alacoque's most unusual life is not devoid of gripping details. Like Catherine of Siena and Magdalena dei Pazzi, she overcame her reticence, her body and her psychological revulsions to better welcome Him. And the three women then described how their souls left their bodies, borne toward raptures *"that cannot be explained in human terms."*

There are celestial love stories, where the Angels, impassive, stand in silent witness to their ecstasies. Apropos of Angels, Sister Marguerite-Marie addressed a letter to the reverend father Jean Croset, dated August 10, 1689, in which she insisted on the importance that He accorded to the relations between men and Angels:

> *God wants the union of Angels and Men. If one could create an association for that devotion, whose members participated for the spiritual good of both, I think that would give great pleasure to this divine Heart; which, it seem to me, would also desire that we feel a special union with and devotion to the holy Angels, who are particularly intended to love, honor and praise Him in this divine sacrament of love, so that being united and associated with them, they represent us in his divine presence, not only to render our homage to him but also to love him for us and for all those who do not love him, and to repair the irreverences that we commit in his holy presence.*

And indeed Christ decided one fine day to give her an Angel, *"a faithful guardian, one of the seven spirits who are closest to the throne of God and who participate the most in the ardors of the Sacred Heart"* that she could only see when Christ was angry (??) On the other hand, when He was in a good mood, the Angel became invisible. Yet one day, the Angel put her in her place: *"Be careful that no grace of God makes you forget what He is and what you are."*

Here is a vision of seraphim written by Sister Alacoque:

> *And one other time, as we worked at the communal task of braiding hemp, I retired to a small courtyard, near the holy sacrament, where doing my work on my knees, I felt first totally meditative, within and without, and saw at the same time a vision of the lovable heart of my adorable Jesus, brighter than the sun. He stood amid the flames of his pure love, surrounded by seraphim who sang in admirable chorus:*

> *"Love triumphs, love delights*
> *Love of the Sacred Heart rejoices."*
> *And when these happy spirits invited me to join them*
> *in their praise of this divine Heart, I dared not do it; but*
> *they begged me again. . . . And after the two or three hours*
> *that it lasted, I have felt the effects all my life, as much for*
> *the help I received as for the sweetness it produced and still*
> *produces in me; I was totally overwhelmed and confused;*
> *and in praying to them I never again called them anything*
> *but my divine associates.*

Up against the mistrust and hostility of the convent's Mother Superior, the nun waited almost twenty years before the first mass in honor of the Sacred Heart was celebrated by her convent.[53]

Marguerite-Marie rejoined Him forever at the age of forty-three, after eighteen years of martyrdom. Doctor Billet, who followed her and cared for her as well as he could, has left us a wonderfully (and unintentionally) comic commentary, considering the circumstances (the body is still lying on the bed):

> *Since this girl had lived by a miracle a life of so many*
> *mortal and desperate illnesses, which she was able to resist*
> *naturally, I was not surprised that by another miracle she*
> *had died with no appearance of real sickness.*[54]

Marguerite was buried in the convent's vault, and her remains obeyed nature. And yet we may feel vexed for her that after such a life He did not deign to leave her "incorruptible": on November 26, 1705, when her vault was opened for lack of space to put other "arrivals," that is fifteen years after her death, the sisters found only some bones that they distributed generously. Which proves once again that the bodies of these saints are not the object of any special treatment at their death, as no one suspects at the time that they are headed for beatification.

---

53. Paray-le-Monial was the first town to construct (in 1688) a church in honor of the Sacred Heart. Nevertheless the cult did not become official until after the signing of a bull by Pope Clement XIII in 1765, seventy-five years after the death of Sister Marguerite-Marie.

54. Jean Ladame citing Languet, p. 334, op. cit.

## ANGELA DE FOLIGNO
## 1250–1309
### (Group IIa: Stigmata, Miracles, Angels)
### Italy

The Italian Angela de Foligno (1250–1309), a tertiary Franciscan recluse at Foligno (Umbria), also lived the Passion to the last stroke of the whip. Angela was a beautiful woman, rich, noble, well married, who divided her time among her lovers, her children, her husband, and the pleasures offered by wealth. But when Christ sets his heart on a soul, like any terrestrial lover, He levels all obstacles. Nothing resists love, especially Christ's love. Thus it was—and she had asked it of Him—that Angela lost, one after another, her seven children, her mother, and her husband, nine people altogether. Once the way was clear, He was able to begin his work of transformation. And after she had truly experienced Divine love, she knew that no earthly love could ever satisfy her, and decided then and there, at forty years of age, to distribute all her worldly goods among the needy and to have only a single lover, Christ. An astonishing marriage, in which suffering, beatific ecstasies, mystical raptures, the delights of heavenly ravishment, and dialogues with the Most High flourished like wild poppies along a deserted road. When we read her *Visions and Instructions*, we are literally dumbfounded by it, so much does that rapture in Him transform her, transport her, carry her to extremes, to a kind of trial, deep within her very entrails, of the love that they express.

She has left us a work so strong that her memoir has survived seven hundred years in print without interruption!! What authenticated Angela de Foligno was first her stigmata, visible proofs of the Invisible, and then the mass of testimonies of all those who had occasion to attend her regular mystical weddings in church, as well as the sworn testimonies that she ate nothing for more than twelve years after a communion with the Angels.

In her boundless love for Christ, Angela went much further than the good Padre Pio or Gemma Galgani: She enjoyed herself physically, she moaned, she cried out, she loved Him and He loved her in a Heaven certainly above the seventh. She suffered terribly in reliving the Passion but she suffered with pleasure because she knew that it would ease His sufferings. She even went so far as to offer herself totally nude before the cross. The wonder of feminine love, indestructible, unique; and we understand through her why women reach a new and higher level of emotion when they discover Him.

Angela has never been canonized, but it is easy to imagine,

given the record of her Love, that wherever she is, she couldn't care less. From her ecstasies she has left us her angelic visions and her burning sensations,[55] dictating them to Brother Arnaud, a Franciscan monk, who immediately translated them into Latin. He spent a good part of his life scratching away at these pleasures with a goose quill, these paradisiac raptures that he never felt but saw, supposed, presumed, and above all understood. He was so impressed that he decided to devote his life to Angela. *"Children of our scared mother, be careful of human respect! Learn from our Angela, learn from our Angel, learn from the Angel of good advice, the way of magnificence and the wisdom of the cross! Learn about poverty, suffering, disgrace and obedience to Jesus,"* we may read in the first prologue. In the second, he warns: *"Here is the manifestation of gifts from the Most High, made in the spirit of my mother, Angela de Foligno. Following the word and the promise He made in his Gospel: 'Whosoever loveth me, he will keep My word, and my Father will love him, and we will come to him, and We will remain in him.' and 'He who loveth Me, I will show Myself to him.' . . . I, Brother Arnaud, of the order of Miners, by strong entreaties, have torn from her (Angela) the secret of her eyes and her soul."*

Having become a tertiary Franciscan recluse, Angela allowed herself to be borne off by her God. Her body lived in a tiny cell, regularly brought to heel by the "scourge," an instrument of fetish that, it would seem, helps considerably to calm all desire. In short, as the Franciscans noted, Angela was no longer really of our world. Here are two extracts of her numerous raptures during which the Angels appeared:

> *Then I saw how Jesus Christ came with an army of angels, and the magnificence of his escort let my soul relish it with immense delight. I surprised myself for a moment by being able to take pleasure in looking upon the angels, for as a rule all my joy is centered on Jesus Christ alone. But soon I perceived in my soul two completely different joys, one coming from God and the other from the angels, and they were not alike. I admired the magnificence surrounding the Lord, and I asked what the beings I beheld were called. "They are thrones," the voice said. Their multi-*

---

55. Angela de Foligno, *Le Livre des visions and instructions (The Book of Visions and Teachings)*, Paris, Seuil, collection Points Sagesse, 1991; translated by Ernest Hello.

*tude was resplendent, and so totally beyond enumerating that if number and measure were not laws of creation I would have believed the sublime crowd I saw to be without number and without measure. I saw no end to that multitude in either breadth or length; I saw crowds greater than all our figures.* [56]

*On the other hand I felt such extreme pleasure and such great joy in the presence of the angels; their talk was so pleasing to me that their words had never before brought me such joy. I would never have believed the very holy angels to be so pleasant and capable of obtaining such delights for the soul if they hadn't obtained them for me. As I had prayed to all of the angels but to the seraphs in particular, the very holy angels said to me:*
*"Here and now you receive what the seraphs possess, and share in it."* [57]

## GERTHRUDE D'HELFTA
## 1256–1301
### (Group IIa: Stigmata, Miracles, Angels)
### Germany

Latinists speak of the "Grand Gertrude," who left them an imperishable work, written in a delectable Latin full of verve and poetry. And we are still amazed by this anthology of mystical women all from the same convent—Helfta, a town near Bingen—and from the same space-time since Helfta was also the cradle of Mechtilde of Magdeburg and Mechtilde von Hackenborn. It was the time of Saxon Beguines, Carmelites and Cistercians, all just emerging from the dark years of the Middle Ages. Women on whom The Love of the Most High had melted like a pastry, leaving them drained, mortified and then destroyed by their sufferings. Medical knowledge in that era was not even at the level of Moliere's doctors. We know that Gertrude was born on January 6, 1256, and that as an orphan she was taken in by the abbey of Helfta, where she died November 17, 1301. Educated exclusively by the sisters, Gertrude there learned Latin, letters, music and of course all the religious texts.

---

56. *Le Livre des visions et instructions,* Editions Seuil, p. 114
57. *Le livre de l'expérience des vrais fidéles (The Book of the Experience of the Truly Faithful),* Paris, Droz, 1927. Cited by V. Klee.

She herself acknowledged, *"I took care of my soul like my old slip-pers; I lived like the most pagan of pagans."* In a nutshell, she took advantage of her convent life as a young woman until the day she went through a true depression lasting more than a month. She would never have come out of it if one evening, in the dormitory, an Angel with the features *"of a young man of perfect distinction and beauty"* had not appeared to her, saying: *"Don't give way to grief and sorrow; your health will soon be restored."* She was twenty-five. The Angel announced to her the imminent arrival of Christ. From then on, her life changed completely, going from ecstasies to rap-tures and sufferings to expiations. Gertrude, bride of Christ, benefited from an impressive protection by Angels, according to this testimony:

> The feast day of the Archangel Michael was approach-ing. One day when she (Gertrude) was to take communion, she recalled the good works that, thanks to divine generos-ity, she received from all the blessed spirits, despite her great unworthiness. In her desire to repay them, she dedi-cated to God the invigorating sacrament of her body and blood, saying: "In honor of those grand princes (the Angels) who are yours, O my beloved Lord, I offer you this admirable sacrament in eternal praise for the increase of their joy, their glory and their beatitude." Then the Lord allowed the sacrament that she had offered him into his divinity, there to unite with him in a marvelous and inex-pressible way, and to spread among the blessed spirits such ineffable delights that, if they had never before enjoyed blessedness, this favor would suffice to see them at the height of happiness, in an overabundance of delights. The holy Angels, then, according to their rank, went to bend the knee to her with great reverence, saying:
>
> "You have acted well, doing us the honor of such an oblation, and we will watch over you with special affection."
>
> The hierarchy of Angels said: "In an ineffable joy we are careful to guard you night and day with all solicitude, we will see to it that you lack nothing of what is suitable to adorn you in the expectation of your Spouse."

Gertrude d'Helfta was canonized by Rome in 1677, after pres-sure from the king of Spain. Almost three centuries of patience for that woman who, like Saint Francis of Assisi, received the five wounds of the Passion after a vision of Christ. She left us three works, *The Revelations of Saint Gertrude,* the *Liber Specials Gratie* and the *Spiritual Exercises.*

# CHAPTER 10

# An Ecstasy Like No Other

THIS GROUP OF STIGMATICS AND THEIR ANGELS REQUIRES US TO PAUSE for reflection on these predestined souls. Who are they, and why do they see Angels and other heavenly beings when the common run of mortals, including the religious, remains blind? The French journalist Helene Renard, who studied this mysterious question of stigmata, finally concluded that save for *"the few pretenders or hysterics, we note that the majority of cases of stigmatization do not answer to supposedly 'natural' explanations. The 'supernatural' explanation is the one that believing Catholics advance: the stigmata are given by Christ himself (with the consent of the mystic) so that he may participate in the torment of his Passion with a view to redemption. But to my mind the word 'participate' is badly chosen. Stigmatics do much more than 'participate.' They are the suffering part of the invisible body of Christ. They actualize the Passion. They prolong it by living it from generation to generation. One might say, using another vocabulary, that they are 'somatic,' that is, they imprint in their bodies a reality thenceforth invisible but always present."*[1]

In effect these souls extend the Passion, like the baton in an athletic race that goes on and on in time, transmitted from one soul to another. Not a century passes without these victims, chosen by Him, whom he brings low with sickness and expiated sufferings. And we would have every right to think Christ a sadist if He offered only pains. These "chosen" souls do not spend their lives in expiation, under the blows of the Father and Christ, groaning, drooling, carted from one hospital to the next. Not at all. God recompenses them too, favors them with ecstasies, supernatural

1. *Des Prodiges et des hommes*, p. 83.

graces and celestial visions which, once tasted, erode their desire to stay on this earth.

Once they have discovered this divine ecstasy, they are ready to suffer still more for Him so that He will not abandon them; they have tasted paradise and its Angels and are capable of immolating themselves alive if he were to ask them. It is true that their lives seem horrible to us. But in the end what do we really know about it? If we could just once taste that divine ecstasy, perhaps we would leave wife, mistress and children to live with Him, somewhat like the countess who left her chateau, title, and fortune to live with the gardener because he had shown her sensual pleasure. Is physical orgasm then just a pale imitation of mystical ecstasy? Jean-Noel Vuarnet studied Bernini's statue of Louise Albertoni[2] so carefully that he entitled his chapter *"No doubt about it, she is coming."*[3] Carried away by her lips parted in obvious pleasure and that hand pressed to a swelling bosom, he writes: *"But what is she suffering and what is she enjoying, the happy Ludovica? . . . If it is the divine called to the divan, it is certainly woman whom he visits, a woman who, like Theresa, finds herself completely transformed 'in frozen curves of marble.'"* And he adds the reflection of Lacan, who was also perturbed by the blessed: *"And why is she in the throes? It is clear that the essential testimony of mystics is that they experience it, but know nothing of it."*

Christ one day asked Gemma Galgani: *"Do you love me?"*[4] To which she answered, *"What a question. . . ."* Stigmatics seem to live an even greater ecstasy, ready to receive plague, cholera and cancer together to taste and retaste his Love, a love that only He can offer. Inevitably, I think back also to all those who fused with the Light in a NDE and who, on their return, stated that they were ready to die on the spot to return to this luminous nectar. Moreover don't they say that they did not want to come back?

What then is that ecstasy like none other? Dr. Elizabeth Kübler-Ross, remembering her experience at the Monroe Institute, compared this ecstasy to an *"orgasm to the power of ten thousand."* Gemma Galgani spoke of *"celestial delights,"* but as she was a virgin, we do not know just what she was comparing them to. To nothing, simply because everybody declared as if with one voice,

2. Roman widow, 1474–1533, tertiary Franciscan subject to numerous ecstasies and visions.

3. *Extases Féminines*, pp. 131–2.

4. Read also *Mariette in Ecstasy*, a short novel by Ron Hansen, published by Harper Perennial, New York, 1991.

*"It cannot be described in human terms."* But I defy the reader to describe sexual orgasm in words. It is not easy at all. And if that cannot be described, then imagine an orgasm to the ten thousandth power.

To taste that Love during one's lifetime, one must follow the way of the cross in fourteen stages, to relive it in the flesh, to earn the right to that ecstasy BEFORE the resurrection. These "victims" suffer, certainly, but Christ is far from a mean Spouse. His brides live through what he has lived through, but they also experience his divinity as an everyday matter: bilocations, visions, perfumes, hierognosis, clairvoyance, incorruptibility, healings, seraphim, guardian Angels, levitation, communion from afar, etc. A veritable basket of supernatural wedding presents, and it is true that the most precise visions of Angels always come to us signed and sealed from these souls. The blood they lose each Friday is the blood He lost. The whiplashes they feel are the whiplashes he suffered. How can we ignore these cases? How can we relegate them to some category of autosuggestion? Have we ever seen a corpse remaining incorruptible because its occupant had autosuggested incorruptibility of the physical shell during his lifetime? And even when some psychiatrists succeeded in reproducing Christ's wounds on a patient by autosuggestion, we were a very long way from the characteristics of the true stigmatic. The blood of these sick people gives off a nauseating odor, the wound infects, and when the patient comes out of the hypnotic state, the autosuggested wounds disappear progressively. Was Padre Pio a fake, he who stripped a soul bare in three seconds, confounding the penitent by listing his sins, like a mechanic who peers at a wreck and offers an estimate?

Well?

The stigmatics truly seem to represent Christ on Earth, souls who, in accepting suffering, permit Him to redeem other souls (mine, yours), distanced from their Creator. . . . And perhaps this dialogue of Christ—one day no doubt when He was out of sorts—with Gemma Galgani will enlighten us better than any theological treatise:

> *My daughter, what ingratitude and malice there is in the world! Sinners live on stubbornly clinging to evil. My Father no longer wants to tolerate them. These lazy and degraded souls make no effort to change their bad habits. The afflicted souls fall into discouragement and despair. The ardent souls cool down little by little. The ministers of my sanctuary . . . (here Jesus paused; a moment later he*

*went on), those I had ordered to go on with the good work of redemption . . . (Jesus paused again). My Father can no longer tolerate them either. I give them light and strength continually. And they, in return! . . . Those to whom I have always been partial; those whom I have always considered very precious . . . (Jesus stopped and sighed). I am constantly forgotten, unrecognized by ungrateful creatures. Indifference increases every day; no one improves. And from the heights of heaven, I dispense graces and favors to all; I give light and life to the church; virtue and power to those who govern it; wisdom to him who must enlighten shadowed souls; strength and countenance to whoever walks with me; manifold graces to all the just and even to sinners hidden in their shadowy lairs. Even there, I show them the way; even there, I show them tenderness and do all possible to convert them; and they, in return! . . . Yes, after all that, what do I receive? What response do I find among the creatures I have loved so much? At this spectacle I feel my Heart breaking again! No one cares any more about my love; they behave as though my Heart had suffered nothing for anyone and should be forgotten by all; and this heart is continually saddened. I am almost always alone in the churches; and if a crowd assembles, it is usually for other reasons; so that I suffer the pain of seeing my sanctuary transformed into a place of entertainment. I have seen many too who make a hypocritical show, and betray me by sacrilegious communions.*[5]

And Gemma Galgani, in a faith that can only be compared to that of a child, has her heart broken and wants to relieve Him of His sufferings; she wants to console Him by carrying His cross and putting balm on His wounds. No woman has withstood the sight of His eternal sufferings, and they ask Him then to grant His sufferings to them. One of the examples that best illustrate this will, this determination, is the young Frenchwoman Elisabeth Catez, better known today under the name of Elisabeth de la Trinité. She too knew at the age of fourteen that she would become a nun, and immediately asked her mother for permission to join the Carmelites. Categorical refusal. But when He calls a predestined soul, no one can block the way, and Madame Catez finally gave her consent when she saw that her daughter was truly determined.

5. Letter from Gemma Galgani to her confessor October 13, 1901.

Elisabeth entered the convent at twenty to sacrifice her life in prayer, in order to save souls in His company. She understood equally that a true bride of Christ had to be sacrificed like Him to share His sufferings in the immense plan of the redemption, a sort of holocaust. He heard her prayers, and the young woman was shortly felled by a cancer of the stomach. Five years after joining the Carmelites she died, suffering horribly. A cancer of the stomach at twenty-five is very rare to say the least. Her last wish was *"not only to die as pure as an Angel but most of all to be transformed into Jesus crucified."* Elisabeth of the Trinity achieved her mission and rejoined Him at twenty-five, like Theresa of Lisieux and Gemma Galgani. The three young women went as if struck by lightning, and He doubtless preferred to have them with Him on high rather than here below.

We have also noted that ecstasy "like no other" in the words of Georgette Faniel, answering the question, *"What is a union with God?"* At that moment, her face altered, literally lit up, a bit like when we remember a particularly pleasant memory: *"Almost death, because the soul leaves the body altogether to join Him. So it's the perfect union of two souls. True Love. . . . It cannot be described. I can't compare it to any human joy."* And invariably we come back to the same point, *"it cannot be explained in human terms."* I do not remember now who used the image of vanilla: *"You can write three tomes on vanilla, its taste and its smell, and you can spend your life reading those books, but you will never know what vanilla is, unless you have tasted and smelled it yourself."* I have concluded that this *"ecstasy like no other"* which the mystics and NDE survivors speak of with light in their eyes was a sort of divine dessert, like the vanilla, that we will perhaps taste one day.

Nevertheless, a comparison, and perhaps a commentary, are necessary on these saints, who asked for only one thing—to suffer for the greater pleasure of Christ. It would seem that these men and women are truly the first rank, in suffering, people for whom near-death experiences, out-of-body experiences, fusions with the Light and voyages with their guardian Angels are common occurrences. It is, we might say, their recompense for consenting to be a victim. So the voluntary sacrifice of the saints makes sense: they assist this general plan whose details escape us. In the eyes of God their sacrifice takes on great value and they surely redeem many lost souls. Elizabeth Kübler-Ross told us that *"suffering is like the Grand Canyon. If we said, 'It's so pretty, we must protect it from wind and storm' it would never be sculpted by the wind and we would never appreciate its beauty. That is my answer in regard to suffering.*

*If you don't suffer, you don't grow. You must experience sorrow, loss, tears and anger."* Suffering truly makes sense, and that sends a chill up my spine. With Gemma Galgani, a few months before her death, we find the following statement by Christ, which also casts light on the reason or reasons for suffering, confirming Kübler-Ross's statement almost word for word:

> *Do you know why, my daughter, I am happy to send crosses to souls who are dear to Me? I want to possess their hearts, but entirely. To that end I surround them with crosses. I envelop them with tribulations and so keep them from slipping through My hands. To that end I strew their way with thorns so that, not being attached to anyone, they find in Me alone all their contentment. . . . O, my daughter, how many would already have abandoned Me, if I had not crucified them! The cross is an extremely precious gift, and it is the school of a good many virtues."[6]*

A declaration to freeze the blood, identical to the one He made to Marguerite-Marie Alacoque: *"Here is the bed of My chaste brides where I will have you consummate the delights of My love. Little by little, these flowers will fall, there will remain only the thorns that these flowers hide because of your weakness; soon they will make you feel their points so sharply that you will need all the strength of my love to accept your martyrdom."*

How will these women find the strength to surmount the road to this interior crucifixion, if not by drawing on the memory of the ecstasies that He gave them a taste of? A foretaste of Heaven, a sample of paradise, a model apartment among the many dwellings in the House of the Lord, a specimen demonstration of what His love is. Like the survivors of the fifth NDE stage (according to Professor Ring), this memory of fusion with God is more than we can imagine, and doubtless more than we can even conceive on the smallest scale. The "victims" are God's channels, and Gemma's biographer Jean-François Villepelée justly remarks that *"our contemporaries, prisoners of a humanitarian civilization, rich in science, remain lost before the mystery of existence. Often their lives no longer make any sense, and two possible futures present themselves to their disenchanted expectation: either stupefy themselves in a vain treasure-hunt, or accept suicide in the long or short run. We forget a bit too easily that God lives, and is the source of life. Only he is responsi-*

6. Jean-François Villepelé, *La Folie de la Croix*, Editions Parvis, p. 16.

ble for mankind, which he created with birth and death but also with promises of eternal blessedness. *The saints, on the other hand, know why they are on this earth and why they depart on the day set, because they take into account this unique presence which illuminates them, and in whom all things find their cohesion."* God avenges these voluntary victims of the crucifixion, dead in anonymity, by granting them supernatural powers, available to them who ask and who call for intercession by the saints.

On this point, a friend remarked to me that being a saint cannot be very restful, for as we have seen we do not die, but simply change our reality, a reality more or less close to God. So if one is alive and moreover a saint, one must answer thousands of prayers each day, any time anybody on earth invokes one by asking anything.

Try to imagine for an instant having to answer so many prayers every day. Here we put a finger on the pure essence of divinity, that capacity for being, seeing and understanding everything everywhere at one time, and above all manipulating events (from their point of view, the present and the future do not exist) so that our prayers are answered! On Earth, we call their answers graces, synchronicities, chance or coincidence. More, this seems to be their favorite game, if we judge them by this declaration of the Archangel Raphael himself to the German stigmatic and mystic Mechtilde Thaller, who addressed a prayer to him:

> He (Raphael) said to me smiling: "What 'Deus dedit' to you, which you beg me to bring to pass, will weigh a bit less upon him. But it will remain a continual concern to him, from which the Lord will not deliver him completely. There are needs and concerns from which God never releases us, because He wants us to pray to Him always. That incessant demand, that prayer full of abandon, is what he loves most of all. And as He is infinitely good and merciful toward man, He leaves nothing unrewarded. Even if He seems to grant little or nothing, He offers to him who asks an abundance of grace of which human beings can have no idea. To know the continual kindness of His bounty is one of the greatest joys that God reserves for us in blessed eternity."[7]

7 Friedrich von Lama, Christiana, *The Angels*, Stein am Rhein (Switzerland), 1987, pp. 34–35.

In short, there is no doubt that whoever becomes a saint and who intercedes is not headed for a life of repose in Eternity. And there is one constant: it seems that the younger the future saint dies, the greater is his or her power of intercession, as for example Gemma Galgani or Thérèsa of Lisieux, dead well before the age of thirty-three, who as we have seen, also represents another constant, principally among the stigmatics.

# CHAPTER 11

# Incorruptibles and Angels (IIb)

*The sun bore down upon this rottenness*
*As if to roast it with gold fire*
*And render back to nature her own largess*
*A hundredfold of her desire. . . .*
*And even you will come to this foul shame*
*This ultimate infection*
*Star of my eyes, my being's inner flame*
*My angel and my passion! . . .*
*Speak, then, my Beauty, to this dire putrescence,*
*To the worm that shall kiss your proud estate*
*That I have kept the divine form and the essence*
*Of my festered inviolate*

—Charles Baudelaire, from "La Charogne"
("A Carrion," translation Allen Tate)

THIS CATEGORY PLUNGES US INTO A MYSTERY AS PROFOUND AS THAT OF
the stigmatics, as even the laws of nature seem to bow before
the saintliness of the soul who wore the flesh, making a liar
of the Bible: it is not all ashes to ashes and dust to dust. A registry
of about one hundred cases of incorruptibility has been compiled,
and in this study it has been discovered that this grace is not
reserved merely for the greatest or the humblest. Thérèsa of
Lisieux, for example, the most popular saint of five continents, was
not granted that honor. On the other hand the body of Cardinal
Schuster (whom no one knew), former Cardinal of Milan, dead in
1986, as well as that of the nun Monique de Jésus, dead in 1964,

remains intact.[1] There is no rule, no common denominator for incorruptibility,[2] contrary to the stigmatics. However, in contrast to the personalities we have just discussed, here there are no ecstasies, no delirious crowds surging to touch a living saint, no bilocations, in short no everyday supernatural events unless during a very short period of their lives, during which an Angel *"descends from Heaven"* to announce a bit of news.

With the *"incorruptibles"* Angels act exclusively as messengers, but if their mission seems simple, nevertheless the consequences of their visits on the lives of those "chosen" are felt even today, long after their deaths. The most striking example is Catherine Labouré, the little nun from the Chapel of the Miraculous Medal in Paris. Angels descend to prepare, encourage, and above all, purify him or her who has been chosen by the Most High for this public spiritual revelation. And the incorruptibility of their remains seems to be the divine seal, the post mortem imprint that He leaves on their bodies to prove to us that all mortals (you, me) do not become ashes. *"Behold now, I have taken upon me to speak unto the Lord, which am but dust and ashes,"* we read in Genesis.[3] Those judged worthy of speaking to Him or transmitting His messages thus escape that rule: they do not turn to ashes, as God obeys his own law. He leaves them intact. Suddenly, the bodies of these insignificant beings (according to our modern values), sometimes illiterate, survive, while the bodies of laborers and millionaires are devoured by worms. A paradox. And when we broach the subject of incorruptibility of a cadaver, rationalists will tell you that it is due to atmospheric conditions, and that bodies of Vikings perfectly preserved have been discovered; that if the tomb is well aerated, the cadaver does not rot, etc.

Why not?

But how does biological death act on the body? I wanted to see with my own eyes. After several telephone calls, I arranged an appointment at one of the busiest morgues in the United States, in Los Angeles. In an anonymous building close to the women's pavilion at the hospital of the University of Southern California, thirty-five doctors and twenty-four investigators work around the clock on the fifty bodies that arrive daily at the morgue. Accidents,

1. Shuster's body is not strictly speaking incorruptible. It is a very rare case of mummification!!
2. Do not confuse a "death mask," made after the death of a subject and artistically reworked, with incorruptible flesh.
3. Genesis 18:27.

suicides, homicides and natural deaths[4] all end up there, ranged in refrigerated "crypts." At first you think you've stumbled into a cop movie. Then you expect to see Inspector Columbo in his raincoat, scratching his head. Sheets cover the forms, but the bare, tagged feet that stick out bring you back to reality in a hurry. And even without the corpses, the pungent odor of formaldehyde, death and detergents puts your olfactory sense on red alert. The neon gleam on the tiling, the green walls and the metal tables all work to drag you into the scene. And you discover that a cadaver does not die: all the bacteria, all the microbes are having a high old time. Logically: the body can no longer defend itself. And when you step into the homicide "freezer," where 150 bodies lie mingled, the smell grabs you by the throat. All victims of violent crimes without distinction land there, exactly in the state in which they were found by the police. At first the smell bothers you and your nose wants to go on strike, but the deeper you advance among the cadavers the more the odor goes to your head. "What you see here are recent homicides. We keep their clothes for analysis." explains my guide, a coroner of French-Canadian origin, Lt. Claude Boucherville. Some skins are greenish in spots, others white as paper. But that smell! The skin emits gases like methane and hydrogen sulphide which mix and give off a terrible odor. You would never have guessed that such a stench could exist.

My guide shows me the body of a woman in a state of decomposition. I come closer, but the odor tears at my stomach. *"You know,"* he says to me, as if he were strolling through the aisles of a Walmart, *"a body first becomes rigid. The first thing that we do when we reach a crime scene is to feel the hand. We can make an early estimate of the time of death by its flexibility. Rigor comes approximately twelve hours after death, sometimes more. It's progressive. It begins in the jaw. Then it proceeds down the rest of the body, attacking the arms, the stomach, the thighs, the knees, the ankles and finally the feet. This rigor disappears in the same progressive fashion, between twenty-four to thirty-six hours after death. Only after that do you really smell the work of the bacteria."* Indeed, on certain bodies we see quite clearly green spots on the stomach, the first true and irreversible sign of putrefaction. Considering the concentration of bacteria in the intestine, the bodies cannot resist for long; the bacteria soon perforate the skin and loose their pestilential gases. I was in a hurry to get out of there. But Claude Boucherville wanted to show me what really interested me, the room for the "decom-

---

4. Except for deaths in hospitals and those certified at home by the family doctor.

posed," During the short walk, I thought of the sepulchre of Teresa of Avila, opened because the smell of roses was rising from it. I realized then that the odor of a cadaver is SO appalling that you have to be a fool, or else lacking any olfactory sense, to exhume a body. The nose revolts and keeps you from it. A normal person CANNOT APPROACH a cadaver more than three days old. As if he had guessed my thoughts, the lieutenant continued: *"The police found a hermetically sealed container with the body of a murdered man. He had been there for two years. When it was opened everybody damn near passed out. The smell was atrocious, horrifying. And it was mush; the skin had melted."* Even though the crypt was refrigerated, I could not imagine that worse smells existed than the odors I had just experienced.

*"Have you ever found incorruptible corpses?"* I asked him.

*"Incorruptible, that can't be. During the demolition of a house, workers found a body buried in concrete. A murder. It had been fifteen years. All that was left were the bones, nothing else. In Canada in the springtime they find people every year who got lost in the snow. Those bodies are preserved by the glacial temperatures. But as soon as the temperature goes up to normal, decomposition is triggered. And the warmer it gets, the faster the putrefication. Even here, where it's refrigerated, the bodies melt. You know, we have to keep unidentified and unclaimed bodies for two years. Look at what that produces."*

I approached, but the smell froze me in place, and I began to choke and cough. My stomach turned. The odor was vile. ATROCIOUS. I thought suddenly of the Libyan heat and Charbel Makhlouf. *"And if you place a body in an aerated tomb, what happens?"* I asked him, trying my hardest not to vomit.

The coroner shut the door of the freezer for the "decomposed": *"After two days, the smell would remind you absolutely that a cadaver must be buried."*

I would love to have seen the expression on his face if he had discovered the remains of the Maronite saint, who was not even entitled to a wooden coffin. He was laid on a plank a foot underground. At the least shower, the tomb was inundated and transformed into a quagmire. A year after his death, witnesses were dumbstruck to discover that he was fresh, supple and gave off the odor of a live body! They decided then to bury him properly, and this time placed him in a zinc coffin. Years later, they noticed that a liquid was running out of the coffin regularly. In 1927 he was exhumed again to find out why. Professor Armand Jouffroy of the medical university of Beirut examined the body and wrote a report on the perfect state of the cadaver, which was placed into a new coffin and hermetically sealed. The seepage persisted. In 1950 Doctors Chikri-Bellan and Maroun, respectively director of the Libyan government health service and professor of the faculty of medicine, as well as a House representative, Dr. Joseph Hitti, examined the remains with a microscope and declared that the present state of science offered no reasonable explanation for such a case. The torrid heat of Libya was not able to clean the body of this monk. And Catherine of Siena? In the fourteenth century, formaldehyde[5] did not exist.

So?

I left the morgue and went in search of the nearest bar.

Let's go back to those rare specimens, free samples of God's (black) humor. They lived the life of saints, no shadow of a doubt about that. And not only were their bodies incorruptible but they emitted pleasant scents. Not just one but TWO laws of nature were broken. Examining the biographies of these privileged beings, we discover the following facts:

1. In 80 percent of the cases, the subject dies in anonymity. He is buried in a cave, a tomb, a crypt, or an ossuary without great formality.

2. In 70 percent of the cases, the body of the subject was devoured by various sicknesses during its lifetime.

3. In the majority of cases, these "incorruptibles" lived in warm countries!

4. Sometimes the body is discovered incorruptible fifty years after death because of:
   a) lack of space in the cemetery or ossuary of the convent or monastery
   b) floods
   c) cracked crypt or sinking of the terrain
   d) moving of the remains
   e) transfer of the body to its native country
   f) various miracles around the tomb (perfumes, voices, lights, flow of oil)
   g) the process of beatification, a minimum of forty years after death, resulting in exhumation

5. A chemical product used by embalmers to retard decomposition; it keeps the limbs rigid.

5. All the saints do not benefit from this "privilege." A phenomenon even more curious: the stigmatics, as for
example Marguerite-Marie Alacoque or Gemma Galgani,
did not leave us their bodies as souvenirs.

For the sake of form, let's check for the possibility of embalm-
ing and immediately we come up against the case of Jacinta
Marto. But let's forget it. . . . If the bodies of Catherine of Siena or
Teresa of Avila had been embalmed, then no one would have
sliced them into small pieces. They would have been embalmed in
the official manner and exposed publicly in their churches or convents. Every time we try to find a rational explanation, we come
to a dead end. And practical details are not lacking. Most of the
time, these incorruptibles were poor, or belonged to orders where
poverty was the rule. Another puzzle: few suspected that these
souls would become saints—and all the incorruptibles have not
been beatified, far from it—and the mother superior would never
have spent large sums of money to eviscerate or embalm one,
simply because the sum total might represent the convent's operating budget for six months or a year. And to mention climate
again, Italy, Spain, France and Portugal are not Sweden. Lastly,
why do we find incorruptible bodies of religious people ONLY
and not laymen, as for example a President of the United States,
the founder of IBM or the inventor of Coca-Cola? Yes, really, why?
I can hear the rationalists claiming it is pure hazard. But the
word "hazard" comes from the Arabic for the word dice in a game
called "God's game." Incorruptibility of the soul, incorruptibility
of the body . . .

## JACINTA MARTO
### 1910–1920
#### (Group IIb: Miracles, Angels, Incorruptibility)
#### Portugal

The Marian apparition of Fatima had never impressed me with its
terrible "secrets," widely published and discussed in various sensa-
tionalist periodicals, with much about the end of the world, global
destruction and I don't know what other apocalyptic terrors. Expiation through suffering, destruction of the earth if we go on
sinning, and, miserable earthworms that we are, we will be condemned to burn eternally in hell, broiled by "four-star" demon
chefs armed with pitchforks, until all our sins are expiated in

extenso. Moreover, I detest revelations that first tell us, *"Be good, or papa spank,"* and then assure us (the same "visionaries" speaking) that God is only love. On the one hand we are assured that HE loves us, and on the other that He is ready to reduce us to ashes. They ought to pull themselves together. And then Fatima represents all those sensational books of the type "All about the Secrets of Fatima," or "What No One Dared Tell You About Fatima," or "Fatima's Secrets Unveiled," etc. That popular imagery, loaded for almost eighty years with a series of pompous cliches and buffoonish secrets all mixed together, is heavily fraught with messages and menaces. Who are we, vulgar yokels, that we have not the right to know this weighty secret that the little "clairvoyant" forbade us to read before 1960 (it has never been unveiled, incidentally), when we are the most concerned?

In short, I would never have spoken of Fatima in this book, and that despite the three apparitions of the Angel, if I had not discovered, with photos to back me up, that the body of one of the child "seers," disinterred fifteen years after her death, was discovered . . . incorruptible. In Finland, Siberia or Norway, we might say "that it was the climate." But as this happened in Portugal, we must keep mum. It was September 12, 1935, during a transfer of two children's mortal remains, when this mystery was discovered. A mystery all the more significant because while the body of the young girl was intact, her brother's was not. . . . And it is impossible to suspect manipulation by anyone in this affair, because Jacinta, one of the three "seers," died at the age of ten. She was not saint, nor visionary, nor stigmatic, nor martyr, but the simple young daughter of a couple of poor Portuguese peasants. Besides, after the visions had ended the crowd's interest immediately turned away from the three children, leaving them almost forgotten. As they "saw" nothing more, they no longer interested anyone. And then it is hard to imagine some twisted spirits working desperately (as in a horror movie) to embalm the body of a ten year old youngster, at night in a deserted cemetery in a distant corner of Portugal, the more so since Lucia was still alive. And anyway, people had all but forgotten their names.

To put it plainly, the visions of an Angel by Jacinta Marto (who died in 1920), exactly like those of Catherine Labouré and of Bernadette Soubirous, were validated by the most mysterious of divine signs, incorruptibility. Even more amazing, this is the only case of incorruptibility of the body of a child, and that singularity requires me to take into serious account the three visits of the Angel to that Portuguese hill, to announce one of the most astonishing Marian apparitions of our century.[6]

The children always said they felt the Angel's presence most profoundly in body and soul, unlike the Virgin's presence, which had, if I may say so, little effect on them beyond normal conversation with her. Odd, isn't it? For reasons already mentioned, I will not touch on the pseudo-secrets of Fatima; the interested reader can find a more than abundant literature on the subject.

What is fascinating about the Marian apparitions is that Mary always chooses unlikely spots in which to show herself: in totally unknown backwaters in the middle of nowhere, that even the most snobbish travel agent could not dig up for overworked CEOs trekking about in search of a hideaway. Just the names of these places, Medjugorje, La Salette, Akita, Zeitoun, etc., make you wonder. After all, why not simply choose places like Paris, New York, Moscow or Berlin? Imagine for a moment an apparition like Fatima's on the Champs-Elysées or under the Eiffel Tower or better, during Leonid Brezhnev's time, in Red Square in Moscow, on a Sunday, right in front of Lenin's mausoleum where people wait for hours in single file to admire the mummy—and not the incorruptible body—of Lenin.

We must admit that both population and political system would have taken a serious hit, the more so as at Fatima the Virgin asked that Russia consecrate itself to her Heart. Moreover, all the witnesses at Fatima, and there were around seventy thousand (including about thirty journalists sent to cover it),[7] tell us with one voice that on the day announced (October 13, 1917) by Mary during her previous apparition, the promised miracle took place, towards noon:

> *Suddenly the rain stopped and the clouds, thick all morning, dissipated. The sun appeared at its zenith, like a silver disk. Suddenly it began to turn on itself like a wheel of fire, projecting in all directions a shower of light whose color changed several times. Streaks of yellow, red, green, blue, etc. tinted the clouds, the trees, the hills, lending a strange aspect to the countryside and to all that landscape, bizarrely transformed by its Creator. After several minutes,*

6. The other is that of Zeitoun in Egypt in 1968.
7. They all reported to their papers, but the majority of editors-in-chief, comfortable in their easy chairs, who paid any attention to the contents concluded that their reporters were delirious. Others published the articles in extenso but without comment.

*the heavenly body halted, blazing with a light that did no
hurt to the eyes; then it began its stupefying dance again.
This phenomenon occurred three times and each time a
little faster, with a brighter and more colorful light. And
during the twelve unforgettable minutes that this impressive spectacle lasted, the crowd was held in suspense,
watching open-mouthed this tragic and captivating phenomenon, which could be seen for forty kilometers around.
Abruptly, the spectators had the impression that the sun
was tearing loose from the heavens and falling on them. A
formidable cry rose simultaneously from every watcher.
Some genuflected, others cried out, still others prayed
aloud. . . . Meanwhile it stopped in its tracks, then slowly
returned to its place; then it resumed its normal brightness.
There were no more clouds and the sky was a limpid blue.
The entire crowd rose and recited the Credo. The crowd's
clothes, soaked through by the rain an instant before, dried
immediately. The enthusiasm was indescribable."*[8]

Note that this is the first time in history that Mary announces a
miracle beforehand, a bit like in the music-hall, with all due
respect. The same phenomenon in Red Square would certainly
have marked the country forever. But it's true that she always
decides to appear in the middle of nowhere, and always to little
children or to the humble, so poor and innocent that they are
above all suspicion. Even though it was out of context, the explanation was given by Christ to Marguerite-Marie Alacoque: *"Ah! Don't
you know that I use the weakest subjects to confound the strong, and
that ordinarily I show my power most brilliantly on the humblest and
poorest of spirits, so that they will not claim powers for themselves?"*
And all who tried to bribe witnesses into going back on their statements were wasting their time.[9]

Fatima represents the best documented contemporary visit of
the Angel, along with Garabandal, which we will look into further
along. He makes himself visible to children, who are carried away,
and purifies them to prepare them for the great event, somewhat
like a trainer preparing his athletes for the Olympic finals. The
Angel of Fatima thus appeared three times to Marto and their

8. *Stigmatisés et Apparitions.*
9. Hollywood producers offered a colossal gift to Theresa Neumann's parents to
   make a film of her stigmata. Mr. Neumann treated them with the greatest
   contempt.

cousin, Lucia dos Santos. Before we go on, note that in the history of Marian apparitions, with a few rare exceptions the fact that the Angel precedes the Virgin signifies that the repercussions of the apparition will be important. In view of the number of books published on Fatima, there is no possible doubt. That was colossal. The most valuable testimony on Fatima was given us by Lucia dos Santos' memoirs, since shortly after the death of her two little companions Francesco and Jacinta Marto she decided to enter a convent, following the desire expressed by Mary. And Lucia dos Santos, who had seen the Archangel, *"a light whiter than snow, in which we saw a silhouette like a crystal statue with the sun's rays shining through,"* set down her memories, collected as a small book by Father Louis Kondor,[10] which I prefer to the others. In consulting them, I indeed discovered that the Angel did not always say the same things, no doubt because of translation of translations. It is interesting to note also that according to Lucia's statement at the time of the apparitions, *"the words of the Angel penetrated our spirit like a light that made us understand how much God loved us and how much He wanted to be loved."*

> *Apparition No. 1 in 1915:*
> *We had enjoyed the game for a few moments only, when a strong wind began to shake the trees. We looked up, startled, to see what was happening, for the day was unusually calm. Then we saw coming towards us, above the olive trees, the figure I have already spoken about. Jacinta and Francisco had never seen it before, nor had I ever mentioned it to them. As it drew closer, we were able to distinguish its features. It was a young man, about fourteen or fifteen years old, whiter than snow, transparent as crystal when the sun shines through it, and of great beauty. On reaching us, he said:*
> *"Do not be afraid! I am the Angel of Peace. Pray with me."*
> *Kneeling on the ground, he bowed down until his forehead touched the ground, and made us repeat these words three times:*
> *"My God, I believe, I adore, I hope and I love You! I ask pardon of You for those who do not believe, do not adore, do not hope and do not love You."*

10. *Mémoires de Soeur Lucia,* Fatima, Portugal, Vice-Postulacao dos Videntes, 1991, pp. 64–66.

*Then, rising, he said: "Pray thus. The Hearts of Jesus and Mary are attentive to the voice of your supplications."*

*His words engraved themselves so deeply on our minds that we could never forget them.*

Apparition No. 2 in 1915:

*One day, we were playing on the stone slabs of the well down at the bottom of the garden belonging to my parents, which we called the Arneiro. Suddenly, we saw beside us the same figure, or rather Angel, as it seemed to me.*

*"What are you doing?" he asked. "Pray, pray very much! The most holy Hearts of Jesus and Mary have designs of mercy on you. Offer prayers and sacrifices constantly to the Most High."*

*"How are we to make sacrifices?" I asked.*

*"Make of everything you can a sacrifice, and offer it to God as an act of reparation for the sins by which He is offended, and in supplication for the conversion of sinners. You will thus draw down peace upon your country. I am its Angel Guardian, the Angel of Portugal. Above all, accept and bear with submission, the suffering which the Lord will send you."*

*We note again that these souls were certainly predestined, victims, chosen and designated in advance. "Someone" brings them sufferings. Which is why, well before their death, Jacinta and Francesco Marto explained innocently to their parents that they would go "very soon to Heaven!" The Virgin kept her word, since both were dead at the age of ten.*

Apparition No. 3, Autumn 1916:

*A considerable time had elapsed, when one day we went to pasture our sheep on a property belonging to my parents, which lay on the slope of the hill I have mentioned, a little higher up than Valinhos. It is an olive grove called Pregueira. After our lunch, we decided to go and pray in the hollow among the rocks on the opposite side of the hill. To get there, we went around the slope, and had to climb over some rocks above the Pregueira. The sheep could only scramble over these rocks with great difficulty.*

*As soon as we arrived there, we knelt down, with our foreheads touching the ground, and began to repeat the prayer of the Angel.*

*"My God, I believe, I adore, I hope and I love you . . ." I
don't know how many times we had repeated this prayer,
when an extraordinary light shone upon us. We sprang up
to see what was happening, and beheld the Angel. He was
holding a chalice in his left hand, with the Host suspended
above it, from which some drops of flood fell into the chalice. Leaving the chalice suspended in the air, the Angel
knelt down beside us and made us repeat three times:*

*"Most Holy Trinity, Father, Son and Holy Spirit, I offer
You the most precious Body, Blood, Soul and Divinity of
Jesus Christ, present in all the tabernacles of the world, in
reparation for the outrages, sacrileges and indifference with
which He Himself is offended. And, through the infinite
merits of His most Sacred Heart, and the Immaculate
Heart of Mary, I beg of You the conversion of poor sinners."*

*Then, rising, he took the chalice and the Host in his
hands. He gave the Sacred Host to me, and shared the
Blood from the Chalice between Jacinta and Francisco,
saying as he did so:*

*"Take and drink the Body and Blood of Jesus Christ,
horribly outraged by ungrateful men! Make reparation for
their crimes and console your God."*

*Once again, he prostrated on the ground and repeated
with us, three times more, the same prayer "Most Holy
Trinity . . ." and then disappeared.*

We will encounter this communion with the Angel again several
years later in Spain, in 1962. Independently of the fact that this was
not new in history, there it was a matter of the consecration in
good and due form of three children to be victim souls. Lucia was
to say shortly after the apparitions that at that moment, when the
Angel gave them communion, *"the sense of God's presence was so
intense that it absorbed us entirely and annihilated us completely, so
to speak. That presence seemed to deprive us of our senses for a long
stretch of time. . . . The peace and happiness that we felt were very
great, but they were all interior and intimate, our souls entirely concentrated on God."* Only the two little girls "saw" the Angel. The boy
saw nothing, but only heard him. All three explained that an invisible force held them and forced them to kneel, or to bow their
foreheads to the ground. That period passed as though out of time.
They were carried away by the presence, remaining prostrate and
unaware that night had fallen until they emerged from that
lethargy.

The remaining supernatural indicators prove once again that these visions of the Angel were perfectly authentic. The photo shows clearly that this incredulous witness who gazed upon the face of the remains was not discommoded by the odor. Logically, since there was none.

## CATHERINE LABOURÉ
## 1806–1876
### (Group IIb: Miracles, Angels, Incorruptibility)
### France

Zoe Labouré is better known by the given name of Catherine, a little change due to the Sisters of Charity of Saint-Vincent-de-Paul in Chatillon-sur-Seine, which she joined at the age of twenty-four. Practically illiterate, the daughter of farmers, she was sent to the convent on the Rue de Bac in Paris which has since owed her all its fame. Still, after learning to read and write, the humble Zoe passed forty-seven years of her life quite discreetly, assigned to the most obscure tasks, failing which her little comrades would not have tolerated her at all. Her superiors judged her *"cold," "apathetic," "insignificant," "without interest."*

Doubtless they would have modified their judgment if they had known what happened in the convent shortly after her arrival. But her confessor (or director of conscience) who did not believe a word the young girl told him, swore her to silence. The Sisters of the Rue de Bac learned only upon her death on December 31, 1876, that one evening an Angel had wakened her and ordered her to go to the chapel:

> *At 11:30 at night I hear someone call my name: "Sister, Sister!"*
>
> *Waking up I looked toward where I heard the voice, which was on the side by the hallway. I draw the curtains back. I see a child dressed in white, about four or five years old, who says to me: "Get up quickly, the Holy Virgin is waiting for you!"*
>
> *Immediately the thought comes to me "But they'll hear me." The child answers me (he answers my thought): "It's all right, it's 11:30, everyone's fast asleep. Come, I'm waiting for you."*
>
> *. . . The door opens when the child barely touches it with his finger. . . . It was then that the child spoke to me,*

*no longer like a child, but like a man, stronger, and in
stronger language. . . . Then I was standing up above the
steps to the altar, and I saw the child where I had left him.
He said to me: "She is gone."*

*We retraced our steps, always in bright light, and the
child still to my left. I think the child was my guardian
Angel, who made himself visible to show me the Holy
Virgin, because I had prayed to him often to obtain that
favor for me. He was dressed white, bearing a miraculous
light with him, that is, he was resplendent with light: about
four to five years old.*[11]

With that, Zoe was eligible for a vision of Mary, who gave her
instructions for making a medal in her effigy. We know what followed: even though her confessor enjoined her to stop the madness,
in the end the "miraculous medal" was crafted by Vachette, a jeweler on the Quai des Orfèvres, in a trial run of only 1500. The medal
spread around the world like a train of powder—with no publicity
except "word of mouth"—in several million copies.

We may decline to believe in Zoe-Catherine Labouré's vision
and even in the virtues of her miraculous medal, but not the incorruptibility of her body. It is there to prove the authenticity of what
she lived through and said she saw. She was buried immediately
upon her death, and it took the start of her process of beatification
(due exclusively to the effects of the medal) for the authorities to
decide to give her remains a place worthy of the miracles bestowed
by the medal.

On March 31, 1933, fifty-seven years after her death, an army of
doctors and ecclesiastics attended the opening of her tomb, in conformity with canonical law. When the rags that covered her body
were removed, more than one was frozen in stupor to discover that
the body of this "insignificant" but obedient Zoe was intact. Dr.
Robert Didier, a surgeon, feverishly noted his observations, and
next day, in the presence of the highest civil, medical and religious
authorities, he performed an autopsy and explained that the body
was perfect and could easily serve for dissection as a lesson in
anatomy at the medical school. In other words, it was "very fresh."

And like Teresa of Avila and Catherine of Siena, Zoe-Catherine
Labouré ends up in pieces at various convents of her order, as a
holy relic. Very happily, she remains presentable and still visible in
the rue du Bac, her face covered with a layer of wax. Another effect

11. René Laurentin, *Vie Authentique de Catherine Labouré*, pp. 81–84.

of the Angel's visit was her canonization, which led to a constant queue of faithful pilgrims before her enigmatic face.

Still, one may ask why the Angel chose to appear to a nun in the guise of a five year old? The answer may well be found in the fact that for this gentle farm maid, an Angel could only look like a child, in conformity with the representations of the epoch. And others suggest that the sight of a strong handsome man of thirty-something would have troubled the young woman, which is not unreasonable. Ronda de Sola Chervin, who studied the lives of about two hundred women, noticed that some of them (Catherine of Siena, Marguerite of Cortone, Angela of Foligno, Maria-Magdalena dei Pazzi, Mary of Egypt, Pelagia of Antioch, etc.) were susceptible to extreme sexual temptations. . . .

In any case, the two minor details reported by Catherine that leave no doubt, and confirm that the Angel took only the form of a five year old child, are first its tone of voice, more "virile": *"It was then that the child spoke to me, no longer like a child, but like a man, stronger, and in stronger language,"* and second the response to her question by "thoughts." *"Immediately the thought comes to me, `But they'll hear me.' The child answers me: (he answers my thought): `It's all right. It's 11:30, everyone's fast asleep. Come, I'm waiting for you,'"* confirming to us once more that this is the only method of communication with the Angels.

## MARIA D'AGREDA
### 1602–1665
### (Group IIb: Incorruptibility, Miracles, Angels)
### Spain

*Alas, will they treat me so horribly and cruelly that my body, intact and never corrupted, must today be consumed and reduced to ashes?*
—*Joan of Arc*

Maria Coronel, daughter of a family of Spanish grandees, was twelve years old in 1614 and still playing with dolls when she explained to her parents that she wanted to become a nun. As we have seen, certain souls seem predestined, and Maria Coronel more than any other, since her mother Catherine had a vision showing that the family chateau must be converted to a convent. Perhaps one of the rare cases in history where father, mother, and three children (one boy, two girls) take the veil in various orders. That extraordinary family vocation was bound to produce one exceptional case: Maria. After mortifications that Catherine of Siena would not have rejected, it was only a short time before the young Spaniard knew God's grace, which often took the form of levitation, or bilocations like Yvonne-Aimee de Malestroit. It was enough for Maria to kneel in adoration before the Blessed Sacrament for her to be carried away by an ecstasy, manifested as a levitation that might last two or three hours.[12] As we have noticed, this type of mystic always leaves an immortal literary work and Maria Coronel, who became Maria d'Agreda, is no exception to this rule, since she left us the Ciudad de Dios (The City of God), a true marvel of the genre.

One of four volumes totalling almost three thousand pages, the Mystical City is the book of the life of Christ, told to the Spanish nun by the Virgin Mary herself. No need to emphasize that in this inspired work, Angels abound: the house of the Spanish virgin was almost like an international airport, with Angels, Archangels, Powers, Seraphim and other Dominations landing and taking off without pause. One suspects, and her incorruptible body proves to us, that Sister Maria was truly inspired.

In 1637, now mother superior of her convent, Maria d'Agreda received Christ's order to write the life of his Mother according to visions and statements that will be vouchsafed to her. The nun explained all that in her introduction, a model of its kind:

> If in these last centuries someone should hear that a simple girl, by her sex ignorant and weak, and by her sins the most unworthy of all creatures, dared to decide that she would write of divine and supernatural things, I would not be surprised if they called me bold, presumptuous and flighty: especially in a time when our mother the Holy Church is full of doctors, of very wise men enlightened as to the doctrines of our Holy Fathers, who have elucidated all the most hidden and obscure aspects of the mysteries of religion. . . . But what can serve much better as a guarantee of all that I have just said to excuse my enterprise, is the matter I deal with in this divine history, which, being loftier than the human spirit, must make us conclude that

12. On this subject we note a detail, minor certainly, but interesting: the men who observed the levitations of Catherine of Siena, Teresa of Avila or Catherine dei Pazzi all noted that the folds of their robes arranged themselves in natural fashion!

*a superior cause is its animating principle, and that only*
*the divine spirit could have dictated the concepts and sub-*
*lime verities it comprises.*[13]

With her goose quill, she will write in this manner every day for more than fifteen years, covering almost three thousand sheets that describe in detail all the feelings, emotions, fears and joys of Mary of Nazareth. Yet first she held off for ten years, and during those ten years Angels would visit her regularly asking her to go to work. For example, the Archangel Michael often paid her a visit, and one might as usual attribute that claim to hallucination if not for her incorruptible body:

> *The holy Angels destined to lead me in this work, held*
> *forth to me in this manner. The principal of them, Saint*
> *Michael, stated to me on several other occasions that it was*
> *the will and commandment of the Most High. And I dis-*
> *covered, through the interpretations, favors and constant*
> *instruction of this great prince, some magnificent myster-*
> *ies of God and the Queen of Heaven.*[14]

Let us make no mistake about Maria d'Agreda. Like Catherine of Siena, she was a bride of Christ, who lavished innumerable favors upon her. One of them was putting six Angels at her disposition to assist her and direct her in that work, a number that increased to eight when two other Angels of a *"superior hierarchy, very mysterious,"* charged with revealing *"profound secrets,"* joined her. The Angels even warned her:

> *You must divest yourself of all appetites and all pas-*
> *sions to arrive at these exalted mysteries which are far from*
> *according with the perverse tendencies of nature. You must*
> *put off thy shoes from thy feet as Moses did when com-*
> *manded to, so that he might see the burning bush. . . . It*
> *would be demanding a very difficult thing of you if you had*
> *to accomplish this by your own powers alone; but the Most*
> *High wishes and requires these preparations: He is*
> *omnipotent, and He will not deny you His help . . . Soul,*
> *obey the commandments given you; divest yourself of your*

13. Marie d'Agreda, *La Cité Mystique (The Mystical City)*, Paris, Editions Tequi, 1970, pp. 303–304.
14. *La Cité Mystique*, p. 312.

*self, and what is hidden will be revealed to you.*

So Maria d'Agreda humbled herself, and put herself entirely in the hands of Christ, who gratified her with a vision very close to a testimony we saw in the chapter "Tunnels and Angels":

> *The Lord told me, "Take care, and see." Having done which, I saw a very beautiful ladder of several rungs, a great multitude of Angels gathered about it and others descending and ascending. And His Majesty told me, "This is the mysterious Jacob's ladder which is the house of God and the gateway to Heaven. If it is your wish, and if your life is such that I find nothing in it to reprobate, you will come to Me by way of it."*
>
> *That promise excited my desire, animated my will, raised my spirits, and I grieved to feel such contraries within me. . . . I saw the ladder still, but I did not yet understand the mystery of it. I promised the Lord to set myself even farther from all worldly vanities. . . . And having passed some days in these sentiments and these preparations, the Most High said to me that this ladder was life, the virtues and the mysteries of the very holy Virgin Mary; and His Majesty said to me, "My dear bride, I want you to climb this Jacob's ladder, and to pass through this gateway to Heaven, to know my attributes and to contemplate My divinity. Climb, then, and come up. The Angels gathered about it, and ascending and descending, are those I have destined to guard it and to defend this holy city of Zion."[15]*

King Philip IV of Spain, who kept up a lively correspondence with the young woman, learned that she was writing the life of the Virgin under Her direction and asked for a copy as soon as she had finished it. Reading it enchanted him, and he took great care of the precious work.

But Divine Providence herself was to authenticate these memoirs: a little after sending a copy of the manuscript to Philip IV, the nun's spiritual director was replaced, and the new one asked her to burn the three thousand sheets, explaining that a *"women of the Church did not have to write!"* Particularly humble and obedient, Maria d'Agreda obeyed and threw the manuscript in the fire without blinking. Her celestial interlocutors had likewise demanded

15. *La Cité Mystique*, p. 336.

obedience to this order. Some weeks later, however, another confessor ordered her to start all over again.

Without argument, on December 8, 1655, she recommended writing these memoirs, which had been communicated by Mary, from the beginning. The second "edition" was faster than the first since it took "only" five years. Finished in May 1660, the manuscript was immediately compared to the first, jealously guarded at the Spanish court, which made Pope Benoit XIV say that it was a true "miracle, for there was no difference between the two, after an interval of five years, since Maria d'Agreda had burned the first." This detail hardly impresses me, as she could simply have kept a copy, but four other circumstances plead in her favor: (1) Maria de Jésus did not have a secretary at her side charged with noting down her visions and her speeches, as did Hildegarde von Bingen, Angela de Foligno and especially Anne-Catherine Emmerich, who had at her disposal more than a clerk, namely a real writer in the person of Clemens Brentano; (2) at that time, carbon paper and photocopying did not exist; (3) she was under permanent surveillance; (4) a nun of that stature does not lie to her spiritual director.

It should be emphasized that the publication of the four volumes of the Cuidad de Dios naturally provoked a scandal among theologians, who called Maria d'Agreda a crazy mystic, a usurper and a liar. Her work was even put on the Index! But little by little various religious orders, with the exceptions of the Jansenists, adopted La Cuidad and even ended by venerating it as a "cult" book.[16]

And as if God himself wanted to slip his nihil obstat onto the flyleaf of La Cuidad, two years after the Spanish nun's death on May 24, 1665, her body was discovered incorruptible, which made a strong impression on the Spanish court, where they felt they had missed a new Teresa of Avila. From this "perfect" cadaver we may suppose that the work was indeed authentic, guaranteed so by the impenetrable mystery of incorruptibility.

Maria d'Agreda's angelic visions are innumerable and almost interminable, and it seem to me difficult to integrate them into this work. The interested reader would do well to procure the three or four volumes[17] of the City of God. In the meantime, one of her visions is interesting as it is about the Annunciation. Not the Annunciation to Mary, but the other, less well known, of the Archangel Gabriel:

16. There is an excellent abridged version of *The Mystical City of God* (794 pages) by Tan Publishers, Rockford, Illinois.
17. The number depends on the edition.

*The blessed Mary lived to be sixty-seven. But as an end to the mortal career of our great Queen was inevitable, the decree of glorification of the blessed Mother was (to use the language of our day) handed down in divine consistory, where the love due to her alone was considered. . . . Consequently the very holy Trinity appointed the holy Archangel Gabriel with several courtiers of the celestial host, to announce to their Queen when and how the term of her mortal life would arrive, and she pass to eternal life. The holy prince descended with the other Angels. . . . Hearing the celestial music and sensing the presence of the blessed Angels, she fell to her knees to listen to the divine ambassador and his companions, garbed in dazzling white robes. . . . [Gabriel] first addressed her with the salutation of the Ave Maria, and going on he said, "August Empress of us all, the Almighty and the Holy of Holies have sent us from their court with orders to inform you on their behalf of the very happy end of your pilgrimage and your exile in mortal life. Soon the day will come, divine Queen, soon will come the hour so much desired, when by means of natural death you will acquire the eternal possession of the immortal life which awaits you at the right hand of your very holy Son, our God. From this day forward there remain only three years for you to live on earth, after which you will be exalted and received into the Lord's eternal joy. . . ."*[18]

## SANTA CECILIA
## ?–177
### (Group IIb: Incorruptibility, Miracles, Angels)
### Italy

Another angelic apparition with plainly tragic results: that of the guardian Angel of Cecilia, a Roman patrician of high rank, a Christian who wanted to remain a virgin even after her marriage so she could become a nun. Some claim that Cecilia never existed. Others hold to the legend and information dating from the sixteenth century. History tells us that on her wedding night she explained to her husband that if he touched her, her Angel would be very very angry, an objection that Valerian, her husband demanded to . . . see. Cecilia is said to have agreed solely on condition that he convert.

18. *The Mystical City*, vol. 3, pp. 542-545.

As we may imagine, the baptism was expedited after only the briefest delay, and—a deal is a deal—the guardian Angel appeared to him as well as to his brother Tiburtius. The latter converted immediately afterward, Valerian wrote off his carnal delights, and all three spent their days burying Christian martyrs, numerous enough at the time (Cecilia is said to have died in the year 177). The two men were haled before the prefect Almachius, who condemned them to death. Cecilia buried their bodies and was in turn haled before the prefect, who, considering her rank, wanted a discreet execution and condemned her to die elegantly, by suffocation at home, in her steam bath. After a day and a night, the executioner went to the site for the coup de grace, but, overcome by pity, three times running botched the stroke that should have decapitated the young woman. She lay there, head half detached from her body, and died after three days of agony. The house is said to have been transformed into a church (later the Basilica Santa-Cecilia) and Cecilia is buried in the exact position of her death in the catacombs of Saint-Callistus. The sculptor Stefano Medreno immortalized the saint's death throes with his chisel, working from her intact cadaver. Legend? Considering the more than supernatural facts about our various preceding saints, we may grant Santa Cecilia the benefit of the doubt. She became the patron saint of musicians because she preferred the voice of the Angel to the nuptial melody, which reminds me of the words of Geoffrey Scott: *"Virgin and martyr, it's a pleonasm."*

# CHAPTER 12

# Visionaries and Angels (III)

NOT ALL THE MYSTICS LEFT US TESTIMONY ON THE ANGELS, AS FOR example Julienne of Norwich (1342–1416) of whom the theologian Thomas Merton, as if writing of a holy box of soap, said:

> *in the old days I used to be crazy about St. John of the Cross, I would not exchange him now for Julian if you gave me the world and the Indies and all the Spanish mystics rolled up in one bundle.*[1]

On reading Julienne of Norwich, I told myself I would have no problem swapping her for Catherine of Siena or Theresa Neumann; but it is all a matter of taste. Or of passion. You may be sure that mystics without stigmata, whose flesh was "corruptible," have left us real treasures in the realm of angelic visions. As usual, the women are in the majority, and we can only marvel at their perseverance in setting their visions down on parchment, by God's order. In those dark days, they had no right to express themselves, and even less to do it in writing. *"Everything happens,"* notes Jean-Noel Vuarnet, *"as if, writing being in these Middle Ages forbidden to females and reserved to men, it needed all these human and supernatural authorizations for them to become writers, as if the act of writing itself could never take place for them except in a trance or during an ecstasy. Ecstasy as escape: leave the world, but also leave, in the name of the Father, the rhetoric of theologians and of the*

1. *Seeds of Destruction*, by Thomas Merton, New York: Farrar, Straus and Giroux, 1964, page 275.
2. *Extases Féminines*, pp. 42–43.

*Fathers . . . No Virginia Woolf, no Emily Brontë, without an antecedent Elizabeth.*"[2]

In those days women could not attend Mass during their "period of impurity," so we better appreciate the obstinacy that enabled Hildegarde and her emulators to publish the visions of their ecstasies. They brandished the name of God as a guarantee, a little like Joan of Arc, who, coming out of nowhere, but having heard the voice of an Angel, succeeded in convincing the Dauphin to give her an army. So in the Middle Ages only God's favorites could leave their imprint on history. And even in the seventeenth century, wasn't Maria d'Agreda obliged by her confessor to burn her three thousand pages of manuscript because a *"women of the Church did not have to write?"*

Today, this strain of mystics has clearly survived. It has even been modernized, and offers us some fascinating personalities. Marie Valtorta posed for the photographers, Yvonne-Aimée Malestroit[3] was decorated with the American Medal of Freedom; Jean Edouard Lamy was a cyclist; sister Faustina Kowalska took the train; Gemma Galgani levitated before her spiritual director.

You'd think that when a soul pleased God, He decides to marry her in order to make her immortal. The list of Christ's brides is long. Jean-Noel Vuarnet recounts in his work *Extases Féminines*[4] that on September 8, 1979, when he was in Rome, he himself also heard a voice (it's contagious!): *"Here are the names of those who loved me the most. They are dead, but in my heart they live, and in a garden more beautiful than any earthly garden,"* accompanied by a vision: *"I then saw a cathedral,"* he recounts, *"in which they were all gathered together. In the choir, under the blue cloak of the Virgin, they were singing. The brides and the fiancées were there, and so white, and so flowery and attentive that they seemed even more numerous. . . .*

---

3. A French nun whose "exploits" (there is no other word) were so incredible that the church forbade talk of them at the time. General de Gaulle personally presented her with the Legion of Honor, which was added to the Croix de Guerre with palms, the King's Medal, the Medal of the Resistance and the American Medal of Freedom. Mother Yvonne-Aimée appeared in two places at once, and appeared in concentration camps to help prisoners escape or even went to seek out desecrated hosts. She herself escaped in a supernatural manner from the Gestapo, which had arrested her in Paris. It may be of interest to refer to the book *Bilocations de mère Yvonne-Aimée* (Paris, Oeil, 1990). Yvonne-Aimée Malestroit and Maria d'Agreda represent the two best documented cases of bilocation in the history of mystics.

4. *Extases Féminines,* pp. 188–190.

*The dark robes of the Carmelites, the brown robes of the Franciscans, the white robes of the Dominicans. All of them were singing. All of them were waiting for Him who had been promised them."*

The vision (incomplete since it lacked the sublime Galgani) of our academician reminds me of a concert by the Australian rock group INXS: the arrival of the blond singer to stir them up. *"And I heard,"* continued Vuarnet, *"his voice saying, 'Here are those who loved me most and whom I loved even more. They are dead, but now I come, summoned by the wedding I promised them. . . .' And the saints, jealous goddesses, jostled one another at the foot of the altar and cried out like birds. On the steps the nuns cried out also. They tore their robes and stretched out their hands to him."*[5]

We can only bow humbly before the memoirs of these brides who, even though not stamped with the divine seal of incorruptibility or marked by stigmata, succeeded in reaching us across centuries of editions. That fact in itself is already surprising enough. Memoirs by "Masters" of the French Academy, despite their "immortal" works, do not even survive. Yet the work—fifteen hundred pages—of Saint Bridget of Sweden (1303–1373), or the four volumes by Sister Jeanne de la Nativité (1731–1798) or the five volumes containing thirty-five hundred pages of Maria Valtorta (1897-1961), whom no one called "Master," are regularly reissued. The Sister of the Nativity confided one day to her director of conscience, the Abbé Genêt: *"God makes me see, however confusedly, that this little opus, which is His, will one day be received by more than one nation and in more than one realm. It must follow the flame of faith to the end, with those who walk in its light, even if I cannot see where it will end. It will be read until the last century of the world and to the last days of the Church of Jesus Christ."*[6] To put it plainly, if you want to write an immortal work, it is in your interest to have God Himself as your agent. But don't Claudel, Bossuet, Fénelon, Racine and many others, even Pascal, recite theirs rosary?

And what should we think of the brave French country priest Jean-Edouard Lamy (1853–1931) who wrote nothing, but whose memory survives the more prolific "Immortal" academicians of his ear? The writings and the memory of some men of God survive much better than any Pulitzer or Nobel price. And among them, Angels are impossible to avoid.

---

5. Ibid.
6. *Vie et visions de soeur de la Nativité,* Editions Résiac, p.3.

## Vassula Ryden
## 1942–
### (Group III: Visionaries, Angels)
### Switzerland

The case of the Swiss Vassula Ryden, a member of the Orthodox Church, is of surpassing interest. With those we have previously discussed, we always have a sense of the past, and we tell ourselves that this sort of thing no longer happens nowadays. Vassula Ryden, a modern "mystic," epitomizes the invisible power that unexpectedly takes possession of an anonymous soul to transform it. *"Here is a woman who pays no attention at all to God for almost thirty years,"* notes Patrick de Laubier in the preface to *La Vraie Vie en Dieu*,[7] *"and finds herself, worldly and prosperous, suddenly hailed by an Angel who for three months prepares the direct intervention of Christ through the writing of notebooks, accompanied by visions and of almost permanent supernatural presences."* In effect, wife of an international businessman, Vassula follows the career of her husband and travels from country to country, finally landing in Switzerland in 1987. Vassula was not a bigot, she was exactly the opposite: she lived like a diplomat's wife, her week sprinkled with worldly invitations to cocktails and dinners in "high circles."[8] In short, she lived like the majority of us, in complete insouciance. Religion did not interest her and she never went to Mass, except for the social obligations of weddings and funerals. Nothing very extraordinary or tragic.

And yet one day in November 1985 when she was still living in Bangladesh, she was jotting down a banal list of errands when she felt within her *"something like a supernatural vibration:"* and her hand became independent like the hand of the anonymous Capuchin of Turin, suddenly controlled by her guardian Angel. Father René Laurentin asked her the question *"how did you know that it was your guardian Angel?"* Vassula's answer: *"Because he wrote in English, with my hand, 'I am your guardian Angel,' He called himself Daniel."*[9]

Automatic writing is a fairly frequent phenomenon in private revelations and a number of quite serious studies of it are available. Here we will simply note that the various analyses made of both Vassula's normal handwriting and "the other" confirm that

---

7. *Oeil*, ed., Paris, 1990.

8. Patrick de Laubier's term.

9. To those who ask *"why not Maurice, Bill, or Fifi?"* the answer is very simple: the names of Angels end in "el," like Michael, Gabriel, Uriel or . . . Marcel, even if Gustav Davidson (author of *Dictionary of Angels*) has not found an Angel named Marcel.

*"the subject is imbued with a power that surpasses her own."* The graphologist did not speak English and had no idea what he was dealing with. And even if he had known English, he would only have read what amounted to a love letter. The Angel drew also and one of his "works" was used for the cover of the book. This design is interesting as it clearly illustrates the difference between an Angel and his protégé: Daniel holds Vassula in his hands and the difference in size is like a five year old child in the arms of an adult. *"The Angel prepared me for three months,"* explained Vassula. As familiar were her relations with her guardian Angel, so much was she intimidated by Christ: *"The day when He took the Angel's place without my knowing it, He said to me: 'There, that is how you must be, intimate with Me.'"* Little by little, Christ was to educate her, grant her visions, walk her through his kingdom; and it is curious to note that while eight centuries separate Vassula Ryden from Hildegarde von Bingen, the content is still similar.

The fact that Vassula Ryden had met her Angel intrigued me highly, as you might suspect. After various phone calls to Europe, I finally got her telephone number. I dialed immediately, and heard a serious, low voice. She said to me, *"I'll be in the United States in a week, in Tulsa where I've been invited to a meeting."* We made an appointment. I wanted to meet this new version of Anne-Marie Taigi.[10] A week later in Tulsa, I met a woman with a good head on her shoulders who explained to me with good humor that she too was once prodigiously irritated by the dolorist aspect of "professional" Catholics. But, she added, *"He slowly made me understand that it was a necessity, an obligation if one wants to love Him."* I objected: *"Don't you feel that from a marketing point of view the slogan 'come to me, you will suffer' is not the best way to attract customers?"* She burst into laughter and answered simply, *"Do I look like a martyr?"*

No, she seemed serene rather, glowing with a certain "quiet strength;" the heavens might have fallen about her and she would not have batted an eye. She displays an assurance that few priests

10. An Italian visionary (1769–1837), married, mother of seven children, bride of Christ, famous at that time for her gift of sight from afar. She saw the future with such clarity that even Popes Leon XII and Gregory XVI regularly consulted her in their affairs. Her case is largely documented—she was beatified in 1920—and I believe that Anne-Marie Taigi is the only one who one day replied to Christ, worn out from her ecstasies: *"Lord, leave me, I can't go on. Why don't you look for a young virgin instead of hounding an old woman? Let me work!!!"* Her body was discovered incorruptible during the process of beatification.

possess. A reporter friend remarked to me that there were plenty of people, mainly in psychiatric hospitals, who claimed to talk with God. That was true, and I wondered how she had been able to hurdle all the inevitable obstacles reserved for those who pride themselves on such a privilege. The answer is simple: the celebrated René Laurentin had accredited her. And here I discovered the importance of that French priest, about as humorous as a confessional door. He is despite that an internationally prominent person, respected throughout the world, as he is to Marian apparitions what Jacques Cousteau is to the oceanic deeps. Incidentally the two men resemble each other physically: the same hairline, the same steely impersonal look, the same shape face, the same way of wearing "civvies." There is no apparition of the Virgin in the world without René Laurentin soon in the area to inquire about it, like Sherlock Holmes, examining, weighing, comparing, scrutinizing all the witnesses under a microscope. If he gives a positive opinion, the apparition, even before the benediction of the local religious authorities, is almost immediately validated by his approval. You might call him a certified expert on the apparition of the Virgin Mary before the bar of supernatural phenomena. And René Laurentin is a precious ally of Mary: she must certainly hold him in affection, seeing him constantly at her heels—a little like the celebrities who, seeing the same journalist everywhere they go, end by forming cordial ties. In short, René Laurentin establishes a benchmark, a bit like a film critic. It is he who "launched" Vassula Ryden, by his introduction.

So I wanted to know more, mainly about her meeting with her guardian Angel, which she does not discuss in her book, and especially why she had been chosen. Why she, who had not set foot in a church in thirty years, instead of someone who prayed to him every day? Her response was disarming: *"Because of my misery, my poverty. He said to me 'you are miserable.'"*

I was not certain how to interpret the word "miserable." *"What does He mean by miserable in your case?"*

*"I was almost an atheist. I say 'almost' because I believed in God but I never prayed, I never went to mass. And then suddenly he chose me, just like that, in my complete lack of spirituality and totally transformed me. He said to me, 'I come not only for the just but also for those who are outside.' He wants to show me his power, to prove that He can transform someone from nothing and even give him a mission. It is He who opened the doors for me, you know? I am only his pen, if you like, as He tells me regularly: 'You are My notebook.'"*

*"Do you always write 'automatically'?"*

Vassula looks daggers at me. *"First, it's not 'automatic'. Automatic writing means that the person waits for his hand to move. That's not the case with me, it's totally different: as soon as I hear His voice, I write down his words. Only the handwriting changes. Then, these messages have meaning, there's a coherence, a teaching and a theology."*[11]

*"What do you say to people who ask for proof of the authenticity of your relations with Christ?"*

*"Proof? There will never be concrete proof. It's like the death of Jesus. People wanted proof of His resurrection. Anyway the people who ask me for proof don't come to my conferences because they're not believers. And no one has ever asked me for a 'miracle.' And no one has ever asked me to prove that it is indeed Jesus. Never."*

We were eating. She tastes her Oklahoma French fries with some distrust. I wondered if she had enemies. *"Have you been attacked by priests?"*

She made a face. *"Yes, yes. There have been several attacks by priests and also by laymen. They accuse me of being a false prophet. I don't say a word. I let it go, because Jesus has taught me that He is master of all. It is He who gave me this mission, I didn't really choose. He will protect and defend me, and it works very well like that. I don't attach any importance to the attacks."*

*"What do you think of people who say they have seen and talked with Christ during a near death experience?"*

*"I believe they're telling the truth, and those are real experiences. These people have no reason to lie or make up stories. They can't invent that kind of thing. And if they come back, that's because they have their testimonies to pass along."*

*"Is it a reality very near or very far?"*

*"The invisible world is much more material than ours. It is a reality more real than reality, I dare say. We don't perceive it here because we're in the physical world, but the invisible world is infinitely more rich than the one here. So we have to believe that there exists a life after death and that this one is only a prelude, a pilgrimage on earth in preparation for eternal life. You know, we really have nothing to lose by coming close to God. On the other hand, we have a lot to lose if we ignore him."*

Since she spoke with Christ, I ventured onto suffering: *"What is the point of suffering in the Catholic Church?"*

She laughs as if it were a huge misunderstanding. *"I was against*

---

11. Her books have been published in United States by Pat Calhan from Trinitas Publishing, tel: (806) 254-4489

*it too; I found it 'macho.' It was beyond me. But afterward, the more I discovered Him the more I understood the reason for suffering and His suffering. Suffering is divine. I'll go even further: mortification pleases God. People never understand that point and even fight it, so seldom do they love God as they should. You have to love Him prodigiously to be able to understand suffering, why Jesus suffered so much and why He wants victim-souls. To put it very simply: right now there are lots of atheists and especially people who reject God and will not change, even at the moment of their death, and who will tumble into what is called hell. I saw in a vision what hell is. It exists. That's why Jesus asks for generous souls, and that's why I say to Him now 'Make me suffer if You wish, if that will pay for the redemption of other souls who fall.' So one offers oneself as victim. But you have to love Him enough to offer yourself to redeem other souls. That's suffering. But there is also joy, and if you don't experience joy in suffering, then it does not come from God. I can tell you, it was a long time before I understood, and you can't understand without accepting the idea that He suffered for us on the cross."*

This subject always puts me ill at ease. I wanted to change it. *"Tell me about the meeting with your guardian Angel. Did you believe in Angels at that time?"*

*"Oh yes; at that time, you see, if someone had told me the moon was pink, I would have believed it with no problem. I was open to everything. They said there were guardian Angels so I believed I had an Angel but really I was unimpressed, like everyone else. It took that day in November 1985 to interest me in it. I was jotting down a shopping list when I felt a vibration in my body. It was as if the pencil wanted to write all by itself. I let it happen and it drew a rose coming out of a heart. Then it wrote: 'I am your guardian Angel and my name is Daniel.' I was startled but at the same time I said to myself 'Why not?' Then I understood that he was answering my question before I even asked it. Later I asked my Angel why I was hearing his voice and he told me 'Because I'm speaking so you hear me.' I did not yet know the word locution. Later, I saw him. He asked me, 'Discern me, and look well upon me,' and I saw him inwardly. We took great pleasure in these exchanges. One day I asked him to draw something, and all he could find to draw was churches and cathedrals."* She laughed. *"At the beginning of this story, I thought I was the only person in the world to talk with my guardian Angel, because I didn't know that there existed what are called 'private revelations.'"*

*"What does he look like?"*

*"You know, the Angels are different from us. Catherine Labouré saw the Angel in the guise of a five year old. To each his own image, if*

*I may put it that way. I see my Angel as a human being: he takes the shape of a human being and always wears something like a dalmatic, a small cape, made of silver brocade. His skin is matte. His hair is shoulder-length. An Angel is quite perceptible. Sometimes I see another Angel beside him, immense, six feet tall, well-proportioned, with a luminous white robe and white wings. Very very luminous."*

"And the Archangel Michael?"

*"He is an immense brilliant light. That's all."*

"What is the role of the Angel?"

*"Christ told me, in notebook forty-eight, 'I have given you an Angel to guard you, to console you, and to guide you.' And my Angel asked me one day, 'Do you know who was present on the day of your birth?' My answer was obvious: my mother, the doctor, the midwife, not my father because at that time men were not allowed to attend the birthing. The Angel added: 'I too.' He has been with me from the beginning. Then I asked him if he had chosen me. 'No, it was He,' he answered. The Angels are the servants of God before all else. They must protect us and lead us as close to God as possible."* Vassula pauses a moment, then goes on.) *"One time I surprised my Angel saying, 'Oh God,' as if lamenting a bit, 'let her follow you.' I asked him what he was doing and his answer was almost sullen: 'I am praying.' 'But for whom?' 'For you,' he told me."*

She stops a moment, pensive, and looks at me. *"My Angel brought me flowers, did you know that?"*

I confessed that I wasn't aware of it.

*"One day he brought me a bouquet of real flowers. I was passing through Pakistan, awaiting a plane for Switzerland. I was spending the day in the hotel, waiting for the plane, when he said to me, 'You know, it's almost Christmas and I'm going to offer you a gift, I'm going to offer you flowers.' I was stunned: 'Real flowers, not spiritual flowers?' 'Yes, real ones, you'll see.' I heard him with surprise and wondered how I was going to know that they really came from him. 'I'll sign them, you'll see my signature,' he told me. Several hours later, in the evening, I went down to the restaurant for dinner. I was alone in the room. When I finished my dinner, a man in a hotel uniform approached me without saying anything, and I thought he was bringing me the check to sign. He took my hand and placed in it a garland of red Pakistani roses. He turned and left, still without saying a word. I immediately thought about the roses. Instinctively I smelled the bouquet and at the same moment I saw the silver threads of what is called in English 'Angel's hair,' waving gently before my eyes. It was his signature. It was very pretty; I still have them. I dried them."*

"How do you live now?"

*"I let myself be carried along by the flow. I no longer fight the current, because I've learned that it does no good. Besides, Jesus told me that I must always consult Him before making a decision. So I pray and I put myself in His hands."*

*"Do you receive letters from readers begging you to ask Him personal questions?"*

*"Yes, but I don't answer. I don't ask; that's not my mission."*

*"Why this title,* La Vraie vie en Dieu [Real Life in God]*?"*

*"He chose it."*

*"What have you learned from your angelic experience?"*

*"That we must not pray to the Angels only to ask them to find parking places. We must put them really to work and thank them. But above all, during a difficult interview don't ever forget to send your Angel to the interviewer's guardian Angel. That avoids a lot of problems and clears up a lot of situations. And it always works."*

## KATSUKO SASAGAWA
## 1931-
### (Group III: Visionaries, Miracles, Angels)
### Japan

Who could have imagined that the land of high speed microchips, of electronics and especially of Buddhism, would be the cradle of the most startling guardian Angel story of our day, for what is more difficult than to authenticate a "miracle" in Japan? We find as many Catholics on those islands as Mormons in France or Italy. Considering what follows here, we can only bow (very low) before the Most High, for whom nothing is impossible, including making himself heard in the country of miniaturized electronics: no less than twenty million Japanese viewers have watched the statue of Mary weep, live on television. And in a country of Buddhists and Shintoists, there is no need to emphasize that this constitutes an event far surpassing the "classic" European miracle.

Even better, at Akita we have a mixture of Catherine Labouré, Jacinta Marto and Gemma Galgani: stigmata, revelations, so many Angels that there is hardly room for them all, an NDE type of light, the apparition of Mary and a statue that cries warm tears. Examinations, re-examinations, private detectives, Japanese commission of inquiry, Episcopal commission of counter-inquiry, academic analyses, counter-analyses, X-rays, spectrographs, members of parliament, doctors, and as grand finale "detectives" from the Vatican. All were obliged to accept the evidence, against their will: what happened at Akita certainly arose from the supernatural world, perfectly illustrating Father Jacques Fournier's statement in *Time* magazine, September 1991: *"The apparitions of Mary have embarrassed priests since Vatican II."* Yes indeed! Priests do not like it when their God involves himself in their affairs.

It all began two hundred kilometers northwest of Tokyo, in the Tohoku, in a suburb of the city of Akita, as usual in the middle of nowhere, at the top of a nondescript hill where a religious community made up of about twenty sisters had established itself. There was little religious about this convent of Yuzawadai except its purpose, since at that time the Vatican did not even recognize their existence. We must emphasize that these women did not have an easy task: the neighborhood did not hesitate to retail the most dubious rumors about them. A community of women living together, in the name of a "barbarian" religion, could only draw suspicion. Nevertheless, and as always, it was through a woman, Katsuko Sasagawa, that Japan found itself at the center of an episode that would stir up the whole country. And yet Katsuko is ten times more timid and self-effacing than any Italian nun, since she is . . . Japanese. She speaks so softly that a butterfly could perch on her lips without being disturbed. The sound of her voice resembles the slow rustle of silk paper: melodious, down, as if timeless: each word comes out like a feather swinging slowly in the air, falling to rest on your ear. She is a mystic. A real one, in the pure tradition of the contemplative mystics. But with her Buddhist past, Katsuko Sasagawa's serenity would make any French or Italian contemplative seem like a Rock 'n Roll dancer, so gently do her gestures reflect the lightness of a bird and her features the serenity of a Zen monk. It takes more than a dash of holy water to wash out generations of Japanese female submission and Buddhist contemplation.

And then, she is beautiful. This is not Gemma Galgani or Eve Lavalliere, but she possesses the kind of beauty that fills us with a supernatural quietude and peace when we see it. Remarkable. Examining Sister Sasagawa's life, we discover a strange similarity to the childhood (predestined) of stigmatics: sick from her early days, carted from hospital to hospital without knowing exactly what was wrong, worried parents, and so forth. When she was nineteen a doctor operated on her for appendicitis, but the surgeon damaged nerves and she was paralysed. Once more she went from hospital to hospital and from operation to operation. During a convalescence at Myoko, she met a Japanese nurse who befriended her and gave her some books to read on Christianity. Bedridden, the

young woman has nothing to do but read. In 1969, she is persuaded, and decides to convert. More, she feels drawn to this
barbarian God who loves everyone. Momentarily recovered, Katsuko informs her parents that she wants to become a Catholic nun.
The shock in the family, Buddhist for centuries, is severe. But it
worked out in the end, and they let her leave. Besides, what Japanese husband would want a wife who was constantly sick? Katsuko
Sasagawa was converted and became Sister Agnes Sasagawa.

No sooner did she enter the community of the Sisters of Jun-
shin of Nagasaki than she collapsed. Back to square one, the clinic
at Myoko. Four days of coma and what Dr. Moody would call an
NDE. A priest even gave her extreme unction. But Sister Agnes
remembers her "dream":

> I remember that I saw a beautiful person in a place
> which seemed like a pleasant field. This person, with a
> movement of the hand, had invited me to approach her.
> But I was hindered from doing it by people as thin and
> living skeletons who gripped at me. Looking beyond, I saw
> a crowd of persons who were fighting each other to reach a
> level of pure water, but one after the other they fell into a
> river of dirty water. Filled with compassion for these poor
> people, I prayed also for them. I said especially the myster-
> ies of the Rosary. Then I suddenly saw on the right side of
> my bed a gracious person whom I did not know and who
> began to pray the Rosary with me. After the first decade she
> added a prayer I did not know. Surprised, I repeated it after
> her. Then she counseled me to add this after each decade.[12]

She came out of her coma. The Nagasaki sisters, who live on
divine love and fresh water, have just sent her water from Lourdes!
She drinks it with great difficulty, but the effect is immediate: she
recovers soon after. The modification suggested by that *gracious
person*" is the decade of Fatima, that is, the prayer the Angel taught
to Jacinta Marto. One might say that as at Fatima, Garabandal and
the rue du Bac in Paris, the Angel came to prepare her, though the
major event would not occur until six years later.

Agnes Sasagawa leaves the Nagasaki sisters and settles into a
tiny cell in the convent of "the Servants of the Blessed Sacrament."
She feels fine, and for once is not tormented by a variety of illnesses. But in January 1973 she notices that her ears are starting to

12. Teiji Yasuda, *Akita, The Tears and Message of Mary*, 101 Foundation, 1989, p. 200.

play tricks on her and her eardrums aren't working as they used to. On Friday, March 16, 1973, the telephone rings. She picks up the receiver and says, "Moshi-moshi." But she does not hear either the speaker or the buzz of the telephone, which she hangs up. Sister Agnes collapses. The priest finds her prostrated by shock. He sends her to the hospital in Niigata. Dr. Sawada examines her several times and hospitalizes her for forty-three days. In the beginning he was not sure, but now he is: an incurable condition. It is all over: Agnes will never hear again. After the psychological shock, she studies and learns to read lips to maintain social contact. Dr. Sawada, amazed by his patient's reaction, says to her: *"It is very difficult to live in a world without sound. You are fortunate to have faith. I think that it will help you. Do not become discouraged."*[13] Agnes goes home. Her family asks her to give up her vocation and to stay home, now that she is deaf. In May 1973 she realizes that she misses her convent life, and she decides to go back. Living in permanent silence, there is nothing better than the contemplative life. Two months later, on June 12, the sisters leave her alone and the mother superior asks her to pray before the Blessed Sacrament in their absence. Sister Agnes goes into the chapel to open the tabernacle, and she has hardly touched it when an extremely brilliant light bursts forth and blinds her: *"Subjugated by a power which overhelemed me, I remained immobile, incapable of raising my head, even after the light had disappeared."* She thinks she's going crazy. The next morning, she goes back. This time, she opens the tabernacle cautiously, but there is no light. Two days later, when she finds herself in the chapel with the other sisters, the light appears again. Yet only she sees it. The mother superior orders her to keep her visions to herself. Nevertheless, the nun will experience that Light a third time, and her description of it in her diary corresponds in all respects with the Light at the end of the tunnel in NDE: *"The dazzling Light suddenly, and, as before, something like fog or smoke emerged around the altar and the Light. At the same time, a multitude of beings appeared in this fog. They were not human beings, but one could see very clearly that it was a crowd made up of spiritual beings, a multitude, in a space which seemed to open out into infinity. Transfixed by this extraordinary spectacle, I knelt in admiration. Then the thought came to me that there was a fire outside. I turned to look through the glass opening, but there was no fire. It was that mysterious Light that enveloped the altar. The radiance of the host was so bright that I couldn't look at*

---

13. Extract from her journal, cited by Teiji Yasuda in *Akita, The Tears and Message of Mary.*

*it. Then, closing my eyes, I prostrated myself."* She remained there until a sister tapped her on the shoulder. But on leaving the chapel she became aware that the palm of her hand hurt.

This Light will change her life. On June 23 there will occur a sort of apotheosis. During an act of adoration (the Blessed Sacrament was exposed): *"Suddenly, the blinding light shone from the Blessed Sacrament. As previously, something like fog or smoke began to gather around the altar and the rays of light. Then, there appeared a multitude of beings similar to angels who surrounded the altar in adoration before the Host. These were not human beings, but one could see very clearly that they were an adoring crowd of spiritual beings . . . a multitude because . . . the space around seemed to open up into a sort of infinite depth. . . . Absorbed by this surprising spectacle, I knelt down to adore. Then, I was seized with the thought that there could be fire outside. Turning around to look through the bay window in the back, I saw that there was no fire outside. It was indeed the altar which was enveloped in this mysterious light. The brightness from the Host was so brillant that I could not look at It directly. Closing my eyes, instinctively I prostrated myself."*[14] She stayed there until a sister tapped her on the shoulder. But on leaving the chapel she discovers that the palm of her hand hurts badly. The nun is terrified when she sees the palm of her left hand: it is as if someone has made a cross with a razor blade, but the skin is not cut. The wound is interior. The pain becomes more and more insistent. She panics, wondering what is happening to her, fearing the worst after her sudden deafness. She says nothing and suffers in silence. After the visions, this is too much. Convinced that she is the victim of hallucinations because of the many medical treatments she has had to undergo, Sister Agnes confesses to Bishop Ito, who does not judge her and simply asks her not to talk about it, and to tell him if there are fresh visions.

A week later, on Friday June 29 (we note again here the importance of Friday), the sister is attending a Mass—it is the feast of the Sacred Heart—said by the bishop. When she grasps her rosary to begin the recitation, a person appears suddenly to her right. Sister Agnes has a shock: it was the *"same heavenly person who had come to my side in the hospital in Myoko."* The Angel, it is a woman, made of light, accompanies her in her prayer and her voice, *"beautiful and pure . . . resounded in my ears like a true echo of paradise."*[15] The

14. When she told Bishop Ito about it, Sister Agnes was embarrassed to use the word Angel. Page 17 in *Akita, The Tears and Message of Mary.*
15. Page 22, op. cit.

Angel recites a prayer that dedicates sister Agnes as a victim-soul, exactly as Father Gamache consecrated Georgette Faniel. As usual, no one sees anything. Next day, the other sisters notice that Agnes is keeping her hand closed. The superior, Sister Kotake, questions her. She is stunned, does not understand. *"Sister Agnes showed me her wound,"* she recounts. *"She wept and wondered what had happened to her. It was a cross in her left palm. I ran to the statue. It was clearly marked on the right hand; there, a black cross could be seen. I was sad and unnerved to think that we could have wounded our Mother. I prayed all day long. The sister also seemed to suffer. The wound in her palm was perfect, the lines were straight. Someone thought it was a children's prank, but it would be impossible to draw the lines in the hand without a ruler. I didn't talk about it. I waited silently for God to give us a sign."*

It did not take long. On July 5, 1973, in the chapel, the Angel met with Agnes to recite the rosary. According to the nun, to pray with an Angel at your side is an unforgettable and unique experience, and the prayer increases tenfold in power. The pain in her palm also. When she leaves the chapel, the wound begins to bleed. It is no longer possible to hide the stigma. Besides, it is not the stigmata we usually hear about. Agnes shuts herself in her cell to change the bandages in privacy. She is lost, she does not understand. This is not Catherine of Siena or Anne-Catherine Emmerich: so she starts praying, and asks for an explanation. Toward three in the morning a voice echoes in her head. It is the Angel. She asks her not to complain about her wound, Mary's having been much deeper and much more painful. Sister Agnes stares at her, and sees an odd resemblance to her sister, dead several years earlier. She has barely formed the thought when the Angel, smiling, answers her: *"I am the one who is with you and who watches over you."* The Angel sparkles. It is impossible to really describe him/her, except that he/she gives an impression of sweetness and is swathed in light white as snow. The celestial being shows her the way to the chapel, adding: *"A wound like yours will develop in the right hand of the statue of the Virgin and that wound will be infinitely more painful than yours."* Sister Agnes dresses. We might think this a Japanese copy (!) of the rue du Bac. Except here, there are no benches in the chapel but six tatamis[16] with black borders and little cushions. The Angel has disappeared. Agnes is alone before the statue of Mary, thinking again of the Angel's voice, which touched her heart. This statue, soon to become the center of Catholic renewal in Japan, has

16. One tatami, or mat = 1.82 m. x 0.91 m.

a history important to know for the events that followed.

In 1965 the superior of the convent, Sister Kotake, almost died but recovered suddenly and, not knowing how to thank the Virgin, decided to order a statue for the chapel. One of the nuns owned a picture executed by a German painter to the specifications of a Dutch visionary to whom Mary, during one of her frequent apparitions in 1946 in Amsterdam, had declared, *"I am Our Lady of All Peoples."*[17] She liked the picture, and went to a wood-carver in Akita, Saburo Wakasa, a forty-five year old artist. He was a Buddhist. He examined the small painting and took the job. He would explain later: *"When I began to work, I wanted to recreate the calm and serenity of his face. I don't know how to explain it. But you see the sweetness and the calm. I owed it to myself to give the statue that sense of peace."* Saburo Wakasa finished his work. His Virgin's features were just perceptibly but unmistakably those of an Asian. He could not quite sculpt the features of a European. No problem: his statue was a success precisely because of that weakness, which produced a Japanese Virgin. Now back to Agnes: she was in front of the statue, to the right of the altar, when it seemed to come alive. The Japanese woman gazed, incredulous. Later she said that Mary, bathed in a sparkling light, addressed her in these words: *"My daughter, my novice, you have obeyed me well in abandoning all to follow me. Is the infirmity of your ears painful? Your deafness will be healed, be sure. Be patient. It's your last trial."* The Angel was there too. Then they disappeared and the statue returned to its normal state. The next day Sister Agnes went back to the chapel and found the mistress of the novices before the statue. She signaled Agnes closer, and showed her the wooden hand bleeding. This time, it was no hallucination. The right hand was bleeding like a human hand.

Until then everything could be explained theoretically: the nun was sleepwalking, she had hallucinated, she had cut herself on the palm, or maybe even it was a trick played by the whole cloister to attract attention. But now the bleeding statue filled the convent with fear. The sisters who doubted their companion's mental stability—after all, she was already deaf—were all shaken. Bishop Ito, head of the diocese, rushed to the scene. *"When such events occur, the bishop must investigate, but as this was the first time this had happened to me I didn't know how to judge the matter,"* he explained in an interview. *"I didn't know how to judge it expediently. I told*

17. According to an expert in Marian apparitions, Father Laurentin, that apparition was classified as an isolated incident by the Congregation for the Propagation of the Faith, one "department" among many in the Vatican.

*Sister Sasagawa not to speculate and to remain silent. The wound appeared every Thursday and bled on Friday, and on Saturday only a scar remained. She tried to nurse the wound and hide it by wrapping it in cotton. I saw it. But that didn't change anything."* Much later, materialistic minds explained that Sister Agnes had *"ectoplasmic powers,"* that is, she could transfer her wound and/or her blood to the wooden statue by willpower.[18] Her stigma became violently active also, plunging the nun into pain so atrocious that on July 27, a Friday again, the sisters wanted to send her to the emergency room. But Sister Agnes sought refuge in the chapel and prostrated herself before the altar. Immediately, a familiar voice, that of the Angel, rang in her head: *"Your sufferings will end today. Carefully engrave in the depth of your heart the thought of the blood of Mary. The blood shed by Mary has a profound meaning. This precious blood was shed to ask your conversion, to ask peace, in reparation for the ingatitude and the outrages towards the Lord."*[19]. And the Angel disappeared with a smile. The statue bled until . . . September 29, 1973, the feast day of the Archangel Michael, patron saint of Japan. We may also note that if Sister Agnes had been bamboozling, she would obviously have spoken of an apparition of the Archangel, which would have been no more than logical on his feast day. But no. She had no vision on September 29.

On the other hand the Angel continued his unexpected manifestations, and on October 2, the feast day of guardian Angels,[20] the petite nun was granted a detailed vision:

> *It was during the Mass at 6:30 in the morning, at the moment of Consecration. A dazzling light suddenly shone forth. It was the same as I had seen during three days beginning on the twelfth of June and which had so much overwhelmed me. . . .*
>
> *At the same moment there appeared the outline of Angels in prayer before the shining Host. They were kneeling all around the altar in a semi-circle, their backs toward us. There were eight of them. Evidently they were not human beings and when I say kneeling, that doesn't mean*

18. I tried: cutting out a photo of a Ferrari, I concentrated and told myself that I was going to transfer the shape, the color, the options, etc., of the Ferrari to my car. But it didn't happen.

19. Page 54 in *Akita, The Tears and Message of Mary*, op. cit.

20. October 2 is the feast day of Guardian Angels. The 29th of September is the feast day of all Angels, which means that there is a huge party in paradise.

*to say that I saw their legs or how they really were. It is dif-
ficult precisely to describe their clothing. All that one can
say is that they seemed to be enveloped in a sort of white
light. Certainly they resembled human beings, but they did
not have the air either of children or adults, how to say . . .
finally, beings to whom one could not give the age. This
said, one could see also that they were not the fruit of an
optical illusion and that they were truly there. They did not
have wings, but their bodies were enveloped in sort of a
mysterious luminescence which clearly distinguished them
from humans.*

*Amazed, not believing my eyes, I widened and closed
them, rubbed them, but nothing changed. All eight were
there to adore the Most Blessed Sacrament in an attitude of
great devotion. . . .*

*At the moment of Communion, my guardian Angel
approached me to invite me to advance to the altar. At that
moment, I clearly distinguished the guardian Angels of
each member of the community close to their left shoulders, and of the height a little smaller than each. Like my
guardian Angel they gave truly the impression of guiding
and watching over them with sweetness and affection. This
scene in itself opened my eyes to the profound meaning of
the guardian Angel, better than had any theological explanation, even the most detailed.*[21]

On October 13, Sister Agnes was to be privileged to witness
Mary's third and last appearance. The date corresponds with that of
Fatima. Nevertheless, Father Yasuda, who had just been named
priest of the community, had his doubts. *"A sister who speaks with
her guardian Angel. . . . In vain was I a priest: never have I heard tell of
Angelic apparitions. In vain did I know that the Bible mentions them. I
was nonetheless unable to believe in them. The guardian Angel
belonged to pure faith,"* he was to say.[22] *"Without categorically chal-
lenging his existence, I prayed for a sign that would allow me to believe
Sister Agnes, as I thought even so that the Angel was a hallucination
rising out of her unconscious."* A few days later, the sign would literally pierce his soul when the sister delivered to him a message on
behalf of the Angel. The spiritual director's doubts would disappear.

---

21. *Akita, The Tears and Message of Mary,* pp. 75–76.
22. We note a reaction similar to Jean Derobert's when Padre Pio was asked if he
    prayed to his guardian Angel.

Seven months passed. On May 18, the nun went to morning Mass as usual. During the adoration her guardian Angel appeared and smilingly announced to her that her ears would open in August or in October: *"You will hear, you will be healed. But that will last for only a moment."* The Angel's expression became particularly severe and made the nun shudder: *"Because the Lord still wishes this offering and you will become deaf again."* On May 8 in the middle of her prayers Sister Agnes was taken so violently sick to her stomach that she was hospitalized. Her spiritual director began to doubt that she would be healed as the Angel had promised. She stayed in the hospital until September 4. But the celestial being returned on September 21, 1974, and asked Sister Agnes to start a novena of her choice, followed by two others made before the *"Lord truly present in the Eucharist"* and promised that when the three novenas were over, she would recover from her deafness. The Angel even specified that the first sound she would hear would be the Ave Maria and the second, the bell signalling the benediction. On October 13, the anniversary of the apparition at Fatima, the Angel's prophecies were fulfilled in every way. She heard again. The bishop immediately sent her to the Red Cross Hospital and the municipal hospital of Akita to obtain two separate diagnoses. They confirmed that Katsuko Agnes Sasagawa's auditory system was functioning normally. Five months later she lost her hearing again. And the doctors once more announced, on March 7, 1975, that her deafness was incurable. But Sister Agnes would henceforth pay no attention to them.

In the meantime, on January 5, 1975, for the first time, the statue of Mary shed tears, kicking off the first miracle certified by hundreds of Japanese of diverse denominations. The miracle lasted until September 15, 1981, the 101st and last day of weeping. Mitsuo Fukushima, a journalist with the press agency "Fuji News Service," remembers that two television stations set up cameras before the statue twenty-four hours a day to testify to the miracle. After two days of waiting, they managed to film a fit of weeping and broadcast the report: tens of millions of Japanese witnessed the miracle. The bishop almost wept with emotion: *"I went to the convent, and I saw I was stupefied, even though I knew miracles were frequent in the Bible. But that was in the Bible. Witnessing one myself bothered me to the point where . . . I can't express it. At the same time, moreover, it seemed to me too much. By then we had put Sister Sasagawa under surveillance and checked out her entire past."*[23] Nothing. *"She was stable, balanced and honest, known for*

23. A development repugnant to us but quite common in Japan. Japanese enter-

*her excellent memory. Nothing of that kind,"* the bishop was to say.

Father Yasuda sent several samples of tears to the laboratory for analysis. The first analysis by Professor Sagisaka, a pathologist on the Faculty of Forensic Medicine, identifies the group of the blood running from the statue: AB. The blood group of the tears on the other hand is B. A second analysis of tears that fell on August 22, 1981, classifies them in Group O! Sister Agnes could not possibly have manipulated so many different blood groups. Never mind; the witnesses, Buddhists or Shintoists most of them, verified the weeping. Kasai Monkudo, member of the Japanese parliament and municipal councillor in the city of Akita, decided to visit the site of the miracle together with the mayor: *"A tear ran across the cheek and stopped on the chin. We watched the phenomenon without understanding. We were astonished."*

Another witness, Gijido Fujimoto, was present at another lachrymation and, driven by his incredulity, tasted one. Verdict: *"It was very salty."* A university professor, Saimon Miyata, was overwhelmed when he saw tears forming in the corner of the statue's eye. There is no lack of testimonies, and they were certified under oath. And in Japan the sense of honor has a profound significance; each year debtors commit suicide because they cannot repay their debts and students, sometimes even school children, take their own lives, having flunked their exams. Just two years ago an athlete committed suicide because he had failed to climb a mountain, making fools of his sponsors. Japan is not Italy, one reason why the events at Akita are as important as the apparitions at Fatima.

On September 15, 1981, the lachrymations ended. In all the sisters had counted 101 supernatural manifestations by the statue of Mary sculpted by Saburo Wakasa. Sister Agnes still saw her Angel, who confirmed that there would be no more miracles. Two weeks later, while she was lost in adoration before the Blessed Sacrament, her Angel's voice made itself heard. But the nun was surprised because she did not see him. She was even more surprised when a Bible appeared before her eyes, floating in the air and surrounded by a "celestial" light, open to a page in Genesis,

prises regularly spy on their employees and, before hiring them, engage detectives to examine their "past" in the minutest detail: childhood, parents, neighborhood, friends, university, people's opinions, etc. This mania has become so common that many rising executives get a jump on the firm and take the precaution of hiring their own detectives to investigate their own pasts so they know what goes into the report that will be made to their employers!

chapter 3, verse 15. The Angel gave her a rough explanation of the text: *"There is a meaning to the figure 101. This signifies that sin came into the world by a women and it is also by a women that salvation came to the world. The 0 between the two 1s signifies the Eternal God who is from all eternity until eternity. The first 1 represents Eve and the last the Virgin Mary."*[24]

On March 25, 1982, the guardian Angel brought her some good news. Certainly; that day was the Annunciation.

> *Your deafness causes you to suffer doesn't it? The moment of the promised cure approached. By the intercession of the Holy and Immaculate Virgin, exactly as last time, before Him who is truly present in the Eucharist, your ears will be definitely cured in order that the work of the Most High may be accomplished. There will still be many sufferings and obstacles coming from outside. You have nothing to fear. In bearing them and offering them,*

24. At the end of *Dialogues avec l'Ange* there is an index of themes touched on by the Angels in their conversations. One day I wondered if they had mentioned the Virgin Mary. So I looked, but found no reference to either "Marie" (Main, Maison, Mal, Maladie, Malédiction, Manque, Matière, etc.), or to "Vierge," or to "Mère de Dieu." It struck me as odd that the authors of the index had ignored Mary; the Angels do speak of her, just one time, but what they say repeats word for word what Sister Agnes Sasagawa's guardian Angel said, and the mention was in 1944! Page 478 of *Dialogues avec l'Ange*, extract from dialogue 87, November 17, 1944:

But the immaculate, virgin matter remains: MARY
Upon her head, the crown of stars,
at her feet, the moon;
her dress, the rays of the sun.
MARY—the smile of creation,
miracle hovering above the waters.
In matter: virginity.
In Light: matter
LIGHT-MATTER, RESPLENDENT, DWELLS IN YOU.
The Son of Light, the Seven, is born of MARY,
Her Name is Thirst, her Name is eternal Love.
The new Name of MARY is: Light-Awareness.
She is the eternally fruit-bearing tree,
there above and here below.
In place of the poisoned apple
this tree bears the Apple of Light.

*you will be protected. Offer up and pray well.*[25]

On Sunday May 30 Sister Agnes was indeed cured, and the doctors would never understand.

This Angel that we have followed in Japan appeared one last time to Sister Sasagawa who, having been attacked, asked her if she was the product of her imagination. The Angel answered: *"Not at all. I have shown myself to you up to this day to guide you, but I will not appear anymore."* And on those words, the Angel disappeared for good in a celestial light. The work of the petite Japanese woman was over. The Land of the Rising Sun could claim an authentic miracle, a wooden statue that wept, during the great economic and technological expansion of the 1970s and 1980s. Millions of Japanese had observed the lachrymation. By extension, we can conclude that Sister Agnes's angelic visions are just as authentic as those of Catherine Labouré, whose body, more than fifty years after her death, has been found incorruptible.

But we leave the conclusion to Father Teiji Yasuda, the nun's spiritual director: *"In the course of the nine years that I have known her, this person appeared to her many times, guiding her, advising her, sometimes even reprimanding. And she assured me over and over that his person was not just an image, but a beautiful and very real being who appeared especially during prayer. And it is clear that this person's teachings and counsels in no way translated the subjective desires or wishes of the Sister. Sifting through my long experience as a priest, I believe that these numerous interventions and the advice received could come only from an Angel."*[26]

And we'd bet, since it is another constant factor, that Agnes Sasagawa will become an "incorruptible" as well, joining Maria d'Agreda, Catherine Labouré, Bernadette Soubirous, and Jacinta Marto.

## JOHN HEIN
## 1924–
### (Group III: Visionaries, Angels)
### United States

We find Angels everywhere, including Texas! Here is the testimony of John Hein, an American born in 1924, looking just like a business-

---

25. *Akita, The Tears and Message of Mary,* p. 178.
26. Page 23 in *Akita, The Tears and Message of Mary,* op. cit.

man of the 1950s in an ad for horn-rimmed glasses. I have included his Angel story because on the one hand he gives his name, and on the other hand what happened to him lends considerable weight to his testimony. It is for example relatively easy to find the testimony of someone who explains that an Angel came to save him in such and such circumstances. In 99 percent of the cases, there are no witnesses. John Hein's file is unanswerable, unquestionable. Like all American men he devoted his life to his business, working almost eighteen hours a day. Otherwise, he goes to church on Sunday with his wife and that's about all. The humdrum routine of the ordinary life of an average Yankee from Kansas. But in 1980 everything changed in a single day. After the malfunction of one of his machine-tools, a poison gas (zirconium dioxide) spurted out at seven thousand degrees Fahrenheit while John Hein was checking the dials. The gas burned his lungs instantly, and poisoned other workers in the shop. He was rushed to the emergency room with violent cramps. He had almost ceased to breathe. The doctors examined him and told him he would never again be able to use his lungs. Also, half his brain was gravely damaged when he inhaled the gas. In 1988, he was at the end of his rope. After a coma, he was hospitalized again. *"I remember hearing the doctors talk at my bedside,"* he recounts, *"and they were saying, No hope for this one. He's dying. Maybe a month or two to live, no more. We'll try to stabilize him to make him comfortable and then send him home. What else can we do? They'd already told me they couldn't do much, other than help me bear the pain. They gave me a bottle of oxygen. I couldn't take a step without that bottle. I had to have it with me twenty-four hours a day to survive, and take medicine every day to clear my nasal passages and windpipe, in short, to keep my lungs open. But a little later, new problems came along on top of the old. They discovered that this medicine raised the level of my blood sugar considerably. And when they tried another treatment, the level dropped too low. I became hypoglycemic as well as hyperglycemic. Then I began to fall into a coma regularly, and lose my memory, weight, and so on. So the doctors told me to use more oxygen. That forced me to wake several times a night to breathe it in. But the problems continued, every day. I went from bad to worse."*

If he survived, it was thanks to his family circle. But the former businessman, with his bottle of oxygen, looked like a cosmonaut who has lost his space shuttle. And he felt himself dying, heading toward the unknown. So, like many people, when he saw death approaching he began to go to church regularly. The priest of the little parish of Fedony, Kansas, remembers this worshipper well: *"He always came to Mass. One could not help noticing him always trailing his bottle of oxygen. He depended entirely on that bottle. He couldn't walk straight, needed help, and couldn't stand upright for long. I believe this was in July 1988."* Going to church was all he had left, as he saw himself consumed slowly. *"You know, before that I went to mass every Sunday like everybody else,"* John Hein explained to me. *"God was not of primary importance. Money was the main thing, and I'd always put money before God. My life had been a permanent chase after money. True, I got rich with my two companies. I founded them in 1950. I loved money, I ran after money, I was preoccupied with money. But money didn't give me back my lungs. Everything I'd saved, a half-million dollars, went for medical care. At one point I even believed that we were going to lose our house. Then one day in church during a Mass, I had the feeling that it was my last. I felt I couldn't go on. Leaving the church after Mass, a woman saw me with my bottle of oxygen and said to me 'Why don't you go to Lubbock in Texas?' I'd never heard of it. So-called apparitions of the Virgin occurred there. I answered, 'Sure, why not?' I had nothing to lose at that point. But at the same time I wondered, 'What would happen if I had a bad spell along the way?' A Canadian friend spoke up: 'Don't worry, if you want, I'll take you down there.' Then we had to time the trip carefully, because I depended on those bottles. Finally we had the idea of installing a reservoir of liquid oxygen in the car. Oddly enough, I had no bad spells during the eleven hours of the trip from Kansas to Texas, though usually I had three or four a day. I found that really remarkable. But once we reached Lubbock, my body fell apart. I was so weak from losing weight that I couldn't climb stairs any more. We went to Mass in the evening and then went back to the motel. Suddenly I was hungry. Terribly hungry. A hunger like none I had ever known. I ate day and night, about every two hours.*[27] *It was an absolute, vital need. I had to eat and eat and eat. Next day we stayed in church all day to say the rosary. I still had no bad spells. It was more and more miraculous. In the chapel, towards 5:30 P.M., I reached the last rosary and this time I prayed for Mary to intercede with Jesus in my favor because I wanted to live and I had four children. As I began the Crucifixion, a woman dressed in white appeared beside me. She was magnificent. I remember that I didn't see her feet. Suddenly I felt a hand on my shoulder. I turned, but there was no one but my wife and me in the chapel. But the hand was still there. I said to myself, 'I've*

---

27  That desire to eat at any price, right away and anything they set before you, is a common factor with Betty Malz, whom we met in an earlier case. Her stomach had gone bad. But barely out of the hospital after her luminous NDE, she made love and became pregnant. With never a trace of cancer again.

*lost half my brain, and this time I'm really going crazy,' and I said to my wife 'Listen, take me on back, I think I'm not well.' In fact, I believed that I'd gone mad, and that was how you went mad, you understood what was happening at first. As I crossed the threshold of the chapel, I passed out. Someone just had time to catch me and to set me in an armchair outside, in the garden. Later, when I came to, this man explained that he was convinced that I was going to die on the spot, so he rushed to the font for some holy water and sprinkled me with it from head to toe. I got up without thinking, took my reservoir of oxygen and walked toward the church, and at that moment I realized that I could walk alone. But at the time I wasn't really paying attention. Only later did I truly realize that something had happened: I was walking alone, when usually fatigue overcame me after a few steps, and I now could climb stairs without a problem. Gradually something told me I no longer needed oxygen, and I removed the tube. A priest saw me and rushed toward me. He forced me to put it back, saying I must do exactly as usual. I did replace the tube but cut off the oxygen. I knew I didn't need it any more because usually I felt terrible right away without oxygen. The face is, I recovered completely on October 9, 1988, the lungs as well as the brain. When I got home to Kansas, the doctor gave me a breathing test and the needle oscillated between 575 and 600 when before I never went over 350. One month later I hit 675. The doctor told me, 'It's impossible.' But I was breathing perfectly and he saw the dial. He did not understand. He even called the nurse who knew me. Nobody could get over it, nobody understood, nobody could believe me, even though I was cured; it was as if they refused to believe their own eyes. Even my hair had darkened again. No more low sugar level. My brain was fully functioning, and my stability and lung capacity were just fine. When the doctor looked at the X-rays he had a shock: no trace of spots, problems, nothing. I was like new. He couldn't believe it was the same patient."*

The recovery passes all medical understanding. They opened a file on him, for inquiry. I was a bit disappointed. Nevertheless I asked the question: *"And you never saw any Angels?"* which made me feel as if I were asking *"You never saw a pink elephant?"*

But his answer surprised me: *"Yes, once, during the feast of the Assumption in 1989 when I went back to Lubbock. They were all standing around the font, about three in the morning."*

I showed my surprise: *"At three in the morning?"*

John Hein answered as if I had asked the most idiotic of questions. *"Yes, it was a night of prayer. The Angels encircled Mary around the font. They were white. In fact I did not pay special attention to them at that time because when you have Mary in front of*

*you, you don't notice much else. All your attention is concentrated on
her. The Angels were behind her, floating. They were like bodyguards.
She's very petite, you know."*

No, I did not know much about Her except that she was Queen of
the Angels. John Hein looked at me with his faraway expression and
said, *"Listen: that was the only time I saw Angels. I didn't see Christ, or
God, or the Devil, I only saw the Virgin and when I see Her, it's always
a sudden apparition. And also, the first time, I really thought I was
insane. But today I know it was real, my lungs are the proof."*

*"Did she ask you anything?"*

*"Yes, she asked me to talk to people and tell them they should say
the rosary."*

*"Why does She want people to recite the rosary?"*

*"Because she adores it and I imagine that Christ likes it also. It's
the strongest weapon we have. Most of the time apparitions of Mary,
in private or in public, take place during the recitation of the rosary."*

The mystery of the rosary escaped me somewhat and I truly
wanted to know more about it.[28]

*"Why is it so powerful?"*

28. After a while I understood the "functioning" of a rosary: the penitent must meditate on the life of Christ, divided into three parts. The first includes five stages of
his public life, the second the stages of his agony and the last the stages of his resurrection. A rosary is recited by telling one's beads and interspersing "Our
Fathers" and "Ave Marias." According to the historian Jean-Mathieu Rosay, the
rosary arrived in Europe with the crusades, and *"it was the Dominicans who
made it a form of devotion to the Virgin in the Twelfth Century."* The historian just
quoted seems not to know or wants to ignore how really widespread is the use of
the rosary in the Christian community. Indeed I was not at all satisfied with that
explanation, which implies that Catholics copied this form of devotion from the
Muslims or the Hindus, and I wanted to know how the rosary established itself.
What I found is frankly startling: Rosay says "It was the Dominicans who made it
a form of devotion." True. It is even precisely St. Dominic who started it, and this
is how. That monk identified himself so closely with the sufferings of Christ that
he did not hesitate to mortify himself with lashes from a scourge to participate in
His flagellation. Nothing really new in what we know, except for one detail, a very
important detail which that pleased Dr. Maurice Rawlings very much. One day
when Dominic was sharing the agony more than usual, he overdid the scourge so
much that he lacerated himself badly and fell into a coma. Well then! Did he
make a short round trip to the end of the tunnel with the Light at the end? It
would seem that he did, as, still according to Dominic himself, during the coma
he had a vision. There we are. And what does Dominic tell us about that vision?
That he saw three Angels in company with the Virgin Mary, who asked him, *"My*

John Hein reflected a moment. *"I don't know anything about that. No doubt because it was given to the mother of God by an Angel. I don't know why that prayer is efficacious, but it's infallible."*

*"Do you recite it every day?"*

*"Since my recovery yes, and especially because She asked me to recite it three times a day. The first time, I recite it at three in the morning and then go back to sleep. And if I don't wake up, someone wakes me, I don't know how. Once it was a phone call that woke me. And if I sleep, someone recites it for me. I do what She asked me to do. The half-million dollars I spent in hospitals didn't restore my lungs. The rosary did. So now I don't care about money, because my health is more important. I don't drive beautiful brand new cars but little second-hand workhorses. It's all the same to me. I'm alive and I have far fewer worries. I pray. Don't ever worry about that: pray, pray, because God really exists."*

## JACINTA GONZALES
## 1959–
### (Group III: Visionaries, Miracles, Angels)
### Spain

And now we come to one of the most astonishing Archangel stories of these end-of-the-century years. I say most astonishing because what happened at Garabandal, in Spain, has been filmed several

---

*dear Dominic, do you know what weapon the Trinity wants you to use to reform the world?"* We can imagine Dominic's expression. She then explained to him that the angelic salutation was that power and she him thenceforth to preach the rosary, explaining in fifteen points which graces would fall upon anyone who recited it. Dominic then spent his life preaching the rosary and in explaining how it worked. In all her private and public apparitions after that, the Virgin always encouraged and asked for the recitation of the rosary. But it was at Pompeii (Italy) that she gave more precise explanations. For thirteen months Fortuna, daughter of the commandant Agrelli, suffered extremely painful cramps, vomiting, and other physical tortures. The family had all possible and imaginable doctors come but they all withdrew in defeat. On February 16, 1884, the sick girl started on a novena of rosaries, and the Virgin appeared to her on March 3, surrounded by Angels and Saint Dominic and . . . Saint Catherine of Siena. Then She explained that if one called upon her, using the name Our Lady of the Rosary, in making three novenas, one obtained everything one wished, followed by three novenas in thanks. The young girl was instantly healed and that profoundly impressed Pope Leon XIII, who then officially urged that form of prayer.

times, and the scenes of children suddenly falling into ecstasy are frankly terrifying. They make us shiver. First let's locate Garabandal: as usual in the middle of nowhere, which the Virgin has accustomed us to, a village of seventy houses, tucked into a hill five hundred meters high. Not even high enough to ski down. The locals are farmers or cattlemen. Poverty is the rule in this lost corner of Spain four hours by road from Bilbao, and I tell myself it's a dead certainty that we won't soon be seeing an apparition of the Virgin on the Rue du Faubourg St. Honoré in Paris, or on Rodeo Drive in Los Angeles (near the boutique Chanel) or even in the lobby of the Plaza Hotel in New York. Almost always isolated spots, whipped by wind or rain or both, or parched by the sun. And if we study her preferred audience, we notice that she never appears to the children of bankers, industrialists or doctors or lawyers, but to the children of the poor, so miserable and underprivileged that they possess only a single richness, namely indestructible faith. It is all a paradox. And She appears to them and to no one else.[29] To put it plainly, at Garabandal we find all the ingredients of a Marian apparition with, however, one detail leading us to believe that Garabandal is much more important than we wanted to think. We know about hundreds of Marian apparitions, but rare are those preceded, or more exactly prepared, by an Angel, the best known and most important being the one at Fatima, with the three little shepherds. And even if this present event has not been recognized by the Vatican, what I have seen on various films of the time has frankly changed my mind. It is quite staggering, and personally I have not a shadow of a doubt about what happened on that hill. Too many witnesses, too many journalists, too many photos, too many films and above all too many proofs that we are going to examine, which validate that altogether exceptional apparition of the Archangel Michael.

Once more we note the importance of women: Jacinta Gonzales, Conchita Gonzales, Mari-Loli Mazon, all twelve years old, and Mari-Cruz Gonzales, eleven, were bored on this Sunday, June 18,

29. We know of only one exception, that of the Jewish banker Ratisbonne who converted immediately, causing one of the most famous scandals of the nineteenth century. He found himself with a miraculous medal around his neck and in a curious series of circumstances was led to enter a church for the first time in his life to pay his final respects to one of his acquaintances. And in visiting the church as he would a museum, he saw her in a chapel. The news of his conversion definitively confirmed the power of the little medal we owe to the angelic visit to Sister Catherine Labouré.

1961, and decided to go play at the edge of a stony path. I do not know who dared to write[30] that, because of the isolation of their village, their mental development was well below that of children of the same age living in cities. . . . In short, they talked among themselves and decided to go and discreetly swipe some apples (Granny Smiths?) in a neighbor's orchard. What a grave sin! No need to emphasize that all the priests have seen here a repetition of the forbidden fruit in the Garden of Eden, ruminating on the beastly object that is woman, even little girl. Afterward the little girls gave various versions of what happened, each of course more pious than the other, but we may forget that, as it is of no interest compared to what happened later. Here all four of them affirm the same thing: *"We heard a noise, like thunder all around us."* They looked at the sky but saw no sign of a storm. Then they were afraid and ran off. A few moments later they stopped and, reassured, began to play again when suddenly Conchita fell to her knees. The three girls looked at her, tried to make her move and, unable to, decided to go get her mother, thinking she was having a *"nervous fit."* But they too fell to their knees when they discovered what Conchita had been the first to see, the Angel.

Before going on I must note that, as in the television series "Mission Impossible," the Archangel Michael possesses a whole wardrobe of various appearances or exteriors. In the month of June, and no doubt to avoid frightening the children, he materialized as another "child," a little like Catherine Labouré's Angel. The four little girls disclosed excitedly that the Angel *"was dressed in a long, loose, blue robe without a belt. . . . The wings, pink(!), bright, fairly large, very pretty. His face neither long nor round, a handsome nose, black eyes, his countenance dark. The hands delicate, the nails clipped, the feet invisible. He appeared to be about eight or nine years old. So young, but he gave an impression of invincible power."* The Angel disappeared[31] without speaking. Back to normal, the girls gazed at one another without understanding and then dashed to the village to hide. At first they wanted to hide in the church, but they didn't dare enter, and found a hiding-place behind the chapel. They were weeping. Other

30. After research, it is a French priest, Father Robert François in *Tout le peuple l'écoutait* (in English *Oh Children Listen to Me*).

31. If the girls had been telling stories, logically they would have said that he had flown off, since he had wings . . . pink wings! I know of only one other representation of an Angel with "pink" wings, in the chapel Altare Privilegatum, of the Church of Saint-Thomas Aquinas in Paris, the work of the painter Luc-Olivier Mersou, 1887.

children asked them why, and little by little the whole village was brought up to date. Of course the story was amplified, and ended with an Angel as big as an airplane. Few people lent credence to their story. But the Angel came back three days later, on June 21. This time the four little schoolgirls were followed by several curious people, including the priest in charge of the village chapel.[32] The Angel appeared suddenly, and immediately the onlookers were also plunged into the supernatural: they noticed for example that the children's faces went white, almost shining, and that their heads were flung back violently, at a forty-five-degree angle, as if someone had suddenly pulled them back by the hair. Then they began to walk, not blinking, not seeing the spectators, not watching where they stepped, which from a practical point of view was already a feat. Another curious phenomenon: the girls were perfectly synchronized, almost like the synchronized swimming competitions. The Angel, still unspeaking, vanished. But he came back the next day. The crowd around the girls grew, and immediately skeptics were pleased to prove to the others that it was nothing but a huge masquerade. From the moment the Angel arrived, the girls *"disappeared,"* they were elsewhere, in ecstasy. Then the doctors who were present pinched them, passed flaming lighters before their eyes, tried to push them, etc., but no one of the four reacted. General anesthesia, a surgeon would say. In one of the documentary films, three doctors tried to lift Jacinta, no taller than three apples and weighing no more than thirty kilos. But three men tried to pick her up. Couldn't do it. It was as if she'd had concrete poured into her limbs, and that manifestation reminds us of Maria-Magdalena dei Pazzi: *"One day when her sisters wanted to make her leave the chapel,"* Hélène Renard tells us, *"and could not, they tied together some floorboards to transport her and testified that she was 'light as a feather.' In contrast, Marguerite Parigot, subject to numerous levitations, became extremely heavy."*[33] And, exactly like Marie d'Agreda, when the Virgin was leaving them, they lifted one another up to embrace her as if they were picking up a pen![34]

Obviously the whole village kept that appointment with the girls, and about two hundred people saw that "luminosity." The Archangel stayed about two hours, but when they came out of their ecstasy the girls thought it had lasted no more than two minutes. As we have seen, an ecstasy always occurs "outside time." The Angel still said nothing, content to smile gently. Finally on July 1st

32. San Sebastian de Garabandal did not have its own priest.
33. *Des Prodiges et des Hommes*, p. 117.
34. Photos are available.

he opened his mouth to say, *"Do you know why I am here?"* The girls gazed upon him dumbstruck. *"To announce to you that tomorrow Sunday the Holy Virgin will appear to you as Notre-Dame of Carmel."* Note that he did not ask them, as at Fatima, for prayers and sacrifices. On D-day, the village counted many more curiosity-seekers than inhabitants, and toward 6 P.M. the Virgin appeared,[35] flanked by two Angels. The first was Michael,[36] but the second has never been identified. "We did not know the other; he was dressed like St. Michael and resembled him like a twin brother." It doesn't matter. Over almost three years apparition followed apparition, and the Virgin granted the children the gift of hierognosis, that is of recognizing sacred objects from afar, this being a two-edged sword, as we shall see. From the beginning of the apparitions, the local ecclesiastical authorities proved extremely distrustful; they even closed the church to keep the children, in ecstasy, from entering. Then the priests dressed in civilian clothes and mixed with the crowd. They had no luck: when they approached the girls, one of them would rise and say, *"You are a priest."* The fathers, quite embarrassed, wanted to find a hole and hide in it. It was the same with objects. Mary had instructed the children to ask pilgrims for objects to kiss. They ran from wedding or engagement rings to rosaries by way of images and of course all sorts of medals. Several wiseacres in the crowd came back next day and for the second time gave the girls the same ring or medal to kiss. Two precautions were better than one. But when they offered them to the Virgin, she said, *"No, that has already been done!"* And what fascinates me most is to see Jacinta and Mari-Loli, each with forty or so rosaries in her hands, going back then to the considerable crowd and returning the objects to their owners! This detail alone is worth pondering. It's a bit like a waiter in a restaurant. If you're in a group, say of ten

35. Brother Paul-Marie notes in his work *Les Apparitions de Garabandal* (Editions Hovine) that one *"could not talk of suggestion: the girls had never heard of the apparitions of Fatima, for one thing, and modern representations of the Virgin of Carmel, very common in Spain, do not at all resemble the children's vision. Notre-Dame of Carmel is most often shown clothed in brown, with a black or white veil—like the Carmelites—or even red with a blue or white veil. Therefore the girls' vision is at once perfectly original and conformable to the most ancient representations of Notre-Dame of Carmel in the traditional iconography, iconography that they could not know."* Remember also that in 1961, the village was cut off from everything, with neither electricity nor telephones.

36. That was confirmed when one of the Virgin's requests was the construction of a sanctuary in honor of the Archangel who *"weighed souls."*

people, he takes the order and when he comes back he always asks, *"Who's the smoked salmon? The beef marrow rare? Well done?"* Even in Paris, where we find the best waiters, the real "pros," none of them remember who has ordered what. So imagine a girl of twelve with forty rosaries. What's more alike than any two rosaries, especially at night, where, as everybody knows, all rosaries are gray.[37] But not for them. The same for the rings, medals, etc. We agree that this violates our ordinary sense of reality. Conchita will explain in 1970 that she lost this gift some time after apparitions ceased. Another interesting detail, reminding us of section 2 in the chapter "Of Supernatural Interventions," how the four children were always together at the apparitions. Well before you, dear reader, many people thought they were given the word. But several times they were in a way "kidnapped" and forbidden to go out, under strict watch. These strictures notwithstanding, Jacinta, Mari-Loli, Conchita, and Marie-Cruz fell into trances at the same hour and minute. They said that when an apparition was programmed, they heard an inner voice during the day that put them on their guard. At the second "voice" they prepared, because the third was imminent, and at the third they rushed to the spot of the apparition.

Beginning in the month of August 1961 the supernatural phenomena grew wilder and wilder, and what I saw on the documentary films of those days sometimes gave me goose bumps: I saw the four girls arm-in-arm walking fast, heads flung back looking at the sky, going backwards! It is frankly startling to see these girls walking that way, necks back, their feet never hitting a stone, when the path is made of them! Other times, people saw them running backwards! People also saw them fall suddenly and violently to their knees, on those stones, without the least scratch. Witnesses affirmed that the children in ecstasy read their minds. More, when you study the films frame by frame you discover that in one frame Conchita is standing and in the next frame she's kneeling. Of the many books written about Garabandal, one alone stands out, no doubt because it's worthy of a story by a good journalist. It is by the lawyer and professor of history Sanchez-Ventura y Pascal who went to the village out of curiosity to observe this buffoonery obviously organized by the church. Professor Sanchez-Ventura y Pascal has never really understood how, but he was convinced on the spot, and became one of Garabandal's most fervent and brilliant defenders. He tells us that during the vision of August 4, someone in the

---

37. *"Dans la nuit, tous les chats sont gris"* (at night all cats are gray) is an old French
    proverb. —Ed.

crowd came with a tape recorder, one of the first, with its reels (the cassette did not yet exist), to record the murmurs of the four girls. By gestures the spectators indicated his microphone and machine. Jacinta, Mari-Loli, Conchita, and Mari-Cruz wanted to see, and the owner was explaining how it worked, when suddenly Mari-Loli and Jacinta went into "ecstasy" holding the microphone. Everyone could hear her asking the Virgin to speak into the mike. In the whole history of the press, this is surely the first time a reporter, even an amateur, managed to win a few words from the Virgin! In brief, hardly into her ecstasy, Mari-Loli came out of it, and the spectators made an immense circle around the recorder and its operator. When he rewound the reel and put in on "Play," the crowd heard the girl very clearly asking the Virgin to speak, and a *"soft feminine voice"* answering: *"I shall not speak!"* To the crowd this was an apotheosis, and the tape was played over and over again until suddenly no one could hear it. The passage was mysteriously erased.

Certainly the Virgin has a sense of humor.

As we have seen, the events of Garabandal present enough supernatural signs to validate the June apparition of the Angel. Even the specialist René Laurentin notes, *"We are still perplexed by the abundance of extraordinary events that occurred at Garabandal."* [38] The Vatican has never authorized the cult of Notre-Dame of Garabandal because of the retraction squeezed out of the children and especially because the predicted signs never appeared. But at the time of the events, Padre Pio assured everyone who asked him that it was indeed a truly authentic apparition. And as we have seen, Padre Pio carries enough clout, especially since his death, for us to believe what he said while alive! The doctors who examined the little girls might prick them with needles, burn them with matches or try to twist their necks; nothing, absolutely nothing, brought them out of their ecstasy. If it was a question of some fakers, we might understand, but for my part I cannot doubt twelve year old children.

Now we touch on one of the most amazing documents we have, the communion made by the Archangel Michael. Let us acknowledge that it is a true privilege to be served by the first of the Archangels. These communions took place because of the priest's absence, and when the four girls began to receive the host at the hands of the Archangel, it gave rise to serious doubts, mainly

38. *Multiplication des apparitions de la Vierge aujourd'hou*, third edition, Fayard, 1991, p. 148.

because only a "human" priest can give communion according to traditional dogma. The Virgin, in one of her two thousand apparitions, explained that the Angel took the hosts from earthly tabernacles. In the films of that time we see the girls fall suddenly to their knees, put out their tongues and swallow. "Enlargements" were made but naturally there was no trace of the host. One might say they were pretending and one might be right. In fact, that's what everybody was saying at Garabandal, to the point that the "see-ers" asked the Archangel to *perform a miracle so everyone could believe them.*" The Archangel agreed and said to Conchita: *"Through my intercession and yours God will perform one. On July 18* [1962], *Our Lord will make the host visible so that people may see and believe."* That day, it was a triumph: thousands of people went to the village and awaited the announced miracle. But it was not until almost midnight, after three "inner calls," that Conchita left her house and went to the path, followed by an immense crowd. She fell into ecstasy and saw the Angel. The crowd made a circle around her. Conchita gazed at the Archangel: she opened her mouth and a deathly silence fell around her. Her tongue came out, waited for three seconds and suddenly the host, a host as white as new snow, materialized. No tricks, no magic, the Archangel Michael had kept his promise.

I have talked briefly with Conchita but she shuns reporters, and I had no wish to hunt her down in New York, a city I dislike. But she was kind enough to give me a phone number for Jacinta, who lived a half-hour from my apartment, which excited me extremely. Interviewing one of the four girls who had taken communion at the hands of the Archangel Michael seemed to me a good idea. I hopped into my car and drove down the Pacific Coast Highway to Oxnard, a sort of desolate suburb of the missile testing base at Point Mugu, on the shore of the Pacific. And I wondered what Jacinta was doing there, in that out-of-the-way corner of the world. I found her Garabandal-Oxnard itinerary more than strange. I parked in front of a small gray house, a little apart from other buildings, almost deserted, like a haunted house. I even wondered if I'd made a mistake jotting down the street number. Her husband, a gray-haired man of about forty with a chubby face and deep-set eyes, opened the door to me. Then Jacinta arrived. I was agreeably surprised: she was a typical Spaniard, black hair pulled back, black eyes, rosy cheeks, dressed in a blue shirt and black skirt. You'd have guessed she was thirty-seven years old but she was actually forty-seven. No makeup other than lipstick, a pretty figure with a welcoming smile and a body made for love. Her husband had me sit down on a large couch and sat down beside me.

I wanted to hear a description of the Angel with pink wings from Jacinta's mouth.

*"What was the Angel like?"* I asked her.

*"You know, it was so long ago, and I can't deny that the memories have faded as the years passed. We gave descriptions at the time and I can't really add anything. A light, a child with pink wings. He didn't want to frighten four little girls of twelve."*

*"But when the Angel gave you communion did he look the same?"*

*"Yes, he was the same, he told us his name, Saint Michael, the Archangel, he was a child, as in the beginning."*

Then a question crossed my mind: perhaps that host had a strange, other-worldly taste. *"Did the host have a different taste?"*

*"I don't remember if it had a different savor. In any case, it came from tabernacles here on earth. But now that we're talking about it, I remember that the Virgin asked us, 'If you meet a priest talking with an Angel, whom do you greet first?' We all answered, 'The Angel, of course!' but she checked us, smiling. 'No, not the Angel first, but the priest because he ranks higher than the Angel and he can offer blessings at Mass, which the Angel cannot do.'"*

Jacinta's melodious voice had charmed me. *"And the photo of the visible wafer?"*

*"It was an onlooker from Barcelona, Damien, who was there and took a lot of pictures, and that was one of them. Many people saw what happened there."*

I thought suddenly of the tape-recorder and the Virgin's voice. *"Do you remember the tape recorder?"*

Jacinta smiled. *"I was with Mari-Cruz. We held the microphone up to the Virgin and asked her to speak into it. And She said, 'I shall not speak.' Then they heard the tape many times before her voice was mysteriously erased."*

*"Did the Virgin have a sense of humor?"*

Jacinta's face lit up. *"Oh, yes, it was like talking to your mother. Sometimes we even played hide and seek with Her. She always found us! Or She sent us to find the place where one of the four of us was hidden. She was truly a mother, but at the same time commanded immense respect. She laughed often. Once, at the start of the apparitions, someone asked us to throw holy water on the apparition to be certain that it wasn't the devil. She asked us, 'What are you doing?' and we answered, 'We're throwing holy water on you to be sure you aren't the devil.' She burst into laughter and said to us, 'Go ahead, throw holy water on me.'"*

*"Well, since the ecstasies, have you had 'locutions,' have you*

*heard inner voices?"*

*"No, but on the other hand I began to have premonitory dreams of weird accuracy quite often. I remember for example one morning waking up and telling my husband, 'Your father is going to die.' He had no reason to die and showed no signs of illness or anything. But he died two days later of a heart attack. I have lots of dreams like that. It's amazing, because sometimes I see the future in precise detail."*

*"Have you talked with your guardian Angel since then?"*

*"No, I just pray to him every night, for a long time now, and I always say the rosary, every day."*

## GABRIELLE BOSSIS
## 1874–1950
### (Group III: Visionaries, Angels)
### France

Gabrielle Bossis provides us with unarguable proof of the predestination of certain souls to a cloistered life. An actress and playwright, she ranged all over the world playing roles she had created without ever shutting herself away in a convent. Logic: He didn't wish it. And if today her plays have fallen into total oblivion, her seven volumes of "dialogues" with Christ have, by contrast, survived perfectly, and are now in their 50th edition! What novelist, even after being publicized by David Letterman, can boast of such a *post mortem* success. And while she was pursuing an actress's career, a little like Eve Lavalliere, Gabrielle Bossis went through two world wars in His company. No lovers, and no other husband but Him, He who spoke to the young woman through "internal words" that she regularly noted down in little black notebooks. It was not, however, that she didn't hesitate to enter a convent, but that after four years of prayers she ended by perceiving *"that such was neither her destiny nor her path."* And if she was not made to join a religious order, instead, as with the great mystics, Christ spoke to her from her childhood on.

Gabrielle Bossis and Christ were a bit like "A Man and a Woman" by Claude Lelouch. He follows her, He speaks to her, He loves her, He teaches her and leads her progressively toward higher and higher levels of spirituality. It is not passion, if I dare say it, as with Gemma Galgani or Marie-Madeline de Pazzi. Nevertheless He envelops her in His divine protection and leads her by supple steps toward realities that are not of our world. It is a marriage of peaceful, tranquil love. I imagine Christ lying stretched out in a deck chair in Gabrielle

Bossis's garden, sipping a pastis and taking a little rest after a soul-hunt. Doesn't He ask her *"Take Me out on the terrace, Surround Me with your flowers. Think Me with your delicacies. When you see Me you will say: I recognize You, You whom I have never seen?"*

As one might have guessed Gabrielle Bossis had no supernatural manifestation in the manner of Marie-Madeline de Pazzi or an Yvonne Aimee de Malestroit, no vision like Hildegaarde von Bingen and Vassula Ryden and no messages like those to Sister Josefa Menendez or to the splendid Sister Marie-Angelique Millet. She heard Him, that was all. But as we shall see, the style of His dialogues were easily identified, since His style is inimitable.

There are very few Angels in the seven volumes of Gabrielle Bossis. Does one concern oneself with the employees when one frequents the CEO? On the other hand, she knew she possessed a guardian Angel: *"My dear friend,"* she wrote a woman acquaintance, *"I know you are suffering and weak. I turn this knowledge to account to love you even more, and to pray for you with all my heart. And to ask my guardian Angel to be at your side as I can't be there."*[39] Here are her few rare references to Angels:

> *223.—In the country*
> *—Honor and hail the Angels of the terrace. They are there because you have invited them. Honor the Angels of your house. Ah! if you believe, you will live more with invisible beings than with visible ones.*
>
> *And I remembered that before leaving, I said to the Angels, "Come sit on these benches and praise God for so many marvelous horizons."*[40]
>
> *228—Confidence regarding saints and Angels. When one is a little child, one finds oneself in everybody's arms. One lets oneself be cherished, and it's all quite natural."*[41]
>
> *178—July 7—Postwar return to the country.*
> *—Invite the Angels and the saints to accompany you in your inspection—they are there, you see, to be with you in all your activities. They are your older brothers."*[42]

39. Page 99 in *Liu et moi*, vol. VI, op. cit.
40. Page 62 in *Lui et moi*, vol. I, Beauchesne, Paris
41. Page 63 in *Lui et moi*, op. cit.
42. Page 58 in *Lui et moi*, vol. II, op. cit.

*271—August 17—Holy hour. Church of Fresne. I said,
"Hello, my most beautiful Love."*
*—"Yes, My little girl, nothing is more beautiful than I and
thou: God is a soul, God marrying a soul. The human eye
has never seen the like. It is a sight for Angels. Ask your
Angel to play your role in this fete. It's a fete that can last all
one's life if the soul lends itself to it by its poor goodwill.
Very often, I ask nothing more of you than your goodwill. It
is a loving gesture confidentially summoning My aid."*[43]

This unmatchable style that one discovers in the pages of the
eight volumes of Gabrielle Bossis is to be found, too, in diverse
works, always veritable mysteries of publication as, for example, in
that manuscript published by the Editions du Paris, *If Thou Openest
the Door to Me*, which displays enough points of correspondence
with the various feminine mystics we have dealt with hitherto to
attest to its authenticity. These messages, Don Renzo Del Fante
explains to us in the introduction, were confided to *"a Capuchin
nun who probably lived alongside Sister Consola Betrone."* The content of the dialogues, so scrupulously taken down by the sister, was
handed to her director of conscience, who awaited the last instants
of her life, to entrust them to a publisher for eventual publication.
Nothing more is known about that woman, or when that happened,
over how much time, how, etc. This little book presents, as well, a
great many similarities to the American *God Calling*, another work
of Christly dialogues received by two anonymous women, which
has sold millions of copies without any publicity on the part of its
publisher, A.J. Russel. The tone, the content, the poetry and especially the style are familiar, even while being, however, original. The
testimony of the Italian Capuchin merits our slowing down, for
Christ's references to Angels are four in number:

> . . . *All the love of the seraphim and the saints can never
> equal a single beat of my Heart.*

> . . . *My Heart, inflamed with love for you, would wish a
> response on your part. While it could be tranquil in heaven
> with the Angels and the saints, it has chosen to be anxious
> for the honor and the love of mortals.*

> . . . *If I asked my Angels, as I ask you, to intensify their*

43. Page 169 in *Lui et moi*, vol. III, op. cit.

*love for me, I could not retain them.*

> *Courage! Your guardian Angel gathers in everything and stores it for Paradise. Not the slightest suffering and the smallest fatigue passes unnoticed: everything is noted down by the omniscience and wisdom of God.*[44]

## JEAN-EDOUARD LAMY
## 1853–1931
### (Group III: Visionaries, Miracles, Angels)
### France

From this country priest born in 1853 we have a great many documents, because his reputation extended far beyond the communist city of La Courneuve.[45] His case is exemplary for all those who doubt these "gifts from heaven," granted sparingly, to be sure: but why to him and not to another priest? More, if this is merely legend, then why not make up other legends, even more supernatural, more extraordinary, in such a way that every region, and why not, every church, can have its own saint to stimulate, exalt and encourage popular fervor. If we think about it a bit, we see the evidence: no such thing is happening, and the churches are emptier every day. The priests themselves are much to blame, many lacking faith. So how do we explain that the memory of Father Lamy, an ordinary country priest and not even stigmatic, has survived better than that of any "immortal" academician, when he never even published a book? His biographer, Count Paul Biver, can hardly be suspected of fantasy. When this doctor of letters, specialist in art history, and aristocrat met the priest in 1923, he was immediately captivated by his personality and thereafter constantly helped him, with financial aid as well as in his administrative duties. One of the events that the count would never forget was that night when, after accompanying Father Lamy to his room, since he had more and more difficulty moving, he heard him a little later talking with someone. An aristocrat listening at doors hardly implies an education worthy of his rank, but the case was so curious, that we would certainly have done the same thing:

> *At a quarter to ten, I am in bed and I put out my light.*
> *Perhaps two or three minutes pass, when, through the two*

---

44. Page 73, op. cit.
45. A suburb of Paris.

*flimsy doors, I hear a lively conversation in the old priest's room. Three men's voices participate, sharp and quite distinct in the absolute silence of the night. This phenomenon intrigues me immediately and extremely, and I am aware of its possible significance. No one else has climbed the stairs since I did. The steps of fir are so flimsy and the house so resonant that from my room I could distinguish the sound of a mouse. Also when I left the old man at the threshold of his room twenty minutes before, I could see that the room was empty. Father Lamy spoke from time to time, answering someone whose voice was dry, warm, of a very virile and agreeable timbre, who talked without a trace of accent and in a positive tone.*[46]

You guessed it: Father Lamy was talking with his Angels, and saw these celestial beings with the regularity of a metronome, as if it were second nature:

*When you have fifty or so Angels together, you're rather stunned, and you don't think about praying to God. These gilded mirrors that never stop moving are like so many suns! What a marvelous spectacle heaven must be, with millions of Angels in flight! . . . Angels are more striking to look at than the Holy Virgin. With those beautiful reflections shimmering incessantly on the white robes, they seem like brilliant officers around Her, so simple. I speak of the very Holy Virgin herself, independent of Her light. When She shows herself in what I might call her great glory, she is a little terrifying, for the sun is only a light. What I was saying applied when She holds back her glory. . . . With what simplicity and affection the Angels surround her! God has given her thousands and thousands of them. She knows them all by name. They know Her only by the name 'Queen.' Each of them has his particular physiognomy, but they too are all beautiful. The Angels call her 'Queen' in a very respectful tone, and when she talks to the Archangel, She calls him simply 'Gabriel' in a very maternal tone. She contemplates the Angels with a soft and direct gaze.*[47]

The Virgin Mary is called Queen of the Angels, but few mystics

46. Paul Biver, *Père Lamy, apôtre et mystique*, Editions de Serviteur, pp. 179–80.
47. Ibid., p. 171.

have described her exercising her rule. Privileged among the privileged, Father Lamy constantly sees Her surrounded by her "heavenly host." This is a rare privilege, and even Padre Pio was not granted a similar "panoramic" view. Yet Father Lamy, priest of guttersnipes and the proletariat, was not a stigmatic, a quality almost required to gain access to that other eye which can see the mysteries of Heaven. He was unaffected, a rustic, a poor man, even poorer than his parishioners, and he told Count Biver, *"I have only lived among workers; I tell things as they are and I don't know how to disguise them as you do."* Father Lamy was unquestionably a saint, an old-fashioned priest, a priest who moved about on a bicycle and who, even while blessing a rosary, wondered what he was going to have for dinner that night. He was a Specialized Workman among priests, earning half the minimum wage, but opening the doors to the supernatural by his humility; even communist workers find him hard to reject. As for the Angels, they truly whirled around this almost blind old man, and it is only thanks to the admirable tenacity of the well-bred aristocrat that we have these memories of him. Thanks to Count Paul Biver for leaving us the biography of this unusual priest, for without him, one of the most startling testimonies of the Virgin Mary and the Angels would never have come down to us. Indeed, it is thanks to Father Lamy's descriptions that we have been able to establish a portrait of the Virgin, more exactly a sketch, which portrays Her not only as a woman shedding eternal tears but also as true stateswoman, lacking neither humor nor relevance.

In short, Father Lamy moved about the supernatural on his bike, with a loaf of bread under his arm. Toward the end of his life he had so great a reputation that innumerable people came to visit him and ask for advice, cures, favors and prayers. This was not the crowd who came at 3 A.M. to wait for Padre Pio's Mass, but no doubt if this priest had lived a little longer, it would have come to that. Like many other mystics, Father Lamy read minds and often answered questions even before his visitors had had time to ask them. These two points alone impressed a good number of the faithful, to the point where the wildest stories began to circulate about him. Father Lamy did not become famous until he had renounced everything, including himself, and was preparing to die tranquilly. One of his major visions came on September 9, 1909, twenty years before his death, in Grey's chapel; when Count Biver took his notes, the priest often said to him, *"Be careful, none of this must appear before my death."*[48] His

48. His biographer respected his wishes and the book did not appear until 1933, two years after the priest's death.

descriptions of Angels agree wonderfully with those we discovered in the chapter "Of Angels and the Tunnels."

> *We do not pray often enough to our guardian Angels. What do we do for them? A scrap of prayer in the morning, a scrap of prayer in the evening, and that's all! Their mercy to us is great, and most often we do not use them enough. They regard us as poor little brothers; their good will toward us is extreme. Nothing is as faithful as an Angel. . . . Angels, like saints, do not have bodies similar to the real bodies of the Virgin and Our Father; they have bodies that are not of our world. Every Angel has his special physiognomy. . . . Their robes are white, but of a white that is not earthly. I do not know how to describe it, as it is not at all comparable to our color white; it is a white much gentler to the eye. But these holy personages are swathed in a color so different from ours that everything else seems dull and somber. When you see fifty or so Angels, you are filled with wonder: you think no more of praying to God. Those golden plates shimmering perpetually: you would say so many suns! The flight of millions of angels in heaven must be a marvelous spectacle! I have never seen them with wings, but always looking like young men. . . . All these personages, like the devil, are with us, all around us. We do not see them, but we are so near to seeing them! It is as if only a film separates us from them.*[49]

Father Lamy is one of the principal mystics whose visions perfectly corroborate the testimonies of NDE survivors, and we highly recommend that the reader read the biography by Count Biver. His prudence, his respect for the inimitable style of this "poor people's" priest, and especially the accounts that he managed to elicit while the priest was alive, are terribly surprising in their realism, which is why the "Servants of Jesus and Mary" have noted a growing interest in the life of this truculent religious man, who reminds us in many ways of Don Camillo as interpreted by the actor Fernandel, with the major difference that Father Lamy truly existed.

49. *Père Lamy, apôtre et mystique*, pp. 182–184.

## Marie Lataste
## 1822-1847
### (Group III: Visionaries, Angels)
### France

Dying "in the odor of sanctity" at the age of twenty-five, this French nun would be almost unknown if Editions Tequi had not deemed it useful to reissue her diary, her correspondence and her memoirs, which she wrote by order of her spiritual director. This young pre-destined girl's notebooks were released to the bookshops in 1862 and went through four editions before fading into oblivion during wartime. But "notebooks" like Marie Lataste's or Marie-Angelique Millet's cannot fall permanently into oblivion since, as it seems, Divine Providence takes care of keeping them relevant. And again, I was fascinated by the survival of such books. This humble nun pre-served for us a veritable treasure, worthy of the *Dialogues* of Catherine of Siena, since it is in her words that we find a detailed explanation of the guardian Angel given by Christ. Consequently it is also with Marie Lataste, whose body reposes in London today, that the most precise details are found, all issuing from various visions, internal conversations or ecstasies, or, as we say today, "out of body" trips.

Yet this candid young woman was auscultated, judged, weighed and above all humiliated by various priests and spiritual directors who needed to assure themselves of the young nun's authenticity. But Marie Lataste, like Maria d'Agreda, never issued a single com-plaint or protest: she welcomed any humiliation as a gift from God, which she could thus share with Christ.[50]

Well before donning the veil, Marie Lataste remembers that she had only one pleasure, to go to her village church and contemplate Him beside the altar. She was like Sister Agnes Sasagawa or Padre Pio: she saw Him, surrounded sometimes by his Angels. But Christ put her on her guard, sometimes very severely, so that she would not drift into pride because He appeared to her: *"Beware boasting, beware thinking yourself above others because of that. My word alone will not save you, you must cooperate. . . . Know that you must humiliate yourself before Me, as you are only ashes and dust, sin and corruption, and I am God Almighty. . . . I make kings. I make mon-archs and potentates tremble on their thrones. I probe hearts and bodies; nothing done among men escapes me; I know their most*

---

50. That approach is quite frequent among (future) saints, the best examples being Anne-Catherine Emmerich and the nun Ulrique Nisch von Hegne, whose biogra-phy was published by Editions du Parvis.

*secret thoughts.*"[51] Finally, like Helene Kowalska, He leads her to a convent, among the Sisters of the Sacred Heart, where the young girl yields herself wholly to Him. With Marie Lataste, there are innumerable Angels, but what interests us most is found in "book four," entitled *Les Anges et les Hommes.*[52] Christ stresses and develops the minuscule element common to both Angels and men, the soul: *"Through his soul, he (man) is linked to the Angels; through sensation, to the animals; through existence, to the diverse elements of nature,"* and he makes clear that:

1) this union of man with all of creation is a reality which permits him to participate in two creations, terrestrial and celestial;

2) guardian Angels existed well before His coming to earth and are assigned at the moment of man's birth.

> *(Chapter I:)*
> *Man's most intimate union is with the Angels, because that union must endure always, for all eternity. Union with the brute creation is of a much lower order because that union is only transitory, lasting only long enough to enter Eternity. Moreover, my daughter, the union of soul and Angel is the strongest, because that union is not a passive union but a working and highly active union. There is communication between man and the Angels; there is an understanding, and this communication, this understanding become such that man finally comes to resemble the Angel and takes a stand with him.*

> *(Chapter II:)*
> *You remember what I told you about communications between Angels and men. Listen well to this, it is very important. I want to speak to you of two effects Angels have on men. The first is the illumination of intelligence, the second is the impulse of will. . . . Angels, my daughter, enlighten men in three ways: by announcing divine mysteries to them, by instructing them, by exhorting them, they enlighten them, manifesting themselves to them visibly or invisibly. . . .Invisibly, when they use no perceptible object*

51. Pascal Darbins, *Vie et oeuvres de soeur Marie Lataste*, Paris, Editions Téqui, 1974, p. 15.
52. Ibid., pp. 211-22.

*in revealing themselves to man, when they deal directly,
soul to soul, when they speak to him as spirit to spirit, as
Angel to Angel; and that, whether he whom they speak to is
awake or is asleep, as they speak to all those they care
about and who entrusted to them for inspiration to good
thoughts. . . . But this impulse bears no resemblance to the
impulse, for example, that you would communicate to
some object; no, my daughter, because will remains always
free, and as it is free, neither the Angels nor God can impel
it toward the good if it does not desire it. This impulse is a
disposition toward good, an aptitude, a facility to do good.
To that effect the Angels remove, eliminate or diminish
obstacles that would inhibit or block the will, and in that
sense they lend it impulse.*

*(Chapter III:)*

*My daughter, God governs, directs and leads all imme-
diately by His providence. Nothing escapes Him; as He has
created all, so He saves all, so He keeps vigil over all and
watches over all. Nevertheless, it has pleased Him to assign
the performance of his providential acts to ministers He
has given himself. These ministers are the Angels. . . . He
created the world and entrusted it to His Angels. He created
man and entrusted him to them also. They are always at
man's side, they are always with him, they watch over him,
they guard him, and because of that they are called
guardian Angels. Every man has a guardian Angel. . .
because that is the will of our Father in Heaven, doing
everything for man's good and salvation. The guardian
Angels were not given to men only when I came to this
world, but from the very beginning all men have received
an Angel from God to watch over them.*

*(Chapter IV:)*

*Here is what a guardian Angel does for you and what
you must do for him. The guardian Angel drives away the
ills of the body and of the soul; he fights against your enemies, he encourages you to do well; he carries your prayers
to God and records your good works in the book of life; he
prays for you, he follows you until death, and will carry
you to into God's bosom, if you live justly while you are on
earth. . . . A little thing can afflict your body forever, and an
accident can ravage the life of your soul forever. You are*

*not nearly wise enough to fend off and drive away all the*
*dangers; and if you were, you would often be unable to do*
*it alone. What you do not see, your guardian Angel sees for*
*you, and he protects your body and soul by driving off all*
*that might harm them; he does it without your knowledge. If*
*you were to reflect on this at times, and ask yourself how*
*you escaped this or that accident or misfortune, you would*
*put your finger on your good Angel's function. . . . And lastly,*
*my daughter, your guardian Angel will follow you every-*
*where; he will follow you all the days of your life, and when*
*God calls you from this world, he will present you to Him.*

As we might imagine, Marie Lataste did not wait to be in
heaven to see her Angel. He revealed himself regularly, but his role
is somewhat muted since she, like Helene Kowalska, saw Christ
above all. Consequently her Angel remained in the shadows. What
remains fascinating in her work is the spirit that animates it.
Indeed, Marie Lataste was never educated in letters, which is an
elegant way of saying what she never hesitated to avow: *"I am a*
*poor and humble country girl, who knows only what my mother*
*taught me; and all my learning in nature's ways consists of know*
*how to read, to write, to sew and to spin."* Consequently, she also
warned her spiritual director, from the very start of the locutions
and visions, that she could never express all that He said and
showed to her. As for the clergy, they were amazed by the profundity of the texts written by this *"good farm girl"* and examine her
writings as minutely as they wished, they never found a single
error of dogma slipping into the content. As the Abbé Pascal
Darbins noted, *"This serious examination of the manuscripts per-*
*mits no doubt as to the authenticity of the works of Marie Lataste."*
In that, this young nun resembles almost exactly Maria d'Agreda or
Catherine of Siena. And if her body did not remain incorruptible to
"guarantee" her work, we note just the same that her death did not
pass unnoticed, despite her modesty and her willingness to hide
her special graces from the other sisters: *"Those who took care of*
*her upon her death even asserted that her limbs retained their flexibil-*
*ity. We heard one of them attest to it: seeing that the Marie's body bent*
*with the greatest suppleness, she testified her astonishment at that to*
*the assistant Mother, adding that she had always thought the dead*
*were rigid: 'That is usually true,' she replied, 'but saints are not like*
*other people.'"*
We add simply that Marie Lataste has never been canonized.

## HILDEGARDE VON BINGEN
# 1098–1179
### (Group III: Visionaries, Miracles, Angels)
### Germany

Germany has left us, "Mein Gott" alone knows why, four visionary Gothic nuns who made indelible marks on their times and whose memoirs or visions continue to be printed even today, even after eight centuries. The most famous among them, Hildegarde Von Bingen (1098–1179), occupies a curious place in the history of the Church and also of Tower Records, for we find her among the "Flowers of the Saints" (her feast day is September 17) although she has never been canonized, nor even beatified. According to the documents of the time, crowds came all the way from France as well as Germany, made pilgrimage to the convent founded by Hildegarde, whose gift of prophecy as well as her visions and especially her ecstasies were known throughout Europe. Hildegarde Von Bingen, a musician who composed a number of hymns,[53] was assailed by a sort of inner voice and felt a pressing need to set down these messages on parchment. She herself had doubts at first and, after being confessed by her director of conscience the monk Godefroy, she received the assent of the ecclesiastical authorities, who sent her a kind of secretary/spy ordered to make sure that this was not a case of diabolical possession. This secretary, named Volmar, wrote down then what would become known worldwide under the name Scivias. Volmar spent ten years at her side and under her dictation wrote twenty-six visions concerning the relationships among man and God, the Apocalypse and the Angels:

> Then omnipotent God established different orders in his celestial militia, as was suitable, so that each order fulfilled its function, and in such a way that each order was the reflection and seal of its neighbor. Each of these reflections harbored as well divine mysteries that these same orders nevertheless could not see, know, taste or define absolutely. Also, their admiration rises from praise to praise, from glory to glory, and their action is eternal, as they can never reach

---

53. CDs from Hildegarde Von Bingen (my favorites):
- *Symphoniae & Sequantia*, Editio Classica, Deutsche Harmonia Mundi, #77020-2-RG. This CD is absolutely amazing....
- *Canticles of Ecsatsy*, WDR, Deutsche Harmonia Mundi, #05472-77320-2
- *A Feather On The Breath of God*, Hyperion, #CDA66039
- *Vision*, Angel (of course), #CDC 7243-5-552-46-21

*their goal. These Angels are the spirit and the life of God.
They never renounce divine praises, they never cease to contemplate the light lit by God, and that divine light imparts to
them a brilliance as of flame. May the faithful receive these
words with all the passionate devotion of their hearts,
because they come from him who is the first and the last,
for the greater benefit of those who believe!*

A contemporary of Hildegarde, Elisabeth de Schönau,
(1129–1165) also a Benedictine, visited her often. She too lived
somewhat like a phantom and was permanently bedridden by fear-
some illnesses, after her request to Christ that she share his
sufferings, to which she added to her daily sessions with the
scourge. The least we can say about her is that she was quite preco-
cious, as she entered the convent at the age of twelve. And it is this
German, the first bride of Christ, who will herald the future line of
great mystical brides like Catherine of Siena or Angela of Foligno.
Jean-Noel Vuarnet reports *"that an Angel which was in the habit of
paying her visits and carrying her off to the empyrean heights
instructed her one day to write and make known to the world what
she saw during her ecstasies. That Angel, like us, saw in Elisabeth a
daughter of Saint Hildegarde:*[54]

> *He showed me a large number of books, saying to me:
> "Do you see all these books? They must be written before
> Judgment Day." And taking up one of those books, he said
> to me: "This is the book of the ways of God that you must
> write when you have visited Sister Hildegarde and have
> heard her."*

Doubtless the two women had innumerable stories to exchange.
In the same category as Hildegarde Von Bingen and Elisabeth de
Schönau, it would be difficult not to mention the two Mechtildes,
von Magdebourg and von Hackenborn. Born at the beginning of
the thirteenth century in Saxony to a rich and educated noble
family, Mechtilde von Magdebourg at the age of twelve felt the
physical presence of the Holy Ghost (!), which thenceforth pushed
her ceaselessly toward the life of a nun. At twenty she left her
chateau and closeted herself at first with the Beguines, consisting
of widows, before changing her allegiance and joining the Cistercians of Helfta, a place that saw the birth of three mystics one after

54. *Extases féminines*, p. 42.

another. Few data remain to us on Mechtilde's life, aside from her writings regularly published down the centuries. The eminent angelologist Vincent Klee gives a reference concerning her works published in France—*Révélations de la soeur Mechtilde. La lumière de la divinité*, Poitiers, Paris, H. Oudin Freres, 1878.

It was the young woman's confessor who forced her to set down on parchment the raptures that she describes as unspeakable joy. She was one of the first to denounce debauchery in the church, among the priests and monks of her time, which had forced her to leave her convent of Beguines. Like the other mystics, she fell victim to all possible illnesses and even went blind toward the end of her life. She died between 1282 and 1294 at Helfta in Saxony. In her Cistercian convent she was not the only one of know intimacy with God since the other Mechtilde—of Hackenbourn—born in 1241, shared in this divine privilege, as well as Sister Gerthrude of Helfta. The second Mechtilde died shortly after the first, in the same convent, on November 19, 1299, she too leaving her "Revelation (of Sainte Mechtilde)" that Gerthrude of Helfta, whom we have met before in these pages, edited for her. All these ecstasies in the same cloister are a bit confusing, but in their raptures Angels appeared regularly and engaged them in conversation. It is Mechtilde of Magdebourg who explains to us why she was never interested in Angels, thus joining herself to Saint Paul's famous declaration:

> *The least soul is daughter of the father, sister of the son, friend of the Holy Spirit and the true bride of the Holy Trinity. But if we go higher, we see who tips the balance. The greatest of the Angels, Jesus Christ, who is raised above the seraphim, who is with his father one indivisible god—I take him, negligible soul that I am, in my arms, I eat him, I drink him, and I make of him what I want; that will never happen to an Angel, however far above me his station. The divinity of Jesus Christ will never be so far above me that I cannot unite my limbs with his forever. I could not possibly dare more; why then should I burden myself with what might happen to Angels?*

For her part, Mechtilde von Hackenborn was careful not to ignore these spiritual Beings and she even asked Christ, a few days before September 29, feast of the Archangels, how she should render them homage. She received the following—divine—answer:

*"Recite the Our Father nine times in their honor, that being the number of angelic choirs."*

She recited them, and wanted to offer them to her Angel, on his feast day, so he himself could present them to the other spirits; but Jesus said to her with a certain dissatisfaction:

*"You must leave me the responsibility for that, for I would take pleasure in fulfilling it; know that any offering dedicated to me arrives in heaven ennobled by my mediation and transformed with great benefit, just as a thread dropped into molten gold would mingle with the precious metal, cease to be what it was and appear as what it had become, that, gold."*

CHAPTER 13

# Conclusion: Angels Prefer Women (But Men Prefer Flight Attendants)

NOT ALL ANGELIC ENCOUNTERS ARE AS DRAMATIC AS SAINT CECILIA'S, but we note all the same that they are quite frequent; the encounters in the Dialogues of Budapest are an excellent example. In the Dialogues, the Angels prepare their interlocutors for the Holocaust, for death in the Nazi camps. With the saints, either they prepare them for a life of suffering, or they stimulate them to prepare for an apparition of the Virgin Mary or of Christ. The two little shepherds of Fatima died shortly after the apparition of the Angel and Mary. In our day, Angels sometimes appear to children: Dr. Elizabeth Kübler-Ross has noted throughout her career that little children explained to their parents that they were going to disappear, with some such phrase as *"You know mommy, I'm going away today, an Angel told me that."* Nobody pays any attention at the time, but after the accident, the prediction remains an indelible memory for the parents. So the symbolic representation of the Angel of Death is not devoid of all sense; far from it. And according to our hypothesis, these are the same Angels, since many people, a few minutes before drawing their last breath, "see" either the "playmate" of their earliest days, or a "marvelous" Angel waiting for them, as we saw in the chapter "Of Angels in the Tunnels."

With the mystics, they allow themselves to be seen and discussed, to chat and even to laugh, as we saw with Padre Pio. But oddly enough there are few male mystics who have seen Angels or their guardian Angel during their lifetimes, like Padre Pio or Father Lamy. On the other hand, among female mystics it is a very frequent phenomenon, as if through some mysterious grace they were more favored by the Most High, or perhaps judged more worthy to see them. So in Volume 2 of Vincent Klee's *Plus beaux textes sur les*

337

*saints Anges*[1] we notice that of the eighty-one authors selected by this priest, fifty-four were men and twenty-seven were women, a ratio of 67 percent to 33 percent.

On the masculine side, the writings are strictly and exclusively speculative.[2] But among female authors, 70 percent saw their guardian Angel in particular or Angels in general during their ecstasies. In our own study, it is even more flagrant: in Group I—Incorruptibles, Stigmata, Angels—we find four women out of four; in Group IIa—Stigmata, Angels—the ratio comes to nine women for one man, Padre Pio, a little lost among all those veils; in Group IIb—Incorruptibles, Angels—there are no men, and in Group III—Visionaries, Angels—we find ten women and only two men.

Why do Angels appear so seldom to men and so often to women? Are women more contemplative, more open, more sensitive to the immaterial and spiritual character of an Angel? As all reality is translated by numbers, the answer seems to be found among the stigmatics, the most pathetic and most mysterious of divine signs. In his book *Stigmata*, which appeared in 1989,[3] the British journalist Ian Wilson took a census, in a very spotty way, of eighty-eight people authentically marked by the wounds of Christ, examined by surgeons, psychiatrists, clergymen and observed by innumerable witnesses.[4] But just as in our study, in Wilson's book, devoted to a totally different subject, the ratio of women reaches the incredible level of 89 percent! And well before him, in 1824, after studies of more than three hundred cases of stigmatisation, Dr. Imbert-Goubeyre found the same ratio: 280 women, that is, 87 percent, against only 41 men, 13 percent.

We knew that women were more intuitive, more receptive, in short more sensitive than men, but the mystics offer another proof,

1. Nouvelles Editions Latines, Paris.
2. Padre Pio and Father Lamy left no writings.
3. An inquiry into the mysterious appearance of the wounds of Christ on hundreds of people from the Middle Ages to modern America; New York, Harper & Row, 1989.
4. An incomplete study, as the Frenchwoman Marthe Robin for example is totally ignored, probably because no work on her has been translated into English. Father François Brune and Joachim Boufflet counted other stigmatics, like Anna-Maria Goebel (d. 1941), Berthe Petit (d. 1943), Lucia Mangano (d. 1946), Yvonne-Aimée de Malestroit (d. 1951), Edwige Carboni (d. 1952), Alexandrina Maria de Costa (d. 1955), Barbara Brutsch (d. 1966), Adrienne von Speyr (d. 1967), Augustin Hieber (d. 1968), Maria Bordini (d. 1978), Marthe Robin (d. 1981), and Symphorose Chopin (d. 1983).

crushing and indisputable. Is it also because men are less at ease in their relations with God? *"Male mystics,"* Jean-Noel Vuarnet remarks very justly, *"can only become women (the bride-soul theme) or children. As for the women, bound to God with no strain on their gender, they live in mysticism with greater happiness, as daughters, brides or mothers: daughters of the Father, brides of the Father, mothers of the Father. . . ."* So the Angels, just like God, reveal themselves much more often to women than to men. I have thus only a wee chance of "seeing" my Angel. Let us not forget that never in all the Dialogues of Budapest did Gitta, Lili, Hanna or Joseph see so much as a wingtip. And in the end seeing your Angel is not so important, because the most important thing is to believe in him. As the Gospel puts it, *"Happy is he who believes without seeing."*

But how can we establish contact with our guardian Angels, in what circumstances, how can we symbolically show our desire to meet with him (or her) and, above all, how can we interpret his answers? The Angel is only waiting for our goodwill, and his response can at times be blinding or painful; also, it is only normal that we find it hard to believe in his invisible existence. That is only human, and he/she makes no objection, realizing that it is extremely difficult for us to believe in somebody we cannot see, while the Angel surely sees us!!! For example: one of my acquaintances heard talk of my projected book on Angels, and, one thing leading to another, he finally asked if he could read my work, in this case the first part of this book. Delighted to find a guinea pig on which to test my first chapters, I promised to bring the manuscript to his store. Before we go on, a few details are important for an understanding of what followed. Xavier is a former ambulance driver. Because of his ex-profession he has seen so many horrors, tears, blood, lacerated bodies, and children decapitated in auto accidents, that his spirit has shaped him a character of total and absolute cynicism. As a general rule, rare are the ambulance drivers for whom God, and worse, the guardian Angels, can exist. . . .

When I got to his store on Melrose Avenue in Los Angeles, I handed him the book, which he started reading on the spot, there being no customers. After three or four pages he stopped short and fired at me, *"I don't believe in these coincidences; they're just plain stupid. And I'll tell you why. A month ago I bought a car. And from that moment on, I began to notice everybody on the road who was driving the same car as I was, but before that I hadn't paid any attention to that model. It is just chance, nothing more."* Disappointed, and somewhat deflated by his argument, I said to him, *"Well, I don't know, read some more and tell me what you think."* And I went home.

That same evening, Xavier telephoned, totally overexcited, so overexcited that he had to repeat his story twice before I understood what had happened: *"I went on reading your manuscript after you left and about seven at night I told myself it was time to make tracks. I shut the shop's metal blinds and went down the street to buy something on Melrose. While I was walking someone passing me pressed some object into my hand. Immediately I thought it was some drug. When I opened my fist, I found a small metal object, and when I looked closer I was stupefied: it was an Angel. I stood there in the middle of Melrose Street, examining that metal Angel. Never in my whole life had anyone stopped and pressed anything into my hand, just like that, for nothing. But something really happened there!!!"*

The three or four days after that incident were strange for Xavier, so impressed was he by the unlikelihood of that "coincidence" and the real possibility that his guardian Angel might exist with all that implied. The metal Angel was his way of revealing himself, of proving his presence in a very material way. Xavier had experienced much more directly what I had noted at the beginning of my interest, since the Angel had beaten him at his own game.

Perhaps Xavier needed a brutal answer, no doubt because some place deep inside, he wanted to believe on condition of some "palpable" proof, if he couldn't have coin of the realm raining from the sky!!

Whatever happens in our lives, the Angel is there. And even if his job is to guard us, that does not mean that he will keep us from dying, since we also saw that when our time has come, nothing can keep us from "passing" to the other side. But at least we know, now, that we will have someone to come look for us with a bottle of Dom Perignon.[5]

And finally, which is more important, to die well or to live well? As the bewitching Annie Lennox put it, *"Dying is easy, it's living that scares me to death."*[6] The guardian Angel's task is above all to guide us, to help us benefit from our existence on earth and not fear living. Of course the Angel will never put a coin in the parking

---

5. Champagne was invented by three Benedictine monks, mystics of the pious bottle, Dom Perignon, Dom Ruinart, and Frere Oudart.
6. In "Cold," album *Diva*, Arista Records.

meter if you have no change; But to go on from that to say that with the Angels, Life is rosy, kind, sweet, sugary, and full of flowers with birds singing in the fields—sweet chariot—is utterly false, enormously false, and makes Life and the Angels seem what they are not, a candy bar—but in 99 percent of cases they reveal themselves at a time of blood, tears and despair, since we have seen that guardian Angels only materialize fully when:

1. we are in an accident, or at the end of our rope

2. we die with a round-trip ticket (NDE)

3. we die with one way ticket (Deathbed Visions).

To find the right way among these three possibilities is easy: discover the Angel BEFORE these three cases, in other words BEFORE he reveals himself. Those who have discovered this principle are numerous. But they don't talk about it, for fear that they'll make fools of themselves. Others, perhaps a little less sensitive, feel the presence and try to explain it. So the ex-rock star Patti Smith sang "Ask the Angels, Ask the Angels," while David Bowie thanked his and Alice Cooper wanted to see one over his shoulder. With musicians as with writers, with painters as with poets, the Angel (good or bad) is inevitable, omnipresent, eternal. And among those granted the gift of seeing him, from Maria Rilke to Mika Waltari, or from Valery Brysov to Charles Peguy, his imprint in indelible.

And we can't deny the obvious: Annie Lennox had no need of stigmata to write the most powerful song dedicated to a guardian Angel. It is austere and powerful, elevating and rhythmic, inspired but material, to the point that the Angel who emerges from these notes is no longer a *precious little Angel* but a brilliant Being of Light, intense and melancholic as well as terribly majestic, as if the Archangel Gabriel himself were blowing the trumpet held by Dave Defries. In a word, the day we discover that an immaterial but living Being is linked to us, Annie Lennox's words and music are transformed into so many thorns reminding us of all the years we have lived without ever addressing a single thought to him:

*Precious little angel*
*Take a look at what you have done*
*Well I thought my time was over*
*But it's only just begun*
*Precious Little angel*
*You're my own sweet turtle dove*
*Won't you stay with us for ever*
*In a bundle full of love.*

*I was lost until you came*
*Precious little angel*
*Won't you spread your light on me*
*I was locked up in darkness*
*Now you've come to set me free*
*I was covered up with sadness*
*I was drowned in my own tears*
*I've been cynical and twisted*
*I've been bitter all these years.*

*I was lost until you came*

*THE END*

# CHAPTER 14

## Epilogue, Bibliography, and Sources

IN THE HISTORY OF FRANCE THEY CERTAINLY LOOK DOWN THEIR NOSES AT the king Saint Louis, who once, in all innocence, bought some very expensive feathers supposedly fallen from the Archangel Michael's wings. This good king, overly "credulous" in our eyes, was, as they say, "had." Nevertheless, after five years of reading and nine months of writing, I have formed the absolute certainty that in the eyes of the Creator, of the Father, and certainly of the Angels, faith is the most precious thing in life that a man can possess. *"I am like the sun, which one can see less the brighter it shines,"* He declared to Maria-Magdalena dei Pazzi during one of her ecstasies, *"And just as one cannot see the sun in any other light than its own, so I too can be known only by the light I diffuse. . . . The soul believes as if it sees, but he who sees no longer has faith, since faith is to believe without seeing."* In other words, it is up to each of us to create and maintain his own faith, without waiting for the visible manifestation of a guardian Angel. For that, we must pass through an NDE, and as we know, every accident does not give rise to such a personal experience.

To believe that you are born "under a lucky star" or that you are "protected" is a seed of faith, but it is not enough. If that quite justified presumption could be translated into a dialogue with your Angel, then your life would undergo a radical change. It is a bit like positioning a cannon: if you are off only a couple of inches at the point of aiming, these inches may become several miles at the point of impact. The point of impact is somewhere else, far from the initial objective. So it is that we can illustrate the arrival of an Angel in everyday life. It is only a year later, when you look back, that you discover profound modifications. And if you ask him every morning to guide you and advise you on the course of your day, then the connection can only blossom. Never forget that the Angel loves most of all to converse with his protégé, and that he has a phenomenal sense of humor, as the Angel lives in a smile:

> *The smile symbolizes mastery over matter.*
> *If you read a book, you hold it close enough*
> *to read it easily.*
> *If you want to read me,*
> *come close to me:*
> *I DWELL IN THE SMILE*
> *I cannot weep*[1]

It was this book's aim to convince, but alas, I have no idea whether I have achieved my goal, and I will only advise you, like the writer San Antonio, that *"if you do not believe in the efficacy of the guardian Angel after this, you have only to carry this book back to the bookstore and exchange it for a cookbook."*[2] If you have read this book without preconceived notions, you will perhaps think more often of him who is close to you, of your guardian Angel, and if you decide to speak regularly with him, which is the condition sine qua non, the essential will be achieved, and he will then begin replying to you by signs, winks of the eye and fantastic synchronicities. Then you will discover that you have a friend "in very high places."

14 September, Los Angeles, California.

---

1. *Dialogue avec l'Ange,* Friday, February 18, 1944, p. 252.
2. *Des Clientes pour la morgue.*

PRIORITY READING ON NDE:

- Dr. Melvin MORSE, *Closer to the Light*, Ivy Books

- Pr. Kenneth RING, *Heading Toward Omega*, Quill Books

- Dr. George RITCHIE, *Return From Tomorrow*, Chosen Books

- Dr. Maurice RAWLINGS, *Beyond Death's Door*, Bantam Books

- Betty EADIE, *Embraced by the Light*, Bantam Books

- Martin CAIDIN, *Ghosts*, Bantam Books

- *TALKING WITH ANGELS, (Dialogue Avec l'Ange)*,
  Atrium Publishing, 11270 Clayton Creek Road,
  Lower Lake, CA, 95457
  Phone: 707 995-3906   Fax: 707 995-1814

- Bernard RUFFIN: *Padre Pio, the True Story*,
  Expanded Ed. OSV Publishing, Huntington, Indiana.

And above all:
*The Visions Of Tondal:* quite beautiful and in color, printed by the J. Paul Getty Museum. It deals with the NDE of the Irish Chevalier Tondal who recounts, in a fifteenth-century manuscript, his trip from "the other side" in the company of his guardian Angel. This sublime manuscript of forty-five pages is, of all the versions available in the world, the only one to be entirely illuminated. Written in Middle French by the scribe David Aubert and marvelously illuminated by the master Simon Marmion de Valenciennes, *Visions of Tondal* was commissioned in 1474 by Duchess Marguerite of York. Here we have a real treasure (which escaped the French Bibliotheque Nationale) of inestimable value, as much as an oil painting by Leonardo da Vinci. At the Getty Museum it can be viewed only on a screen using cd-rom. It goes without saying that the screen cannot reproduce the fine quality of the miniatures, nor the almost celestial delicacy of the colors invented by Simon Marmion. During a private visit, curator Thomas Kren allowed me to examine the manuscript from the first page to last. The tale told by Tondal (1149) conforms perfectly to modern near-death experiences; I think particulary of Georges Ritchie's, and Robert Monore's story. We cannot recommend too highly the acquisition

of this work of seventy pages. Moreover, few NDE specialists, theologians, angeologists, or bibliophiles know of the existence of this
remarkable book, published in 1990, on the manuscript. The color
miniatures are reproduced on the same scale as those of the original manuscript.

It can be purchased by mail by sending a check for twenty dollars (postage included) to the J. Paul Getty Museum.

Write to:

Curator Thomas Kren

J. Paul Getty Museum

17985 Pacific Coast Highway

Malibu, CA, 90265

# BIBLIOGRAPHY

Angela de Foligno. *Le Livre des Visions et instructions*. Paris: Seuil, 1991. (REVEL)

Antier, Jean-Jacques. *Marthe Robin: le voyage immobile*. Paris: Perrin, 1991. (HAGIO)

Attwater, Donald. *The Penguin Dictionary of Saints*. 2d. ed. London, New York: Penguin Books, 1983. (HAGIO)

Atwater, Phyllis. *Coming Back to Life*. New York: Ballantine Books, 1989. (NDE)

Auclair, Marcelle. *La Vie de Sainte Thérèse d'Avila*. Paris: Seuil, 1960. (HAGIO)

Ball, Ann. *Modern Saints Book 1*. Rockford, IL: Tan Books, 1983. (HAGIO)

———. *Modern Saints Book 2*. Rockford, IL: Tan Books, 1990. (HAGIO)

Balwin, Anne. *Catherine of Siena*. Huntington, IN: O.S.V., 1987. (HAGIO)

Barbier, Jean. *Trois Stigmatisés de notre temps*. Paris: Téqui, 1987. (STIGMATA)

Barret, William. *Death Bed Visions*. Aquarian Press, 1986. (NDE)

Biver, Paul. *Le Père Lamy*. nouv éd. Chiry-Ourscamp: Editions du serviteur, 1988. (HAGIO)

Boniface, Ennemond. *Therese Neumann la crucifiée*. Paris: P. Lethielleux, 1989. (HAGIO)

Bossis, Gabrielle. *Lui et Moi*, vol. I. Paris: Beauchesne, 1985. (REVEL)

———. *Lui et Moi*, vol. II. Paris: Beauchesne, 1950. (REVEL)

———. *Lui et Moi*, vol. III. Paris: Beauchesne, 1952. (REVEL)

———. *Lui et Moi*, vol. IV. Paris: Beauchesne, 1953. (REVEL)

———. *Lui et Moi*, vol. V. Paris: Beauchesne, 1953. (REVEL)

———. *Lui et Moi*, vol. VI. Paris: Beauchesne, 1957. (REVEL)

———. *Lui et Moi*, vol. VII. Paris: Beauchesne, 1979. (REVEL)

Boufflet, Joachim. *Encyclopédie des Phénomènes extraordinaires dans la vie mystique*, volume 1. Paris: FX de Guibert—OEIL, 1992.

Bouyer, Louis. *Figures Mystiques féminines*. Paris: Cerf, 1989. (THEOL)

Brune, François. *Les Morts nous parlent*. Paris: Le Félin, 1988. (NDE)

Burnham, Sophy. *Angels' Letters*. New York: Ballantine Books, 1991. (ANGELS)

————. *A Book of Angels*. New York: Ballantine Books, 1990. (ANGELS)

Caidin, Martin. *Ghosts of the Air.* New York: Bantam Books, 1991. (AFTERLIFE)

Callanan & Kelley. *Final Gifts*. New York: Poseidon Press, 1992. (NDE)

Catherine de Sienne. *Le Livre des Dialogues.* Paris: Seuil, 1953. (REVEL)

Chervin, Rhonda De Sola. *Treasury of Women Saints.* Ann Arbor, MI: Servant Publications, 1991. (HAGIO)

Chevalier and Gheerbrant. *Dictionnaire des Symboles.* Paris: Bouquins, 1982. (SYMBOL)

Choppy, Etienne. *L'Annonciation.* Marseille: AGEP, 1991. (ANGELS and ART)

Cony, Cecilia. *Je dois raconter ma vie, l'Ange gardien mon ami.* Paris: Téqui, 1988. (HAGIO)

Cruz, Joan Carroll. *Eucharistic Miracles.* Rockford, IL: Tan Books, 1987. (MIRACLES)

————. *Relics.* Huntington, IN: O.S.V., 1984. (THEOL)

————. *The Incorruptibles.* Rockford, IL: Tan Books, 1977. (INCOR-RUP)

Curtayne, Alice. *Catherine of Siena.* Rockford, IL: Tan Books, 1980. (HAGIO)

d'Agreda, Marie. *Cité Mystique.* Paris: Téqui, 1970. (REVEL)

Daniélou, Jean. *Les Anges et leur mission.* Paris: Desclée, 1990. (ANGELS)

Darbins, Pascal. *Vie et Oeuvres de Soeur Marie Lataste.* Paris: Téqui, 1974. (HAGIO)

Davidson, Gustav. *Dictionary of Angels.* New York: The Free Press, 1967. (ANGELS)

Delaney, John. *Dictionary of Saints.* New York: Image Books, Doubleday, 1983. (HAGIO)

Delaney, Selden. *Married Saints.* New York: Longmans, Green and Co., 1935. (HAGIO)

Derobert, Jean. *Padre Pio témoin de Dieu.* Marquain, Belg.: Jules Hovine, 1986. (HAGIO)

————. *Passons sur l'autre rive: anges et démons.* Marquain, Belg.: Jules Hovine, 1983. (ANGELS)

Devlin, Pat. *One Family Experience.* Lubbock, TX: Self-published, 1989. (APPARI)

Dickson, Marie-Pascal. *Jubilation das la lumière divine de Françoise Romaine.* Paris: OEIL, 1989. (HAGIO)

Dolto, Françoise. *Enfances.* Paris: Seuil, 1986. (AFTERLIFE)

Dreyer, Elisabeth. *Passionate Women: Two Medieval Mystics.* New York: Paulist Press, 1989. (HAGIO)

Ducaud-Bourget, François. *Vie de Saint Michel Archange.* Bléré, Fr.: Forts dans la foi, 1976. (ADVENTURES)

Duchet-Sucheaux/Pastoureau. *La Bible et les Saints.* Paris: Flammarion, 1990. (HAGIO)

Eersel, Patice van. *La Source Noire.* Paris: Librairie générale française, 1991. (NDE)

Emmerich, Anne Catherine. *The Dolorous Passion of Our Lord Jesus Christ.* Rockford, IL: Tan Books, 1983. (REVEL)

———. *The Life of the Blessed Virgin Mary.* Rockford, IL: Tan Books, 1970. (REVEL)

Englebert, Omer. *La Fleur des saints.* Paris: Albin Michel, 1990. (HAGIO)

Farmer, David Hugh. *The Oxford Dictionary of Saints.* Oxford: Oxford University Press, 1987. (HAGIO)

Faure, Philippe. *Les Anges.* Paris: Cerf, 1988. (ANGELS)

Ferguson, George. *Signs and Symbols in Christian Art.* New York: Oxford University Press, 1989. (SYMBOL)

Fox, Robert. *The World and Work of the Holy Angels.* Alexandria, SD: Fatima Family, 1991. (ANGELS)

Freze, Michael. *They Bore the Wounds of Christ.* Huntington, IN: O.S.V., 1989. (STIGMATA)

Galgani, Gemma. *Ecrits.* Paris: Editions Téqui, 1988. (HAGIO)

Gallup, George, Jr., and Proctor, William. *Adventures in Immortality.* New York: McGraw-Hill, 1982. (NDE)

Germano and Félix. *La Bienheureuse Gemma Galgani.* Paris: Librairie Mignard, 1933. (HAGIO)

Gibson, Arvin. *Glimpses of Eternity: NDE.* Bountiful, UT: Horizon Publishers, 1992. (NDE)

Girard, Guy and Armand. *Mary, Queen of Peace, Stay with Us.* Montréal: Editions Paulines, 1988. (HAGIO)

*God Calling.* New York: A. J. Russel: Jove Books, 1978. (REVEL)

Godwin, Malcolm. *Angels, An Endangered Species.* New York: Simon & Schuster, 1990. (ANGELS and ART)

Graham, Billy. *Angels: God's Secret Agents.* Dallas: Word Publishing, 1986. (ANGELS)

Greeley, Andrew. *Angel Fire.* TOR Books. (NOVEL)

Grey, Margot. *Return from Death.* London, New York: Arkana, Penguin, 1985. (NDE)

Grof, Stanislav. *Beyond Death.* New York: Thamson & Hudson, 1980. (NDE)

Guidici, Maria-Pia. *Qui sont les anges*. Paris: Nouvelle cité, 1985. (ANGELS)

Guiley, Rosemary. *Harper's Encyclopedia of the Mystical & Paranormal*. San Francisco: Harper, 1991. (MISC)

Haddad, Jean-Pierre. *Charbel, un saint du Liban*. Paris: Maison-Neuve, 1978. (HAGIO)

Haffert, John M. *The Meaning of Akita*. Asbury, NJ: 101 Foundation, 1989. (MIRACLES)

Hampe, Johann. *Sterben ist doch ganz anders*. Stuttgart: Kreuz Verlag, 1977. (REVEL)

Harlow, Ralph. *A Life after Death*. New York: McFadden Bartell, 1968. (NDE)

Harris, Barbara. *Full Circle*. New York: Pocket Books, 1990. (NDE)

Hastings, Arthur. *With the Tongue of Men and Angels*. Fort Worth, TX: Holt, Rinehart & Winston, 1991. (NEW AGE)

Hildegard Von Bingen. *Le Livre des Oeuvres Divines*. Paris: Albin Michel, 1982. (REVEL)

Huber, Georges. *Mon Ange marchera devant toi*. Paris: Saint Paul, 1986. (ANGELS)

Humann, Harvey. *The Many Faces of Angels*. Marina del Rey, CA: Devorss Publications, 1986. (ANGELS)

Hunter, Charles. *Angels on Assignment*. Kingwood, TX: Hunter Books, 1979. (ANGELS)

Jeffrey, Francis. *John Lilly, So Far*. Los Angeles: Jeremy Tarcher, 1990. (BIO)

Julienne de Norwitch. *Le Livre des Révélations*. Paris: Cerf, 1992. (REVEL)

Jung, C. G. *Synchronicity*. Princeton: Princeton University Press, 1973. (PSY)

Kerlys, Antoine. *L'Ange de la présence: essai sur le maitre intérieur*. Terre blanche, 1989. (ANGELS)

Klee, Vincent. *Les Plus beaux textes sur les Saints Anges*. Paris: Nouvelles Editions Latines, 1984. (THEOL)

Komp, Diane. *A Window to Heaven*. Grand Rapids, MI: Zondervan, 1992. (NDE)

Kondor, Louis. *Mémoires de Soeur Lucie*. Fatima, Portugal: Vice-Postulaçao dos Videntes, 1991. (BIO)

Kowalska, Hélène. *Petie Journal de Soeur Faustine*. Marquain, Belg.: Jules Hovine, 1985. (BIO)

Kren, Thomas, and Wieck, Roger. *The Visions of Tondal*. Malibu, CA: J. Paul Getty Museum, 1990. (NDE)

Kübler-Ross, Elisabeth. *La Mort est un nouveau soleil*. Paris: Press-Pocket, 1990. (NDE)

————. *La Mort, porte de la vie.* Paris: Editions du Rocher, 1990. (NDE)

————. *On Children and Death.* New York: Collier Books, 1985. (NDE)

————. *On Death and Dying.* New York: Collier Books, 1969. (NDE)

————. *Questions and Answers on Death and Dying.* New York: Collier Books, 1974. (NDE)

Kübler-Ross, Elizabeth, and Preston, Heather. *Remember the Secret.* Berkeley: Celestial Arts, 1982. (NDE)

Kushner, Harold. *When Bad Things Happen to Good People.* New York: Avon Books, 1981.

Ladame, Jean. *La Sainte du Paray Marguerite-Marie.* Monsurs, Fr.: Résiac, 1986. (HAGIO)

Laffineur, M., and le Pelletier, M. T. *Star on the Mountain.* New York: Lindenhurst, 1969. (APPARI)

Lama, Friedrich von. *Les Anges.* Stein am Rhein, Switz.: Christiana, 1987. (HAGIO)

Laurentin, René, and Mahéo, P. *Bilocations de Mère Yvonne-Aimée.* Paris: OEIL, 1990. (HAGIO)

————. *Les Stigmates d'Yvonne-Aimée de Malestroit.* Paris: OEIL, 1988. (HAGIO)

Laurentin, René. *Multiplication des apparitions de la Vierge aujourd'hui.* Paris: Fayard, 1991. (APPARI)

————. *Vie de Catherine Labouré.* Paris: Desclée de Brouwer, 1981. (HAGIO)

*Le Nouveau Testament.* Translated by d'Osty & Trinquet. Paris: Seuil, 1978.

Lebrun, Maguy. *Médecins du ciel, Médecins de la terre.* Paris: Robert Laffont, 1987. (BIO)

Lemoine, Jo. *Rita, la sainte de impossibles.* Paris: Médiaspaul, 1990. (HAGIO)

*Life of Mary as Seen by the Mystics, The.* Rockford, IL: Tan Books, 1991. (REVEL)

Lilly, John. *The Center of the Cyclone.* Julian Press, 1972. (BIO)

————. *The Scientist.* Berkeley: Ronin Publishing, 1988. (BIO)

Lindmayr, Marie-Anne. *Mes relations avec les âmes du purgatoire.* Stein am Rhein, Switz.: Christiana, 1986. (REVEL)

Lorimerm David. *Whole in One.* Londres: Arkana, 1990. (NDE)

Madsen, Truman. *Joseph Smith, The Prophet.* Salt Lake City: Bookcraft, 1989. (HAGIO)

Mallasz, Gitta. *Az Angyal Vàlaszol.* Zurich: Daimon Verlag, 1976. (ANGELS)

————. *Dialogue avec l'Ange, Intégrale.* Paris: Aubier, 1990. (ANGELS)

————. *Talking with Angels.* Zurich: Daimon Verlag, 1988. (ANGELS)

Malz, Betty. *Angels Watching over Me.* New York: Chosen Books, 1986. (ANGELS)

————. *A Glimpse for Eternity.* New York: Chosen Books, 1977. (NDE)

————. *Touching the Unseen World.* New York: Chosen Books, 1991. (NDE)

McDonald, Hope. *When Angel Appear.* Grand Rapids, MI: Day Break Books, 1982. (ANGELS)

*Méditations sur les 22 arcanes majeurs.* Paris: Aubier, 1980. (THEOL)

Menendez, Soeur Josefa. *The Way of Divine Love.* Rockford, IL: Tan Books, 1972. (REVEL)

Mercier, Evelyne-Sarah. *La mort transfigurée.* Paris: L'Age du Verseau, 1992. (NDE)

Michel, Aimé. *Metanoia.* Paris: Albin Michel, 1986. (STIGMATA)

Miller, Vernon. *Mysterious Shroud.* New York: Image Books, 1988. (SHROUD)

Millet, Marie-Angélique. *Dis.. Ecris..* Montsurs, Fr.: Résiac, 1981. (REVEL)

Monroe Institute. *The Gateway Experience.* Faber, VA: Monroe Institute, 1989. (OUT-OF-BODY)

Monroe, Robert. *Fantastiques expériences de voyage astral.* Paris: Robert Laffont, 1990. (OUT-OF-BODY)

————. *Le Voyage hors du corps.* Paris: Garancière, 1986. (OUT-OF-BODY)

Moody, Raymond, and Perry, Paul. *La Lumière de l'au dela.* Paris: Robert Laffont, 1988. (NDE)

————. *La Vie après la Vie.* Paris: Robert Laffont, 1975. (NDE)

Moolenburgh, H. C. *A Handbook of Angels.* C-W Daniel Co. Ltd., 1984 (ANGELS)

Morse, Melvin, and Perry, Paul. *Closer to the Light.* New York: Ivy Books, 1990. (NDE)

————. *Des Enfants dans la Lumière.* Paris: Robert Laffont, 1992. (NDE)

O'Sullivan, Paul. *All about Angels.* Rockford, IL: Tan Books, 1990. (ANGELS)

Osis, Karlis and Haraldsson, Erlendur. *At the Hour of Death.* New York: Avon Books, 1977. (NDE)

————. *Ce qu'ils ont vu au seuil de la mort.* Paris: Editions du Rocher, 1982. (NDE)

Ouvrage Américain Collectif. *Angels & Mortals.* Quest Books, 1990. (ANGELS)

Ouvrage collectif. *L'Ange et L'Homme.* Paris: Albin Michel, 1978. (ANGELS)

Parente, Allessio. *Send Me Your Guardian Angel.* San Giovanni Rotondo, 1984. (ANGELS)

Peat, David. *Synchronicity, The Bridge between Matter and Mind.* New York: Bantam Books, 1987. (SCIENCES)

Pélagius. *L'Anacrisie, pour avoir la communication avec son Ange gardien.* Paris: Cariscript, 1988. (ANGELS)

Pelletier, Joseph A. *God Speaks at Garabandal.* Worcester, MA: 1970. (APPARI)

Perez, Ramon. *Garabandal, The Village Speaks.* New York: Lindenhurst, 1985. (APPARI)

Pernoud, Régine. *Petite vie de Jeanne d'Arc.* Paris: Desclée de Brouwer, 1990. (HAGIO)

Perrin, Odet. *Paroles de Jeanne d'Arc.* Lausanne, Switz.: Mermod, 1961. (HAGIO)

Peyret, Raymond. *Petite vie de Marthe Robin.* Paris: Desclée de Brouwer, 1988. (HAGIO)

Prieur, Jean. *Les «Morts» ont donné signe de vie.* Paris: Lanore, Sorlot, 1984. (BEYOND)

Pseudo-Dionysius. *Pseudo-Dionysius: The Complete Work.* New York: Paulist Press, 1987. (THEOL)

Raquin, Bernard. *Messages de l'après vie.* Paris: L'age du verseau, 1990. (AFTERLIFE)

Rawlings, Maurice. *Beyond Death's Door.* New York: Bantam Books, 1979. (NDE)

Regamey, R. P. *Anges.* Paris: Pierre Tisné, 1946. (ANGELS and ART)

Renard, Hélène. *Des Prodiges et des Hommes.* Paris: Philippe Lebaud, 1989. (STIGMATA and INCORRUP)

Ring, Kenneth. *En route vers Omega.* Paris: Robert Laffont, 1991. (NDE)

———. *Life at Death.* New York: Quill, 1982. (NDE)

———. *The Omega Project.* New York: William Morrow, 1992. (NDE)

———. *Sur la frontière de la Vie.* Paris: Robert Laffont, 1982. (NDE)

Ritchie, George G. *My Life After Dying.* Norfolk, VA: Hampton Roads, 1991. (NDE)

———. *Return from Tomorrow.* New York: Chosen Books, 1978. (NDE)

Roberdel, Pierre. *Marie-Julie Jahenny.* Montsurs, Fr.: Résiac, 1987. (HAGIO)

Rogo, Scott. *Miracles.* London: Aquarian Press, 1991. (MIRACLES)

Ronner, John. *Do You Have a Guardian Angel.* Mamre Press, 1985. (ANGELS)

Rose, Elisabeth. *I Speak and Heal for the Angels*. Sedona, AZ: Light Technology, 1990. (ANGELS)

Rosey, Jean-Mathieu. *Dictionnaire du Christianisme*. Alleur, Belg.: Marabout, 1990. (THEOL)

Rossi, Fausto. *Teresa Musco*. Hauteville, Switz.: Parvis, 1991. (HAGIO)

Rouch, Dominique. *Dieu seul le sait; enquête sur les miracles*. Paris: Hachette Carrere, 1990. (MIRACLES)

Ruffin, Bernard. *Padre Pio, The True Story, Expanded Edition*. Huntington, IN: O.S.V., 1991. (HAGIO)

Ryden, Vassula. *La Vraie vie en Dieu*. Paris: OEIL, 1990. (REVEL)

Sabom, Michael. *Recollections of Death*. Harper & Row, 1982. (NDE)

*Saint Michael & the Angels*. Rockford, IL: Tan Books, 1977. (THEOL)

Sanchez-Ventura, Pascal. *Stigmatisés et apparitions*. Paris: Nouvelles Editions Latines, 1967. (STIGMATA and APPARI)

*Santa Gemma e il suo sanctuario*. Lucca, It.: Monastero Passioniste. (HAGIO)

Schmöger, Carl. *Life of Anne-Catherine Emmerich*. Rockford, IL: Tan Books, 1976. (HAGIO)

Schroeder, Hans-Verner. *L'Homme et les Anges*. Paris: IONA, 1986. (ANGELS)

*Si tu m'ouvres la porte*. Hauteville, Switz.: Parvis, 1977. (REVEL)

Siena, Giovanni. *Padre Pio: «l'heure des anges»*. San Giovanni Rotondo, It.: Editions Arcangelo, 1977. (ANGELS)

Simma, Maria. *Les Ames du purgatoire m'ont dit*. Stein am Rhein, Switz.: Christiana, 1969. (REVEL)

Siwek, Paul. *Riddle of Konnersreuth, Theresa Neumann*. Milwaukee: Bruce, 1953. (HAGIO)

Slaviat, Thor. *Gemma Galgani, Vierge de Lucques*. Paris: Maison de la Bonne Presse, 1936. (HAGIO)

Steiner, Johanes. *The Visions of Thérèse Neuman*. Alba House, 1975. (HAGIO)

Stockton, Bayard. *Catapult, A Biography on R. Monroe*. Norfolk, VA: Donning, 1989. (BIO)

Talor, Terry Lynn. *Messengers of Light*. Triburon: HJ Kramer, 1990. (ANGELS)

Tangari, Katharina. *Le Message de Padre Pio*. Versailles: Publications du Courrier de Rome, 1990. (HAGIO)

Teyssèdre, Bernard. *Ange, Astres et Cieux*. Paris: Albin Michel, 1986. (ANGELS)

Thérèse de l'Enfant Jésus. *Poésies*. Paris: Cerf, 1979. (MISC)

Upinsky, Arnaud-Aaron. *La Science à l'épreuve du linceul.* Paris: OEIL, 1990. (SHROUD)

Vernier, Jean-Marie. *Les Anges chez saint Thomas d'Aquin.* Paris: Nouvelles Editions Latines, 1986. (THEOL)

*Vie authentique de Catherine Labouré.* Paris: Desclée de Brouwer, 1981. (HAGIO)

Villepelée, J. F. *Folie de la croix, Gemma Galgani.* Hauteville, Switz.: Parvis, 1977. (HAGIO)

Vuarnet, Jean-Noël. *Extases Féminines.* Paris: Hatier, 1991. (THEOL)

Walsh, Michael. *Butler's Lives of Saints.* New York: HarperCollins, 1991. (HAGIO)

Walsh, William Thomas. *Our Lady of Fatima.* New York: Image Doubleday, 1954. (APPARI)

Warner, Marina. *Alone of All Her Sex.* First Vintage Books, 1983. (HAGIO)

White, Kristine. *A Guide to the Saints.* New York: Ivy Books, 1992. (HAGIO)

Wilkerson, Ralph. *Beyond and Back.* Anaheim, CA: Melodyland, 1977. (NDE)

Willmore and Sorensen. *The Journey Beyond Life.* Midvale, UT: Sounds of Zion, 1988. (NDE)

Wilson, Ian. *The After Death Experience.* New York: Quill, 1987. (NDE)

———. *The Bleeding Mind.* London: Weidenfeld & Nicolson, 1988. (STIGMATA)

———. *The Shroud of Turin.* New York: Doubleday, 1979. (SHROUD)

———. *Stigmata.* New York: Harper & Row, 1989. (STIGMATA)

———. *Super-moi.* Paris: Press-Pocket, 1991. (NEW AGE)

Winowska, Maria. *Le Vrai visage de Padre Pio.* Paris: Fayard, 1955. (HAGIO)

Woodward, Kenneth. *Making Saints.* New York: Touchstone Books, 1990. (THEOL)

Yasuda, Teiji. *Akita, the Tears and Message of Mary.* Asbury, NJ: 101 Foundation, 1989. (APPARI)

Zaleski, Carol. *Otherworld Journeys.* New York: Oxford University Press, 1987. (NDE)

# INDEX